U. Panther

THE NEW SUMMIT

Texts and Methods

Herausgegeben von: Dr. Karola Schallhorn

Erarbeitet von: Dr. Karola Schallhorn, Dr. Michaela Banzhaf, Heidrun Ferch, Jochen Fritz, James Martin, Rainer Saalfeld und Christina Waltz

Anhang: Dr. Karola Schallhorn unter Mitarbeit von Dr. Klaus Hinz

Sprachliche Betreuung: James Martin

Best.-Nr. 040019 5

Schöningh

www.schoeningh.de
Schöningh Verlag, Jühenplatz 1–3, 33098 Paderborn

Druck A 6 5 4 / Jahr 2007 06 05
Alle Drucke der Serie A sind im Unterricht parallel verwendbar.
Die letzte Zahl bezeichnet das Jahr dieses Druckes.

Umschlaggestaltung: INNOVA, Borchen unter Verwendung eines Fotos von Pictor. Fotos oben (v. l. nach r.): © European Communities, 1995–2001; Anthony/Pfeiffer; Drawing by James Montgomery Flagg; Reinhild Kassing/Verlagsarchiv Schöningh; Royal Shakespeare Theatre Collection, Stratford-upon-Avon
Druck und Bindung: westermann druck GmbH, Braunschweig

ISBN 3-14-040019-5

Contents

The World of English

Great Britain: Past—Present—Future

William Shakespeare—Who Can Beat The Bard?

Appendix

Dear student,

This textbook wants to be your guide through the various topics of the "Sekundarstufe II". It will be your companion when you are looking for methods of planning and carrying through creative and traditional tasks.
You will probably not read this book from cover to cover, but you will profit a lot from knowing how it is organized. It can be a real "method and language kit" for you. The appendix offers you help in most situations: The "Method kit", e.g. provides information on how to work effectively in a team, how to do an Internet research, organize an interesting presentation and so on. The "Language kit" helps you to improve the vocabulary you need for analysing texts or writing compositions.
You will find narrative texts dealing with the cultural and historical background of English speaking countries as well as short non-fictional texts for basic information on special subjects. Cartoons, songs and poems add some fun and motivate you to be more critical of things you take for granted and to be inventive and active yourself.
The convention in this book is to use British English (Brit) in all the tasks, instructions and annotations. Since the texts are authentic texts, American English (US) is to be found as well (color US / colour Brit; -ise US / -ize Brit, etc).
Most of the texts have some while-reading tasks in the margin. The information you need is to be found in the sentence or passage where the arrow points at: directly in the line ➤, in the passage above ▲, or below ▼. These questions or comments help you concentrate on special details or to pay special attention to some facts. They want to help you with understanding.
You find the vocabulary at the bottom of the page. New words are marked by footnotes.
We, the authors, hope that this book will be your "text and method kit" providing the tools ready at hand to climb the summit of your English studies: a good command of the English language, the joy of communicating in the foreign tongue and a successful graduation.

The authors, the editor and the publisher

Some icons or symbols are used to show you immediately what to do, the methods are explained to you in the "Method kit":

- Literary text
- Info-text
- CD: Listen to the text or song
- The door: pre-reading activity
- The feather: creative writing (write a diary; answer in a letter to …)
- Act it out! (role play, freeze frame and other forms of playing a scene)
- Hot seat activity
- Work with your partner
- Work in a team
- Fish bowl
- Make a discussion or hold a debate
- Exchange information in a double circle

The following abbreviations have been used:

arch	=	archaic (not used anymore)
Brit	=	British English
cf.	=	compare
coll	=	colloquial
derog	=	derogative (offensive)
e.g.	=	for example
esp	=	especially
euph	=	euphemic (e.g. "to pass away" for "to die")
fml	=	formal English
idm	=	idiomatic expression, phrase
infml	=	informal
joc	=	jocular (meant as a joke)
poet	=	poetic
sb	=	somebody
sth	=	something

The World of English

In what way does the illustration visually take up the double meaning of the English word "tongue"?

In German, one of these two meanings is preserved in certain, rather old-fashioned expressions and idioms. Can you give examples?

Listen to the following samples of quite different World Englishes and identify the varieties. Take into account various aspects: sounds, grammar, words and context.

English Around The World

Lewis Carroll

Jabberwocky

'Twas brillig, and the slithy toves
Did gyre and gimble in the wabe;
All mimsy were the borogoves,
And the mome raths outgrabe.

"Beware the Jabberwock, my son!
The jaws that bite, the claws that catch!
Beware the Jujub bird, and shun
The frumious Bandersnatch!"

He took his vorpal sword in hand:
Long time the manxome foe he sought—
So rested he by the Tumtum tree,
And stood awhile in thought.

And as in uffish thought he stood,
The Jabberwock, with eyes of flame,
Came whiffling through the tulgey wood,
And burbled as it came!

One, two! One, two! And through and through
The vorpal blade went snicker-snack!
He left it dead, and with its head
He went galumphing back.

"And hast thou slain the Jabberwock?
Come to my arms, my beamish boy!
O frabjous day! Callooh! Callay!"
He chortled in his joy.

'Twas brillig, and the slithy toves
Did gyre and gimble in the wabe;
All mimsy were the borogoves,
And the mome raths outgrabe.

Recitation

1. Recite the poem in different ways, so as to make it resonant of the following moods:
   - joy
   - depression
   - triumph
   - sadness
   - …
2. Which tone do you consider most suitable for the poem?
3. Compare your preferences to the professional recording.

Grasping pecularities

1. Guess when and where the poem was written and obtain information on the author.
2. Summarize the contents of the poem in one sentence.
3. There are many words here you will not find in an English dictionary, yet they still sound English. Why?

Style

Find examples of the following stylistic devices:

- alliteration
- onomatopoeia
- internal rhyme

→ Language kit, Terms for text analysis, p. 316ff.

Writing your own poem

Replace all nonsense words with real ones. Which effect is evoked?
or
Write your own nonsense poem by replacing the nonsense words (e.g. in a stanza of your choice) with your own word creations, so that a different atmosphere emerges.

Example: *'Twas sonoric, and the moony plies*
Did drowse and pender in the lulls;
All nappy were the snorabies,
And the droopy ploads begull.

Switching into German

This is Christian Enzensberger's German version of "Jabberwocky":

Der Zipferlake

Verdaustig wars, und glasse Wieben
Rotterten gorkicht im Gemank;
Gar elump war der Pluckerwank,
Und die gabben Schweisel frieben.

Divide into groups and translate the remaining five stanzas.

The Spread of English

Here is a family tree representation of the way English has spread around the world, showing the influence of the two main branches of American and British English.

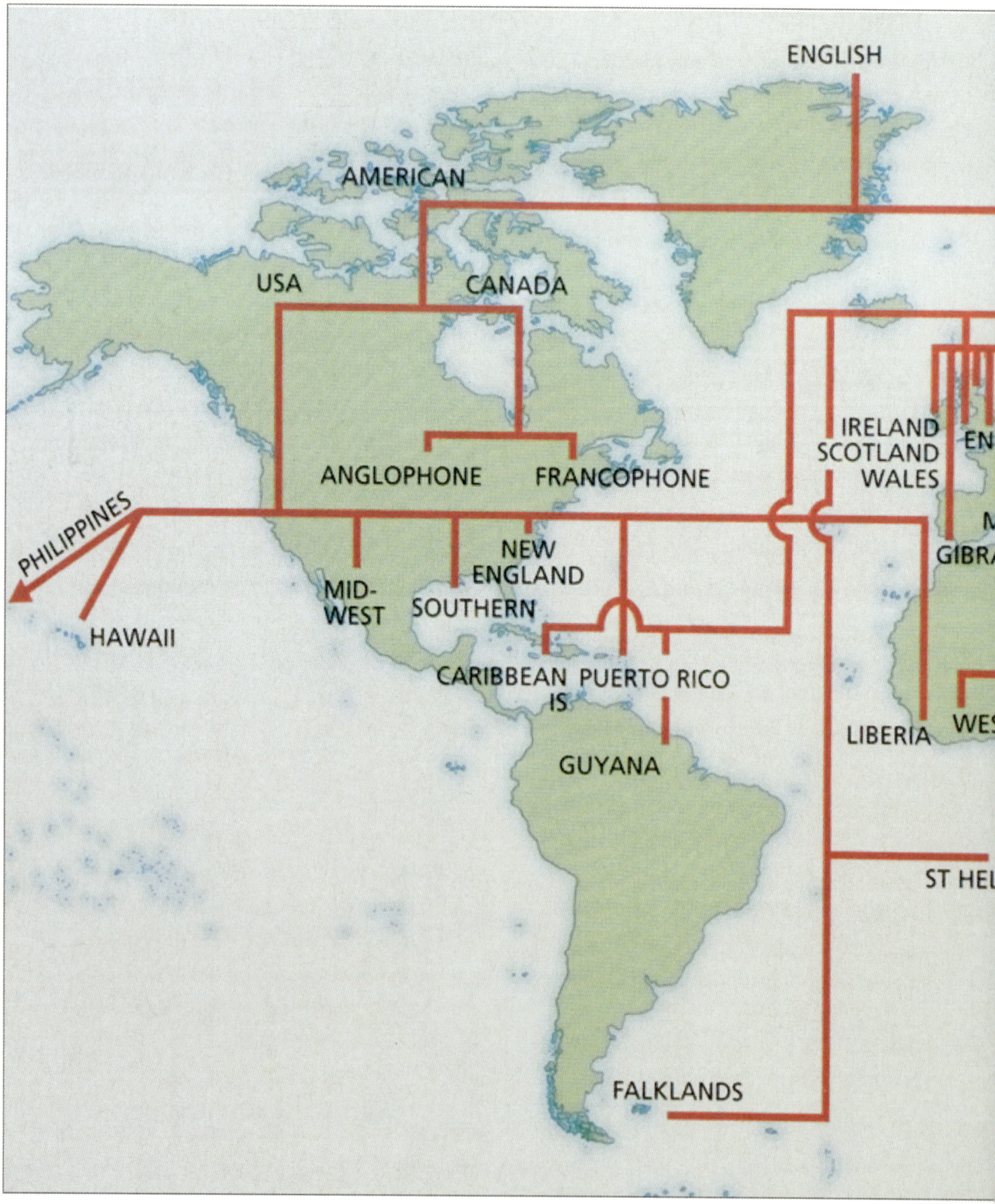

World Englishes

Why do you think English is spoken in all these countries? Find out more about the status English has in these parts of the world.
The Internet might help:
http://www.ethnologue.com
or use an almanac.

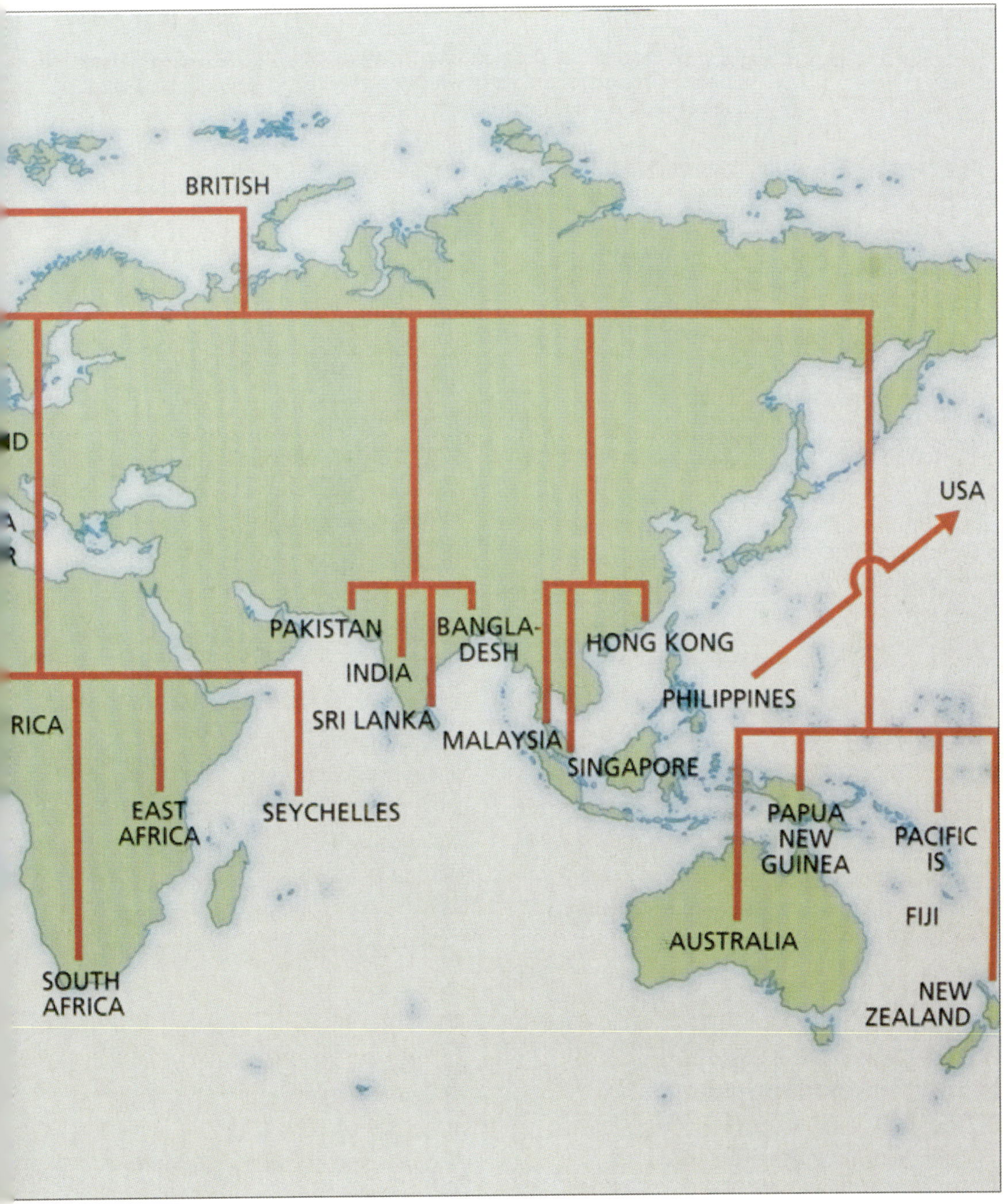

David Crystal

Why Do People Everywhere Learn English?

There are more and more English learners in the world every year. Get together in groups and compile your personal reasons for studying English.
Design an ad that promotes the study of English. Then present your posters in class and decide which one you believe would best attract future learners of English.

Below, there is a set of general reasons for the ever-increasing attractiveness of the English language.

a) Most of the scientific, technological, and academic information in the world is expressed in English, and over 80 per cent of all the information stored in electronic retrieval[1] systems is in English. Closely related to this is the concern to have access to the philosophical, cultural, religious, and literary history of Western Europe, either directly or through the medium of an English translation. In most parts of the world, the only way most people have access to such authors as Goethe or Dante is through English. [...]

b) The USA's dominant economic position acts as a magnet for international business and trade, and organizations wishing to develop international markets are thus under considerable pressure to work with English. The tourist and advertising industries are particularly English-dependent, but any multinational business will wish to establish offices in the major English-speaking countries.

c) English is the main language of popular music, and permeates[2] popular culture and its associated advertising. It is also the main language of satellite broadcasting, home computers, and videogames, as well as of such international illegal activities as pornography and drugs.

d) Whether the country has imperial antecedents[3] or not, English may have a role in providing a neutral means of communication between its different ethnic groups. A distinctive local variety of English may also become a symbol of national unity or emerging nationhood. The use of English in newspapers, on radio, or on television, adds a further dimension.

[1] **to retrieve** here: to find or extract stored information – [2] **to permeate** ['pɜːmieɪt] to spread to every part of sth – [3] **antecedent** [ˌæntɪ'siːdnt] a thing or an event that existed or comes before another

e) English is the language of international air traffic control, and is currently developing its role in international maritime[1], policing, and emergency services […]. It is the chief language of international business and academic conferences, and the leading language of international tourism.

f) It is sometimes thought that English has achieved its worldwide status because of its intrinsic[3] linguistic features. People have claimed that it is inherently[4] a more logical or more beautiful language than others, easier to pronounce, simpler in grammatical structure, or larger in vocabulary. This kind of reasoning is the consequence of unthinking chauvinism or naive linguistic thinking: there are no objective standards of logic or beauty to compare different languages […]. For example, English may not have many inflectional endings[5] […], but it has a highly complex syntax […]. Languages rise and fall in world esteem[6] for many kinds of reasons—political, economic, social, religious, literary—but linguistic reasons do not rank highly among them.

g) Because of the legacy[2] of British or American imperialism, the country's main institutions may carry out their proceedings in English. These include the governing body (e.g. parliament), government agencies, the civil service […], the law courts, national religious bodies, the schools, and higher educational institutions, along with their related publications […].

h) My own reasons:

Getting the gist

1. Take notes, giving the gist of each clipping.
2. Find appropriate headings for each clipping.
3. Compare the clippings' content with your own internal/external motivation as a language learner.

Ranking

Work with a partner. Rank the clippings in order of importance.

Learning English today

1. When is a good time to start learning English?
2. Bilingual education is gaining more and more ground in European classrooms. What do you think about this development?

[1] **maritime** ['mærɪtaɪm] of the sea, ships or sailing – [2] **legacy** ['legəsi] a thing passed to sb by people who lived before them or from earlier events, etc – [3] **intrinsic** existing within sb/sth, rather than coming from outside – [4] **inherent** [ɪn'hɪərənt] existing as a natural or permanent feature or quality of sb/sth – [5] **inflectional ending** the ending of a word showing its grammatical function in a sentence – [6] **esteem** high regard

Anonymous

Let's Do the Tongue Twist

I take it you already know
Of tough and bough[1] and cough and dough[2]?
Others may stumble, but not you,
on hiccough[3], thorough, laugh and through.
Well done! And now you wish, perhaps,
to learn of less familiar traps[4]?

Beware[5] of heard, a dreadful word
that looks like beard[6] and sounds like bird.
And dead; it's said like bed, not bead[7],
For goodness' sake don't call it 'deed'.
Watch out for meat and great and threat
(They rhyme with suite and straight and debt[8].)
A moth[9] is not a moth in mother
Nor both in bother, broth[10] in brother,
And here is not a match for there,
Nor dear and fear for bear and pear.

And then there's dose and rose and lose—
Just look them up—and goose and choose,
And cork and work and card and ward[11],
And font[12] and front and word and sword[13].
And do and go and thwart[14] and cart[15]—
Come, come, I've hardly made a start!
A dreadful language? Man alive!
I'd mastered it when I was five!

i:	see	/si:/
i	happy	/'hæpi/
ɪ	sit	/sɪt/
e	ten	/ten/
æ	cat	/kæt/
ɑ:	father	/'fɑ:ðə(r)/
ɒ	got	/gɒt/
ɔ:	saw	/sɔ:/
ʊ	put	/pʊt/
u	actual	/'æktʃuəl/
u:	too	/tu:/
ʌ	cup	/kʌp/
ɜ:	bird	/bɜ:d/
ə	about	/ə'baut/
eɪ	say	/seɪ/
əʊ	go	/gəʊ/
aɪ	five	/faɪv/
aʊ	now	/naʊ/
ɔɪ	boy	/bɔɪ/
ɪə	near	/nɪə(r)/
eə	hair	/heə(r)/
ʊe	pure	/pjʊə(r)/

Practicing pronunciation

1. Read the poem out loud. Compare with the professional recording. How could you improve your English pronunciation?
2. Divide into groups, each one focussing on one stanza. How many different pronunciations can you find for the same combination of letters? Consult your dictionary and look up the phonetic transcription of words you don't know, then write them next to the respective sound. The letters 'ough' for example, can have seven different pronunciations: cough /cɒf/, through /θru:/, tough /tʌf/, hiccough /hikʌp/, thorough /θʌrə/, dough /dəʊ/, bough /baʊ/.
   Can you give examples where the American pronunciation and spelling differ from the British?
3. The poem is an excellent example of the use of "eye rhyme". Guess what this is. ➪ Language kit, Eye rhyme, p. 318

[1] **bough** any of the main branches of a tree – [2] **dough** a thick mixture of flour, water etc ready to be baked into bread, pastry etc – [3] **hiccough** *Schluckauf* – [4] **trap** device for catching animals – [5] **to beware of** (used only in the infinitive and imperative) to be cautious of sb/sth – [6] **beard** hair growing on the chin and the lower cheeks of a man's face – [7] **bead** *Perle* – [8] **debt** sum of money owed to sb – [9] **moth** *Motte* – [10] **broth** soup made from water in which meat has been boiled – [11] **ward** a separate part or room in a hospital for a particular group of patients – [12] **font** here: *Becken* – [13] **sword** *Schwert* – [14] **thwart** (esp passive) to oppose a plan successfully – [15] **cart** two-wheeled vehicle pulled by a horse

Robert Mc Crum, William Cran, Robert MacNeil

The Spread of RP

"All varieties of language are equal. But some varieties are more equal than others." (adapted from George Orwell)

Which variety (e.g. class accent, regional dialects) in your own language would you consider "more equal" than others? Estimate the percentage of speakers using this variety in your country.

The years from the end of the First World War in 1918 to the end of the Second World War in 1945 were the heyday[1] of radio in Britain and the United States, the years of Roosevelt's[2] fireside chats to the American people and of Winston Churchill's[3] wartime broadcasts. The establishment in Britain in 1922 of the first radio broadcasting service, the BBC, was a milestone for the English language. As one of its first executives wrote: "The broadcasting of aural[4] language is an event no less important than the broadcasting of visual language [printing], not only in its influence on human relations, but in its influence upon the destinies of the English language." From the first, the BBC had a global—and in those days imperial—attitude towards the English language. Its motto ran "Nation shall speak peace unto nation", and no one doubted what the tongue should be. The question was: what kind of English?

In an era of rapid change, there was, first of all, the question of acceptable vocabulary. New inventions could provoke furious public debate: should *airman* be recognized[5] in favour of *aviator*? A

Why is the BBC considered "a milestone for the English language"?

Rephrase this motto.

How was the importance of radio different 50 years ago?

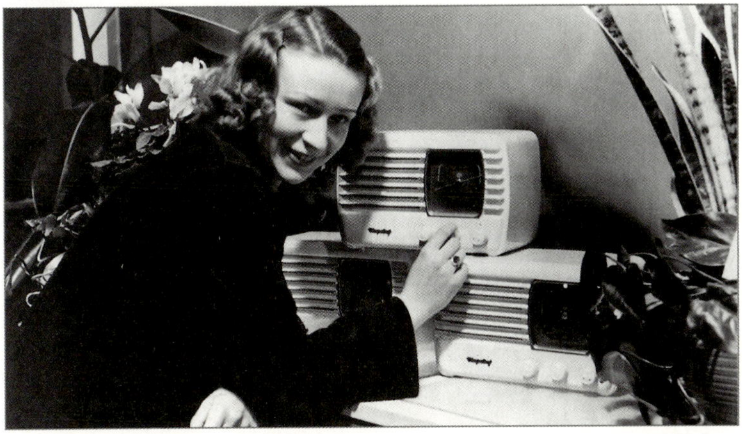

[1] **heyday** the time of greatest success, power, influence etc for sb/sth – [2] **Franklin D. Roosevelt** (1882–1945) 32nd president of the U.S. (1933–1945) – [3] **Sir Winston Churchill** (1874–1965) British Prime Minister (1940–1945, 1951–1955) – [4] **aural** of or concerning the ear or hearing – [5] **to recognize sb/sth** to accept sb/sth as officially valid or genuine

British broadcasting authority would have to make such rulings. Then there were foreign borrowings[1] to cope with. Would a mass radio audience understand *Zeitgeist, Weltanschauung* and *Übermensch*, or should the BBC voice say *time-spirit, world-outlook* and *superman*? And what about that old British bugbear[2], Americanisms? What attitude should the new BBC take towards such coinings[3] as *cocktail, joy-ride, pussyfoot, road-hog* and *sneakthief*? And, perhaps most sensitive of all, what English accent should the BBC adopt?

Look up these expressions in a modern English dictionary.

Explain the function of ACSE.

The approach to a solution, reached in 1926, was to set up the so-called *Advisory Committee on Spoken English* (ACSE). This high-powered group of experts included the poet Robert Bridges, a northerner who argued unsuccessfully for the adoption of a Northern Standard, the American scholar Logan Pearsall Smith, and the Irishman George Bernard Shaw, but was composed chiefly of RP speakers, men such as the lexicographer C.T. Onions; the scientist Julian Huxley; the art historian Kenneth Clark; and Alistair Cooke, then a young journalist. The Committee's declared task was to arbitrate[4] on the usage and pronunciation of words, English and foreign. Decisions were reached by a simple vote, an arbitrary[5] procedure that, in 1936, for example, sensibly favoured *roundabouts* against *gyratory circuses*, but less sensibly, proposed *stop-and-goes* instead of *traffic lights*. Arbitrations on usage were probably much less influential for the evolution of a spoken Standard English than judgements about pronunciation. […]

According to [Lord] Reith [the first Director General of the BBC], "the language, the speech and pronunciation … that the announcers were taught to speak … was the very best thing we could do." He was, of course, describing RP. Bridges alone seriously challenged[6] the implicit[7] assumption[8] that RP was the only socially acceptable accent for radio. The establishment of a uniform BBC English was partly designed to promote a sense of impersonality and impartiality[9]. A sober[10] recital[11], it was felt, would seem more accurate. In the early days, the newsreaders wore dinner jackets and, when nothing newsworthy was deemed[12] to have occurred, they said so—and played classical music instead.

Like many pioneers, Reith was an idealist. His broadcasting corporation reflected his aspirations[13]. First, there was the hope that the BBC would promote English on a global scale. "We cherish[14] the decision," as one pamphlet put it, "that our language will remain as we know it now, the optimistic even seeing in it a future world lan-

Received Pronunciation (RP)—also known as the *Queen's English, Oxford English, public school English or BBC English*—is the regionally neutral, prestige accent of British English, spoken by less than 3 per cent of the population. Today it tells something about a person's educational background and it may even contain some regional characteristics.

[1]**borrowing** here: a word taken by one language from another – [2]**bugbear** thing that is feared or disliked or that causes annoyance – [3]**coining** newly invented word or phrase – [4]**to arbitrate** to make a judgement about or settle an argument between two parties, when asked by them to do so – [5]**arbitrary** based on personal opinion or impulse, not on any reason or system – [6]**to challenge** to question whether sth is true, right or valid – [7]**implicit** implied, but not expressed directly – [8]**assumption** a thing that is thought to be true or certain to happen, but is not proved – [9]**impartiality** neutrality – [10]**sober** serious and sensible – [11]**recital** [rɪ'saɪtl] from *to recite* to read something aloud or repeat something from memory, especially for an audience – [12]**to deem** to consider, to regard – [13]**aspiration** a strong desire or ambition – [14]**to cherish** to keep a feeling or an idea in one's mind or heart and think of it with pleasure

guage." Much more potent[1], and much more pervasive[2], was this belief: "It would appear ... that the higher a community climbs on the social scale, the greater is the degree of uniformity in speech. Whenever language is spoken, there is present in the minds of the speakers the notion that there is a "right way." Accent was one of the factors that perpetuated[3] social inequality, sustained[4] class barriers, and put the lower classes at a disadvantage. "You cannot raise social standards without raising speech standards," observed one member of the Committee. Overseas, BBC English—transmitted by eight so-called Empire announcers, and later by the World Service—was intended to unite the colonies, later the Commonwealth. Gradually, the English of the airwaves took over from the English of the imperial Civil Service, a vital means of communication among people without a common language.

Within the British Isles, the spread of RP by the BBC, first on radio, then on television, helped to reinforce what was an already strong connection in many people's minds between education and "Standard English" [...].

◄ Guess what people could mean by "the right way".

Investigating correspondences

1. Consult an encyclopedia (e.g. *Brockhaus*, *Meyer's*, etc) and find out how the standard variety of German evolved.
2. Find out whether there are correspondences between the standards spoken in England and Germany as regards
   - situational usage, register
   - emergence and spread
   - teaching practices
   - connections between education and the standard variety, and
   - attitudes towards the standard variety.

Appointing committee members

Suggest German personalities that you would consider competent to serve on an "Advisory Committee on Spoken German." Can you think of anyone who would be completely out of place there? Present your favourites and give reasons for your choice.

Translation

Translate ll. 54–72 ("Like many pioneers ... without a common language") in teams of two, one of you working on ll. 54–63, the other on ll. 63–72. Be careful with English abbreviations; translate only when there is a German equivalent.
Then exchange your paragraph with your partner and correct each other's translations.

[1] **potent** here: convincing – [2] **pervasive** present and seen or felt everywhere – [3] **to perpetuate** to make sth continue – [4] **to sustain** to keep sb/sth alive or in existence

A Literary Journey in the English Speaking World

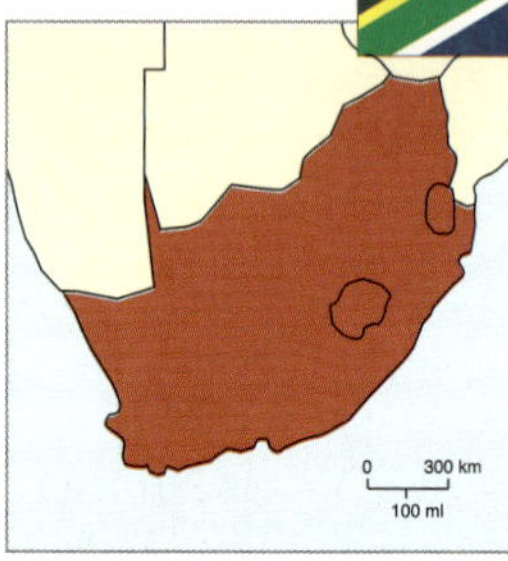

Alan Paton

Growing Apart

In his novel *Cry, The Beloved Country* South African author Alan Paton depicts a type of initiation of the Zulu Reverend Stephen Kumalo into urban life and its effects on attitudes and ways of life. In 1995, the novel was turned into a movie which received international acclaim.

Having never left the small village of Ndotsheni where he leads a pious life and upholds tribal values, Kumalo had to witness the subsequent departures of his brother, his sister and his only son to Johannesburg. None of them has ever sent word from there, so Kumalo considers them irretrievably lost: "When people go to Johannesburg, they do not come back. They do not even write any more."

However, when he is urgently called to the city on behalf of his sister, he starts on the journey and in Johannesburg is confronted with violence, prostitution, greed and racial tension.

Aerial view of Johannesburg

Calling on his brother John in the company of a new-found friend, Reverend Msimangu, proves to be one more unsettling encounter for Kumalo: his brother has rid himself of his communal and tribal roots and changed so much that he has grown estranged from Kumalo.

Charles S. Dutton as John Kumalo in the 1995 film version of the novel

His brother John was sitting there on a chair, talking to two other men. He had grown fat, and sat with his hands on his knees like a chief. His brother he did not recognize, for the light from the street was on the backs of his visitors.

– Good morning, my brother.

– Good morning, sir.

– Good morning, my own brother, son of our mother.

John Kumalo looked closely at him, and stood up with a great hearty smile.

– My own brother. Well, well, who can believe! What are you doing in Johannesburg?

Kumalo looked at the visitors. I come on business, he said.

– I am sure my friends will excuse us. My own brother, the son of our mother, has come.

The two men rose, and they all said stay well and go well.

– Do you know the Reverend Msimangu, my brother?

– Well, well, he is known to everybody. Everybody knows the Reverend Msimangu. Sit down, gentlemen. I think we must have some tea.

He went to the door and called into the place behind.

– Is your wife Esther well, my brother?

John Kumalo smiled his jolly knowing smile. My wife Esther has left me ten years, my brother.

– And have you married again?

– Well, well, not what the Church calls married, you know. But she is a good woman.

– You wrote nothing of this, brother.

– No, how could I write? You people in Ndotsheni do not understand the way life is in Johannesburg. I thought it better not to write.

– That is why you stopped writing?

– Well, well, that could be why I stopped. Trouble, brother, unnecessary trouble.

– But I do not understand. How is life different in Johannesburg?

– Well, that is difficult. Do you mind if I speak English? I can explain these things better in English.

– Speak in English then, brother.

– You see I have had an experience here in Johannesburg. It is not like Ndotsheni. One must live here to understand it. He looked at his brother. Something new is happening here, he said.

He did not sit down, but began to speak in a strange voice. He walked about, and looked through the window into the street, and up at the ceiling, and into the corners of the room as though something were there, and must be brought out.

– Down in Ndotsheni I am a nobody, even as you are a nobody,

Is there anything that strikes you about this reunion of two brothers?

Investigate John Kumalo's true motive in not writing to Ndotsheni.

Comment on John Kumalo's use of rhetorical skills.

my brother. I am subject[1] to the chief, who is an ignorant man. I must salute[2] him and bow to him, but he is an uneducated man. Here in Johannesburg I am a man of some importance, of some influence. I have my own business, and when it is good, I can make ten, twelve pounds a week.

He began to sway[3] to and fro, he was not speaking to them, he was speaking to people who were not there.

– I do not say we are free here. I do not say we are free as men should be. But at least I am free of the chief. At least I am free of an old and ignorant man, who is nothing but a white man's dog. He is a trick, a trick to hold together something that the white man desires to hold together.

He smiled his cunning[4] and knowing smile, and for a moment addressed himself to his visitors.

– But it is not being held together, he said. It is breaking apart, your tribal society. It is here in Johannesburg that the new society is being built. Something is happening here, my brother. […]

His voice grew louder, and he was again addressing people who were not there. Here in Johannesburg it is the mines, he said, everything is the mines. These high buildings, this wonderful City Hall, this beautiful Parktown with its beautiful houses, all this is built with the gold from the mines. This wonderful hospital for Europeans, the biggest hospital south of the Equator, it is built with the gold from the mines.

There was a change in his voice, it became louder like the voice of a bull or a lion. Go to our hospital, he said, and see our people lying on the floors. They lie so close you cannot step over them. But it is they who dig the gold. For three shillings a day. We come from the Transkei, and from Basutoland, and from Bechuanaland, and from Swaziland, and from Zululand. And from Ndotsheni also. We live in the compounds[5], we must leave our wives and families behind. And when the new gold is found, it is not we who will get more for our labour. It is the white man's shares that will rise, you will read it all in the papers. They go mad when new gold is found. They bring more of us to live in the compounds, to dig under the ground for three shillings a day. They do not think, here is a chance to pay more for our labour. They think only, here is a chance to build a bigger house and buy a bigger car. It is important to find gold, they say, for all South Africa is built on the mines.

He growled, and his voice grew deep, it was like thunder that was rolling. But it is not built on the mines, he said, it is built on our backs, on our sweat, on our labour. Every factory, every theatre, every beautiful house, they are all built by us. And what does a chief know about that? But here in Johannesburg they know.

He stopped, and was silent. And his visitors were silent also, for there was something in his voice that compelled[6] one to be silent. And

James Earl Jones as Stephen Kumalo in the 1995 film version

[1] **subject to sth/sb** here: required to obey sth/sb; under the authority of sth/sb – [2] **to salute** to make a gesture of greeting, respect or loyalty – [3] **to sway** to move or swing slowly from side to side – [4] **cunning** clever at deceiving people – [5] **compound** here: an enclosed group of buildings for the segregation or restraint of a particular group of people – [6] **to compel** to make sb do sth; to force sb

Stephen Kumalo sat silent, for this was a new brother that he saw.

John Kumalo looked at him. The Bishop says it is wrong, he said, but he lives in a big house, and his white priests get four, five, six times what you get, my brother.

He sat down, and took out a large red handkerchief to wipe his face.

– That is my experience, he said. That is why I no longer go to the Church.

– And that is why you did not write any more?

– Well, well, it could be the reason.

– That, and your wife Esther?

– Yes, yes, both perhaps. It is hard to explain in a letter. Our customs[1] are different here.

And Msimangu said, Are there any customs here?

John Kumalo looked at him. There is a new thing growing here, he said. Stronger than any church or chief. You will see it one day.

– And your wife? Why did she leave?

– Well, well, said John Kumalo with his knowing smile. She did not understand my experience.

– You mean, said Msimangu coldly, that she believed in fidelity[2]?

John looked at him suspiciously[3]. Fidelity, he said. But Msimangu was quick to see that he did not understand.

– Perhaps we should speak Zulu again, he said.

The angry veins stood out on the great bull neck, and who knows what angry words might have been spoken, but Stephen Kumalo was quick to intervene.

The Reverends Stephen Kumalo and Msimangu in the 1995 film version

What is the new thing John Kumalo repeatedly talks about?

Characters

Write a brief characterization of the three men.

Method kit, Characterization, p. 289

Changing perspectives

Describe life in Johannesburg from either of the two Reverends' points of view. Choose one of the following tasks:

- On the evening after his encounter with his long-lost brother, the Reverend Steven Kumalo writes a letter to his wife in Ndotsheni and tells her in his own words about John's experience in the city.
- After accompanying his friend Stephen Kumalo to his brother's, Reverend Msimangu writes a diary entry about the visit, voicing his private feelings about John Kumalo's "definition" of life in Johannesburg.

Method kit, Letter writing, p. 295 and Diary entry, p. 294

[1] **custom** a traditional and generally accepted way of behaving or doing things – [2] **fidelity** loyalty, a faithful attitude towards sth; loyalty towards one's husband or wife in not having any other sexual partner – [3] **suspicious** *misstrauisch*

Switching codes

1. Twice during the conversation a switch of language is suggested—from Zulu to English and back again. Find these places and explain the respective speaker's motivation to change languages.
2. These two different languages are expressions of the speakers' identities. Contrast the two different ways of living and the corresponding identities as represented by language preference.

Zulu (Stephen Kumalo, Msimangu)	the language of	English (John Kumalo)
– tribal reverence		– business
– customs ...		– ...

Tracing figurative language

Find examples of similes in the text and explain their function.

→ Language kit, Similes, p. 319

Covering a novel's major issues

1. Describe and compare the two covers, reflecting on the different thematic focus that is taken in each. What additional information about the novel's plot can you gather here?
2. Which cover do you prefer?
3. Create a collage that covers the issue of language raised in the extract. Give equal weight to text and pictures.

Cover of a pocketbook edition of *Cry, The Beloved Country*

Suggested book cover for *Cry, The Beloved Country* by a German student

Nissim Ezekiel

All Men Are Brothers, No?

Listen to the poem and guess who the speaker is.

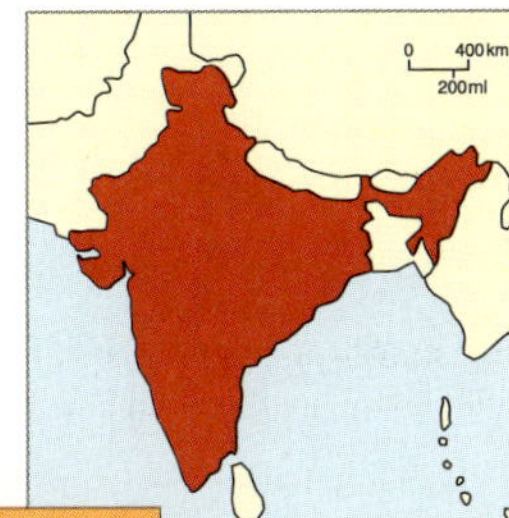

I am standing for peace and non-violence.
Why world is fighting fighting,
Why all people of world
Are not following Mahatma Gandhi
I am simply not understanding.
Ancient Indian Wisdom is 100 % correct.
I should say even 200 % correct.
But modern generation is neglecting—
Too much going for fashion and foreign thing.

Other day I'm reading in newspaper
(Every day I'm reading Times of India
To improve my English Language)
How one goonda[1] fellow
Throw stone at Indirabehn[2].
Must be student unrest fellow, I am thinking.
Friends, Romans, Countrymen, I am saying
(to myself)
Lend me the ears.
Everything is coming—
Regeneration[3], Remuneration[4], Contraception[5].
Be patiently, brothers and sisters.

You want one glass lassi[6]?
Very good for digestion[7].
With little salt lovely drink,
Better than wine;
Not that I am ever tasting the wine.
I'm the total teetotaller, completely total.
But I say
Wine is for the drunkards only.

Nissim Ezekiel (*1924)

[1]**goonda** (from Hindi) a dishonest man or one without principles – [2]**Indirabehn** Indira Gandhi, prime minister of India (1966–1977, 1980–1984), assassinated in 1984 – [3]**regeneration** process of making sb/sth strong and vigorous again – [4]**remuneration** reward, payment – [5]**contraception** methods used in preventing a woman becoming pregnant – [6]**lassi** Indian refreshment drink containing yoghurt and mangos – [7]**digestion** [daɪˈdʒestʃən] *Verdauung*

What you think of prospects of world peace?
Pakistan behaving like this,
China behaving like that,
It is making me very sad, I am telling you.
Really, most harassing[1] me.
All men are brothers, no?

In India also
Gujaraties[2], Maharashtrians[3], Hindiwallahs[4]
All brothers—
Though some are having funny habits.
Still, you tolerate me,
I tolerate you,
One day Ram Rajya[5] is surely coming.

You are going?
But you will visit again
Any time, any day,
I am not believing in ceremony.
Always I am enjoying your company.

Voicing unspoken replies

1. It appears the speaker is having a conversation, yet one part of it is missing. Read the poem carefully, pausing where you think a reply seems natural.
2. Work with a partner and compare your suggestions. Then insert possible responses made by the addressee. Practice reading your conversation and pay special attention to gestures and facial expressions.
3. Act out your dialogue in front of your classmates and together decide which one you like best.

Giving your opinion

Taking into account your personal experience what would be your answer to the speaker's question 'All men are brothers, no?' (l. 35)?

Spotting the difference

1. If you were an English teacher, what would you mark wrong? Why?
2. Identify characteristics of Indian English. Focus on grammar, choice of words and sentence structure.

[1] **to harass** ['hærəs, hə'ræs] to worry, to trouble – [2–4] **Gujaraties/Maharashtrians/Hindiwallahs** peoples of India – [5] **Ram Rajya** the rule, or kingdom of Rama, an incarnation of the god Vishnu

Benjamin Zephaniah

Dis Poetry

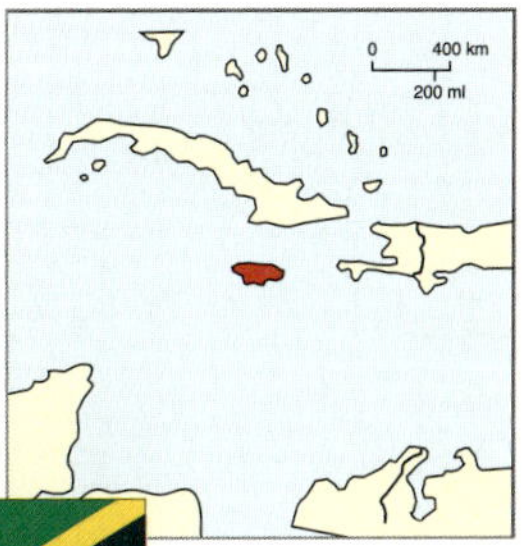

Dis poetry is like a riddim dat drops
De tongue fires a riddim dat shoots like shots
Dis poetry is designed fe rantin[1]
Dance hall style, big mouth chanting[2],
Dis poetry nar put yu to sleep
Preaching[3] follow me
Like yu is blind sheep,
Dis poetry is not Party Political
Not designed fe dose who are critical.
Dis poetry is wid me when I gu to me bed
It gets into me dreadlocks
It lingers[4] around me head
Dis poetry goes wid me as I pedal me bike
I've tried Shakespeare, respect due dere
But dis is de stuff I like.

Dis poetry is not afraid of going ina book
Still dis poetry need ears fe hear an eyes fe hav a look
Dis poetry is Verbal Riddim, no big words involved
An if I hav a problem de riddim gets it solved,
I've tried to be more romantic, it does nu good for me
So I tek a Reggae Riddim an build me poetry,
I could try be more personal
But you've heard it all before,
Pages of written words not needed
Brain has many words in store[5],
Yu could call dis poetry Dub[6] Ranting
De tongue plays a beat
De body starts skanking[7],
Dis poetry is quick an childish
Dis poetry is fe de wise an foolish,
Anybody can do it fe free,
Dis poetry is fe yu an me,
Don't stretch yu imagination
Dis poetry is fe de good of de Nation,

Benjamin Zephaniah (*1958)

[1] **to rant** to speak in a very loud, aggressive, or bombastic way, usually at length and repetitively – [2] **to chant** to sing or shout sth repeatedly, using the same rhythm – [3] **to preach** to try to persuade people to accept, follow or support a belief, a method, etc – [4] **to linger** to stay for a time – [5] **in store** kept ready for future use – [6] **dub** a style of popular music, originating in reggae in the 1970s, involving remixing records to bring some instruments into the foreground while causing others to echo – [7] **to skank** to dance to reggae music, especially in a jerky way

Chant,
In de morning
I chant
In de night
I chant
In de darkness
An under de spotlight,
I pass thru University
I pass thru Sociology
An den I got a dread[1] degree
In Dreadfull Ghettology.

Dis poetry stays wid me when I run or walk
An when I am talking to meself in poetry I talk,
Dis poetry is wid me,
Below me an above,
Dis poetry's from inside me
It goes to yu
WID LUV.

Getting into "de riddim"

1. Listen to the recording of the poem and enjoy it.
2. Play it a second time and join in, "chanting" along.
3. "Dis poetry is designed fe rantin dance hall style" (ll. 3f.). Does it fulfill this purpose? If so, explain how.

"Dis poetry" and "dat poetry"

1. In which way is this poem different from other poems you know?
2. Which special qualities does the speaker attribute to "dis poetry"?
3. What makes "dis poetry" superior to "dat poetry" in the speaker's opinion?

Creating your own rhythm

Write your own "rhythm poem". You can either choose a rhythm you know or create your own.

Taking a look at Jamaican English

Find some of the distinctive features of Jamaican English.

[1] **dread** inspiring fear and respect or awe in equal measure

The Wor(l)d Formation of English

The English Language Tree

The photograph printed below was taken in the Immigration Museum on Ellis Island. It depicts quite a common image of language formation and illustrates the assimilation of words into English from the mother tongues of American natives, settlers and immigrants. According to David Crystal, author of *The Cambridge Encyclopedia of the English Language*, English "has always been a vacuum cleaner of a language. It sucks in words from everywhere."

Why is the image of a tree quite an appropriate one for the formation of language—in more than one way?

The lexicon of the English language has been enriched by over 120 languages, starting centuries back with the incorporation of Celtic, Latin, Norman French and Scandinavian loan words and becoming increasingly polyglot, e.g. with the age of exploration, and subsequently, the waves of immigration into America. Thus, Asian, Dutch, German, Indian, Irish, Italian, Eastern European, Latino, African and countless other borrowings were moulded into English.

Examples of foreign words included in the English lexicon

ombudsman, coyote, sauna, amok, safari, parka, marmalade, penguin, whiskey, geyser, fjord, anonymous, coffee, bagel, shampoo, tycoon, kangaroo, tattoo, puma, anorak, potato, poncho, hamburger, goulash, circus, opera, chocolate, apartheid

Filling the leaves of the language tree

1. Trace the origin of the words above with the help of an extensive English-English dictionary (e.g. *The Encarta World English Dictionary, Webster's Dictionary,* etc) or an English encyclopedia. Group the borrowings according to the language they derive from. After copying the image of the language tree, fill in the other foreign languages the words above sprang from, then attach the "leaves" to the appropriate "branches."
2. Think of more examples of foreign loan words in the English language and add them to your drawing.

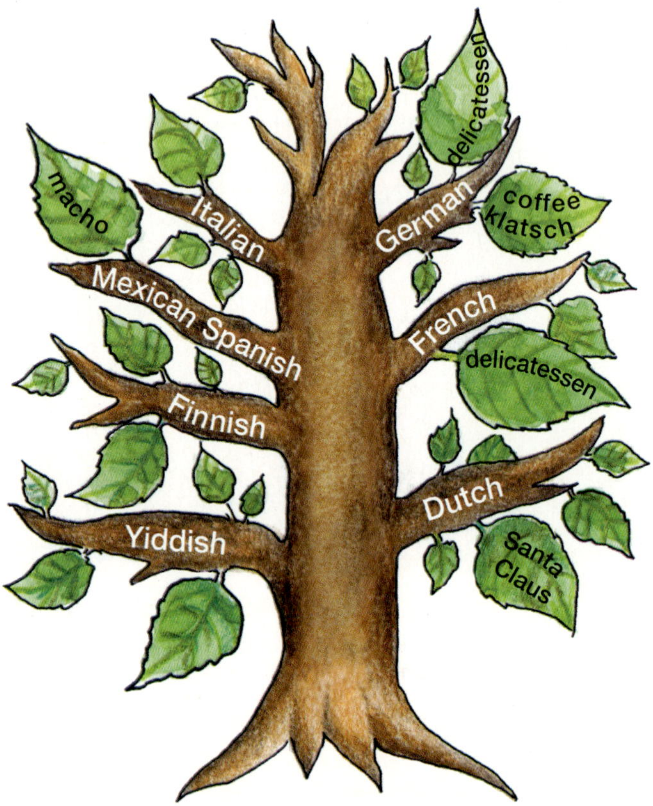

Word-Formation

Info

Due to the constant development of new conditions in society, the English lexicon[1] is undergoing continual change. As linguist Anne H. Soukhanov puts it: "New words are the birth certificates of change—change in attitudes, in mores, in human relations, in technology, in the social and economic landscape, in the natural world."
Apart from the integration of words from other languages (subsequently called *borrowings* or *loan words*), various linguistic processes within a language prevail in enlarging its vocabulary. All of these together are known as word-formation.
Some of the major processes in lexical construction are listed below (in alphabetical order):

Abbreviations

The habit of abbreviating words has been noticeable for more than 150 years and is usually attributed to the desire of achieving linguistic economy. Different types of abbreviations can be traced:

AIDS

Acronyms: Items are pronounced as words, e.g. *NATO* (North Atlantic Treaty Organisation), *AIDS* (Acquired Immune Deficiency Syndrome), *OPEC* (Organisation of Petroleum Exporting Countries), etc. Some of them are no longer recognized as abbreviations and so are not written in capital letters, such as laser (Light Amplification by Stimulated Emission of Radiation), *yuppy* (Young Urban Professional), etc.

flu

Clipping: A part of a word serves as a substitution for the whole, e.g. *ad* (advertisement), *fridge* (refrigerator), *phone* (telephone), *flu* (influenza), *exam* (examination), *cello* (violoncello), etc.

BSE

Initialisms: Items are spoken as individual letters, e.g. *EU* (European Union), *BBC* (British Broadcasting Corporation), *MP* (Member of Parliament), *BSE* (Bovine Spongiform Encephalopathy[2]), UN (United Nations), etc.

Affixation

bio-

Affixes[3] are attached to previously existing words, giving a huge scope of new items and often resulting in an item that belongs to a different word class.
In English, they occur either before the root of the word (prefixes) or after (suffixes). Some of the multitude of samples are un-, in-, pro-, anti-, inter-, ex-, bio-, and Euro- for prefixes and -tion, -ness, -ism, -able, and -ish for suffixes.

[1] **lexicon** here: the entire stock of words belonging to a branch of knowledge or known by somebody – [2] **Bovine Spongiform Encephalopathy** a usually fatal disease of cattle (also: *infml* mad cow disease) – [3] **affix** a letter or a group of letters added to the beginning or the end of a word to change its meaning or the way it is used

Info

Back-formation

Instead of forming new and longer items by adding affixes to words, this process works the other way round, as a shorter word is created by removing a real or imagined affix, as in to *televise* (from television) or to *baby-sit* (from baby-sitter).

to baby-sit

Blends

New words are created by joining parts of other words, e.g. *brunch* (breakfast + lunch), *telex* (teleprinter + exchange), *smog* (smoke + fog), *Eurovision* (European + television), etc.

smog

Coining

Coinings (also: coinages or neologisms) are creations of completely new words or phrases, usually as reactions to altered social circumstances, e.g. cardboard city, couch potato[1], ecofriendly, Trojan horse[2], etc. They usually derive from[3] a compounding process or a new meaning is attributed to an already existing word.

couch potato

Compounding

New terms are composed by two or more formerly separate words, which together convey a unique and quite different meaning from their individual one. Examples are *on-line, roundabout, homesick, scarecrow, African-American, and mother-in-law.*

on-line

Conversion

With this process, words undergo a change of word class without the attachment of an affix, e.g. *to bottle, to paper, a natural, to dirty, the how and the why*, etc.

the why

Finding examples of the word-formation processes

1. Study the processes described above and give at least five more English examples for each. Recent newspaper articles might prove a helpful source.
2. Which one do you consider most productive in enlarging the lexicon?

Inventing new words

A special form of neologisms (see above) are the so-called *nonce-words*, invented words that occur only once and do not spread into general usage, e.g. "brillig" (in *Jabberwocky*).
Create nonce-words yourself, using any of the word-formation processes above, and have your partner guess their meaning.

[1] **couch potato** (*joc* or *derog*) a person who spends a lot of time at home watching television – [2] **Trojan horse** a computer programme that appears to be useful but that actually does damage – [3] **to derive from** to have sth as its source or origin

English Makes the World Go Round

Kim Campbell

American English— The Global Language of Tomorrow

Among the roughly 350 million native English speakers, American English is spoken by about 70 per cent. What impact do you think this fact has on learners of English today?

[…] The "Americanization" of English is happening around the world today, from Africa to Britain itself. American English is seeping[1] into the nooks and crannies[2] of English everywhere thanks to education, business, Hollywood, and the Internet.

Although British English—which many countries consider to be the "real thing"—is widely taught around the world, what those learners use in their private lives is more influenced by the US. As a result, "American English is spreading faster than British English," says Braj Kachru, a linguist[3] in India. […] In television broadcasts alone, the United States controlled 75 percent of the world's programming as recently as 1993, beaming "Sesame Street" to Lagos, Nigeria, for example. Americans also outnumber Britons: People are more likely to encounter[4] one of the 260 million Yanks than one of the 55 million Brits. […]

What makes British English "the real thing" in your opinion?

Why do you think AE is more popular with learners than BE?

The spread of American English began in the decades after World War II. Experts say the simultaneous[5] rise of the US as a military and technological superpower and the receding[6] of the British empire gave many in the world both the desire and option[7] to choose American English. […] "There's no question that Britain made English an international language in the 19th century with its empire," says Bill Bryson, an American author of several books on the history of English. "But it's Americans that have been the driving force behind the globalization of English in the 20th century" because of their commercial and cultural clout[8], he says. […]

What are the reasons for the spread of AE in the 20th century?

Britain has not been immune to the spread of American English, either. More words that were exclusively American are now found in the speech and writing in both countries, says Norman Moss,

[1] **to seep** to flow slowly and in small quantities through sth – [2] **nooks and crannies** every part, everywhere – [3] **linguist** one who makes a scientific study of language – [4] **to encounter** to meet sb unexpectedly – [5] **simultaneous** happening or done at the same time as sth – [6] **receding** here: decline – [7] **option** a thing that is or might be chosen; a choice – [8] **clout** power or influence

English sign in Thailand

compiler of an American-British/ British-American dictionary. [...] "Once 'guy' and 'campus' were almost unknown in Britain," he says. Today they are widely used. Britons are also increasingly saying "movie" instead of "film". Computer-related words are more frequently spelled the American way: program, without the British addition of "me" on the end, for example. And the American phrase "the bottom line" is encroaching[1] on its British equivalent "at the end of the day." [...]

Linguists note that the mixing of British and American English in Europe has given rise to a "mid-Atlantic" English, a more neutral language that is less identifiable with either country.

In some European countries, both kinds of English are now accepted and taught. Some learners prefer American English because they believe it has fewer regional accents and dialects than British English does, experts say, and therefore is easier to understand and to use.

Still, the USIA[2]—which advises countries on English teaching but does not teach it directly—and the British Council[3], argue that the languages are not in competition. "I don't think there is a fierce[4] contest going on between the two kinds of English," says Ms. Kershaw of the British Council. She notes that there are few differences between the two. [...]

But the question of who is teaching the world to speak English is no small matter. The hunger for the language has made English teaching a big business. "English has become an economic commodity[5]," says Dr. Kachru, who runs the Center for Advanced Study at the University of Illinois in Champaign. Some estimates[6] place the revenues[7] of the worldwide industry at about $ 10 billion annually. That includes teaching, textbooks, and materials, and money spent by foreign students who choose to attend schools in English-speaking countries as a result of learning the language. [...]

Currently, much of the English taught in Europe, India, and parts of Asia and Africa is British or British-influenced. American English is favored in Latin America, Japan and South Korea.

But linguists note that often those learning the language just want English—they don't care what kind. English is often studied by people whose primary purpose is not to speak to Americans or Britons, says Dr. Feria of Berlitz[8]. They need to speak with other

[1] **to encroach on/upon sth** to intrude – [2] **USIA** United States Information Agency – [3] **British Council** government-sponsored agency that operates British-English teaching centres worldwide – [4] **fierce** violent and angry, intense, strong – [5] **commodity** useful thing, esp an article of trade – [6] **estimate** calculation, not necessarily detailed or accurate, of the value of sth – [7] **revenue** income, esp of a state or organization – [8] **Berlitz** language school

non-native speakers, using English as a common language, experts say. Many cultures also increasingly communicate in their own forms of English—Indian English, for example. And some countries may reject[1] either American or British English if speaking it is considered undesirable for political reasons. [...]

As English continues to spread, some experts say, a form of it could become the common language of the world. But multilingualism is also on the rise, suggesting that English may not be the only language to prevail[2]. David Crystal, a linguist from Wales and author of *The Cambridge Encyclopedia of the English Language*, says that the way English is changing now, if it does become the global language, "it's going to be American-English-dominated, I have no doubt."

The Christian Science Monitor, September 6–12, 1996, pp. 10–11

Name some countries where you think one of the two varieties might be rejected.

What other tongue could become an international language?

Americanization of English

Compile reasons given in the text for the increasing Americanization of English.

What's the difference?

The linguist Norman Moss is working on an American-British/British-American dictionary called "What's the difference?". Find more examples like the ones quoted (ll. 30–41) for entries to his collection. You may scan English-speaking newspapers or consult a dictionary for more material.

Method kit, Skimming and scanning, p. 278

British English		American English
film ...	**lexicon**	movie ...
programme ...	**spelling**	program ...
at the end of the day What's the matter with ...? ...	**idioms**	the bottom line What's with ...? ...

A plea for British or American English

Which variety of English do you personally prefer? Prepare a short plea for your choice and try to be as convincing as possible.

Method kit, Comment and speech, p. 292

[1] **to reject** to refuse to accept – [2] **to prevail** to be widespread

Starting your own language school

Worldwide, a lot of money can be made with teaching English. Imagine you and your friends started your own language school in your area for people your age. How could you make learning English attractive for your clients and a successful enterprise for yourself? In groups work out a strategy (who would you hire as a teacher, what should your students learn, what methods would you want to use for teaching the language effectively, where should classes take place, how would you advertise for your school, etc). Then prepare an English lesson that suits your objective and give the lesson in class.

Tracing passive forms

Frequent use of the passive voice is quite typical of formal texts. Look through the article and find examples. Then change them into the active voice.

Translation

Translate ll. 58—77 ("The hunger for the language ... undesirable for political reasons."). Remember: In German, more generous use of proper nouns and subordinate clauses might be helpful when translating -ing forms and past participle constructions.

Yasmin Alibhai-Brown

The English Language Is Taking Over the World. But Should We Rejoice?

Which languages do you speak and how did you learn them? Compare your language proficiency with that of your parents and grandparents. Give examples of situations in which you/your parents/your grandparents use a particular language.

Why is there reason for the British to rejoice?

Today, David Blunkett will tell business leaders to rejoice[1] because the demand for one British product has increased massively across the world, and the demand is growing exponentially[2]. No, it is not size-16 Marks & Spencer cardis[3], following their brilliant advertising campaigns using women with real bums[4] and tums[5]. It is the English language. [...]

Some of the happiest years of my life were spent teaching English as a foreign language at the London School of English in Holland Park, owned by Peter Fabian, an eccentric English gentleman with

[1] **to rejoice** (dated or *fml*) to feel or show great joy – [2] **exponential** produced or indicated by multiplying a set of numbers by themselves – [3] **cardis** (*infml*) cardigans – [4] **bum** (*infml* esp Brit) the part of the body on which one sits – [5] **tum** (*infml*) stomach

a wonderful range of bow ties[1] and a passionate mission to spread the word. This was in the Seventies and early Eighties. Students, at first, would be very disappointed to see an Asian standing in front of them. They wanted their own Henry Higgins.[2]

But it didn't last. I was teaching them something they were so hungry for—even then—that the suspicion[3] soon disappeared and all of us, good *and* bad teachers, were adored, spoilt[4] with expensive presents and offered all sorts of other delights, including pleasures of the flesh by randy[5] Italians who picked up the English needed for flirting within hours of starting at the school. Now we have hundreds more schools here and abroad, and this good news needs to be better known.

But even as we celebrate this success, we should be counting the cost of it. There are at present some 6,000 languages spoken around the world. By the year 2025, more than half of these may die. We would worry terribly if this was a statistic for plants or birds or beasts. But cultural and linguistic "biodiversity" is surely just as important.

According to the *New Internationalist*, only 100 languages are actually written down and specialists believe that no language can survive unless 100,000 people speak it.

When languages die, concepts, ways of thinking, self-belief and value systems go, too. Some of the most authoritarian regimes throughout history have understood this and tried to kill languages by forbidding their use in public spaces. The Kurds, Basque people and Native Americans have suffered immeasurably as a result of these all too real culture wars.

When I was growing up in East Africa, most Asian children there spoke at least three languages by the time they were three. We used Swahili when communicating with the local Africans who were (to our shame) the underpaid servants and maids in the homes. Then we spoke the first language of the family, which could be Punjabi, Urdu, Gujarati or Kutchi, and then came Hindi, the language of Bollywood[6] films which we all went to see at least twice a week. English came later and became just another language to be used in our complex daily interactions.

The colonial administration tried to ban "vernacular[7]" languages in school, but this had little effect. We were already well-formed, efficient polyglots[8]. French would have been yet another addition had we not had the misfortune to be taught for years by the slightly mad Miss Lachlan who had clearly fled to Africa after some bounder[9] broke her heart. She wore her dresses the wrong way round, never washed her hair and recited[10] sad poems at us instead of tapping[11] into the obvious talent we had for learning languages.

Which cliché of an English teacher is evoked here?

Rephrase this idiom.

Why do you need 100,000 people to make a language survive?

Imagine what the author means and find further examples.

[1] **bow tie** *Fliege* – [2] **Henry Higgins** character in George Bernard Shaw's (1856–1950) play *Pygmalion* (a professor of phonetics teaching a Cockney flower girl how to speak "proper" English) – [3] **suspicion** *Misstrauen* – [4] **to spoil** (spoilt/spoiled, spoilt/spoiled) to harm the character of sb, esp a child, by lack of discipline or too much attention, praise etc – [5] **randy** (*infml* esp Brit) sexually excited – [6] **Bollywood** film industry in Bombay – [7] **vernacular** a language or form of a language spoken in a particular country or region or by a particular group, as compared with a formal or written language – [8] **polyglot** (*fml*) knowing, using or written in many languages – [9] **bounder** (*derog*) dishonourable person – [10] **to recite** to say a piece of literature aloud from memory, esp to an audience – [11] **to tap** here: to extract or obtain a supply of sth from a source

Today, neither of my children can speak any of my rich, resonant[1] childhood languages. They cannot communicate with their Asian grandmother except in her simple English. They will never know the words which cannot be translated but which mean so much. *Sanskari*, for example, means a combination of cultured, educated, sensitive, thoughtful, caring and much else. Not only do they not know the word, the concept is all but lost to them in this crude world they now inhabit. If they decide at some future date to replant their roots, they will not find it easy to speak the languages properly because many of the sounds are impossibly difficult unless you learn them young and use them constantly. They will sound like foreigners in their ancestral cultures.

My son Ari did speak Kutchi until he was seven. Then he gave up, realising, I think, that our society believes non-European languages and cultures to be inferior. Our languages are not given the status of French, Spanish or even Russian in our education system. One of my most painful memories is of being thrown out of a sports shop with my mother and young son. I was speaking to my mother in Kutchi and the manager didn't want any "bloody foreign Paki lingo[2]" spoken in his shop.

Millions of Britons already believe they have no need to learn other languages and that the whole world should damn well speak English. With so many foreigners now wanting to do exactly that, the danger is that, instead of pride, it is conceit[3] that will grow and with it an indifference to the annihilation[4] of oral traditions, with no DNA to save and resuscitate[5] in the future. *The Independent*, October 31, 2000

Responding to the article

1. "The English Language Is Taking Over the World. But Should We Rejoice?" Which answer to the question is implied in the article?
2. Answer the question posed in the headline from your personal point of view.
3. Outline Alibhai-Brown's "linguistic biography" and that of her children. What has changed and how does she feel about it?

Language and culture

The writer mentions that the Kutchi word "sanskari" cannot be translated into English, since it means "a combination of cultured, educated, sensitive, thoughtful, caring and much else" (ll. 56f.). Can you think of words in your mother tongue that would present the same problem (e.g. "Schadenfreude") because the words convey particular cultural concepts? Try to cluster them by their meaning, e.g.

emotions	philosophy	food	...
...	Dasein	Ersatzkaffee	...
...	...	...	...

Method kit, Mind map, p. 281

[1] **resonant** deep, clear and continuing to echo – [2] **lingo** (*infml, jog* or *derog*) a foreign language – [3] **conceit** excessive pride in oneself or in one's powers, abilities, etc – [4] **annihilation** the act of destroying sb/sth completely – [5] **to resuscitate** [rɪ'sʌsɪteɪt] to bring sb/sth back to consciousness

Translation

Translate ll. 29–63 ("When languages die ... their ancestral cultures.") into German. Pay special attention to the translation of gerunds.

Holding a debate

"We should allow English to take over the world because this would ensure global understanding."
You can either from groups and hold a debate, or exchange your opinions, e.g. by using the fish bowl method. Place three or four chairs for the respective spokesperson and the presenter in the centre of a full circle of seats. Provide one more chair in the centre for members of the audience who want to step forward and give additional contributions in turns.

Tracing figurative language

1. Find examples of metaphors in the text and explain them.
2. Pin down the main image the author uses to describe language. To what effect is it used?
   → Language kit, Metaphor, p. 317

Your thematic vocabulary

Create your own word tree for the word field "The English Language".

1. Working in groups, choose one of the following topics: Varieties of English, The English Lexicon, Learning English, Use of English.
2. Collect words from the texts you have read in this chapter, which deal with your chosen topic.
3. Copy the word tree printed on the right and attach your findings to "your" branch, then present them to the class.
4. Complete the word tree by adding the other groups' findings to your drawing. Now use 15 of these words in informative sentences about the English language.

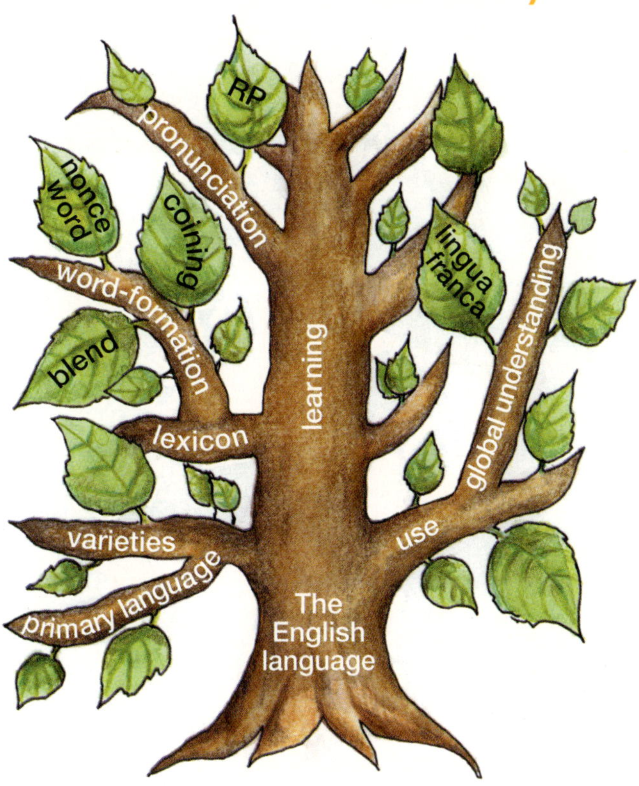

Great Britain:

Past—Present—Future

Manchester 2002

The XVII Commonwealth Games

Great Britain has experienced lots of ups und downs during the last years. Do you remember any special events?

A Multicultural Society

Linton Kwesi Johnson

Inglan Is a Bitch

Linton Kwesi Johnson is a writer, journalist and singer who was born in Kingston, Jamaica, in 1952 and came to Britain in 1963 where he was raised in the Brixton section of London. He was a member of the Black Panthers and published his first poems in the journal *Race Today*. He is regarded to be the inventor of dub poetry. While pure dub is drum and bass reggae music with a strong beat, dub poetry combines the instrumental rhythm track of dub with spoken poetry.

The spelling in this song is for the most part an attempt to transcribe West Indian English phonetically. At first hearing the song is hard to understand, but sometimes you must only change the vowels: e.g. 'rab' means 'rob'.

Listen to the song and note down key words and phrases. Then read the song with the help of the annotations and tell your partner how much you have understood. Then listen again.

w'en mi jus' come to Landan toun
mi use to work pan[1] di andahgroun
but workin' pan di andahgroun
y'u don't get fi know[2] your way aroun'

Inglan is a bitch
dere's no escapin' it
Inglan is a bitch
dere's no runnin' whey fram it

mi get a lickle jab in a big 'otell
an' awftah a while, mi woz doin' quite well
dem staat mi aaf as a dish-washah
but w'en mi tek a stack[3], mi noh tun[4] clackwatchah!

Inglan is a bitch
dere's no escapin it
Inglan is a bitch
noh baddah try fi hide fram it

Linton Kwesi Johnson at the Irie-Festival in Dortmund, Germany (1998)

[1] **pan** (nonstandard) upon – [2] **get fi know** to get to know ('fi' can also mean 'for to' or 'for') – [3] **stack** a large amount of plates, cups etc – [4] **tun** turn

w'en em gi'you di lickle wage packit
fus dem rab it wid dem big tax rackit[1]
y'u haffi struggle fi meek en's meet[2]
an' w'en y'u goh a y'u bed y'u jus' cant sleep

Inglan is a bitch
dere's no escapin it
Inglan is a bitch fi true
a noh lie mi a tell, a true

mi use to work dig ditch[3] w'en it cowl noh bitch
mi did strang like a mule, but, bwoy, mi did fool
den awftah a while mi jus' stap dhu ovahtime
den aftah a while mi jus' phu dung[4] mi tool

Inglan is a bitch
dere's no escapin it
Inglan is a bitch
y'u haffi know how fi suvvive in it

well mi dhu day wok an' mid dhu nite wok
mi dhu clean wok an' mid dhu dutty wok
dem seh dat black man is very lazy
but it y'u si how mi wok y'u woulda sey mi crazy

Inglan is a bitch
dere's no escapin it
Inglan is a bitch
y'u bettah face up to it

dem have a lickle facktri up inna Brackly
inna disya[5] facktri all dem dhu is pack crackry[6]
fi di laas fifteen years dem get mi laybah
now awftah fiteen years mi fall out a fayvah[7]

Inglan is a bitch
dere's no escapin it
Inglan is a bitch
dere's no runnin' whey fram it

mi know dem have work, work in abundant[8]
yet still, dem mek mi redundant[9]
now, at fifty-five mi gettin' quite ol'
yet still, dem sen' mi fi goh draw dole[10]

Inglan is a bitch
dere's no escapin it
Inglan is a bitch fi true
is whey wi a goh dhu 'bout it?[11]

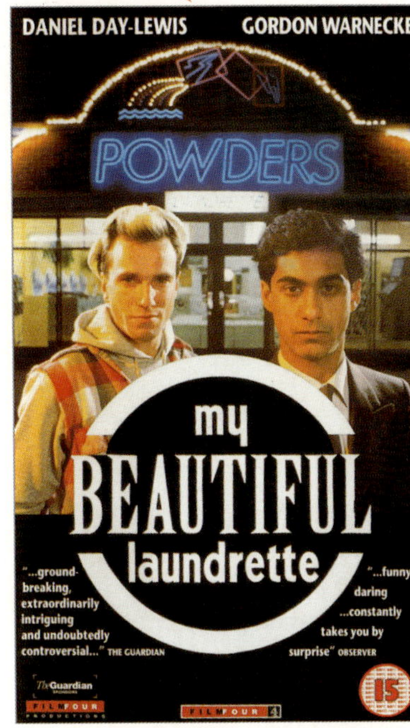

In the film "My beautiful laundrette" H. Kureishi tells the story of Omar, a young Asian, who dreams of turning an old laundrette into a glittering success. Things get complicated when he employs his childhood friend Johny, an ex-National Front member.

[1] **tax rackit** (racket) *Steuerbetrug* – [2] **fi meek en's meet** (to make ends meet) to earn just enough money to be able to buy the things you need – [3] **ditch** a long channel dug in the ground – [4] **dung** done, finished – [5] **disya** this – [6] **crackry** (crockery) cups, plates etc – [7] **fall out a fayvah** (to fall out of favour) to lose one's privileged position – [8] **work in abundant** (abundance) plenty of work – [9] **redundant** unemployed – [10] **dole** *(coll)* unemployment money – [11] **is whey wi a goh dhu 'bout it?** (the question) is what we are we going to do about it?

The immigrant experience

1. What sort of jobs did immigrants have to do in GB?
2. What is Johnson complaining about?
3. "... dere's no escapin it." Do you agree?

Standardizing

Rewrite the first seven stanzas in Standard English.

Music as a means of protest

Dub poetry as well as raps are often the only means underprivileged groups have to express their anger and protest. Write a rap about a similar situation.

J.F.O. McAllister and Helen Gibson

The Importance of Being British

Describe what is going on in the picture on the next page.

As you read, summarize each paragraph in a short sentence.

Say the words "British" or "English" and most people think "enduring"[1]: a royal succession[2] that goes back to 1066, the language of Shakespeare, ancient universities, the mother of Parliaments. But the reality of Blair's post-imperial, globalized Britain—when the royals are tabloid[3] fodder[4], hereditary peers[5] have been kicked out of the House of Lords, and Scotland and Wales have their own assemblies[6]—is better described as fluctuating. And that is giving British politics a case of vertigo[7]. In small ways and large, national identity, and its more prickly[8] cousins immigration and race, keep popping onto the national agenda[9].

They did so with a vengeance[10] two weekends ago in Oldham, a former textile town near Manchester. A skirmish[11] outside a shop between two British-born teenagers, one of Asian descent and one white, triggered[12] fighting between whites and non-whites. The Asian youths then turned on the police. The violence left dozens injured, cars torched[13] and properties smashed. Though Oldham has quieted down, race relations are likely to remain contentious[14] issues even after the election. Says Chris Myant, of the publicly funded Commission for Racial Equality (C.R.E.), "While you have

[1] **to endure** to continue to exist for a long time – [2] **succession** act of taking over an official position or title – [3] **tabloid** less serious newspaper with lots of pictures and short, sensational articles – [4] **fodder** easy target for sb/sth – [5] **hereditary peers** members of the House of Lords who can pass on their title to their children – [6] **assembly** regional parliament – [7] **vertigo** the fear of losing one's balance – [8] **prickly** sth or sb difficult to deal with – [9] **agenda** schedule, detailed plan – [10] **vengeance** ['venʒəns] revenge – [11] **skirmish** short fight – [12] **to trigger** to start, to initiate – [13] **to torch** to set fire to a building or car – [14] **contentious** [-'--] controversial

a picture of significant success in some areas, you still have a vast backlog[1] of problems pulling down a number of groups, and you still have a high degree of racial prejudice among some white members of the public."

Ethnic minorities make up only 6% of the population, but immigrants have more than doubled from the annual 90,000 during the early 1990s. The suffocation[2] of 58 Chinese being smuggled across the English Channel in a refrigerator truck last year added fuel to a debate about who should be entitled[3] to enter and remain in the country. Is Britain a "soft touch[4]"? Does it need more foreign workers, or fewer? There is no consensus. William Hague[5] has made the temporary detention[6] of asylum[7] seekers a central plank of his campaign, responding to anxieties[8] in some towns where asylum seekers are now housed. […]

[1] **backlog** quantity of work that should have been done already – [2] **suffocation** death from lack of oxygen – [3] **to entitle** to give sb the right to have or do sth – [4] **soft touch** a person that you can easily persuade to do sth – [5] **William Hague** Conservative MP since 1989, leader of the Conservative Party from 1997–2001, when he lost the general elections – [6] **detention** state of being kept in prison – [7] **asylum** [ə'saɪləm] – [8] **anxiety** [æŋ'zaɪəti] fear

Even before the campaign started, the C.R.E. asked M.P.s to sign a pledge[1] calling on candidates to refrain[2] from stirring up[3] racial hostility. It sounds harmless, but some refused on the grounds that it was wrong for the group to enforce "political correctness." Shortly thereafter, Foreign Secretary Robin Cook suggested—to some derision[4]—that Britain's multicultural success was shown by chicken tikka masala[5] becoming the country's most popular dish. Then a retiring Tory[6] backbencher raised temperatures when he said the British were becoming a "mongrel"[7] race through immigration. Hague forced him to apologize. The gusts[8] of opinion that these incidents provoked are signs of how hard Britain is finding it to answer the question of who is "really" British.

There is another complicating factor: shifting[9] political institutions and allegiances[10] within the country. The Labour government sold the idea of a new, Scottish Parliament and Welsh Assembly as ways to strengthen the Union. It may be having the opposite effect. [...] Scottish M.P.s at Westminster can vote on English laws, for example, but English M.P.s have no vote on many Scottish matters. [...] A recent survey[11] found that 17% of people in England now saw themselves as English, not British, up from 7% two years ago.

And then there is Europe. Tony Blair recently argued the "patriotic case" for engaging with the E.U., but two-thirds of voters want to stay out of the euro, and half would even leave the E.U., mostly because they feel it threatens British identity.

Despite Oldham, British anxiety about national identity has the virtue[12] of being a mostly peaceful sport. "People's conception of what it is to be British, what it is to be English is an ever-changing one, and so it should be," Home Secretary Jack Straw said recently. But those shifts may not always come without hurt. As Chris Myant says, "Race and identity are very close to people's hearts."

Time, June 11, 2001, p. 35

Britain's national identity

1. What are the current issues in the debate on British national identity?
2. Define "national identity." Consider different concepts: fatherland, country, land, nation, etc.
3. Is Britain's national identity threatened?
4. Explain the headline.

Translation

Translate ll. 11–33 ("They did so ... now housed.") in two groups and compare your translations.

[1]**to sign a pledge** to make a promise – [2]**to refrain from** to stop oneself from doing sth – [3]**to stir up** [stɜ:(r) ʌp] to cause; to encourage – [4]**derision** [dɪ'rɪʒn] *Hohn, Spott* – [5]**chicken tikka masala** a dish from Bangladesh – [6]**Tory** Conservative MP – [7]**mongrel** ['mʌŋgrəl] dog that is a mixture of different races – [8]**gust** a strong expression of emotion – [9]**to shift** to change – [10]**allegiance** [ə'li:dʒəns] loyalty, faithfulness – [11]**survey** statistical study – [12]**virtue** here: advantage

Identifying -ing forms

Look for -ing-forms and classify them. Rewrite the present participle clauses using a different grammatical structure.

Britain's most popular dish: Chicken Tikka Masala

Preparation time: 10 to 30 min
Cooking time: 10 to 30 min
Serves: 4

Ingredients

4 skinless chicken breast fillets, cubed
3 tablespoons vegetable oil
1 red pepper *(Paprika)*, halved, de-seeded and cut into pieces
1 yellow pepper, halved, de-seeded and cut into pieces
450 g tikka masala cooking sauce
250 g Indian basmati rice
plain pappadums (spicy fried crackers)—to serve 2 tablespoons natural yogurt
fresh coriander or parsley *(Petersilie)*, chopped (optional)

Methods

1. Fry the chicken in the oil in a large pan.
2. Add the peppers, stir in the sauce and simmer for 25 minutes, or until chicken is cooked.
3. Cook rice and pappadums following the instructions on the packets.
4. Serve the chicken on a bed of basmati rice, garnished with natural yogurt and herbs.

Zadie Smith

The Burning of Books

Zadie Smith was born in north-west London in 1975 and still lives there. She is the daughter of an English father and a Jamaican mother. Smith studied literature at King's College, Cambridge University.

The following text is an excerpt from Zadie Smith's first and highly acclaimed novel *White Teeth*, a satire about what it means to be English. It's a tale that spans 25 years of two families' assimilation in North London: the Joneses (from England and Jamaica) and the Iqbals (from Bangladesh)—an unlikely pairing of families, but their destinies, which are very closely connected, condense the British Empire's history and their hopes into a multiethnic future. In his search for identity Samad Iqbal's son Millat, 14, joins an ultra-Muslim activist group.

Zadie Smith

How is Millat introduced?

14 January 1989

Millat spread his legs like Elvis and slapped his wallet down on the counter.

'One for Bradford[1], yeah?'

The ticket-man put his tired face close up to the glass. 'Are you asking me, young man, or telling me?'

'I just say, yeah? One for Bradford, yeah? You got some problem, yeah? Speaka da English. This is King's Cross[2], yeah? One for Bradford, innit[3]?'

Millat's Crew[4] (Rajik, Ranil, Dipesh and Hifan) sniggered[5] and shuffled[6] behind him, joining in on the yeahs like some kind of backing group.

'Please?'

'Please what, yeah? One for Bradford, yeah? You get me? One for Bradford, *Chief*[7].'

'And would that be a return? For a child?'

'Yeah, man. I'm fifteen, yeah? 'Course I want a return, I've got a barii[8] to get back to like everybody else.'

'That'll be seventy-five pounds, then, please.'

This was met with displeasure by Millat and Millat's Crew.

'You what? Takin' liberties[9]! Seventy—*chaaaa,* man. That's moody[10]. I ain't payin' no seventy-five pounds!'

'Well, I'm afraid that's the price, Maybe next time you mug[11] some poor old lady,' said the ticket-man, looking pointedly at the chunky[12] gold that fell from Millat's ears, wrists, fingers and from around his neck, 'you could stop in here first before you get to the jewellery store.'

'Liberties!' squealed[13] Hifan.

'He's cussin'[14] you, yeah?' confirmed Ranil.

'You better tell 'im,' warned Rajik.

Millat waited a minute. Timing was everything. Then he turned around, stuck his arse in the air, and farted long and loud in the ticket-man's direction.

The Crew on cue[15] *'Somokami*[16]!'

What do you think about the ticket-man?

'What did you call me? You—what did you say? You little bastards. Can't tell me in English? Have to talk your Paki language?'

Millat slammed his fist so hard on the glass that it reverberated[17] down the booths to the ticket-man down the other end selling tickets to Milton Keynes[18].

'First: I'm not a Paki, you ignorant fuck. And second: you don't need translator, yeah? I'll give it to you straight.' [...]

'You want to thank God for the glass between us, boy.'

[1] **Bradford** Northern English town of 300,000 inhabitants, west of Leeds – [2] **King's Cross** London train station – [3] **innit** (*sl*) isn't it – [4] **crew** here: gang – [5] **to snigger** to laugh in a quiet, unpleasant way – [6] **to shuffle** to walk without lifting one's feet – [7] **chief** (North London slang) fool – [8] **barii** (Bangladeshi) home – [9] **to take liberties** to be too friendly with s.o. – [10] **moody** bad-tempered, here: impertinent, outrageous – [11] **mug** attack and rob – [12] **chunky** thick and heavy – [13] **to squeal** to speak in a very high voice – [14] **to cuss** (*infml*) to swear at sb – [15] **on cue** on command – [16] **Somokami** (Bangladeshi; *derog*) homosexual – [17] **to reverberate** to echo – [18] **Milton Keynes** town north-west of London

'Yeah, yeah, yeah. I thank Allah, yeah'? I hope he fucks you up wicked[1], yeah? We're going to Bradford to sort out[2] the likes of you, yeah? *Chief!*'

Halfway up platform 12, about to board a train they had no tickets for, a King's Cross security guy stopped Millat's Crew to ask them a question. 'You boys not looking for any trouble, are you?'

The question was fair. Millat's Crew looked like trouble. And, at the time, a crew that looked like trouble in this particular way had a name, they were of a breed[3]:

Raggastani.

It was a new breed, just recently joining the ranks[4] of the other street crews:

Becks, B-boys, Indie kids, wide-boys, ravers, rude-boys, Acidheads, Sharons, Tracies, Kevs, Nation Brothers, Raggas and Pakis; manifesting itself as a kind of cultural mongrel[5] of the last three categories. Raggastanis spoke a strange mix of Jamaican patois[6], Bengali, Gujarati[7] and English. Their ethos, their manifesto, if it could be called that, was equally a hybrid[8]

I've been wonderin' why
People livin' in fear
Of my shade
(Or my hi top fade)
I'm not the one that's runnin'
But they got me on the run
Treat me like I have a gun
All I got is genes and chromosomes
Consider me Black to the bone
All I want is peace and love
On this planet
(Ain't that how God planned it?)

(From the song "Fear of a Black Planet", Des Jam Music Inc., Bring the Noize Inc., Bridgeport Music Inc. Corp., Universal Music Publ. GmbH/MCA Music GmbH, Hamburg, Sauerwald Musikverlag GmbH + Ingo Kleinhammer OHG, Bridgeport Switzerland)

[1] **wicked** (*sl*) severely – [2] **to sort sb out** to punish – [3] **breed** race, sort – [4] **to join the ranks** to become a member of a particular group – [5] **mongrel** ['mʌŋgrəl] a mixture of different breeds – [6] **patois** ['pætwɑ:] local dialect – [7] **Bengali, Gujarati** languages spoken in Pakistan – [8] **hybrid** mixed breed

thing: Allah *featured*[1], but more as a collective big brother than a supreme[2] being, a hard-as-fuck *geezer*[3] who would fight in their corner if necessary; Kung Fu and the works of Bruce Lee were also central to the philosophy; added to this was a smattering[4] of Black Power (as embodied by the album *Fear of a Black Planet*, Public Enemy) [...]. They looked like trouble in stereo. Naturally, there was a uniform. They each dripped gold[5] and wore bandanas[6], either wrapped around their foreheads or tied at the joint[7] of an arm or leg. The trousers were enormous, swamping[8] things, the left leg always inexplicably[9] rolled up to the knee; the trainers[10] were equally spectacular, with tongues so tall they obscured[11] the entire ankle[12]; baseball caps were compulsory, low slung[13] and irremovable, and everything, everything, everything was Nike™ [...].

'No trouble, yeah?' said Millat to the security guy.

'Just going—' began Hifan.

'To Bradford,' said Rajik.

Describe the Raggastani.

'For business, yeah?' explained Dipesh.

'See-ya! Bidayo!' called Hifan, as they slipped into the train, gave him the finger, and shoved their arses up against the closing doors.

'Tax[14] the window seat, yeah? Nice. I've *blatantly*[15] got to have a fag[16] in here, yeah? I'm fuckin' *wired*[17], yeah? This whole business, man. This fuckin' geezer, man. He's a fuckin' coconut—I'd like to fuck him up, yeah?'

'Is he actually gonna be there?'

All serious questions were always addressed to Millat, and Millat always answered the group as a whole. 'No way. He ain't going to be there. Just brothers going to be there. It's a fucking protest, you chief, why's he going to go to a protest against himself?

'I' m just saying,' said Ranil, wounded, 'I'd fuck him up, yeah? If he was there, you know. Dirty fucking book.'

For what reason do they go to Bradford? What does Millat know about the book?

'It's a fucking insult[18]!' said Millat, spitting some gum against the window, 'We've taken it too long in this country. And now we're getting it from our own, man.

Rhas clut[19]! He's a fucking bador, white man's puppet.'

'My uncle says he can't even spell,' said a furious Hifan, the most honestly religious of the lot. 'And he dares to talk about Allah!'

'Allah'll fuck him up, yeah?' cried Rajik, the least intelligent, who thought of God as some kind of cross between Monkey-Magic[20] and Bruce Willis. 'He'll kick him in the balls. Dirty book.'

'You read it?' asked Ranil, as they whizzed past Finsbury Park[21].

There was a general pause.

Millat said, 'I haven't exackly read it exackly—but I know all about that shit, yeah?'

[1] **featured** here: was included – [2] **supreme** highest in rank – [3] **geezer** (*infml*) old man – [4] **smattering** small amount – [5] **to drip gold** to wear a lot of gold chains – [6] **bandana/bandanna** piece of cloth worn around the head – [7] **joint** *Gelenk* – [8] **swamping** here: extremely wide – [9] **inexplicable** unexplainable – [10] **trainers** shoes you wear for sports – [11] **obscure** here: cover up – [12] **ankle** *Fußknöchel* – [13] **low slung** hiding the face – [14] **to tax** (North London slang) to occupy – [15] **blatant** ['bleɪtnt] urgent – [16] **fag** (*infml*) cigarette – [17] **wired** excited – [18] **insult** ['--] offence; *Beleidigung* – [19] **rhas clut** (Bengali) shit – [20] **Monkey-Magic** bizarre characters in a Japanese multimedia game – [21] **Finsbury Park** district in London

Arabian women protesting against Rushdie (1989)

On January 14, 1989, Salman Rushdie's book 'Satanic Verses', which won the Whitbread Book Award in 1988, was burned by outraged Muslims in Bradford, India and South Africa after the former Iranian spiritual leader Ayatollah Khomeini had banned this book and called on all zealous Muslims to execute the writer. Rushdie, an Indian born Muslim, was accused of having insulted the Prophet Muhammad. He was forced into hiding until 1998, when the holy war (fatwa) officially ended and lives in New York now.

To be more precise, Millat hadn't read it. Millat knew nothing about the writer, nothing about the book, could not identify the book if it lay in a pile of other books […].

But he knew other things. He knew that he, Millat, was a Paki no matter where he came from; that he smelt of curry; had no sexual identity; took other people's jobs; or had no job and bummed off[1] the state; or gave all the jobs to his relatives; that he could be a dentist or a shopowner or a curry-shifter[2], but not a footballer or a filmmaker; that he should go back to his own country; or stay here and earn his bloody keep[3]; that he worshipped[4] elephants and wore turbans; that no one who looked like Millat, or spoke like Millat, or felt like Millat, was ever on the news unless they had recently been murdered. In short, he knew he had no face in this country, no voice in the country, until the week before last when suddenly people like Millat were on every channel and every radio and every newspaper and they were angry, and Millat recognized the anger, thought it recognized him, and grabbed it with both hands.

'So … you ain't read it?' asked Ranil nervously.

'Look: you best believe I ain't buying that shit, man. No way, star.'

'Me neither,' said Hifan.

'True, star,' said Rajik.

'Fucking nastiness[5],' said Ranil.

'Twelve ninety-five, you know!' said Dipesh.

'Besides,' said Millat, with a tone of finality […], you don't have to read shit to know that it's blasphemous[6], you get me?'

What reasons does the narrator give for Millat's journey to Bradford?

[1] **to bum off** (*infml*) to try to get money – [2] **curry-shifter** sb who sells curry – [3] **keep** (n) wages – [4] **to worship** to idolize, to adore – [5] **nastiness** very bad or unpleasant thing – [6] **blasphemous** ['blæsfəməs] not showing respect for God

Millat, the bad boy

1. Write a short character portrait of Millat and his use of language.
   ➔ Method kit, Characterization, p. 289
2. To what extent does the narrator's comment on Millat help you to understand the boy a little bit better?
3. Millat's mother sees him on TV burning the *Satanic Verses* while he should be attending school. Millat tries to defend himself while his mother scolds him for being rude and not attending school. Put Millat on the hot seat.

Muslims in Britain

1. Find out where Muslims live in GB. The text "Britain—A Multicultural Society", p. 53 will help you.
2. Bradford is a place where racial emotions run high. The year 1989 marks the beginning of a chain of racially motivated incidents. Find out what happened in 1995 and 2001 and which groups were involved. *The Guardian Online* (http://www.guardian.co.uk—see Special Report on Race) is a good starting point.
3. Bradford City Council has tried to appease the residents. Contact http://www.bradford.gov.uk. What has been done to decrease racial tensions? Hold a discussion. Representatives from all groups involved should take part.

The immigrant experience

The following excerpt from the same novel depicts a typical problem of New Commonwealth immigrants:

> "These days it feels to me like you make a devil's pact when you walk into this country. You hand over your passport at the check-in, you get stamped, you want to make a little money, get yourself started ... but you mean to go back! Who would want to stay? Cold, wet, miserable; terrible food, dreadful newspapers—who would want to stay? In a place where you are never welcomed, only tolerated. Just tolerated. Like you are an animal finally housebroken. Who would want to stay? But you have made a devil's pact ... it drags you in and suddenly you are unsuitable to return, your children are unrecognizable, you belong nowhere."

What is the "devil's pact"? Apply this experience to Millat and immigrants who have come to Germany.

Britain—A Multicultural Society

Info

As British subjects[1], people from the Empire were expected to fight in all Britain's wars, and the part they played in both World Wars made a decisive difference to Britain's future prospects[2]. Faced with the massive task of reconstruction after the Second World War and acute labour shortages, the British government encouraged immigration, first from among European refugees displaced[3] by the war, and then from Ireland and the Commonwealth. Before long, in some factories the great majority of workers were Asian or black: Afro-Caribbeans from the West Indies as well as from the mainland territories of Guyana and Belize, and immigrants from Hong Kong and the Indian subcontinent. Until 1962 Commonwealth citizens had always been free to enter Britain. Since many British people complained that their "homogenous" Anglo-Saxon society had been seriously undermined by the massive immigration, the government decided that it was necessary to limit the influx of immigrants to a number the country could absorb, both economically and socially. Further Immigration Acts followed. The majority of those who are now allowed to settle in Britain are spouses[4] or dependants of people who are British citizens. People from the New Commonwealth countries make up more than 55% of the total number accepted.

Population by ethnic group, 1998

	No. in 1000s
White	53,079
All ethnic minorities	3,663
Black groups	1,160
Black Caribbean	510
Black African	353
Black other	297
Indian subcontinent	1,678
Indian	944
Pakistani	568
Bangladeshi	166
Chinese	166
Other groups	659

Nationwide, non-whites make up about 6% of the population. The highest concentration of ethnic minorities is in Greater London, where nearly 50% of all minorities live, making up approximately 20% of the capital's population. It is home to over 30 ethnic communities of more than 10,000 residents each. In this city, over 300 languages are spoken. The settlement patterns within the ethnic minorities are quite diverse: whereas nearly 60% of Afro-Caribbeans live in London, only about 35% of South Asians do. Many South Asians live in the West Midlands, Leicestershire and West Yorkshire. The ethnic minorities, as elsewhere in Europe, are mainly represented in the large cities and towns and are rarely found in small towns or rural[5] areas. In Scotland and Wales ethnic minorities make up just over 1% of the population.
The great pluralism contributes to the cultural and economic vitality of the British nation. For example hundreds of thousands of visitors are attracted by London's Caribbean Notting Hill carnival every year.
Britain continues to be the preferred location for multinational companies setting up in Europe because of the linguistic variety of the staff that they can recruit there. Today, curries and Chinese takeaways are as popular as fish and chips.
Members of the ethnic minorities as a whole, though, experience a greater number

[1] **subject** person who has the right to belong to a particular country, especially one with a monarch – [2] **prospect** chance – [3] **displaced** driven away – [4] **spouse** husband or wife – [5] **rural** in the countryside

Info

Notting Hill Carnival

of social disadvantages than other groups. Their children are more likely to need special help in education; unemployment is higher among the ethnic minorities than among the population at large, particularly among the younger age group, and racial discrimination is often experienced on a daily basis. In the 1980s, there were riots and urban disorder in Brixton, Birmingham and Liverpool, which highlighted the breakdown in confidence between the police and certain members of the community, both black and white. Recent racial clashes[1] have occurred in the industrial towns of Oldham (May 2001) and Bradford (July 2001). As among the whites, forces of conservatism also exist in the non-white population of Britain. Many black and Asian Britons feel that they will lose their roots if they become too British. Above all, they argue for special schools and spaces.
However, despite some negative aspects of life in Britain for ethnic minorities, they are probably better integrated into society than ethnic minorities in other European countries. The percentage of mixed-race relationships is among the highest in the world. The Indian food industry produces a turnover that is higher than coal, steel and shipbuilding combined. Virtually[2] everyone has British citizenship, and even citizens of Commonwealth countries who are not British citizens may vote in elections if they reside in Britain. However, only five of the 659 Members of Parliament are Black or Asian.
Like many other European nations, Britain has to cope with an increasing influx of asylum[3] seekers, refugees and illegal immigrants. People trafficking[4] is a fast growing criminal business. In many cases organised crime is involved in that migration. The most brutal incident occurred in June 2000 when fifty-eight Chinese suffocated[5] in a lorry in an attempt to reach Dover.

[1]**clash** violent confrontation – [2]**virtually** practically – [3]**asylum** [ə'saɪləm] – [4]**people trafficking** smuggling people illegally into a country – [5]**to suffocate** to die because there is no air to breathe

From Empire to Commonwealth

Margaret Atwood

Rule Britannia

Margaret Atwood was born in 1939 in Ottawa and grew up in northern Ontario, Quebec, and Toronto, where she still lives. Throughout her career, Atwood has received numerous awards. She is the author of more than thirty volumes of poetry, non-fiction and fiction, including children's books and short stories. Her most recent works include *The Handmaid's Tale* (1986), *Cat's Eye* (1989), and *Alias Grace* (1996).
The following text is an excerpt from her most autobiographical work, *Cat's Eye*. Atwood's critically acclaimed seventh novel is the story of Elaine Risley, who returns to her home town Toronto and becomes consumed by vivid images of her past.

Margaret Atwood

The school room is high-ceilinged, yellowy-brown, with blackboards at the front and along one side and tall many-paned[1] windows above the radiators on the other side. Over the door to the cloakroom[2], so that you feel you're being watched from behind, there's a large photograph of the King and Queen, the King with medals, the Queen in a white ballgown[3] and diamond tiara[4]. High wooden desks that sit two, with slanted[5] tops and holes for inkwells[6], are arranged in rows. It's like all the other school rooms at Queen Mary, but it seems darker, possibly because there's less decoration. Our old teacher brought paper doilies[7] to school in her many efforts at appeasement[8] and her windows were always crawling with paper vegetation.

But although Miss Lumley observes the seasons in this way too, the

▼ Describe the school room.

Coronation of King George IV and Elizabeth in 1937. Children: left: Princess Margaret, right: the future Queen Elizabeth II (1952–present)

[1]**paned** cf. **pane** sheet of glass – [2]**cloakroom** room where coats, hats, etc may be left – [3]**ballgown** dress worn at a ball – [4]**tiara** [ti'ɑ:rə] diadem – [5]**slanted** not straight – [6]**inkwell** ink container – [7]**doily** *Spitzendeckchen* – [8]**appeasement** act of making sb quiet or calm by making concessions

plants we bring forth under her glittering steel-rimmed[1] eyes are smaller, shriveled[2]-looking, so that there are never enough of them to cover the bare spaces of wall and glass. Also, if your fall foliage[3] leaf or your pumpkin[4] is not symmetrical, Miss Lumley won't put it up. She has standards.

Things are more British than they were last year. We learn to draw the Union Jack[5], using a ruler and memorizing the various crosses, for St. George of England, St. Patrick of Ireland, St. Andrew of Scotland, St. David of Wales. Our own flag is red and has a Union Jack in one corner, although there's no saint for Canada. We learn to name all the pink parts of the map.

"The sun never sets on the British Empire," says Miss Lumley, tapping[6] the roll-down map with her long wooden pointer. In countries that are not the British Empire, they cut out children's tongues, especially those of boys. Before the British Empire there were no railroads or postal services in India, and Africa was full of tribal warfare[7], with spears, and had no proper clothing. The Indians in Canada did not have the wheel or telephones, and ate the hearts of their enemies in the heathenish[8] belief that it would give them courage. The British Empire changed all that. It brought in electric lights.

What does Miss Lumley tell her pupils about countries before they belonged to the British Empire?

Every morning, after Miss Lumley blows a thin metallic note on her pitch pipe[9], we stand up to sing "God Save the King." We also sing,

Rule Britannia, Britannia rules the waves;
Britons never, never, never shall be slaves!

Because we're Britons, we will never be slaves. But we aren't real Britons, because we are also Canadians. This isn't quite as good, although it has its own song:

In days of yore[10], from Britain's shore
Wolfe[11], the dauntless[12] hero, came
And planted firm Britannia's flag
On Canada's fair domain[13]
Here may it wave, our boast[14], our pride
And join in love together
The thistle[15], shamrock[16], rose entwine[17]
The Maple Leaf[18] forever.

Miss Lumley's jaw quivers[19] in a frightening way when we sing this. Wolfe's name sounds like something you'd call a dog, but he

The poem "Rule Britannia" by James Thomson (1700–1748) is sung as an unofficial national anthem in GB today.

[1] **steel-rimmed** glasses with a steel frame – [2] **shriveled** (US) **shrivelled** (Brit) *welk* – [3] **foliage** leaves of a tree or plant – [4] **pumpkin** *Kürbis* – [5] **Union Jack** national flag of the United Kingdom – [6] **to tap sth** to knock gently on sth – [7] **tribal warfare** fighting between different racial groups – [8] **heathenish** [i:] not believing in God – [9] **pitch pipe** *Pfeife zum Angeben einer Tonhöhe* – [10] **yore** [jɔ:] long ago – [11] **James Wolfe** (1727–1759) British general – [12] **dauntless** not easily frightened – [13] **domain** [dʌ'meɪn] lands – [14] **boast** thing that one is proud of – [15] **thistle** [θɪsl] *Distel*; symbol of Scotland – [16] **shamrock** *weißer Feldklee*; symbol of Ireland – [17] **to entwine** [-'-] to wind one thing round another – [18] **Maple Leaf** *Ahornblatt*; here: national flag of Canada – [19] **to quiver** to tremble slightly

conquered the French. This is puzzling, because I've seen French people, there are lots of them up north, so he couldn't have conquered all of them. As for maple leaves, they're the hardest part to draw on our red flag. Nobody ever gets them right. Miss Lumley brings newspaper clippings about the Royal Family and sticks them to the side blackboard. Some of them are old clippings, and show Princess Elizabeth and Princess Margaret Rose, in Girl Guide uniforms, making radio and other speeches during the Blitz[1]. This is what we should be like, Miss Lumley implies: steadfast[2], loyal, courageous, heroic.

There are other newspaper pictures too, showing thin-looking children in scruffy[3] clothes, standing in front of piles[4] of rubble[5]. These are to remind us that there are many starving[6] war orphans[7] in Europe, and we should remember that and eat our bread crusts and potato skins and everything else on our plates, because waste is a sin. Also we should not complain. We are not really entitled[8] to complain, because we are lucky children: English children got their houses bombed and we did not. We bring our used clothing, from home, and Miss Lumley ties it up into brown paper packages and sends it to England. There isn't much I can bring, because my mother tears our worn-out[9] clothing up for dusters[10], but I manage to salvage[11] a pair of corduroy[12] pants, once my brother's, then mine, now too small, and a Viyella[13] shirt of my father's that got washed wrong by mistake and shrank[14]. It gives me a strange feeling on my skin to think of someone else, someone in England, walking around in my clothes. My clothes seem a part of me, even the ones I've outgrown.

All these things—the flags, the pitch pipe songs, the British Empire and the princesses, the war orphans, even the strappings[15] are superimposed[16] against the ominous[17] navy-blue background of Miss Lumley's invisible bloomers[18]. I can't draw the Union Jack or sing "God Save the King" without thinking about them. Do they really exist, or not? Will I ever be in the classroom when she puts them on or—unthinkable—takes them off.

The Union Jack

Canadian flag 1922–1957

The present Canadian flag

Miss Lumley's lessons

1. What does Miss Lumley teach her pupils and what are her teaching methods? Compare with teaching in our time.
2. Tell your partner how the narrator experienced the lessons.
3. Ask Miss Lumley questions about her job as a teacher and about her philosophy of life.

[1]**the Blitz** intensive German air raids on Britain in 1940 – [2]**steadfast** firm and not changing – [3]**scruffy** dirty and untidy – [4]**pile** number of things lying one upon another – [5]**rubble** bits of broken stones or bricks – [6]**starving** suffering severely from hunger – [7]**orphan** child whose parents are dead – [8]**to be entitled to** to be given the right to – [9]**worn-out** very damaged by use or wear – [10]**duster** cloth for cleaning furniture, etc – [11]**to salvage** to save – [12]**corduroy** ['kɔ:dərɔɪ] strong cotton cloth with parallel soft raised ridges – [13]**Viyella** (brand name) made of artificial fibres – [14]**to shrink** (shrank, shrunken) to become smaller – [15]**strappings** beating with a strap – [16]**to superimpose** to put sth on top of sth else – [17]**ominous** suggesting that sth bad is about to happen; threatening – [18]**bloomers** underpants

Miss Lumley and the British Empire

1. According to Miss Lumley, what are the benefits of the British Empire for its various subjects? Make a list and add new items.
2. Work in groups. List the problematic aspects of British rule. Compare your results with those of other groups, filter out the less important aspects and rank the others.

Civilization Begins at Home (1898)

The blessings of civilization

1. The cartoon is called "Civilization Begins at Home" and the map reads "The Philippine Islands." Analyze the pictorial elements of the cartoon and evaluate them in the context of the Imperialist Age.
2. Can you imagine why in former times so many well-educated Britons went to work in the British colonies either as soldiers, civil engineers, magistrates or in other government functions?

George Orwell

A Hanging

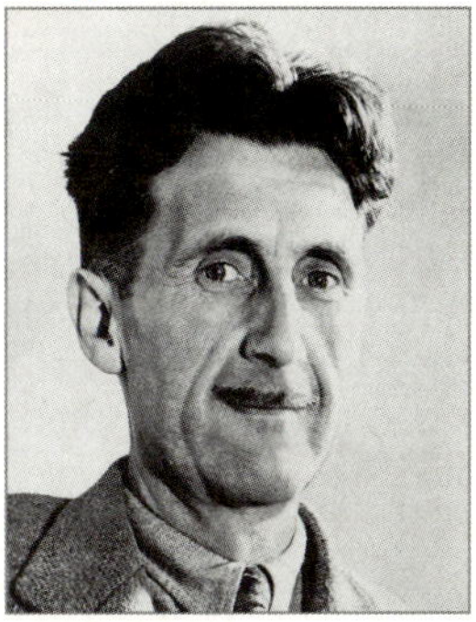

George Orwell

George Orwell was the pseudonym of the English writer Eric Arthur Blair. He was born on June 25, 1903, in Mothari, Bengal. His father was a Government of India employee in the Opium Department. In 1904, his mother moved back to England with Eric and his sister to raise them there as it was the custom. From 1917–1921 Orwell attended Eton College as a King's Scholar, but did not go on to a university.
He served in the Indian Imperial Police in Burma from 1922–1927. There were many ups and downs in his life as a writer, which began in Paris in 1928. He worked as a dishwasher, became a tramp, taught at a private school, actively took part in the Spanish Civil War in 1936, became a BBC talks producer and finally worked for *The Tribune* and *The Observer*. His first great literary success, which made him famous overnight, was *Animal Farm* (1944). He ended his literary career with *Nineteen Eighty-Four* (1949). Orwell died on January 21, 1950.

It was in Burma, a sodden[1] morning of the rains. A sickly light, like yellow tinfoil[2], was slanting[3] over the high walls into the jail yard. We were waiting outside the condemned cells, a row of sheds fronted with double bars[4], like small animal cages. Each cell measured about ten feet by ten and was quite bare within except for a plank bed and a pot of drinking water. In some of them brown silent men were squatting[5] at the inner bars, with their blankets draped round them. These were the condemned men, due to be hanged within the next week or two.

▲ Describe the atmosphere at the outset of the story.

One prisoner had been brought out of his cell. He was a Hindu, a puny wisp of a man[6], with a shaven head and vague liquid eyes. He had a thick, sprouting moustache, absurdly too big for his body, rather like the moustache of a comic man on the films. Six tall Indian warders[7] were guarding him and getting him ready for the gallows[8]. Two of them stood by with rifles and fixed bayonets, while the others handcuffed[9] him, passed a chain through his handcuffs and fixed it to their belts, and lashed his arms tight to his sides. They crowded very close about him, with their hands always on him in a careful, caressing[10] grip, as though all the while feeling him to make sure he was there. It was like men handling a fish which is still alive and may jump back into the water. But he stood quite unresisting, yielding[11] his arms limply[12] to the ropes, as though he hardly noticed what was happening.

▼ Reflect on the way the condemned man is treated.

Eight o'clock struck and a bugle call[13], desolately thin in the wet air, floated from the distant barracks. The superintendent[14] of the

[1] **sodden** extremely wet – [2] **tinfoil** aluminium foil – [3] **to slant** *hereinfallen* – [4] **bar** metal barrier – [5] **to squat** to sit on one's heels – [6] **puny wisp of a man** *zerbrechlicher kleiner Mann* – [7] **warder** person who works in a jail – [8] **gallows** hanging platform – [9] **to handcuff sb** to put metal rings round the wrists of a prisoner – [10] **to caress** to touch softly – [11] **to yield** to stretch out – [12] **limply** weakly – [13] **bugle call** *Hornsignal* – [14] **superintendent** chief of police

jail, who was standing apart from the rest of us, moodily[1] prodding[2] the gravel[3] with his stick, raised his head at the sound. He was an army doctor, with a grey toothbrush moustache and a gruff voice. 'For God's sake hurry up, Francis,' he said irritably. 'The man ought to have been dead by this time. Aren't you ready yet?'

Francis, the head jailer, a fat Dravidian[4] in a white drill suit and gold spectacles, waved his black hand. 'Yes sir, yes sir,' he bubbled. 'All iss satisfactorily prepared. The hangman iss waiting. We shall proceed.'

'Well, quick march, then. The prisoners can't get their breakfast till this job's over.'

Can you understand the bad mood of the superintendent?

We set out for the gallows. Two warders marched on either side of the prisoner, with their rifles at the slope; two others marched close against him, gripping him by arm and shoulder, as though at once pushing and supporting him. The rest of us, magistrates and the like, followed behind. Suddenly, when we had gone ten yards, the procession stopped short without any order or warning.

A dreadful thing had happened—a dog, come goodness knows whence[5], had appeared in the yard. It came bounding among us with a loud volley of barks, and leapt round us wagging its whole body, wild with glee[6] at finding so many human beings together. It was a large woolly dog, half Airedale, half pariah[7]. For a moment it pranced round[8] us, and then, before anyone could stop it, it had made a dash for the prisoner, and jumping up tried to lick his face. Everyone stood aghast[9], too taken aback[10] even to grab at the dog.

What effect has the dog's appearance got on everybody present?

The bugle call

'Who let that bloody brute in here?' said the superintendent angrily. 'Catch it, someone!'

A warder, detached from the escort, charged[11] clumsily[12] after the dog, but it danced and gambolled just out of his reach, taking everything as part of the game. A young Eurasian jailer picked up a handful of gravel and tried to stone the dog away, but it dodged the stones and came after us again. Its yaps echoed from the jail walls. The prisoner, in the grasp of the two warders, looked on incuriously, as though this was another formality of the hanging. It was several minutes before someone managed to catch the dog. Then we put my handkerchief through its collar and moved off once more, with the dog still straining[13] and whimpering[14]. It was about forty yards to the gallows. I watched the bare brown back of the prisoner marching in front of me.

He walked clumsily with his bound arms, but quite steadily, with that bobbing gait[15] of the Indian who never straightens his knees. At each step his muscles slid neatly into place, the lock of hair on his scalp danced up

[1] **moody** depressed, in a bad mood – [2] **to prod** *herumstochern* – [3] **gravel** *Kies* – [4] **Dravidian** sb from southern India – [5] **whence** (*arch*) from where – [6] **glee** happiness, joy – [7] **pariah** [pəˈraɪə] outcast; here: half-breed – [8] **to prance round** to dance around – [9] **aghast** shocked, horrified – [10] **taken aback** extremely surprised – [11] **to charge after** to attack – [12] **clumsy** not very elegant – [13] **to strain** *zerren* – [14] **to whimper** *winseln* – [15] **bobbing gait** *tänzelnder Schritt*

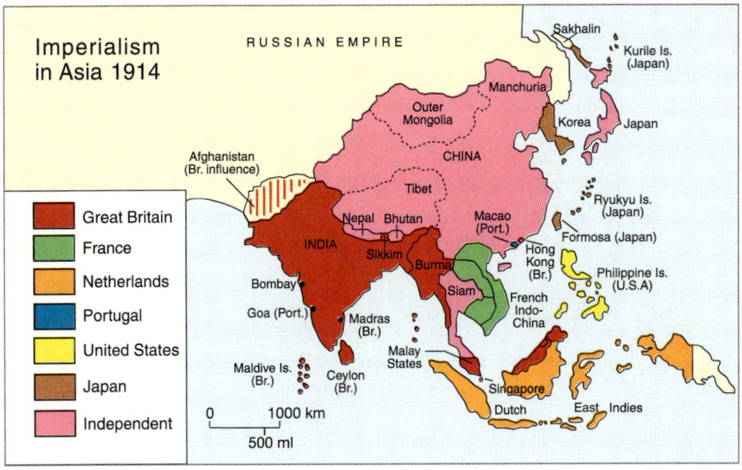

In three wars (1824, 1852, and 1885), the British conquered the territory of the Burmese kings. British Burma was administered as part of India until 1937 when a separate government was created. It became independent in 1948.

and down, his feet printed themselves on the wet gravel. And once, in spite of the men who gripped him by each shoulder, he stepped slightly aside to avoid a puddle[1] on the path.

It is curious, but till that moment I had never realized what it means to destroy a healthy, conscious man. When I saw the prisoner step aside to avoid the puddle, I saw the mystery, the unspeakable wrongness, of cutting a life short when it is in full tide. This man was not dying, he was alive just as we were alive. All the organs of his body were working—bowels[2] digesting food, skin renewing itself, nails growing, tissues[3] forming—all toiling away[4] in solemn foolery. His nails would still be growing when he stood on the drop, when he was falling through the air with a tenth of a second to live. His eyes saw the yellow gravel and the grey walls, and his brain still remembered, foresaw, reasoned—reasoned even about puddles. He and we were a party of men walking together, seeing, hearing, feeling, understanding the same world; and in two minutes, with a sudden snap, one of us would be gone—one mind less, one world less.

The gallows stood in a small yard, separate from the main grounds of the prison, and overgrown with tall prickly[5] weeds. It was a brick erection like three sides of a shed, with planking on top, and above that two beams and a crossbar with the rope dangling. The hangman, a grey-haired convict[6] in the white uniform of the prison, was waiting beside his machine. He greeted us with a servile crouch[7] as we entered. At a word from Francis the two warders, gripping the prisoner more closely than ever, half led, half pushed him to the gallows and helped him clumsily up the ladder.

◀ Why should the condemned man want to avoid the puddle?

▼ In what way does this paragraph differ from the rest of the story?

◀ "One mind less, one world less." Comment on this phrase.

[1] **puddle** small pool of water – [2] **bowels** ['baʊəlz] *Eingeweide* – [3] **tissue** *Gewebe* – [4] **to toil** (away) to work hard – [5] **prickly** with pricks like a cactus – [6] **convict** prisoner – [7] **crouch** the act of bending down

Modern Burma

Then the hangman climbed up and fixed the rope round the prisoner's neck.

We stood waiting, five yards away. The warders had formed in a rough circle round the gallows. And then, when the noose[1] was fixed, the prisoner began crying out on his god. It was a high, reiterated[2] cry of 'Ram! Ram! Ram! Ram!', not urgent and fearful like a prayer or a cry for help, but steady, rhythmical, almost like the tolling of a bell. The dog answered the sound with a whine. The hangman, still standing on the gallows, produced a small cotton bag like a flour bag and drew it down over the prisoner's face. But the sound, muffled by the cloth, still persisted[3], over and over again: 'Ram! Ram! Ram! Ram! Ram!'

The hangman climbed down and stood ready, holding the lever[4]. Minutes seemed to pass. The steady, muffled crying from the prisoner went on and on, 'Ram! Ram! Ram!' never faltering for an instant. The superintendent, his head on his chest, was slowly poking the ground with his stick; perhaps he was counting the cries, allowing the prisoner a fixed number—fifty, perhaps, or a hundred.

Everyone had changed colour. The Indians had gone grey like bad coffee, and one or two of the bayonets were wavering[5]. We looked at the lashed, hooded man on the drop, and listened to his cries—each cry another second of life; the same thought was in all our minds: oh, kill him quickly, get it over, stop that abominable[6] noise!

Suddenly the superintendent made up his mind. Throwing up his head he made a swift motion with his stick. 'Chalo[7]!' he shouted almost fiercely.

There was a clanking[8] noise, and then dead silence. The prisoner had vanished, and the rope was twisting on itself. I let go of the dog, and it galloped immediately to the back of the gallows; but when it got there it stopped short, barked, and then retreated into a corner of the yard, where it stood among the weeds, looking timorously[9] out at us. We went round the gallows to inspect the prisoner's body. He was dangling with his toes pointed straight downwards, very slowly revolving, as dead as a stone.

The superintendent reached out with his stick and poked[10] the bare body; it oscillated[11] slightly. 'He's all right,' said the superintendent.

[1] **noose** *Schlinge* – [2] **to reiterate** to repeat – [3] **to persist** to continue – [4] **lever** *Hebel* – [5] **to waver** to move in an unsteady way – [6] **abominable** extremely unpleasant – [7] **chalo** (Hindi) come on – [8] **clanking** *klirrend* – [9] **timorously** cowardly, timidly – [10] **to poke** *(herum)stochern* – [11] **to oscillate** ['ɒsɪleɪt] to rotate

He backed out from under the gallows, and blew out a deep breath. The moody look had gone out of his face quite suddenly. He glanced at his wrist-watch. 'Eight minutes past eight. Well, that's all for this morning, thank God.'

The warders unfixed bayonets and marched away. The dog, sobered[1] and conscious of having misbehaved itself, slipped after them. We walked out of the gallows yard, past the condemned cells with their waiting prisoners, into the big central yard of the prison. The convicts, under the command of warders armed with lathis[2], were already receiving their breakfast. They squatted in long rows, each man holding a tin pannikin[3], while two warders with buckets marched round ladling out rice; it seemed quite a homely, jolly scene, after the hanging. An enormous relief had come upon us now that the job was done. One felt an impulse to sing, to break into a run, to snigger[4]. All at once everyone began chattering gaily[5].

Explain the reaction of the officials.

Why are they suddenly in such a happy mood?

The Eurasian boy walking beside me nodded towards the way we had come, with a knowing smile: 'Do you know, sir, our friend (he meant the dead man), when he heard his appeal had been dismissed, he pissed on the floor of his cell. From fright. Kindly take one of my cigarettes, sir. Do you not admire my new silver case, sir? From the boxwallah[6], two rupees eight annas. Classy European style.'

Several people laughed—at what, nobody seemed certain.

Francis was walking by the superintendent, talking garrulously[7]. 'Well, sir, all hass passed off with the utmost satisfactoriness. It wass all finished—flick! like that. It iss not always so – oah, no! I have known cases where the doctor wass obliged to go beneath the gallows and pull the prisoner's legs to ensure decease[8]. Most disagreeable!'

'Wriggling[9] about, eh? That's bad,' said the superintendent.

'Ach, sir, it iss worse when they become refractory[10]! One man, I recall[11], clung to the bars of hiss cage when we went to take him out. You will scarcely credit, sir, that it took six warders to dislodge[12] him, three pulling at each leg. We reasoned with him. "My dear fellow," we said, "think of all the pain and trouble you are causing to us!" But no, he would not listen! Ach, he wass very troublesome!'

I found that I was laughing quite loudly. Everyone was laughing. Even the superintendent grinned in a tolerant way. 'You'd better all come out and have a drink,' he said quite genially. 'I've got a bottle of whisky in the car. We could do with it.'

We went through the big double gates of the prison, into the road. 'Pulling at his legs!' exclaimed a Burmese magistrate suddenly, and burst into a loud chuckling. We all began laughing again. At that moment Francis's anecdote seemed extraordinarily funny. We all had a drink together, native and European alike, quite amicably[13]. The dead man was a hundred yards away.

What is so funny about that?

What effect has the last sentence got? Could it be left out?

[1] **sober** serious and sensible – [2] **lathis** (Hindi) wooden stick – [3] **pannikin** a little pan – [4] **to snigger** to laugh in an unpleasant way – [5] **gay** happy, joyful – [6] **boxwallah** (Hindi) (*derog*) white businessman – [7] **garrulous** to talk too much – [8] **decease** [dɪ'siːs] the death of a person – [9] **to wriggle about** *zappeln, sich winden* – [10] **refractory** stubborn, difficult to control – [11] **to recall** to remember – [12] **to dislodge** to remove – [13] **amicably** in a friendly manner

Finding the theme

What is the basic theme of the story? In your view, is the author's way of dealing with this theme convincing? Give reasons for your opinion.

Plot and structure

1. Work out the structure of *A Hanging* and give each part a heading. Try to present it in a graph showing the development of the action.
2. Is this story a "classical short story"? Compare it to "The Definition of the Short Story" by Edgar Allan Poe.

The execution

1. All the characters in the story have just witnessed an execution. Analyse what impact this experience has on the officials and the first person narrator.
2. One of the prison inmates—also a Hindu—has watched the execution. What account of the condemned man's behaviour might he give?

The superintendent

1. Characterize the superintendent. What does he do and say? What might he be thinking? What impression does he make on you?
   → Method kit, Characterization, p. 289
2. Place the superindentent on the hot seat and ask him what he felt like during the execution.

The condemned man

Write a fictional biography of the condemned man's earlier life, job, social status, family life, his crime, etc or write a diary entry for the condemned man.

→ Method kit, Diary entry, p. 294

The defense of British law

One of the spectators is a reporter for *The Times*, an ardent supporter of British colonial rule. Transform the short story into a newspaper report. (150–200 w)

→ Method kit, Newspaper article, p. 298

Improve your vocabulary

1. In order to enlarge your vocabulary, write down new words and phrases from the text. You can either make a list or arrange items in a mind map or cluster.
   → Method kit, Mind map, p. 281
2. If you prefer to make a list, start a page for each new word field. Put the pages in a vocabulary folder and add to them when you come across new words/phrases from the same word fields.

From Empire to Commonwealth 2001

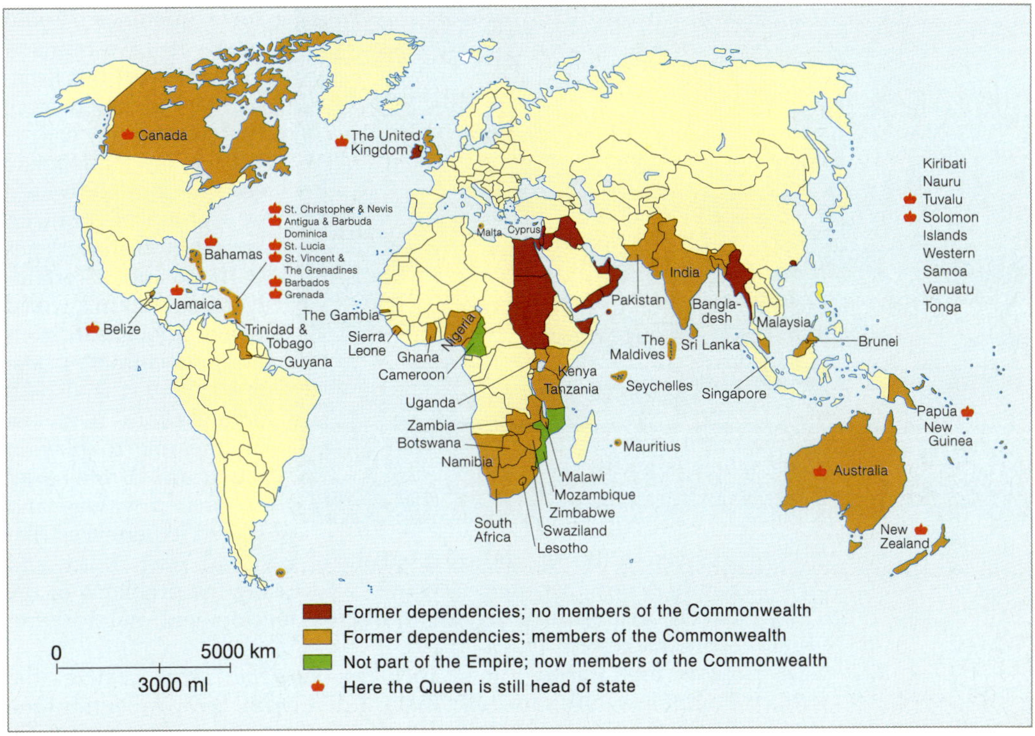

Tony Blair

The Commonwealth Today

This text is from the Prime Minister's speech, which he delivered at the opening of the Commonwealth Parliamentary Association Conference on 21 September 2000 at Westminster Hall.

Have a look at the map above and find out which of the countries are members of the Commonwealth.

It is an honour to welcome a major Commonwealth Conference to the United Kingdom. The Commonwealth Parliamentary Association Conference is a unique[1] event, bringing together elected parliamentarians from around the world who share a respect for—and common tradition of—Parliamentary democracy. It is

[1] **unique** [ju:'ni:k] unlike anything else, being the only type

therefore a source of great pride for me that this Millennium year the conference should open in Westminster Hall, the seat of parliamentary democracy in this country.

There is a tendency to see the Commonwealth as a group of countries bound by historical ties of friendship. It certainly is that. But in a world where globalisation is bringing countries closer together it is also an organisation with a unique role to play in the future. A role based on shared values and shared experiences that cuts across the traditional divisions of East and West, North and South. A role that offers a way of addressing the problems of the twenty-first century together: poverty, development, political and economic reform. [...]

We are rightly now focusing on the areas where the Commonwealth can really make a difference, complementing[1] the work of other international organisations. One such area is in strengthening democracy in member countries. The Commonwealth has led the world in defining the fundamental political principles of good governance[2], the principles upon which the Commonwealth was founded.

The Commonwealth's unique institution, its Ministerial Action Group, plays an increasingly important role in this process of deepening democracy. The Ministerial Action Group has proved its worth several times over in upholding[3] the values of the Commonwealth to which we, as parliamentarians, are all committed[4] – good governance, the rule of law and human rights.

But reform is not just a political question. The Commonwealth has great potential to help drive forward the world's economic and social reform agenda[5]. I am delighted with the emphasis the Commonwealth is placing on debt relief[6]. This is one of the foremost international challenges we face[7]. Historically the Common-

[1] **to complement** ['kɒmplɪment] to add to – [2] **governance** government – [3] **to uphold** to support – [4] **to commit oneself to sth** *sich für etw. einsetzen* – [5] **agenda** [ə'dʒendə] schedule, detailed plan – [6] **debt relief** (*det*) *Schuldenerlass* – [7] **to face sth/sb** to be confronted with sth/sb

wealth has led the way in international efforts to secure a lasting exit from debt for the poorest countries in the world. […] We must continue this work together, offering debt cancellation[1] based on the commitment to economic policies which benefit the poor, promote responsive[2] government and bear down[3] on corruption.

There are other challenges where the Commonwealth needs to be at the forefront. The Commonwealth is rightly playing a leading role in international efforts to respond to the devastating[4] social and economic impact[5] of HIV/AIDS. […]

The Commonwealth also has a vital contribution to make in areas such as trade and investment, environment, IT[6], education. Work is already in hand[7]. […]

Commonwealth leaders place great value on the CPAs input to the Commonwealth agenda. These conferences provide a unique opportunity for Parliamentarians throughout the Commonwealth to exchange ideas and to reach conclusions on the challenges we jointly face. And I look forward to hearing the results of your discussions.

I hope this week will be a productive and stimulating one. And that it will allow you to strengthen the networks between our countries, as well as helping to shape the Commonwealth's evolving[8] role for this new century.

Prime Minister's speech at the opening of the Commonwealth Parliamentary Association Conference at Westminister Hall, London, September 21, 2000

The future role of the Commonwealth

1. According to Tony Blair, what is the future role of the Commonwealth?
2. Which tasks do you think are most important? Make a ranking list and explain your choice.
3. Could the Commonwealth be a role model for a globalized world?

Working with the language

Find the corresponding nouns:

a) unique
b) to complement
c) to strengthen
d) to deepen
e) to prove
f) committed
g) poor
h) to devastate
h) vital
i) to provide
k) to exchange
l) productive
m) to stimulate
n) to evolve

Translation

Translate ll. 32–54 ("We are rightly now … bear down on corruption."). Work in two groups, with each group concentrating on one paragraph. Discuss your translations together. Pay special attention to idiomatic German.

[1] **debt cancellation** the end of paying back one's debts – [2] **responsive** reacting quickly and in a positive way – [3] **to bear down (on)** (US) to fight against – [4] **to devastate** to destroy, to ruin – [5] **impact** effect, influence – [6] **IT** Information Technology – [7] **to be in hand** *erledigt werden* – [8] **to evolve** to develop gradually

Info

How the Empire Became the Commonwealth

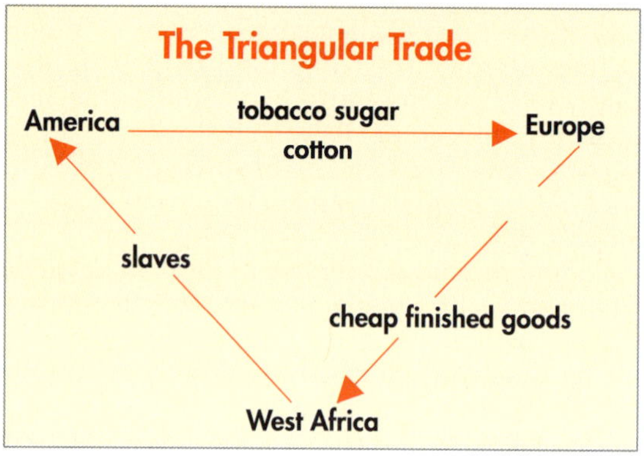

After the loss of the American colonies in 1783, British colonialism expanded around the whole globe, with India being the most cherished[1] colony. While Canada, Australia, New Zealand and the Cape Colony were settlement colonies, most of the other ones were used for trading (India: spices, cotton, tea) or were regarded as important strategic locations (Gibraltar, Malta, Cyprus and the Suez Canal acted as a chain of communication through the Mediterranean to India). All the colonies were under direct rule of Britain.

The Commonwealth gradually evolved out of this imperial past, mainly through decolonisation, the effects of two world wars and changing patterns of international relations.

Today, from Africa to Asia, from the Pacific shores to the Caribbean, the Commonwealth's 1.7 billion people in 54 countries make up 30% of the world's population. Officially, it helps to advance democracy, human rights and endurable[2] economic and social development within its member countries. It is loosely bound together by a common working language and similar systems of law, public administration and education.

The modern Commonwealth has its roots in the 19th century. In 1867, Canada became the first colony to be transformed into a self-governing Dominion; a status which came to imply[3] equality with the United Kingdom. In Australia in 1884, the British politician Lord Rosebery described this changing empire as a Commonwealth of Nations. Australia became a Dominion in 1900, New Zealand in 1907, South Africa in 1910 and the Irish Free State in 1921. At the Imperial Conference of 1926, prime ministers adopted the Balfour Report, which defined the Dominions as:

... autonomous, communities within the British Empire, equal in status, in no way subordinate one to another in any aspect of their domestic or external affairs, though united by common allegiance[4] to the Crown, and freely associated as members of the British Commonwealth of Nations.

This definition was adopted into British law in 1931 as the Statute of Westminster.

In 1930, the first Empire (later Commonwealth) Games were held as a means to strengthen the ties between the member countries.

The Second World War changed the face of the modern world forever. It also changed the nature of the British Commonwealth, marking its transition to a multiracial association of sovereign and equal states. That process began with India's

[1] **to cherish** to love, to treasure – [2] **endurable** tolerable – [3] **to imply** to mean – [4] **allegiance** support of or loyalty to a government or ruler

Info

and Pakistan's independence in 1947. With India's desire to become a republic yet remain in the Commonwealth, the principle of Commonwealth membership had to be rethought. A conference of Commonwealth prime ministers in 1949 revised[1] this criterion[2] and decided to welcome India as the Commonwealth's first republican member. They all agreed, however, to recognize[3] King George VI as the "symbol of their free association and thus Head of the Commonwealth." At the same time, the word *British* was dropped from the association's title to reflect the Commonwealth's new reality. Committed to racial equality and national sovereignty[4], the Commonwealth became a natural association of choice for many new nations emerging[5] out of decolonisation in the 1950s and 1960s. Ghana achieved independence in 1957 and became the first majority-ruled African member. From 1960 onwards, the Commonwealth expanded rapidly with new members from Africa, the Caribbean, the Mediterranean and the Pacific. Today, 33 members are republics and five have national monarchies of their own (Brunei Darussalam, Lesotho, Malaysia, Swaziland and Tonga). Sixteen are constitutional monarchies which recognize Queen Elizabeth II as their Head of State. All, however, accept the Queen as Head of the Commonwealth.

In the 19th century, under the rule of Queen Victoria (1837–1901), "the sun never set on the British Empire."

The Commonwealth's opposition to all forms of racism, and especially apartheid, led to the withdrawal[6] of South Africa in 1961. In 1994, following the end of apartheid and the establishment of a non-racial government, South Africa rejoined the association. In 1965, another milestone[7] was reached when Commonwealth leaders established the Commonwealth Secretariat in London to be the association's own independent civil service, headed by the Commonwealth Secretary General.

Queen Elizabeth II at the XVI Commonwealth Games, Kuala Lumpur, 1998

[1] **to revise** to change, to alter – [2] **criterion** (pl. criteria) – [3] **to recognize** to accept and approve of sb/sth officially – [4] **sovereignty** ['sɒvrənti] – [5] **to emerge** to appear or become known – [6] **withdrawal** act of no longer taking part in sth – [7] **milestone** important event

Info

In 1991, the Harare Commonwealth Declaration set the association firmly on a new course for a new century: that of promoting[1] democracy and good government, human rights and the rule of law, as well as the equality of women, universal access[2] to education and sustainable[3] economic and social development.
At their 1997 summit in Edinburgh, Commonwealth leaders agreed on a similar set of economic principles and practical activities. In the same year the last important British Crown Colony, Hong Kong, was handed back to China.
The British Prime Minister Blair has recently formulated new goals for the Commonwealth, including fighting AIDS, avoiding economic downturns[4] and ending terrorism.

Hyllus Maris

Spiritual Song of the Aborigine

I am a child of the Dreamtime[5] People
Part of this Land, like the gnarled[6] gumtree[7]
I am the river, softly singing
Chanting our songs on my way to the sea
My spirit is the dust-devils
Mirages[8], that dance on the plane
I'm the snow, the wind and the falling rain
I'm part of the rocks and the red desert earth
Red as the blood that flows low in my veins
I'm eagle, crow and snake that glides
Through the rain-forest that clings to the mountainside
I awakened here when the earth was new
There was emu, wombat, kangaroo
No other man of a different hue[9]
I am this land
And this land is me
I am Australia

Australia is the ➤ home of many unique species. Do you recognize this one? Do you know others?

Your reaction to the poem

1. What is your first reaction to this poem?
2. Who is the speaker?

[1] **to promote** to encourage, to advocate – [2] **access** the opportunity to use sth or see sth/sb – [3] **sustainable** *nachhaltig* – [4] **downturn** a time when the economy becomes weaker – [5] **Dreamtime** term often used to refer to the 'time before time,' or 'the time of the creation of all things,' while 'dreaming' is often used to refer to an individual's or group's set of beliefs or spirituality – [6] **gnarled** [nɑ:ld] twisted and rough – [7] **gumtree** eucalyptus tree – [8] **dust-devils mirages** ['mɪrɑ:ʒ] images produced by dust storms – [9] **hue** colour

Matthew Kneale

Sunday Services

This is an excerpt from the novel *English Passengers*, which was written in 2000.
In 1857 Reverend Geoffrey Wilson set out for Tasmania, hoping to find the Garden of Eden there. What he found, however, wasn't Paradise but the Tasmanian Aboriginals fighting a desperate battle against British invaders.

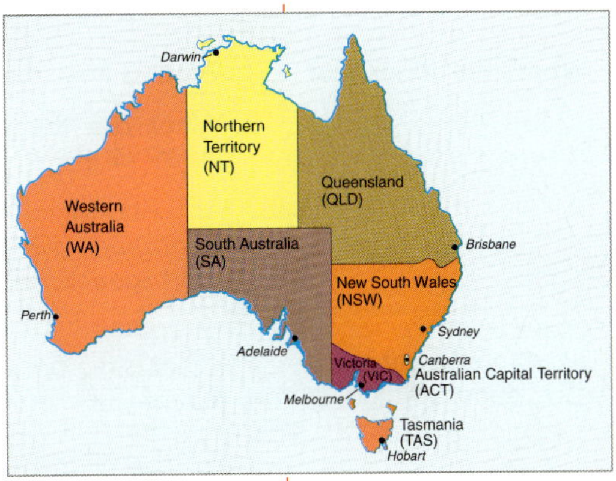

The greatest cause of our difficulties did not, however, lie with white men, but, I regret to say, with the blacks themselves. It may seem harsh and yet I could not help but observe they showed an increasing reluctance[1] to apply themselves to their reformation. There were always a handful, such as the monstrous Mary, who quite refused to attend school classes, but as time passed this number began gradually to increase, almost as if the majority of the blacks had attended only out of curiosity[2], or boredom, and were now growing tired of this novelty. Even those who continued with their learning would suddenly disappear on some foolish hunting expedition. This made their instruction most difficult, especially in the case of the older ones, whose powers of memory were feebler[3]. How frustrating it was after weeks of practice upon, for instance, the Ten Commandments, to have half a class abruptly vanish[4], only to return days later, excitably clutching speared wallabies[5], their commandments all but forgotten.

There was not one among them, if truth be told, who showed a full and enthusiastic devotion to his studies. […]

Here, indeed, lay the fundamental problem. Though some among the blacks might learn lines of the Scriptures[6] tolerably, they seemed obstinately[7] unable to see the bright light of faith. During Sunday services some would even tie handkerchiefs around their foreheads to hide their eyes, so they might sleep unobserved: this, as the very word of God was being brought to them! It was quite as if they imagined that Christian knowledge had little pertinence[8] to their lives. Sad to say, this could hardly have been less true. As time passed the blacks' numbers were diminishing at a perilous[9] rate. The outbreaks of disease, which had seemed to slow when Mr

[1] **reluctance** unwillingness – [2] **curiosity** strong desire to know about sth – [3] **feeble** weak – [4] **to vanish** to disappear – [5] **wallaby** small kangaroo – [6] **Scriptures** biblical writings – [7] **obstinate** stubborn, refusing to change one's opinion – [8] **pertinence** ['---] relevance – [9] **perilous** dangerous

Robson first arrived, had grown more frequent than ever, with several deaths sometimes occurring in a single week. The aborigines, who had comprised[1] some two hundred even in the early days, were now reduced to less than half that number, and their huts, whose crowded conditions had caused Mr Robson great concern when he first arrived, were now all too sadly sufficient[2]. Little by little the settlement began to acquire an aura of sombre[3] emptiness, only the graveyard remaining busy.

What's the difference?

1. What is Reverend Geoffrey complaining about?
2. What are the reasons for the "aura of sombre emptiness"? (ll. 39–40)
3. An Aboriginal leader explains to Wilson why his fellow Aborigines are "unable to see the bright light of faith." Write a short speech. → Method kit, Comment and speech, p. 292

Different ideas about spirituality

1. What is the basic difference between the Aboriginal concept and that of Christianity?
2. In our society many people claim to be indifferent to religious matters. Why isn't it possible for an Aboriginal to hold such a view?

A Letter from England

On January 26, 1988, while white Australians were celebrating the Bicentennial, Burnum Burnum, an Aboriginal activist, in a symbolic gesture above the white cliffs of Dover claimed Britain in the name of the Australian Aboriginals.

How would you have reacted to this event if you had heard about it?

Burnum Burnum, previously called Harry Penrith (1936–1997), took the name of his great grandfather to better express his sense of Aboriginality.

[1] **to comprise** to include, to be composed of – [2] **sufficient** adequate – [3] **sombre** ['sɒmbə] dark; sad

Dear Burnum Burnum,

Seven years ago today (this was written on January 26), you planted the Aboriginal flag on the white cliffs of Dover and claimed our country for your people, (or some of them).

That was 200 years to the day since Captain Phillip[1] claimed your country for our people (or some of them).

I'm writing to you in recognition of your claim, and to offer you homage and loyalty, on behalf of our people (or some of them).

Seven years may seem like a long time for a reply, but so far there have been few signs of an invasion. I hope this doesn't mean you've given up on us.

Maybe you're in no particular hurry to consolidate your claim. Viewed in the long term, seven years is not that long at all, really.

You people have always been good at thinking in the long term, and to me that's part of the attraction. The old regime over here is daft as emus[2]. It can't see more than five years ahead, and so it continues to rip up the land to provide little short-term comforts like roads and houses.

The only sites that are sacred are ones that earn them money. You must see how difficult it is to respect people like this.

Your people have suffered atrociously[3] at the hands of my lot[4]. We tried hard to destroy you, and almost succeeded.

It's easy to say, 'sorry,' and difficult for us to make amends[5], now that we're properly confined to this island.

What we can do is to start showing some real respect by listening to what you Aborigines have to say about looking after the land.

In your book 'Aboriginal Australia,' you describe your race as 'perhaps the most successful people who ever lived on this planet.'

Now some people would say that you're biased[6], but maybe you've got a right to be proud. I do know that my lot have got loads to learn from folk who managed to live in relative harmony with each other and the land, for 50,000 years and more.

That's quite a bit longer than there's been people here in Blighty[7], and plenty of time to get a few things right.

It's no coincidence that the world is now so interested in Aboriginal art, and culture in general. Your culture is being triumphantly vindicated[8], as the rest of us slowly wake up to what you people have been saving for so long.

'In claiming this land, we wish no harm to you natives,' you said as you planted the flag, which is a good deal better than we deserve.

Welcome, then, to the controls of this tarnished[9] but still-beautiful island of ours.

I look forward to your inspiration and guidance. Who knows, maybe one day we natives will have grown Aboriginal enough to look after the place properly for ourselves.

Yours loyally
Adam Stout

The Koori Mail, No. 94, February 8, 1995

- Who might the letter writer be?
- Why does he write to Burnum Burnum?
- What is the writer's attitude towards Aboriginal people?

[1]**Captain Phillip** (1738–1814) Naval Officer who is remembered as being the founder of the first European settlement in Australia – [2]**daft as emus** (*coll*) very stupid – [3]**atrocious** (*infml*) very bad or unpleasant – [4]**my lot** (*coll*) my fellow countrymen– [5]**to make amends** *etw. wiedergutmachen* – [6]**biased** ['baɪəst] full of prejudices – [7]**Blighty** (*sl*) England; used esp by British troops serving abroad – [8]**to vindicate** to justify – [9]**tarnished** which has lost its shine

What's your view of the letter?

1. In what way does the form of this letter correspond to the happening staged by Burnum Burnum?
2. How do you evaluate this way of dealing with the problem?

Find out more about the Aboriginal peoples

Conduct an Internet research on the relationship between white people and the Aborigines in the past and at present and present your findings in class. ➔ Method kit, Internet research p. 304 and Making a presentation, p. 309

What is that in German?

"As daft as emus"(l. 14) is an example of an Australian simile. You must be careful translating similes. A straight translation doesn't work. How would you translate the following similes?

- as good as gold
- as dead as a dodo
- as mad as a hatter
- as daft as a brush
- as dumb as dirt
- as high as a kite
- as happy as a king
- as deaf as a doorpost
- as happy as a pig in muck
- as like as two peas in a pod
- as plain as the nose on your face
- as sure as eggs are eggs
- as thick as two short planks

simile ['sɪməli]: a comparison of one thing with another, e.g. 'as brave as a lion', 'a face like a mask'.

Info

Two Peoples – One Nation: Australia and the Aboriginals

Australia's official flag

In 2001 Australia celebrated the centenary of the Australian Federation: the Commonwealth of Australia. It is a constitutional monarchy with Queen Elizabeth as head of state. She is represented by a governor general. Prime Minister John Howard has been the head of government since 1996. The future of the monarchy has been much debated, but in a referendum[1] in November 2000 whether to turn Australia into a republic, the advocates of monarchy won with 55% to 45%.

Australia has a population of 19,200,000. The percentage of Aboriginals is 1.5%. People of European descent make up 94% and Asians 4%—with the Asian population growing fastest.

About 50,000 years ago the first groups of people from Southeast Asia arrived in Australia. When the last Ice Age ended—c. 8000 BC—the melting ice caused the sea levels to rise to those we know today. From that time on Australia and its in-

[1] **referendum** vote taken on an important issue by all people of a country

digenous[1] population—the Aboriginals—were isolated from the rest of mankind.
In 1770 Captain James Cook discovered the eastern coast of Australia and 18 years later the first English settlers arrived in Botany Bay. They brought with them diseases such as the smallpox[2], which had a devastating effect on the Aboriginal tribes. Since they seemed to be unwilling to cooperate, the English settlers took their land away by force and treated them as inferior human beings, even though there were protection programmes for the Aboriginals, which, however, were rather measures of control and restriction on the Aboriginal way of life.
Until 1967, when the Aborigines were recognized as Australian citizens, forceful assimilation was practised. Aboriginal children were separated from parents who were proclaimed unfit to bring up children. These 'stolen' children were taken to mission homes where they were given Christian names and were no longer allowed to speak their native language or practise their own customs.
In 1991 a Council for Aboriginal Reconciliation was established to guide a ten-year-long reconciliation process. One year earlier, in 1990, the Aboriginal Provisional Government was founded with the aim to create an independent and sovereign Aboriginal state. The APG strongly advocated[3] a separate Aboriginal team for the Olympic Games.
The desire to reconcile the past led to many new designs for a future national flag. The national heritage is represented in the colours. Black symbolizes the Aboriginal people, red, the mother earth, and yellow, the sun, the renewer of life. Red, white and blue represent the British, and more broadly, European heritage. The boomerang design gives the flag a uniquely[4] Australian identity. The southern cross and the seven-pointed Federation Star, representing the six original states with one point for all future states and territories are retained.

The flag of the Aboriginals

The future Australian flag?

Cathy Freeman: The well-known track star lights the Olympic cauldron[5] in 2000. Her emergence as Australia's best hope for a gold medal on the running track comes at a time when Australians are increasingly seeking to reconcile[6] with Aborigines.

Info

[1] **indigenous** native – [2] **smallpox** *Pocken* – [3] **to advocate** to speak publicly in favour of sth, to support – [4] **unique** unlike anything else, being the only type – [5] **cauldron** *Kessel* – [6] **to reconcile** to make people become friends again, e.g. after quarrelling

Robert Hardman

No Red Carpet for the Queen

What special relationship is there between Australia and Queen Elizabeth?
How do you think a monarch expects to be received by her subjects?

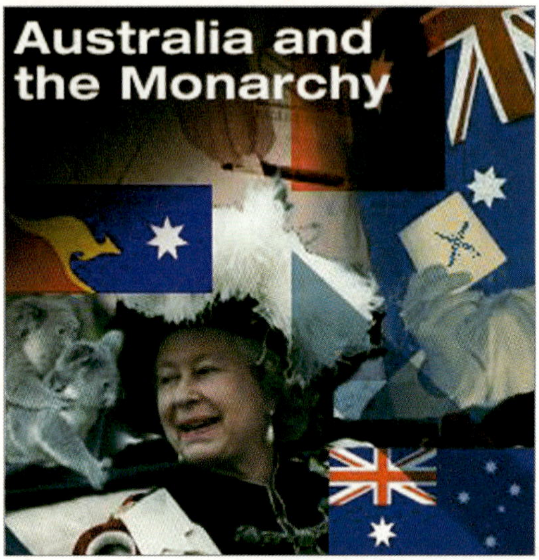

The Queen arrived in Australia last night to find that even referendum[1]-winning monarchs must take second place to an endangered species of lizard[2]. She landed in Canberra at the start of a 15-day tour which will be more of a healing process than a celebration. Just four months after the stormy constitutional plebiscite[3] which endorsed[4] the Crown but split Australia, there was nothing remotely[5] triumphal about the Queen's low-key[6] entry into the capital.

Her arrival in a small Falcon jet of the Royal Australian Air Force summed it up. She had flown from London as far as Sydney in a Qantas[7] 747 chartered by the Australian government. But it was not permitted to land at Canberra. A small, protected lizard called the Eastern lined earless dragon inhabits the grass around Canberra airport and, despite[8] its lack of ears, it dislikes large aircraft. Under Australia's environmental laws, 747s are therefore banned from Canberra and the Queen had to switch planes in Sydney for the final leg[9]. […]

In 1954, she had been cheered into Sydney by a million. Last night, there was a welcoming party of four—the pro-monarchy Prime Minister, John Howard, and the Governor General[10], Sir William Deane, plus wives.

Why is there no red carpet for the Queen?

[...] Neither the recent constitutional unrest[11] nor the long journey from London appeared to have dimmed[12] the Queen's affection for the place as she arrived, smiling, in a cheerful lilac[13] floral-patterned dress. […] The only public welcome last night was provided by nine republicans complaining that they had an "irrelevant" head of state. They carried a banner saying "Republic of the ACT[14] Welcomes The Queen of England". The Queen waved at them. They smiled but did not reciprocate[15]. Robin Poke, 56, once of Isleworth, west London,

[1] **referendum** a vote taken on an important issue by all people of a country – [2] **lizard** *Eidechse, Echse* – [3] **plebiscite** ['plebɪsɪt] *Volksentscheid* – [4] **to endorse** to support – [5] **remotely** to a very slight degree – [6] **low-key** not intended to attract a lot of attention – [7] **Qantas** Australia's largest airline – [8] **despite** in spite of; *trotz* – [9] **leg** here: part of a journey – [10] **Governor General** the representative of the Queen – [11] **unrest** situation in which people are angry or dissatisfied – [12] **to dim** to become less strong – [13] **lilac** pale purple – [14] **ACT** Australian Capital Territory, one of the six states, situated on the east coast – [15] **to reciprocate** here: not to wave back

and the group leader, said: "We didn't wave because we think she's an anachronism. This is not a protest. This is a statement." But their sentiment—that the Queen should be welcomed but treated as someone else's queen—seems to be the prevailing[1] one in republican circles. It is widely accepted that any overt[2] hostility[3] or abuse[4] would do the republican cause no good at all.

James Terrie, of the Australian Republican Movement, said yesterday: "The Queen is head of state and while she remains the head of state, she should be accorded[5] the proper protocol. We are telling people that if they are offended by her presence, they should ignore it. Our official position is not to do anything during this tour but people have every right to make a statement." Just as the republican mainstream[6] is avoiding confrontation, so the monarchist cause is exercising restraint[7] too. [...]

The central themes of the tour, as arranged by Mr Howard, are multi-culturalism, young people, medical progress and the regions. Republicans say the latter is a sop[8] to the non-urban areas which tended to back the monarchy in the referendum.

Monarchists complain that the Queen will spend more time in Canberra, the most republican district in the country, than any-

Why is there such a cool welcome?

During his visit in 1920 the Prince of Wales is overwhelmed by his subjects.

[1]**to prevail** to be dominant – [2]**overt** clear, visible – [3]**hostility** aggressive feelings or behaviour – [4]**abuse** rude and offensive remarks – [5]**to accord** to give – [6]**mainstream** the people whose ideas are most accepted – [7]**restraint** self-control – [8]**sop** a pill that calms you down

where else. The republicans gleefully[1] point out that the Queen arrived on St Patrick's Day[2] and is leaving on April Fool's Day. The monarchists are mobilising their supporters to turn out at every royal event. Church bells will be rung wherever she goes. But other factors may upstage[3] the old debate. More attention will be paid to the Aboriginal community than on any previous tour.

However, one Aboriginal rights group is threatening legal proceedings[4] against the Queen for crimes against Australia's indigenous[5] people. No one is taking it very seriously. But it will certainly be reported.

From "No red carpet as Queen flies into Australia to welcome party of four", *The Daily Telegraph*, March 18, 2000, p. 3

A serious matter

1. Analyze the tone of the newspaper article.
2. How does the Queen see her visit?

> On her 15-day-tour through Australia—the walkabout—the Queen visited a school in Western Australia. All the children were instructed how to behave except one, a boy named Sol. He first hit a classmate so that she started screaming and then looked up and demanded of the monarch: "What's your name?" The Queen, though looking a little startled, said nothing.
>
> *The Guardian*, April 1, 2000

3. How would you have reacted?
4. How might the Queen have felt during her visit? Write a dialogue between the Queen and Prince Philip after the end of their visit.

The Head of Commonwealth

1. Find out what role (political power, functions, personal role model) the Queen plays in the Commonwealth.
2. Hold a debate: The Queen should resign as the formal head of state in all Commonwealth countries except the UK.

[1] **gleeful** happy – [2] **St Patrick's Day** the Irish national holiday; the Irish are often made fun of because they are said to lack intelligence – [3] **to upstage** to make sth less interesting – [4] **proceeding** action, claim – [5] **indigenous** native

The United States of Europe?

The Way We Are

Now that the euro has been introduced, do you think Europe will become one nation? What makes you feel European?

> "Identity has become something completely different since the Berlin wall came down. Young people are looking for an identity."
>
> Joeri Boom, 29, Dutch journalist

As part of TIME'S exploration of European youth in 2001, they surveyed 21- to 35-year-olds in Britain, France, Germany and Italy about their hopes, habits and problems. Here are some of the results:

To what extent do you support or oppose the current trend of globalization?

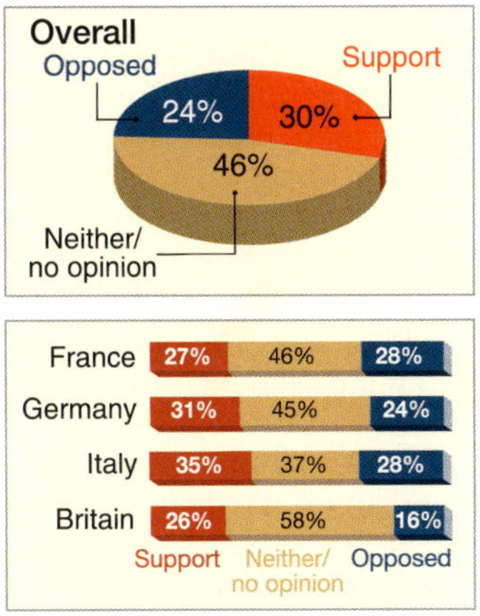

To what extent do you see yourself as European?

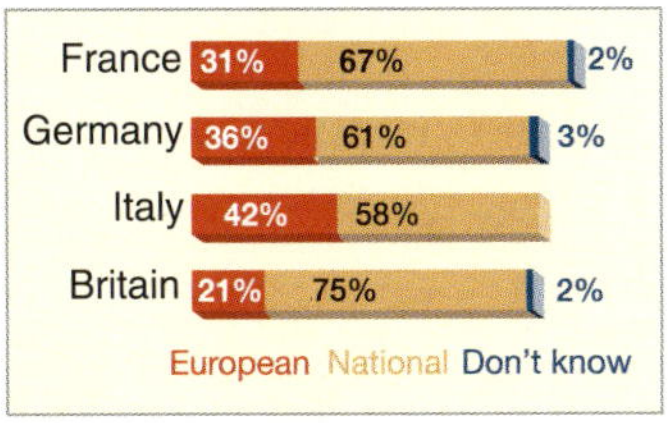

To what extent do you support or oppose further research into genetic engineering?

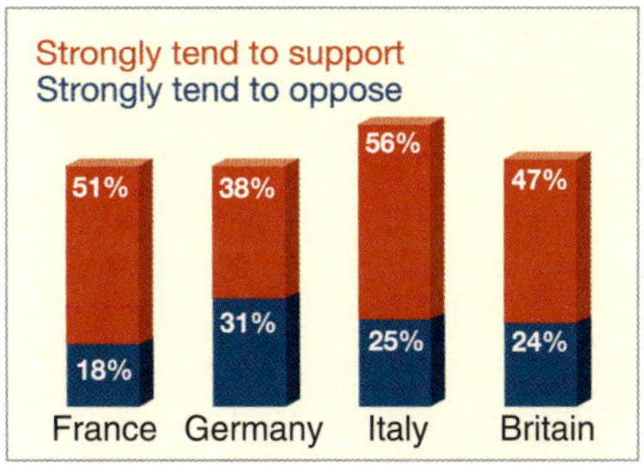

What are your greatest long-term concerns about the future?

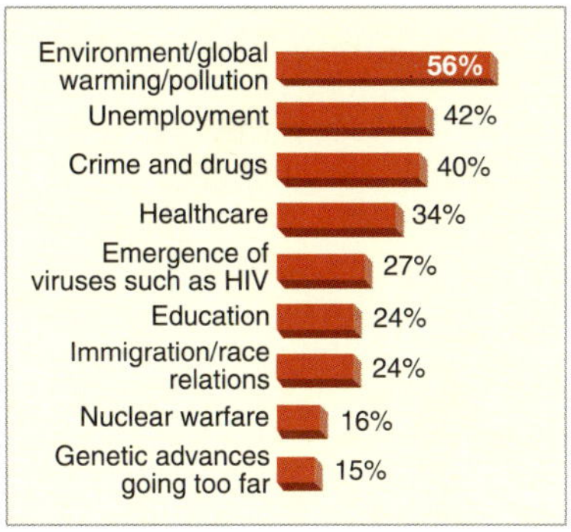

Time, April 2, 2001, pp. 40–41

Talking about charts

- figure – number – percentage – in comparison with – to rise – to increase – to drop – to decrease
- more/less likely the survey illustrates/proves …
- Only/more than ten per cent of …
- The graph/chart shows the attitude/development of …
- The graph/chart provides information about …
- Only/more than half of a third of …
- Compared to …
- It clearly indicates that …
- The percentage of … is very small/large/negligible

1. Prepare a two-minute statement about your findings. The words and expressions in the box will help you.
2. Take your own poll in class.

What things are you concerned about?

Romesh Ratnesar

Generation Europe

They're young, they're cosmopolitan and don't have much use for borders that have divided Europe for centuries.

Where could this picture have been taken?
What does it show about young people today?

A generation is on the move. In burgeoning[1] numbers and with astounding[2] ease, young adults in Europe are hurdling[3] national barriers, dumping[4] old routines and abandoning[5] traditional career choices in search of their own, highly personalized, custom-made[6] paths to have been unimaginable a generation ago. All of this is forming the basis for happiness. And for many, that means leading peripatetic[7], borderless lives that would have been unimaginable a generation ago. All of this is forming the basis for a common European identity in which national and regional ties co-exist with a new and still evolving[8] *esprit d'Europe.*

Says Michael Gillespie, 26, the head of international research at Informer Brand Development in London: "In terms of outlook and attitudes toward life, there are a lot of shared values among young Europeans. It has to do with a sense of being tolerant and open, and a willingness to try new things." It's no longer unusual for someone like the French novelist Frédéric Biegbeder, 35, to profess[9] little desire to leave France but also "feel totally European. And that means I don't give a damn about France. I go along with John Lennon: 'Imagine there's no countries.'"

And as Lennon might assure Biegbeder, he's not the only one. A

[1] **to burgeon** ['bɜdʒən] to grow rapidly – [2] **to astound** to surprise – [3] **to hurdle** to jump over – [4] **to dump** to get rid of – [5] **to abandon** to give up – [6] **custom-made** made for a particular person – [7] **peripatetic** going from place to place – [8] **to evolve** to develop – [9] **to profess** to state openly

TIME poll[1] of 1,225 people between the ages of 21 and 35 in Germany, France, Italy and Britain found that a majority of young adults still identify themselves with their native countries. But close to one-third prefer to call themselves European; in Italy, the number is over 40%. And there are countless others who have tried on so many identities that they simply won't—or can't—choose among them.

Paula Romero, 29, was born in Spain, has an English husband and lives in Brussels, where she is pursuing[2] an arts degree at a Belgian university. "A true European is someone who doesn't feel his or her culture is the only thing in town," she says. "Just one culture is not enough these days." Catherine Rubbens, 34, an environmental consultant in London who left the Netherlands after high school, speaks five European languages and says she feels more European than Dutch. "I notice as I start to adjust somewhere that I speak to myself in the language of that place." [...]

Europe has long had its share[3] of cosmopolitan globehoppers [...]. But now, even those who don't fit into the go-anywhere jet set can now lay claim[4] to a more expansive world. The ease of travel, the advances in communications technology, the ubiquity[5] of multinational brand[6] names, the interdependence of the global economy—all have served to provide young adults with a set of mutual[7] experiences, attitudes and cultural cues[8]. In a Continent where 83% of young West European adults carry mobile phones, this generation's lingua franca[9] is the text message. Europe's nightclubs have made icons[10] out of DJs who spin[11] in different European cities every week, trailed[12] by a transnational community of fans. "There are stronger communions that cut across national identity," says Eric Tong-Cuong, the founder of the French record company Naive. Events like London's Notting Hill Carnival and the Love Parade, the annual threeday outdoor rave in Berlin, have become massive pan-European parties. "Our generation functions tribally[13] but you can belong to several tribes at the same time."

Some young Europeans see a downside[14] to all this cultural convergence: it often feels like homogenization. Paola La Falce, 34, an Italian who works for Universal Music in Paris, recalls[15] her first trip to the U.K. 15 years ago: "It was incredibly different from where I came from. But now the center of London is just like the center of Milan—it's the same *Gap* and *Levis* stores. I'm nostalgic for that period when you really felt like you were somewhere else. I'm all

Imagine

Imagine there's no heaven,
It's easy if you try,
No hell below us,
Above us only sky,
Imagine all the people
Living for today ...

Imagine there's no countries,
It isn't hard to do,
Nothing to kill or die for,
No religion too,
Imagine all the people
Living life in peace ...

Imagine no possessions,
I wonder if you can,
No need for greed or hunger,
A brotherhood of man,
Imagine all the people
Sharing all the world ...

You may say I'm a dreamer,
But I'm not the only one,
I hope some day you'll join us,
And the world will live as one.

John Lennon

(EMI Music Publishing GmbH, Hamburg)

Explain the last sentence in this paragraph.

What's the "downside" of cultural convergence?

[1] **poll** the process of questioning people – [2] **to pursue** to follow, here: to work at – [3] **share** part, portion – [4] **to lay claim to sth** to state that you have a right to own sth – [5] **ubiquity** presence everywhere at the same time – [6] **brand** *Marke* – [7] **mutual** sth shared by several people – [8] **cue** [kju:] signal, key word – [9] **lingua franca** international language – [10] **icon** idol, sacred image – [11] **to spin** (an LP) to move in circles – [12] **to trail** to follow – [13] **tribal** belonging to a large group of related people – [14] **downside** disadvantages – [15] **to recall** to remember

for a united Europe, but I think we're losing something at the same time." That ambivalence about the momentum[1] of European integration—and in a larger sense, globalization—is widely felt.

Europeans in their twenties retain[2] only hazy[3] memories of the ideological struggle that divided Europe for 50 years. As a result, many young adults in the E.U. tend to be enthusiastic about extending membership to Eastern and Central European countries. Says Sara Priem, 24, president of the Young European Movement, a British pro-Europe grassroots group[4]: "It's one of those issues that's easy to be strong on because everyone agrees with it. The Berlin Wall came down when we were 10 or 11, so for us those in the east are part of Europe. There's no divide in our heads." […]

Some researchers say the collapse of communism has also changed the way young adults throughout Europe, East and West, organize their lives and imagine their careers. Stefan Baumann, a manager of the Hamburg-based Trend Bureau, says that the disappearance of "an alternative to capitalism" has made the "primacy[5] of the economy" the governing principle of their lives. Politics and ideology consumed[6] their parents, but Europe's young professionals are now more likely to invest their jobs with social significance.

"Today's workers see work as a way to put their values into practice where your work has become something of a political choice," says Richard Reeves, director of futures at the Industrial Society, a U.K. think tank[7]. "For this generation, which box you put your ballot[8] in on election day may matter less than which desk you put your butt[9] behind every day." With unemployment for 21- to 35-year-old in the E.U. at 11% as of 1999—compared to the overall jobless rate of 9.2%—anxiety[10] about getting and keeping any job at all remains high: in the TIME poll, 42% of respondents[11] cited[12] unemployment as their chief concern for the future. But young workers today are also better prepared to handle uncertainty. Indeed, in the new economy they embrace[13] it. "My dad worked at BNP[14] all his life. For my generation, the trend is to change jobs frequently," says Benoit Cacheux, 26, a French native who works for a Web design agency in London. "There are so many companies starting up that it creates an energy that makes people want to change." […]

Which differences between the older and the younger generation does the author mention?

As time goes on, the desire of young Europeans to pursue those ideals—in essence, the desire for a high quality of life—could have

[1]**momentum** *Triebkraft, Impuls* – [2]**to retain** to keep – [3]**hazy** unclear, vague – [4]**grassroots group** people who are the backbone of a movement – [5]**primacy** ['praɪməsi] priority, sth that is most important – [6]**to consume** to use the energy – [7]**think tank** a group of excellent experts – [8]**to put one's ballot in** to vote – [9]**butt** (*infml*) the part of the body you sit on – [10]**anxiety** great fear – [11]**respondent** a person who answers questions in a survey – [12]**to cite** here: to mention sth as an example – [13]**to embrace** to accept; to hold tight – [14]**BNP** Business News Publishing Company

broader implications[1], strengthening support for the idea that such common aspirations[2] can be realized through pan-European co-operation. Expanding access to the good life, for instance, depends on the preservation of Europe's open market and the easy availability[3] of such delights[4] as French wine, Belgian beer, Italian pasta and Spanish beaches. And in the TIME'S poll of 21- to 35-year-olds, 56% cited the environment, global warming and pollution as their chief long-term concern, and 40% named crime and drugs.

That too reflects the primacy this generation places on the quality of life, and their determination to protect the components of it: safe streets, clean water, fresh air. Those also happen to be the kind of social problems that are best tackled[5] on a supranational[6] level.

Time, April 2, 2001, pp. 28–38

Which new ideals of the young generation does the author present?

Model Europeans

1. Describe a young model European. Write down keywords and then introduce him or her to your class.
2. There is still a large percentage of British people who feel uneasy about a closer European Union like the *Critical European Group* (www.keele.ac.uk./socs/ks40/ceghome.html). Study their arguments and compare them to counter arguments you can find under www.britainineurope.org.
3. Conduct a discussion about the pros and cons of a strongly united Europe.
4. Write a fictional account of the European Union in the year 2100. You can present it as either a utopia or a dystopia. Before you start, make a list of words that describe the situation in the future and generate a mind map. ➡ Method kit, Mind map, p. 281

Utopia: an ideal state.
Dystopia: a state where everything has taken a turn for the worse.

Reported speech

Transform the parts of the text in direct speech into reported speech. Start with an introductory verb in the past tense. (He/she said/pointed out/… that …) Remember: there is no comma before *that*.

Euro-words

Generate a mind map *Europe*. Use the words in the text and go beyond. ➡ Method kit, Mind map, p. 281

Translation

Translate ll. 106–119 ("As time … supranational level.") into German. Work in small groups and compare your translations.

[1]**implication** thing that is suggested or implied – [2]**aspiration** dream, desire – [3]**availability** *Verfügbarkeit* – [4]**delight** a feeling of great pleasure – [5]**to tackle** to deal with or overcome sth awkward or difficult – [6]**supra-** above, beyond

Jonathan Lynn and Anthony Jay

Food is a Weapon

Name five attitudes or characteristics that you think are typically British, Italian, German, French and Dutch. Talk about your views in a double circle.

In *Yes, Prime Minister* Jim Hacker, formerly Minister for the Department of Administrative Affairs, writes down his political advancement in a diary. The book was turned into a very successful comedy in the eighties. Hacker is surprised as anyone when he suddenly finds himself elevated[1] to the post of Prime Minister of the United Kingdom. In his new role, he has the assistance of Bernard Woolley, his Private Secretary, but he has to assert himself against the troublesome Sir Humphrey Appleby, Cabinet Secretary to the Prime Minister and in charge of the entire Civil Service[2].

Sir Humphrey Appleby, Jim Hacker and Bernard Woolley

Explain the comical element of this situation.

January 2nd

There was a drinks'do'[3] at the FCO[4] this evening. It was for our European friends. With friends like them …

I met an EEC[5] official who seemed awfully Teutonic[6], and I asked him where he was from.

"From Brussels I have just arrived," he told me.

I was surprised. "You're from Belgium?"

"Brussels is in Belgium. That is correct." The Teutonic mind!

Bernard came to the rescue. "I think the Minister is asking if you are Belgian?"

The official nodded and smiled. "No, I am German."

"And what are you at the EEC?" I asked pleasantly.

"I am still German."

I reminded myself that patience is a virtue[7]. "I know that," I said, and looked to Bernard to rescue me again.

"I think the Minister means," said Bernard carefully, "what is your job?"

"Ah," said the Kraut. "I am a Chef du Division."

"It's a sort of Assistant Secretary," Bernard whispered to me.

I wondered, to Bernard, if our German friend (as I have to call him) can help us with our sausage problem. Bernard nodded, and asked him exactly what his job was.

He was only too happy to explain. "My job is concerned with the

[1]**to elevate** to give sb a higher position – [2]**Civil Service** people working for the different departments of a government – [3]**drinks'do'** *Umtrunk* – [4]**FCO** Foreign and Commonwealth Office – [5]**EEC** European Economic Community – forerunner to the EU – [6]**Teutonic** qualities typical of German people – [7]**virtue** behaviour that shows high moral standards

Common Agricultural Policy. I have to see that the farmers are paid enough money to produce more food."

This came as a considerable surprise to me. I thought we were producing too much food in the EEC – hence[1] the surpluses[2]. I said as much.

The German nodded significantly. "Too much food to eat, yes!" I was baffled[3]. "What else is food for?" I asked him. His eyes lit up with pleasure.

"We do not produce food for eating. Food is a weapon!"

I couldn't exactly see what he meant. "A weapon," I said. "You mean ...," I searched for the right response, but answer came there none. "You mean ... what *do* you mean, exactly?"

It was obvious to him. "Food is power. Green power,"

I asked if he meant that we fight the Russians with food. He became impatient, and explained that we don't fight the Russians. They are our friends, our customers. We fight the Americans!

I asked him to expand on this theme. He was delighted. His eyes gleamed as he discussed his nation's favourite pastime. "It is a war," he began. "A trade war. Using food we can increase our spheres of influence over Third World countries. You should have seen Dr Kissinger's[4] face when we threatened to sell wheat[5] to Egypt." He chuckled[6] merrily[7]. "He wanted Egypt to himself. You see, if the Third World switches from American to European wheat, the US President loses millions of votes in the vest."

It took me a moment to realize that he was speaking geographically, not sartorially[8].

"The *Mid*-vest," he explained. "So. The Common Agricultural Policy gives us great influence over America, you see? Last war, guns. This war, butter."

"It's better, butter," I remarked facetiously[9] and laughed a little. He did not get the joke. [...] So I asked what, *precisely*, he did in the food war.

"I ensure that our farmers are subsidized[10] to produce all the food that they can. We have underground silos bursting with agricultural missiles." We were standing by the buffet, and he started to set up a dinner-table battlefield as an illustration. "We move a division of butter to Bangladesh, we threaten Egypt with three brigades of wheat. But it is a decoy[11], you see," he cried triumphantly. "We have six airborne divisions[12] of beef waiting to fly into China. Then ..."

He suddenly paused, and then burst out laughing. Bernard and I stared at him, bemused. Finally I asked him what the joke was.

"It's better, butter," he chortled[13]. "Very funny. Very funny."

Bernard took me by the hand and led me quietly away to another part of the reception, where he presented me to a Monsieur Jean Penglet, who is also a Chef du Division in Brussels.

▲ Sum up the German Assistant Secretary's view of the agricultural policy of the EEC.

[1]**hence** for this reason – [2]**surplus** an amount that is more than you need – [3]**baffled** confused – [4]**Dr Kissinger** U.S. secretary of state (1973–1977) during the Nixon and Ford administrations – [5]**wheat** *Weizen* – [6]**to chuckle** to laugh quietly – [7]**merrily** happily – [8]**sartorially** *was die Kleidung betrifft* – [9]**facetiously** [fəˈsiːʃəs] trying to appear amusing – [10]**to subsidize** to provide financial support – [11]**decoy** *Köder* [12]**airborne division** *Luftlandedivision* – [13]**to chortle** to laugh loudly with pleasure

Hacker in front of his new home

I speak no German, but I tried out a little French on Monsieur P. "Vous parlez anglais, Monsieur Penglet?" I enquired poetically.

"I do," he replied with cool politeness.

"And what do *you* do?" I asked.

"My job," he said with a patient smile, "is to deal with food surpluses."

"You mean, export them or store them?"

He was confused. "Non—I pay farmers to see that all surplus food is destroyed." Now I was confused. "Destroyed?" I repeated.

"But of course," he said with a patronising Gallic shrug[1]. "Don't you know the Community produces too much food?"

I kept my temper.

"But look, sorry, I don't want to appear dense[2] but that chap there" – I pointed to our humorous friendly German – "pays farmers to *produce* surplus food. Green power, he says."

"I know," he nodded. "He does a good job. Food is a weapon."

This was making less and less sense. "Then *why*," I demanded, "do you pay people to destroy it?"

There was no contradiction as far as our French friend was concerned. "All weapons must be made obsolete. Then you can pay people to produce more. Simple."

"Can't you just go on storing it?"

He thought that was a silly idea. "*Non*, it is cheaper to destroy the food than to store, liquefy[3] or dehydrate."

"Or send it across the world?" asked Bernard.

"Exactly."

The whole Through-The-Looking-Glass approach[4] was becoming clear to me. "And", I said, "I suppose you can't sell it at the market price because then the price would fall and the farmers would not make enough money."

The Frenchman was delighted that I understood. "Exactly."

I decided to sum up. "So, *he* pays French farmers to grow too much food—*you* pay the same French farmers to destroy it!"

He was grinning now. "Exactly."

There was just one thing left that I didn't understand. "Why," I asked, "don't we just pay the farmers to sit there and not bother[5] to grow the food at all?"

The Frenchman was offended[6]. "Monsieur Hacker," he replied snootily[7]. "French farmers do not want to be paid for nothing. We do not want charity."

Summarize the Frenchman's view in your own words.

[1]**patronising Gallic shrug** the Frenchman raised his shoulders arrogantly – [2]**dense** (*infml*) stupid – [3]**to liquefy** to make sth liquid – [4]**Through-The-Looking-Glass approach** when everything is reversed (reference to Lewis Carroll's book *Through The Looking Glass*, 1871) – [5]**to bother** to care – [6]**to offend sb** to insult sb, *beleidigen* – [7]**snootily** arrogantly

Hacker's diary

1. Characterize Hacker. Will he be a good Prime Minister?
   ➡ Method kit, Characterization, p. 289

2. The British have always been quite uneasy about subsidising the agricultural sector in the same way their continental neighbours have. Add another entry to Hacker's diary, which reflects on his conversation with the two EEC Assistant Secretaries.
   ➡ Method kit, Diary entry, p. 294

Yes, Prime Minister: A satire

1. The excerpt is part of a satire, written as a diary. Give examples of how a satire works. ➡ Language kit, Satire, p. 318

2. We are often prejudiced against people from other countries. Which stereotypical views of German and Frenchmen can you find in the text?

Translation

Translate the following expressions:
- to come to the rescue (l. 11)
- to be only too happy to do sth (l. 25)
- to say as much (ll. 29–30)
- to light up with pleasure (ll. 32–33)
- to get the joke(l. 56)
- to burst out laughing (l. 65)
- to keep one's temper (l. 85)

British diseases

The Beefeater

1. What does the cartoon express? How does it relate to the satire's motto "Food is a Weapon"?

2. Use the Internet to inform yourself about mad cow disease and foot and mouth disease. To what extent did the European countries' ways of tackling these problems differ?
   ➡ Method kit, Internet research, p. 304

Peter Preston

51st State

In his novel Peter Preston throws a daring look at the political future of GB: Roughly thirty years after Tony Blair's first term of office Europe has become a superstate with its own president. Great Britain strongly feels the loss of her sovereignty and there are lots of protests against Britain's staying on in the new superstate. Rupert Warner, the leader of the House of Commons who becomes the next prime minister, devises a way out of this dilemma. In the following excerpt he talks to his fellow countrymen about his plans for Britain as an extension to NAFTA. The speech was written by his political advisors and Warner hadn't seen it before the broadcast. While he is reading it, he makes silent comments to himself.

'Good evening to you all,' said Rupert. He hated TV fireside chats[1]. Try as he may, his eyes still pottered[2], transfixed[3], along the passing lines of text so that, five minutes in, he felt himself drifting into a goggling[4] trance. If you had an interviewer, preferably a woman interviewer, you could make a few jokes and try a touch of charm. Straight to camera was like looking down a black hole. But there was no help for it. Prime ministerial broadcasts of national importance—so important that the BBC had postponed[5] one of its Brazilian soaps—couldn't be unveiled[6] with girls waving their legs at the front of the screen.

'I speak to you tonight in this way because I have something to say that impacts[7] on the future for everyone, which puts us once more at the crossroads[8] of history. [...]

'It is eighteen months since the people of this country, you, the sovereign voters, chose to reassert[9] our national destiny by asking us, your servants, to withdraw[10] from the European Union.' *Nothing to do with me, Jack[11]. I only took orders.* 'I make no pretence[12]. They have not been easy months. We did not expect, and had no reason to expect, the bitterness, verging[13] on malevolence[14], of some of our former partners, who have sought to exclude us from markets traditionally vital to our fortunes[15]' *Blow you[16], Adolf[17], we're not all right.*

[1]**chat** conversation (fireside chats: addresses of President Roosevelt to the American people by radio from 1933–1944) – [2]**to potter** to move slowly – [3]**to be transfixed** to be unable to move – [4]**to goggle** ['gɒgl] to look at sth with one's eyes wide open – [5]**to postpone** to put off to a later time – [6]**to unveil** [ʌn'veɪl] to introduce a new plan, to uncover – [7]**to impact on sth** to have strong effect on sth – [8]**at the crossroads** at an important point in a development – [9]**to reassert** to state again that sth should be done – [10]**to withdraw** to move away – [11]**Jack** a man of the common people; lad, fellow (Warner is talking to himself here) – [12]**to make no pretence** to tell the truth – [13]**to verge on sth** to be very close to an extreme state or condition – [14]**malevolence** the desire to harm or hurt people – [15]**fortunes** wealth – [16]**blow you** (*infml*) be damned – [17]**Adolf** (Hitler) reference to the Germans, who play a leading role in the EU

'I want to make one thing clear tonight. Great Britain has never wished, or chosen, to go it alone in a world of increasing interdependence. We believe in partnership. But we can only be partners with friends who respect us and who recognize the role that our wisdom and our past achievements equip us for.' *King of the knacker's yard*[1]. 'Our erstwhile[2] friends across the Channel could not come to terms[3] with that. But there is one friend who has always been there when needed, asking nothing, giving generously. Ladies and gentlemen, the United States of America.' *Cue*[4]*: stars and stripes.* 'And its great President, Mr Bill Angeli.' *Cue: portrait.*

Rupert took a slow sip of water. 'Many of you may know that, for nearly forty years now, the United States has stood at the heart of a great trading alliance of nations called the North American Free Trade Area. In the beginning, it was joined by Canada, our old dominion[5], and by Mexico, one of the most teeming[6] and vibrant new countries on earth. But now the membership of NAFTA, as it is called, spreads far beyond that original grouping.'

'To the sun-drenched[7] islands of the Caribbean. To Panama and Guatemala at the bridgehead between two continents. To Venezuela, with its riches in oil, and Colombia, emerging[8] triumphantly from the dark shadows of the drug baronies. To the once tumultuous[9] stretch of shoreline and mountain peak called Chile.' *What had they done? He'd asked for a little contexting*[10]*, not a bloody travelogue*[11].

'Ladies and gentlemen, a few days ago my dear friend Bill Angeli came to talk with me at Chequers[12]. I explained our problems. He listened. And then he made the most generous of propositions. "Come live with us in our NAFTA homestead[13]," he said. "There would be no United States if there had not been a United Kingdom. We are bound in blood from our very birth. Together, trading freely, we can find new directions in a new world for all our sons and daughters, and for their children yet unborn."'

That was the hump[14], over. It was, and was intended to be, an utter surprise. The cabinet had only been told at five, and kept locked in Downing Street till the broadcast was finished. Rupert began to relax. We would not be joining some fresh federal superstate seeking to drain[15] us of our freedom, he said. This would be a pooling[16] of economic possibility between equal partners. There was, of course, much work to be done. Detailed proposals had to be

What reasons does Warner give his audience for leaving the EU?

NAFTA: North American Free Trade Agreement. The economic union of Canada, Mexico and the U.S.A. An organization similar to the EU.

What does the "travelogue" allude to?

What is the "hump"?

[1]**knacker's yard** place where old horses are taken to be killed – [2]**erstwhile** former – [3]**to come to terms with sth** to accept sth unpleasant by learning to deal with it – [4]**cue** [kju:] here: *Einblendung* – [5]**dominion** part of the British Commonwealth with its own government – [6]**teeming** full of people moving around – [7]**sun-drenched** with a lot of sunshine – [8]**to emerge** to appear – [9]**tumultuous** loud, noisy – [10]**contexting** to put information into the proper context – [11]**travelogue** film or piece of writing about travel – [12]**Chequers** private residence of the British prime ministers – [13]**homestead** home – [14]**hump** most difficult part – [15]**to drain sb of sth** to take sth away from sb – [16]**pooling** *Bündeln*

prepared and presented to the Parliament of Great Britain and the Congress of the United States. It was for them, in democracy, to decide.

'But, my friends, if there is a will, there is always a way. And with that will on both sides, I see no reason why, by next Christmas, we should not already have signed the necessary protocols and be the most optimistic, the most thrusting[1] new member of the organization that President Angeli has offered to rename the All-American and North Atlantic Prosperity[2] Area. Mark that well. A N A P A, an acronym[3] with Prosperity built in. It is our capital road to better times. Take it and, truly, we can commence[4] a new year together with hope high on our horizon. Thank you. And goodnight.'

Europe or America?

1. Analyze Prime Minister Warner's speech: How does he try to make this enormous step attractive to the British electorate?
2. What might British newspapers have written the next morning? Method kit, Newspaper article, p. 298
3. Devise a speech that the U.S. President might have given at the same time supporting the idea of a 51st state. Another group might list arguments in opposition to such a step. Method kit, Comment and speech, p. 292
4. There is a debate in the U.S. Congress whether or not to make GB the 51st state.
5. Interview the French President/the German Chancellor/a representative of one of the new Eastern members of the EU after the union between Britain and the U.S. has taken place. Method kit, Interview, p. 308
6. What is your vision of a more closely united Europe? What does it offer you?

Finding the humour

Find humorous passages. How do they work?

[1] **thrusting** active and ambitious – [2] **prosperity** economic or financial success – [3] **acronym** word formed from the first letters of several words (e.g. NATO) – [4] **to commence** to begin

British, but how European?

The European Union (EU)—previously known as the European Community (EC)—is an institutional framework for the construction of a united Europe. It was created after World War II to unite the nations of Europe economically so another war among them would be unthinkable. Today fifteen countries are members of the European Union, and some 370 million people share the common institutions and policies that have brought an era of peace and prosperity to Western Europe. The UK was not one of the founding members of the then EEC in 1958, not joining it until 1978 and has ever since been reluctant to become fully integrated into the EU. However, the construction of the Channel Tunnel/ Eurotunnel (completed in 1994) proved Britain's willingness to move closer to the Continent.

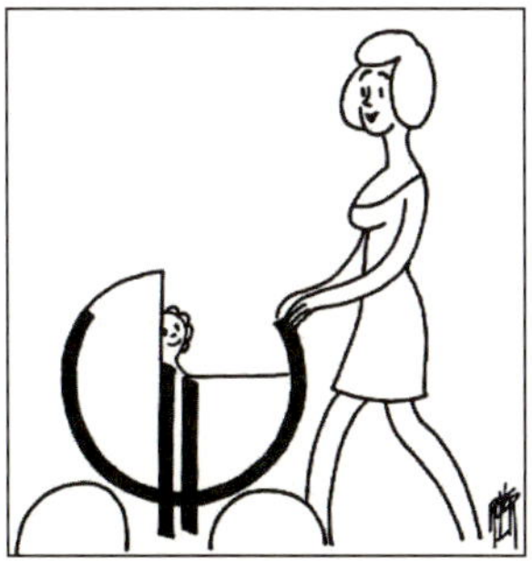

Info

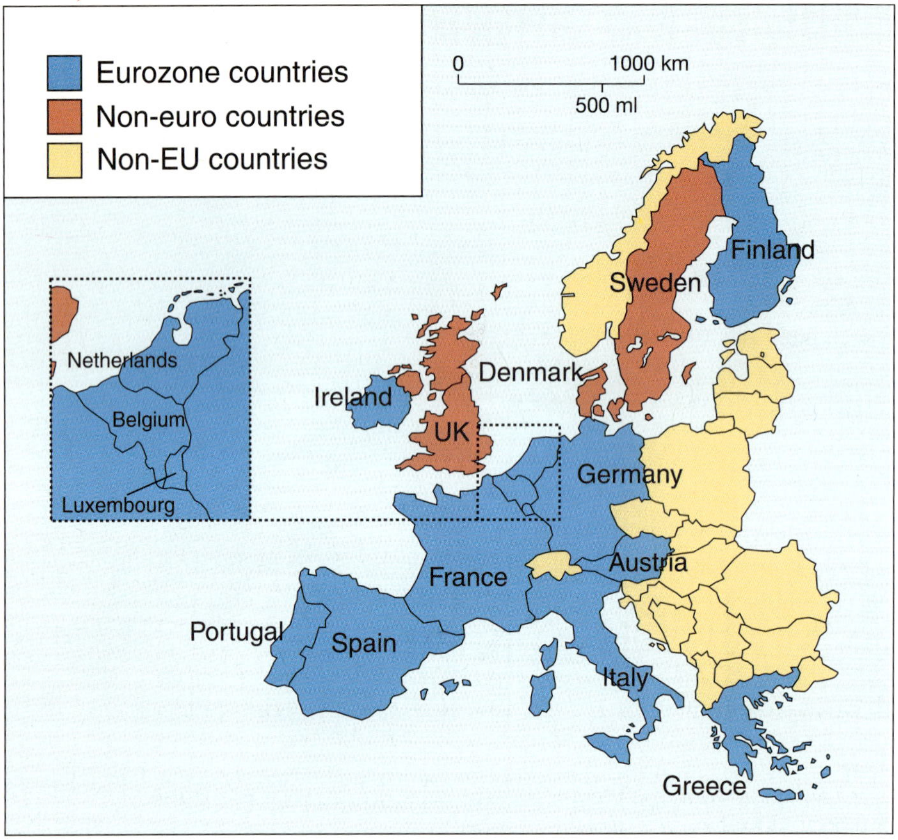

The big issue today is the euro. Though Labour is pro-Europe, it hesitates to join Europe's new single currency, just like Northern Ireland, Denmark and Sweden. Many Britons regard this to be the most important economic and political decision Britain will have to make in the first half of the twenty-first century. Britain's economy is quite stable at the moment and the pound's exchange rate is very high. Therefore, most Britons are unwilling to give up their national currency because they fear higher unemployment, less investment from countries outside the EU, a weakening of ties with the U.S. and a shaky economic stability because of the weaker member states. In particular the loss of national sovereignty is an issue since the European Central Bank is in Frankfurt, and thus Germany's influence might become too great. Britons fear that in the process of unifying taxes Britain's tax policy would be dictated from Brussels. Losing the pound would mean losing an important national symbol and the history behind it. Finally many Britons are perhaps most afraid of monetary union inevitably leading to political union.

The euro

1. Write a caption for each cartoon.
2. Create your own cartoon with the euro sign.
3. Get more information at www.britainineurope.org. ➡ Method kit, Internet research, p. 304

Society and Politics

Tony Blair

Major Changes Ahead

Different from most other democracies, the new British prime minister starts his office immediately after the election results are definite. The British monarch, however, has to confirm him in his office.

Tony Blair

I have just returned from Buckingham Palace, from my audience with the Queen. I want to say what an enormous privilege and honour it is to be trusted with the government of this country and I am deeply conscious of that privilege and honour at this time.

I would like to congratulate all the MPs from whatever political party who have been elected to the House of Commons.

I would like also to say this word about my opponent in the election, Mr Hague[1].

Even though obviously I profoundly[2] disagreed with many of the things he may have said during the course of this campaign, I thought he showed extraordinary stoicism[3] and resilience[4] in very difficult circumstances and I said to him in the early hours of this morning I wish him well, I wish him the very best of luck in the future.

It has been a remarkable and historic victory for my party but I am in no doubt at all as to what it means.

It is a mandate for reform and for investment in the future and it is also very clearly an instruction to deliver[5].

I have learnt many things over the past four years as prime minister. I have, I hope, learnt from the mistakes as well as the good things.

But above all else I have learnt of the importance of establishing the clear priorities of government, of setting them out clearly for people and then focusing on them relentlessly[6] whatever events may come and go.

I believe there is an even greater obligation[7] on us, on me, after re-election to tell people very clearly what are the difficult choices and challenges we face[8] and how we work our way through them and that I will try to do.

So in the course of the campaign we have just had, I set out in a series of speeches the changes that I believe the country needs to see.

[1] **William Hague** Conservative MP since 1989, leader of the Conservative Party from 1997 to 2001 – [2] **profoundly** completely, seriously – [3] **stoicism** act of not complaining when you are suffering – [4] **resilience** flexibility – [5] **to deliver** to give – [6] **relentless** not stopping or getting less strong – [7] **obligation** duty – [8] **to face sth** to be confronted with sth

On the foundation of a strong economy, we need to keep it strong. We need to make sure that mortgages[1] and inflation are as low as possible.

But then on top of that we need to start building the economy of the future based on skills[2] and talents and education and the application of technology, knowing that for this country in the future the forces of global competition and technological change mean that we can only compete on the basis of skill and ability, not low wages.

And then, we have the critical importance of investment in, and reform of, our public services, most particularly our National Health Service[3], our education system and our transport system.

Again here, from talking to people, from meeting them, from hearing their concerns[4] over the past few weeks, that they may applaud the direction in which we wish to go, but they want us to do it as fast and as profoundly as we possibly can and that again is an obligation that we must discharge[5].

In our welfare system we need change too. We need to separate very clearly those who cannot work, who need security and protection and must have it, and those who can work but at present don't, who we must try to help off a life on benefit[6] and into productive work.

Then there is the reform of our criminal justice system. There is no issue that touches our citizens more deeply than crime and law and order on our streets and we need to make the changes there so that we have a criminal justice system that punishes the criminal, but also offers those convicted[7] of crime the chance to rehabilitate and get their way out of a life of crime.

Finally, in respect of Europe and the wider world, we need to make changes there too, so that we are engaged, exerting[8] influence, having the self belief not to turn our back on the world or retreat[9] into isolationism.

These changes will not be easy. But Britain is a very special country and its people are a very special people and our very best quality is our ability, when we need to do so, to face up to and overcome the challenge of change.

All those changes are for one purpose and that again is the purpose I have tried to set out in the few weeks of this campaign and will try to set out again in the years to come.

And the purpose of each and every change that we make must be this—to create a society which is a genuine[10] open, meritocratic[11] nation where we have laid to one side the old adage[12] about knowing your place and where the only place that any man, woman or child knows is the place that their talents take them, where we

[1] **mortgage** ['mɔ:gɪdʒ] *Hypothekenzins* – [2] **skills** abilities, capabilities – [3] **National Health Service** (NHS) public health service in GB that provides free medical care – [4] **concern** worry – [5] **to discharge** here: to carry out – [6] **benefit** money provided by the government to people in need – [7] **to convict** to prove guilty – [8] **to exert** to use – [9] **to retreat** to move back – [10] **genuine** real; honest – [11] **meritocratic** a system where people get power on the basis of their ability – [12] **adage** ['ædɪdʒ] phrase expressing a general truth, proverb

create a country genuinely where not just a few people at the top, but everyone, *every one* of our citizens gets the chance to fulfill their true potential.

I believe in the last four years we have laid foundations. I believe our victory in this election shows the British people understand we have laid foundations but now is the time to build upon them. Thank you.

The Guardian, June 9, 2001, p. 6

The rhetoric of politics

1. Analyze the structure of Blair's speech.
2. What stylistic devices does he make use of? → Language kit, Terms for text analysis, p. 316ff.
3. Write down what Blair promises the British people as a report you might find in a quality paper. → Method kit, Newspaper article, p. 298
4. Politicians are often said to promise everything but not to keep a lot. Comment on that view, referring to current political developments.
5. What do you expect politicians to do for you?

Translation

Translate ll. 44–63 ("Again here ... isolationism."). Pay special attention to the stylistic devices when you translate Blair's speech.

Alistair Heaton

No Second Chance in Politics?

What do you know about the results of the 2001 elections in GB? The cartoon depicts William Hague, the loser of the elections. How is he portrayed?

William Hague in a winner's pose

In a room overlooking Smith Square, William Hague (Conservative MP since 1989), Tony Blair's election opponent, muses about his great success with two party members: Sebastian Coe and Michael Portillo. Not even the bad news broken to him by Portillo, can open his eyes to reality: he is the loser.

HAGUE: Well, all in all, I think we achieved a thoroughly[1] satisfactory result, don't you, Seb?

COE: Um …

HAGUE: A race well run, as you might say. And after all, it's not the winning that matters is it? It's the taking part.

COE: Er, look, William, I …

HAGUE: Of course, there's more work to be done before I get to Number 10[2], I can quite see that. But I think we can allow ourselves a small celebration before rolling up our sleeves[3] and getting down to the business of winning the next election, don't you?

COE: *(Glancing at his watch)* Um, how can I put this, William …?

HAGUE: My only regret is that Ffion isn't here with me to share my moment of triumph. Why do you think she went home to Wales as soon as the results started coming through?

COE: I've to go in a moment, William. It's been a wonderful friendship, and—

HAUGE: What's that noise from the street?

COE: I don't think you should go near that window.

HAGUE: Nonsense. There are hundreds of Conservative Party workers down there, calling for me. *(Opens window)* Look, they're burning an effigy[4] of Tony Blair. Not a very good effigy, is it? It's completely bald[5]. Doesn't look like Blair at all! *(Laughs)* Never mind, it's the thought that counts. *(The sound of booing is heard)* Can you hear that? They're booing somebody! Portillo must be arriving. Can you see him?

Portillo backing up Hague

PORTILLO: I'm already here, William.

HAGUE: Oh! My goodness, you did give me a turn[6], Michael. You really ought not to creep up[7] on people like that.

PORTILLO: I've brought a few friends of the party with me, William.

A number of other people file into the room […]

COE: Must dash! Bye, William! *(Hurries out)*

HAGUE: *(To the newcomers)* Lovely to see you all! Let's crack open a few bottles of good Yorkshire ale[8] and celebrate the night's achievements, eh?

PORTILLO: We've brought you something, William. *(Hands Hague a sealed envelope)*

HAGUE: What is it? No, no, don't tell me, let me guess. *(Weighs the envelope in his hand, holds it up to the light)* It's a congratulation card!

PORTILLO: Not exactly.

HAGUE: Oh, you are a tease[9], Michael! *(Hague opens the envelope, takes out a black-bordered card)* Ah! It's one of those musical cards. *(We hear the strains[10] of Mendelssohn's Funeral[11]*

[1] **thorough** complete – [2] **Number 10** The prime minister's home in Downing Street – [3] **sleeve** part of the shirt which covers the arm – [4] **effigy** ['efɪdʒɪ] statue or model of a person – [5] **bald** hairless – [6] **to give sb a turn** to frighten or shock sb – [7] **to creep up** to move slowly nearer – [8] **ale** type of beer – [9] **tease** person who likes to play tricks and jokes on other people – [10] **strain** tune, melody – [11] **funeral** ceremony for burying a dead person

March) Now what's the tune? No don't tell me, I'll remember it in a minute. Its not Cliff Richards[1] Congratulations, is it? No, no, that's not it. Let me see …

PORTILLO: Are you familiar with the concept of defenstration[2], William?

HAGUE: Oh yes, it's when unloved political leaders are thrown from windows, isn't it.

PORTILLO: You got it.

The rest of the scene is censored for reasons of taste and decency[3].

From "Nonsense. There are hundreds of Tory Party workers down there, calling for me", *Evening Standard*, June 8, 2001, p. 4

The end of a political career

1. Why is Hague going to be thrown out of the window?
2. Characterize Hague, Coe and Portillo.
   → Method kit, Characterization, p. 289
3. Discuss the title question. Do you know similar cases?
4. Write down the missing last scene of this miniature drama and act it out.
5. Would you go for a career in politics? Write a short essay discussing the pros and cons of being a politician.

How the Political System Works

Info

The Constitution

The constitution of the United Kingdom, unlike the constitutions of many other countries, is not written down in any single document. It consists of laws made by parliament, important court decisions (common law) and conventions and practices, which have been established over the years. Britain is a constitutional monarchy. However, the influence of the monarch is mainly informal. The Queen officially appoints the Prime Minister and has the right and the duty to express her views on government matters to him at her weekly audiences. But these meetings—and all communications between the monarch and her government—remain strictly confidential[4]. An important day for the Queen is the State Opening of Parliament, which takes place after parliamentary recess[5] in autumn or immediately after general elections. Her speech, however, does not express her own views but is drafted[6] by the Prime Minister. The Queen is the Head of the Church of England and Head of State. She acts as a focus for national unity, presiding[7] at ceremonial occasions, visiting local communities,

[1]**Cliff Richards** British pop singer for nearly four decades, whose greatest hit was "Congratulations" – [2]**defenstration** act of throwing sb out of a window (the word does not really exist) – [3]**decency** *Anständigkeit* – [4]**confidential** secret – [5]**recess** break, vacation – [6]**to draft** to write a rough outline – [7]**to preside** to lead or to be in charge of a meeting

Info

and representing Britain around the world. She is also Head of the Commonwealth. By visiting all the Commonwealth countries the Queen tries to strengthen the bond between Britain and her former colonies.

Political parties, parliament and the election system

Parliament consists of two chambers: the House of Commons with its 659 elected members who make laws, and the House of Lords with appointed members (life peers[1]) and members who have inherited[2] a title (hereditary peers[3]), who can examine and revise[4] bills from the Commons and delay them for up to a year.
The UK, with a population of 59 million, is divided into 659 areas or constituencies with roughly 69,000 voters each. Every constituency elects one member to the House of Commons. Unlike most other European countries where they have proportional representation, British MPs are elected by majority vote (first-past-the-post-system[5]). This means that the candidate with the most votes in a constituency wins the seat and all the other votes are lost. Such a system results in clear winners and losers. The Prime Minister can call national elections at any time, though no more than five years may pass from one general election to the next. He must give a minimum of three weeks and a maximum of six weeks notice. The leader of the winning party becomes Prime Minister. He appoints the Cabinet of about 20 members, usually the most important ministers. The party that wins the second-largest number of seats is the Opposition, which forms a "Shadow Cabinet".

General Election Results in the UK 2001

Party	popular vote	MPs elected			percentage of seats
		male	female	total	
Labour	40.7%	317	95	412	62.6%
Conservative	31.7%	152	14	166	25.2%
Liberal Democrats	18.3%	47	5	52	7.9%
Others*	9.3%	25	4	29	4.4%

* Scottish National, Ulster Unionist, Plaid Cymru, Democratic Unionist, Sinn Fein, Independent. The Green Party is not represented in the Commons.

Data: House of Commons, Research Paper 01/54 (rev. edition), June 18, 2001, pp. 8, 11

In front of Downing Street No. 10, Tony and Cherie Blair greet the cheering crowd after his electoral victory on June 8, 2001.

In the 2001 general elections Tony Blair won his second landslide[6] victory (see results above). All parties showed great concern for the low voter turnout[7]: 58%, the lowest ever. Young people in particular were blamed for being apathetic. Like in the

[1] **life peer** sb who is given the title Lord or Lady but who cannot pass it on to their son or daughter – [2] **to inherit** to receive by legal right at a person's death – [3] **hereditary peer** sb who is given the title Lord or Lady who can pass it on to their son or daughter – [4] **to revise** to change – [5] **first-past-the-post-system** the winner in a constituency gets the seat; all other votes get lost – [6] **landslide** great (victory) – [7] **turnout** here: number of people who vote in an election

1997 election, more than 50 per cent of the 18- to 24-year-olds did not bother[1] to visit a polling booth[2].

Constitutional reforms

In recent years interest in far-reaching reforms of the British Constitution has grown. Movements like Charter 88—a group of prominent politicians, lawyers and journalists—demanded reforms in some key areas like the House of Lords, decentralized government (devolution), the election system and a written constitution. In his first term (1997–2001) Tony Blair started by reducing the amount of hereditary peers by more than 600 to 92. At present there are 592 life peers, members who are appointed by the Queen at the Prime Minister's suggestion. The system of appointments of life peers is under review. Blair has, however, resisted calls for a fully elected upper chamber, in part because of fears that elections would increase the power of the Lords at the expense of the House of Commons.

Proportional representation (PR) is the biggest issue in the UK. Voting in Scotland, Wales and Northern Ireland has been transformed, but Labour also promised a referendum on how Westminster MPs are elected. Polls show that a majority of English people favour elected regional assemblies[3] in the regions of England, too. There is now decentralized government in Wales and Scotland. On May 6, 1999, elections to the Welsh and Scottish Assemblies were held and in the same years the Scottish and the Welsh Parliaments assumed[4] their full powers. Northern Ireland has its own parliament, too, which, however, has had a long history of closing and reopening because of sectarian[5] terrorist activities going on that have often made direct British rule necessary.

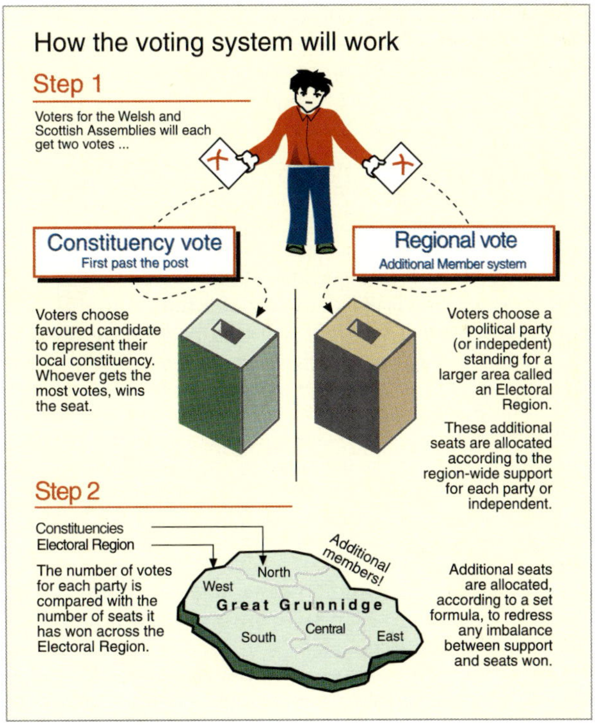

What European election system does the new voting system in Scotland and Wales remind you of?

[1] **to bother** to be concerned, to care – [2] **polling booth** small place where people vote – [3] **assembly** legislature, meeting of parliamentarians – [4] **to assume** here: to begin to have power – [5] **sectarian** people who have different religious views

Sue Townsend

Mrs Windsor

The Queen is one of the richest persons in England but she hardly has any privacy. Should we envy or rather pity her and her family for the life they lead?

In *The Queen and I* Sue Townsend imagines that the last election in GB was won by the People's Republican Party. The royal family has to abdicate[1] and to be relocated. They are given accommodation in a street known to its residents as Hell Close, which is part of a Midlands[2] housing estate[3].

The Queen winced[4] as Jack Barker ground[5] his cigarette out on the silk rug[6]. A faint smell of burning rose between them. Jack fought the urge[7] to apologise. The Queen stared at Jack disdainfully[8]. His stomach gurgled. Her picture had hung in his classroom when he was struggling to learn his nine times tables. In his boyhood he used to look to the Queen for inspiration. Prince Charles bent down and picked up the cigarette stub. He looked for somewhere to put it, but, finding nowhere suitable, he slipped it into his pocket.

Princess Margaret said, 'Lilibet I've got to have a fag[9]. Please!'

'May we open the windows, Mr Barker?' asked the Queen. Her accent cut into Jack like a crystal. He half expected to bleed.

'No chance,' he replied.

'Am I to have a house of my own, Mr Barker, or must I share with my daughter and son-in-law?' The Queen Mother gave Jack her famous smile, but her hands were twisting the full skirt of her periwinkle[10] dress into a knot.

'You'll get a pensioner's bungalow. It's your entitlement[11] as an ordinary citizen of this country.'

'A bungalow, good. I couldn't manage stairs. Will my staff[12] be living in or out?'

Jack laughed and looked at his fellow Republicans. Six men and six women, hand-picked to witness this historic occasion.

They laughed along with Jack. 'You don't seem to understand. There'll be no staff, no dressers, no cooks, secretaries, cleaners, chauffeurs.'

Turning to the Queen he said, 'You'll have to nip in[13] now and then, help your mum out. But she'll probably be entitled to Meals on Wheels.'

The Queen Mother looked quite pleased to hear this. 'So I shan't starve[14]?'

[1] **to abdicate** to give up the position of being king or queen – [2] **Midlands** area between Manchester and Nottingham that includes many industrial towns – [3] **housing estate** area in which a large number of houses are built at the same time – [4] **to wince** *zusammenzucken* – [5] **to grind out** (ground, ground) to put out – [6] **rug** carpet – [7] **urge** impulse, desire – [8] **disdainful** *verachtungsvoll* – [9] **fag** (*infml*) cigarette – [10] **periwinkle** here: green – [11] **entitlement** sth you have an official right to – [12] **staff** personnel – [13] **to nip in** (*infml*) to visit – [14] **to starve** to die of hunger

'Under the People's Republican Party's rule, nobody in Britain will starve,' said Jack.

Prince Charles cleared his throat and said, 'Er, may one, er, enquire as to where …? That is, the location …?'

'If you're asking me where you're all going, I'm not telling you. All I can say at the moment is that you'll all be in the same street, but you'll have strangers as next-door neighbours, working-class people. Here's a list of what you can take with you.' […]

'Mr Barker, there is no mention of dogs here,' said the Queen.

'One per family,' said Jack.

'Horses?' asked Charles.

'Would you keep a horse in a council house[1] garden?'

'No. Quite. One wasn't thinking.'

'Clothes aren't on the list,' said Diana, shyly.

'You won't be needing much. Just the bare essentials. You won't be making personal appearances[2] will you?'

Princess Anne rose and stood next to her father. 'Thank God for that! At least something good has come out of this bloody shambles.[3] Are you all right, Pa?'

Prince Philip was in a state of shock and had been ever since the previous night when he had turned on the television for Election Night Special at 11.25 and seen the announcement of the election of Jack Barker, founder and leader of the People's Republican Party, the member for Kensington West. Prince Philip had watched incredulously[4] as Barker had addressed the joyous crowds in the Town Hall. Middle-aged poll tax[5] payers had cheered alongside young people wearing ragged[6] jeans and nose rings. He had lifted the telephone and advised his wife to watch the television set. Half an hour later, she rang him back. Philip, please come to my room.'

They had sat up until the early hours as one Republican candidate after another had been declared elected in front of cheering crowds of British citizenry. Gradually their children had joined them. At 7.30 a.m. the servants brought them breakfast, but nobody ate. By 11 a.m. the People's Republican Party had won 451 seats and John Major[7], the Conservative Prime Minister, had reluctantly[8] conced-

Describe the neighborhood the Windsors will be moving to.

[1] **council house** house or flat rented from the local town council cheaply – [2] **to make personal appearances** *in der Öffentlichkeit auftreten* – [3] **shambles** mess, disorder – [4] **incredulous** disbelieving, sceptical – [5] **poll tax** very unpopular tax introduced by Prime Minister Margaret Thatcher (1979–1990) in the 80s – [6] **ragged** [rægɪd] old and torn – [7] **John Major** Prime Minister from 1990–1997 – [8] **reluctant** *unwillig*

ed[1] defeat. Shortly afterwards, Jack Barker announced that he was Prime Minister. His first job, he said, would be to go to Buckingham Palace and order the Queen to abdicate.

The thirteen Republicans in a minibus had been waved through the gates of Buckingham Palace by smiling policemen. The soldiers of the Household Cavalry had removed their bearskins and waved them in the air.

Members of the Queen's personal staff had shaken them by the hand. Champagne had been offered, but had been declined[2].

Until his election as member for Kensington West, Jack Barker had been the leader of a breakaway section of the Television Technicians' Union. For the three weeks preceding the General Election, Jack and his disgruntled[3] members had broadcast subliminal[4] messages to the watching public: 'VOTE REPUBLICAN—END THE MONARCHY'.

On the Saturday before polling day, *The Times* had called for the dismantling[5] of the monarchy. A hundred thousand anti-monarchists had walked from Trafalgar Square to Clarence House[6], not knowing that the Queen Mother was at the races. A violent thunderstorm had dispersed[7] them before she returned, but she saw the discarded[8] placards from the window of her limousine.

'GOD DAMN YOU, MA'AM.'

An error, she thought, surely they meant 'God bless', didn't they?

That evening, she noticed that her staff were surly[9] and uncooperative. She'd had to wait half an hour for a servant to draw her bedroom curtains.

On polling day the British people, brainwashed by the television technicians, had made their choice.

We are not amused

1. How can a political nobody win the general elections?
2. How are the members of the royal family and Jack Barker characterized? Write down five key words for each.
3. Develop freeze frames that highlight the atmosphere in this scene.
4. Make role cards for all the characters involved and reenact the scene.
5. Write an article in a pro-monarchy newspaper about this outrageous event. → Method kit, Newspaper article, p. 298

From monarchy to republic

1. Devise a political schedule for Barker for his next six months as prime minister.
2. "Britain without a monarchy." Write a short essay.

[1] **to concede** to admit – [2] **to decline** to refuse to accept sth – [3] **disgruntled** disappointed – [4] **subliminal** *unterschwellig* – [5] **to dismantle** to end sth – [6] **Clarence House** home of the Queen Mother, who died in 2002 – [7] **to disperse** to go away in different directions – [8] **to discard** to throw away – [9] **surly** ['sɜ:rli] bad-tempered

The Queen and her new neighborhood

"If I could only remember where I've seen her before."

1. Analyse the situation in the cartoon.
2. How is the Queen presented?
3. What might the two women on the left be talking about? Write a short dialogue and act it out.

John O'Farrell

What Price a Prince?

Britain's monarchy is regarded to be a costly affair. Find reasons that may justify the great expenses.

When underground trains pull into Green Park station, the electric Tannoy[1] recently began announcing: "Alight[2] here for Buckingham Palace". This is very considerate[3] of them, but I don't think the Queen has started using the tube just yet. On Thursday, Buckingham Palace proudly boasted[4] that the royal family had halved its expenditure[5] over the past 10 years, although most of that was probably achieved when Fergie's[6] credit card was cut in two.

The Queen's treasurer even went so far as to claim that the royal family now actually gives more money than it spends. Those poor royals must be getting really fed up with subsidising[7] our luxury lifestyle. Prince Philip must keep seeing ordinary people in their three-bedroom semis[8] and saying: "Why do they need that ex-

[1] **Tannoy** loudspeakers used for giving information in a public place – [2] **to alight** to get off – [3] **considerate** [kən'sɪdərət] thoughtful – [4] **to boast** *prahlen, angeben* – [5] **expenditure** an amount of money spent – [6] **Fergie** Duchess of York, Prince Andrew's former wife – [7] **to subsidise** to support with money – [8] **semi** (*infml*) semi-detached house, a house that shares one wall with another house

Prince William on his 18th birthday

pensive Ford Mondeo in the car port? You know, in Sweden the subjects cycle everywhere."

"Well, I know these ordinary families are expensive," says the Queen, "but they do a lot for charity. And think of all that money they bring in tourism …"

Sir Michael Peat also listed dozens of cutbacks[1] that the royal family had made over the past year, while insisting that the search for savings would continue. Sir Michael has the job description of the "keeper of the privy[2] purse". Well that's one economy that could be made for a start—why does the Queen need a purse in the privy, let alone[3] someone whose job it is to keep it'? Maybe they still have those old-fashioned lavatories where you have to pay a penny to get into the cubicle[4], and because Her Majesty doesn't carry money, we're paying fifty grand[5] a year for this bloke[6] to stand outside the royal privy all day with a purse full of old one penny coins.

This week's press conference was part of a sustained[7] PR effort to open the royal accounts and justify the huge amounts that are still spent every year. Closer scrutiny[8] of the royal finances had been long overdue[9]. For example, it was discovered that helicopters were being used for journeys of only a few miles—such as going to the bottom of the garden.

Use of the royal train was costing £ 30,000 a trip, although it was only £ 28,000 if they travelled after 9:30 a.m. And less money is now given to the Ogilvys[10] for Lady Marina, since it was discovered that she was in fact a car that they'd bought from British Leyland in the 1970s. […]

"No," said the Queen, "we're going to have to cut back on non-essentials." At which point Prince Edward packed his bag and left. The rest of them sat round the kitchen table and all agreed to try to find a way to make savings.

They let go of the footmen who took the corgis[11] for a walk by carrying them in a sedan chair. But even after they'd cancelled the subscription to the Sky Sports Dressage[12] channel and agreed to stop buying What Castle magazine, they were still £ 30 million over. The Queen thought she could save a few more pence if she simply handed her mum the telegram for reaching 100, but it was still not enough.

Then she looked at her phone bill and realized that she could update her "friends and family" list, as she doesn't ring those numbers in Nepal any more.

[1] **cutback** a reduction in sth – [2] **privy** ['prɪvɪ] an outdoor toilet; **the Privy Council** a group of people who advise a monarch – [3] **let alone** not to mention – [4] **cubicle** small room; toilet – [5] **grand** (*sl*) a thousand pounds – [6] **bloke** (*infml*) man – [7] **sustained** continued – [8] **scrutiny** close examination – [9] **to be overdue** sth that should have been done for a long time – [10] **the Ogilvys** close relatives of the royal family – [11] **corgi** ['kɔːgɪ] a small dog with short legs; the Queen's favourite pets – [12] **dressage** ['dresɑːʒ] *Dressurreiten*

Maybe the only way to make any real dent[1] in the cost of the monarchy is to introduce a public finance initiative. This is supposed to be the solution to everything else, so I don't see why the royal family should be spared[2]. Private companies could be brought in to run the royal family more efficiently. Foreign dignitaries[3] attending state banquets would have to queue up and opt[4] for Chicken McNuggets or Big Mac and fries. […]

This will never happen of course; this is the British royal family we are talking about, not just some school or hospital. Funny how it's only the things that we really value that we can't afford to pay for.

The Guardian, June 30, 2001, p. 22

Financial problems and how to solve them

1. How is the royal family portrayed here?
2. What do they spend their money on and what is the author's suggestion for solving the financial problems?
3. How serious is the writer?
4. If you could advise the royal family where to save money, what would you suggest? Write a list with your partner.

Translation

Translate ll. 31–42 ("This week's press conference … in the 70s.") and ll. 56–66 ("Maybe … to pay for."). Pay special attention to the translation of sentences in the passive voice.

Your thematic vocabulary

Select the semantic vocabulary from the texts of this chapter and cluster them according to the following categories:

Britain: A Multicultural Society	Empire and Commonwealth	Britain and Europe	Political Life in Britain

[1] **to make a dent in sth** to reduce the amount (of money) – [2] **to spare sb** to save sb from having a bad experience – [3] **dignitary** person who has an important official position – [4] **to opt for sth** to choose

The American Way:

From Dream to Reality

Holly Johnson **Americanos**

There's a place
Where a kid without a cent
He can grow up to be president
A magic kingdom filled with Barbie dolls
If you've got time we can make it a good time

Americanos
Blue Jeans and Chinos
Coke Pepsi and Oreos
Americano-oh-ohs
Movies and heroes
In the land of the free
You can be what you wanna be!

They know how to advertise
Sell you anything at any price
Need it or not, that's what you got—yeah
Take no bull from anyone
We just wanna have some fun
We got the queen of soul
Created rock 'n' roll—yeah
(queen of soul oh-oh oh-oh)

Americanos,
Blue jeans and Chinos
Coke, Pepsi and Oreos
Americano-oh-ohs
Low-riding Chicanos
In the land of the free
You can be what you wanna be
(Be what you want—yeah)
(Totally spectacular)
(An educated consumer is our best concern)

Yeah-ea-ea-ea-ea-eah
Take it to the bridge one time—yeah

Satellite stations across the nations
That's cable TV for you and me
I'm cleaning kitchens, washing pots and pans
Everything's organised
From crime to leisure time
High schools and swimming pools
King sharks 'n' fools oh-oh

Americanos
Blue Jeans and Chinos
Coke, Pepsi and Oreos
Americano-oh-ohs
Movies and heroes
In the land of the free
You can be what you wanna be!

How do you see it? How would you describe the picture of America that is portrayed in this song? Positive, negative, subjective, objective? What is your picture of America based on?

The Americans and Their Dreams

Everything is Different in America

What have you heard about the ways American family life and schools differ from those in Germany?

A class of eleventh graders is going to the US with an exchange program organized by their school. Before the trip, Jochen writes his Scottish pen pal Ian about the upcoming adventure and everything he has heard about the Americans.

Freiburg, 30 April 2002

As you may remember from my last letter, next month I'll be going to Harrisburg, Pennsylvania, to live with an American family for three weeks and to go to school there. Our teacher, Herr Kraemer, gave us a list of things we should take into consideration for our stay there. From the sound of it, you would think we were going to another planet! When I visited you last summer in Edinburgh, I didn't feel like an outsider at all. The land of the free and the home of the brave (as we learned from their national anthem) is going to be full of surprises for us if our teacher's tips are any indication!

First of all, he told us that the American teenagers don't have much free time. They spend most of the day in school or participating in school activities or sports and then a lot of them work after that to pay for gas (they all have cars) or to save up for college, if they have to do homework like I do, I doubt they'll have any time for the important things in life.

On Sundays they usually get all dressed up and go to church. We are supposed to bring a sport coat and tie (maybe I'll finally learn how to tie one over there) and the girls have to bring dresses for church and the school dances. My girlfriend Bianca (remember her? she says hi) is going shopping on Saturday to find something to wear. Even on the normal school days we'll probably have to adhere to strict dress codes. Nothing like the uniforms in England, but I guess I'll have to leave my cool "Never mind *the bullocks here's the Sex Pistols" T-shirt at home. Herr Kraemer even <u>strongly</u> suggested that my friend Daniel should get his hair cut before he goes or he might be mistaken for a ... what did he say? ... a dropout—someone who has left high school before finishing. I bet he will cut it because he says he wants to get to know some American girls and Herr Kraemer said his chances will be much greater if he looks "decent."*

Come to think of it, Daniel is going to have a real hard time over there. Here he smokes two packs of cigarettes a day, and on the weekends we go out with a couple of six-packs and hang out in town where there's some action. Now, everyone knows the Americans don't like smokers, which I can understand, but why is it that they can drive a car when they're 16 but can't even drink beer until they're 21? I'll have to remember to ask someone about that.

What we will be drinking—if we are to believe our teacher—is tap water with ice cubes. Sprudel—mineral water—is almost as rare as a guy with long hair, and good coffee can only be found at Starbucks. I wonder what the food will be like—steak and potatoes or hamburgers and French fries all the time? Are there any vegetarians in America? Do the ranchers there have problems with BSE, too?

Oh, and Bianca is going to shave her legs and ... what are they called? ... underarms because that is what the American girls do. Supposedly there is nothing worse for an American guy than a girl with hairy armpits. I'm glad I don't have to worry about that! Herr Kraemer said we'd draw attention to ourselves, though, if we didn't take a shower and change our clothes every day.

Ich bin gespannt – I can't wait to see if he is exaggerating or if the Americans are really as prudish as they are portrayed in the movies and in Herr Kraemer's stories! As they say, if you don't go, you aren't going to know. I'll write you from the USA and let you know what it's like.

All the best,

Jochen

Comparing experiences

1. If you have spent time with an American family, compare your experiences with the information Jochen has been given. If you have never been to America, what information causes you the most concern?
2. Contact an American via e-mail and try to find out the truth behind some of these tips. Try the *Transatlantisches Klassenzimmer* at http://www.tak.schule.de. ➜ Method kit, Internet research, p. 304

How the World Sees America

What ideas do you have about America and the Americans?

Cover of the January 31, 2000 edition of *Newsweek*

Your cover picture does a disservice to the millions of American professional expats[1] who work and live abroad by perpetuating the myth that all Americans wear cowboy hats, belts and denims, are sloppy[2] and overweight and shove their American flag and their values down other people's throats. Thanks, Newsweek, for nothing.
Mike Babb, Rio de Janeiro, Brazil

If America is such a bad place, why are there queues at every visa department at every U.S. Embassy around the world? The truth is that America is an amalgamation[3] of every culture in the world and has thus captured[4] the best and the worst the world has to offer. So far, the best seems to be winning.
Stephen Previs, London, England

I am French, and I don't hate America. I have made two trips to your country, and I study English at university. You Americans complain about not being loved by some people, but you don't accept anything that is not American; you are quite narrow-minded about French culture, our music, our movies. In Europe we're surrounded by American culture—fast foods, beverages[5], brand-name clothes, cinema and music. So who hates whom?
Emilie Blanc, Ales, France

to honk *hupen* → [1] **expat** (an expatriate person) sb who is living in a foreign country – [2] **sloppy** not neat – [3] **amalgamation** mixture – [4] **to capture** to gain possession of – [5] **beverage** sth to drink

The spread of mass culture is wiping out smaller cultures and traditions. The United States, however, is not the sole perpetrator[1] of mass pop culture. It is filling an ugly role that might exist even if America did not. Of course, this is not an excuse for the States to act irresponsibly. Steps need to be taken to preserve cultural identities, but it is a waste of time to hate the United States for producing Micky Mouse.
Lied Eckblad, Iloilo City, Philippines

Yes, the U.S.A. is not perfect, but it is hard to beat, which is why the whole world wants to go there. As a European who has traveled and worked all over the world, I can attest to the fact that America is great because it gives an honest man who is willing to work hard more opportunities to succeed than any other country in the world.
Jacques G. Migeotte, Menlo Park, South Africa

The reason for people's hating America is jealousy and envy at our economic success, technological advances, quality of life, superpower status and freedoms. Frankly[2], I don't see any other country using its international and economic power as morally as the United States does. Consider the alternative. Would you rather have America be the megapower that it is or have North Korea, Cuba, China, Iran, Iraq or Sudan wield[3] this force?
Keith W. Brown, Stara Zagora, Bulgaria

Letters to the Editor of Newsweek, February 28, 2000, p. 12

[1] **to perpetrate** to be responsible for sth – [2] **frank** open and honest – [3] **to wield** [wiːld] to exercise (power or influence)

Listing and categorizing

1. What is America criticized for? What is it praised for?
2. Which of these aspects might apply to other countries as well?

Expatriate thoughts

Imagine you left your native country to live abroad for many years. In groups, discuss the following questions:

- What challenges would you face?
- Would you feel it necessary to assimilate to the new culture? To what extent?
- Would you have to necessarily break with your old culture? To what extent?

After formulating the main challenges your group discussed, present the results to your class on a transparency.

The pen strikes back

Choose one of the letters and write a response to it.

Translation

Translate the letters from England and Bulgaria. Make sure to maintain the tone of the opinion.

Language

Find all the relative pronouns (who, that, which) and the antecedents they refer to.

J. Hector St. John de Crèvecœur

What is an American?

In small groups write down your answers to the title's question before reading the text.

What then is the American, this new man? ... *He* is an American, who, leaving behind him all his ancient prejudices and manners, receives new ones from the new mode of life he has embraced, the new government he obeys, and the new rank he holds. He becomes an American by being received in the broad lap of our great *Alma Mater*[1]. Here individuals of all nations are melted into a new race of men, whose labours and posterity[2] will one day cause great changes in the world. Americans are the western pilgrims, who are

[1]**Alma Mater** (*fml* or *joc*) here: nourishing mother – [2]**posterity** all of a person's descendants

carrying along with them that great mass of arts, sciences, vigour, and industry[1] which began long since in the east; they will finish the great circle. The Americans were once scattered all over Europe; here they are incorporated into one of the finest systems of population which has ever appeared, and which will hereafter become distinct by the power of the different climates they inhabit. The American ought therefore to love this country much better than that wherein either he or his forefathers were born. Here the rewards of his industry follow with equal steps the progress of his labour; his labour is founded on the basis of nature, self-interest; can it want a stronger allurement[2]? Wives and children, who before in vain demanded of him a morsel[3] of bread, now, fat and frolicsome[4], gladly help their father to clear those fields whence[5] exuberant[6] crops are to arise to feed and to clothe them all; without any part being claimed, either by a despotic[7] prince, a rich abbot[8], or a mighty lord. Here religion demands but little of him; a small voluntary salary to the minister, and gratitude to God: can he refuse these? The American is a new man, who acts upon new principles; he must therefore entertain new ideas, and form new opinions.

◀ Just Europe?

◀ Why does he stress *equal*?

Summarizing

What is new about the American, according to the author?

Writing and discussing definitions

1. This selection was written in 1782 by a Frenchman who was trying to define the type of people found in America as contrasting to their European forefathers. Based on Crèvecœur's description, write a description of the European as he must have seen him then.
2. To what extent are these two views still valid today?

Improve your vocabulary

1. Find the corresponding adjectives: posterity (l. 7), sciences (l. 9), vigour (l. 9), industry (l. 10), labour (l. 18), gratitude (l. 25).
2. Find the corresponding nouns: received in (l. 5), incorporated (l. 12), exuberant (l. 21–22), despotic (l. 23), mighty (l. 24), voluntary (l. 25), refuse (l. 25).
3. Find substitutes. You may change the sentence structure: life he has embraced (l. 3), the ... rank he holds (l. 4), by being received in (l. 5), will ... become distinct (l. 13–14), the rewards of his industry (l. 17), who before in vain demanded (l. 19–20), he must therefore entertain new ideas (l. 27).

[1]**industry** hard work – [2]**allurement** temptation – [3]**morsel** small piece – [4]**frolicsome** playful – [5]**whence** from where – [6]**exuberant** produced in excess – [7]**despotic** tyrannical – [8]**abbot** man who is the head of a monastery or an abbey

Anonymous

The Contrapuntal[1] Civilization

I have died
in Vietnam.
But I have walked
the face of the moon.

I have befouled[2] the waters
and tainted[3] the air of a
magnificent land. But I have
made it safe from disease.

I have flown through the
sky faster than the sun.
But I have idled[4] in streets
made ugly with traffic.

I have littered[5] the land
with garbage.
But I have built upon it
a hundred million homes.

I have divided schools
with my prejudice[6].
But I have sent armies
to unite them.

I have beat down my enemies
with clubs[7].
But I have built courtrooms
to keep them free.

I have built a bomb[8]
to destroy the world.
But I have used it
to light a light.

[1]**contrapuntal** [kɒntrə'pʌnt(ə)l] contrasting – [2]**to befoul** to dirty sth – [3]**to taint** to pollute – [4]**to idle** to stand around aimlessly – [5]**to litter** to make untidy – [6]**prejudice** *Vorurteil* – [7]**club** *Schlagstock* – [8]**bomb** [bɒm]

I have outraged[1] my brothers
in the alleys of the ghetto.
But I have transplanted
a human heart.

I have scribbled[2] out
filth[3] and pornography.
But I have elevated[4]
the philosophy of man.

I have watched children
starve[5] from my golden towers.
But I have fed
half of the earth.

I was raised
in a grotesque slum.
But I am surfeited by[6]
the silver spoon of opulence[7].

I live in the greatest country
in the world in the greatest time
in history. But I scorn[8] the ground
I stand upon.

I am ashamed.
But I am proud.
I am an American.

[1]**to outrage** to anger – [2]**to scribble** to write carelessly – [3]**filth** offensive words – [4]**to elevate** to raise – [5]**to starve** to suffer from or die of hunger – [6]**to be surfeited by** ['sɜ:fɪt] to be given too much of – [7]**opulence** great wealth – [8]**to scorn** to despise, to feel contempt for

The poem's structure

1. Think about the title. Comment on the structure of the poem and how it affects your understanding and appreciation of the text.
2. Match up the following newspaper headlines to lines in the poem. It is not necessary to know every term, but try to complete the exercise based on what you do understand.
   - Exxon Valdez runs aground, oil spill harms wildlife
   - Hiroshima flattened by Enola Gay payload
   - Farmers chalk up another year of surplus
   - American scientist wins Nobel prize for medicine
   - National Guard troops escort Little Rock Nine to class
   - Civil Rights demonstrators injured in protest
   - Fifth Avenue shops considered tops
   - Nuclear plants provide "nearly unlimited" power
   - More body bags return from Saigon
   - Neil Armstrong plants American flag in Tranquillity Bay
   - Pilot flies at Mach 2
   - Plessy v. Ferguson provides for separate education facilities
   - Harlem families have fewer chances, study shows
   - New novel banned: labelled obscene
   - Emerson Society awards scholars
   - L.A. Freeway leaves cars little room
   - Trash dumps all full, board says
   - Housing project successful
   - Cardiac patient in "stable" condition
   - Black Panthers riot

Pardoning the unpardonable

In a fish bowl, begin a discussion with one person starting with the following opinion and the others reacting to it:
"I'm never going to the US because I will never pardon the country for ... [choose one of the negative items from the poem]."
After the discussion in the fishbowl has finished, have the observers give the 'fish' input about how some objectivity (perhaps based on the positive items in the poem) can be an aid to intercultural understanding.

The tenses

Look at the choice of the verb tenses in the poem. To what effect are they used?

Info

A Solid Foundation

Every morning before classes begin in America's schools, pupils stand together with their classmates, put their right hand over their heart and recite:

The Pledge[1] of Allegiance[2]

I pledge allegiance to the Flag of the United States of America and to the Republic for which it stands, one Nation under God, indivisible[3], with liberty and justice for all.

First-graders certainly do not understand the meaning or importance of the words, but the symbolic act of standing up together, facing the Stars and Stripes and chanting in a prayer-like rhythm the same thing every day makes reverence[4] for the flag an unquestioned absolute in their minds. Nor do most Americans question the singing of the first verse of the "Star Spangled[5] Banner" before every sporting event:

The Star Spangled Banner (first verse)

Oh, say, can you see, by the dawn's early light,
What so proudly we hail'd[6] at the twilight's last gleaming[7]?
Whose broad stripes and bright stars, thro'[8] the perilous[9] fight,
O'er the ramparts[10] we watch'd, were so gallantly streaming?
And the rockets' red glare[11], the bombs bursting in air,
Gave proof thro' the night that our flag was still there.
O say, does that star-spangled banner yet wave
O'er the land of the free and the home of the brave?

This text, penned by Francis Scott Key during the British bombardment of Fort McHenry in the harbor at Baltimore, MD, on September 13, 1814, is for most young Americans as abstract in its poetry as it is inspiring when sung by a stadium full of sports fans before a game.

The key words of both these patriotic texts are so closely associated with the American flag that it has come to symbolize for most Americans all that is good about their country—its history as a free land where everyone had the opportunity to pursue[12] his or her happiness. In 1776, one year into the War of Independence—or Revolutionary War—the colonists declared their independence from King George III of England. The young Thomas Jefferson drafted[13] an eloquent complaint[14] against the ruler with the following words:

The Declaration of Independence (beginning)

When in the course of human events, it becomes necessary for one people to dissolve[15] the political bands which have connected them with another, [...] a decent respect to the opinions of mankind requires that they should declare the causes which impel[16] them to the separation.

[1]**pledge** promise – [2]**allegiance** [ə'li:dʒ(ə)ns] loyalty – [3]**indivisible** that cannot be divided – [4]**reverence** feeling of respect – [5]**spangled with stars** *mit Sternen übersät* – [6]**to hail** to greet – [7]**to gleam** to shine – [8]**thro'** [θru:] through – [9]**perilous** dangerous – [10]**rampart** *Schutzwall* – [11]**glare** strong light – [12]**to pursue** to follow with the goal of reaching sth – [13]**to draft** *entwerfen* – [14]**complaint** *Klage* – [15]**to dissolve** to break down or destroy – [16]**to impel** to drive or force

Info

We hold these truths to be self-evident[1], that all men are created equal, that they are endowed[2] by their Creator with certain unalienable[3] rights, that among these are Life, Liberty, and the pursuit of Happiness. That to secure these rights, Governments are instituted among Men, deriving[4] their just powers from the consent[5] of the governed. That whenever any Form of Government becomes destructive of these ends, it is the Right of the People to alter or to abolish it, and to institute new Government, laying its foundation on such principles and organizing its powers in such form, as to them shall seem most likely to effect their Safety and Happiness [...].

The Declaration then goes on to list the abuses the colonists had suffered at the hands of what they considered to be a tyrannical king, including his refusal to approve of laws that would be good and necessary for their well-being.
As self-evident as these truths may have seemed to the idealistic founding fathers, the development of the American society over the past two centuries has given cause for some people to question their applicability[6] today. As the difference in the standards of living between the rich and the poor in the US increases, the question presents itself: To what extent are life, liberty and the pursuit of happiness still guaranteed American citizens today?

Developing an ideology

While the Declaration of Independence has no function in the present legislative arena, it did help form the ideology of the members of Congress who drafted what would become the US Constitution a decade later. It probably reflected the overall thinking of America's enlightened elite in the last decades of the eighteenth century. Adopted in 1789, the Constitution had been drafted by 55 delegates from the colonies, including most of the outstanding leaders of the new nation. These Founding Fathers represented a wide range of interests, yet they all agreed on the main objectives expressed in the preamble to the Constitution:

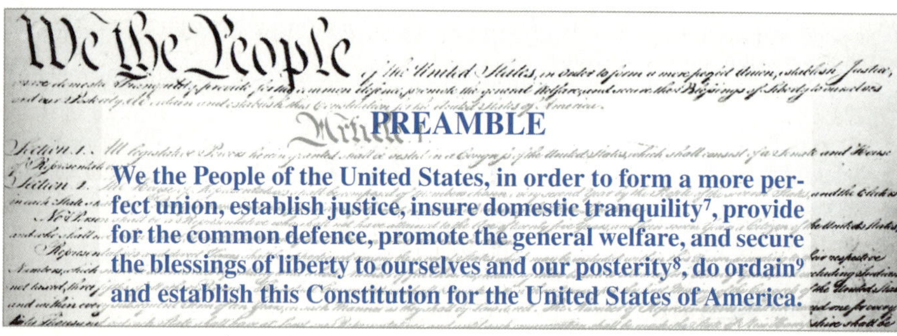
We the People

PREAMBLE

We the People of the United States, in order to form a more perfect union, establish justice, insure domestic tranquility[7], provide for the common defence, promote the general welfare, and secure the blessings of liberty to ourselves and our posterity[8], do ordain[9] and establish this Constitution for the United States of America.

One of the chief aims of the Constitution was to create a strong elected government, directly responsive to the will of the people. The concept of self-goverment did not originate with the Americans; indeed, a certain amount of self-government existed in England at the time. But the degree to which the Constitution committed the United States to rule by the people was unique, and even revolutionary, in comparison with other governments around the world.

[1]**self-evident** *selbstverständlich* – [2]**to endow** to provide – [3]**unalienable** *unveräußerlich* – [4]**to derive** to get, to obtain – [5]**consent** agreement, consensus – [6] **applicable** *anwendbar* – [7]**tranquility** peace – [8]**posterity** later generations – [9]**ordain** *(Gesetz) festsetzen*

Info

System of checks and balances

The seven articles of the Constitution granted powers to the Legislative (House of Representatives and Senate), Executive (President) and Judicial (Supreme Court) branches of the federal government and to the individual state governments. This structure of power was necessary for the new democracy to function and to last. These three branches of government are separate and distinct from one another. The specific powers given to each branch of the federal goverment are balanced by the powers of the other two. In addition, each branch serves as a check on potential excesses of the others. For example, if Congress passes a proposed law, or bill, that the president considers unwise, he can veto it. That means that the bill is dead unless two-thirds of the members of both the House and the Senate vote to enact it despite the president's veto.

Bill of Rights

The delegates from some states, however, felt that a strong federal government might be a threat to the ability of its citizens to govern their own lives. Therefore, the first ten amendments, or Bill of Rights, were added to the Constitution by the new government in order "to prevent misconstruction or abuse of its powers" and to "best insure the beneficent[1] ends of its institution."
Among other things, they guarantee freedom of religion, speech, and the press; they pledged the right of trial by jury, the right to bear arms, and the right to due process of law; and forbade both "unreasonable searches and seizures" and compulsion[2] to testify against oneself in criminal cases.
Given that these basic rights were formulated in an era when democracy was still an idea—or at best, an ideal—and the American frontier lay just behind the Appalachian Mountains, they appear astonishingly modern. However, considering the major changes in technology and in society, some of them seem almost ancient. The Second Amendment, for example, states that "a well regulated militia, being necessary to the security of a free state, the right of the people to keep and bear arms shall not be infringed." In 1789 guns were less effective than they are today. In 1789 a good marksman could fire his rifle twice in two minutes. Today, a 16-year-old gang member can shoot 600 rounds per minute from the AK-47 assault rifle his brother bought at a gun show.
Scientific breakthroughs and technological advancements will certainly continue to challenge the American system. But will stem cell research or the Internet be enough to shake its foundation? Or will the terrorist attacks on New York and Washington be enough to turn the tide? If one judges from the past, some stretching of this relatively flexible system can be expected, but there will probably be no big breaks.

Due process of law is the principle that an individual cannot be deprived of life, liberty, or property without appropriate legal procedures and safeguards. The Bill of Rights and the Fourteenth Amendment to the Constitution guarantee that any person accused of a crime must be informed of the charges, be provided with legal counsel, be given a speedy and public trial, enjoy equal protection of the laws, and not be subjected to cruel and unusual punishment, unreasonable searches and seizures, double jeopardy, or self-incrimination.

[1] **beneficent** [-'---] doing good – [2] **compulsion** condition of being forced

Dreams in a Land of Opportunity

"I like the dreams of the future better than the history of the past."

Thomas Jefferson

Thomas Jefferson, 3rd President (1801–1809). He drafted the Declaration of Independence (1776).

Alexander Hamilton, the first U.S. secretary of the treasury (1789–1795)

Ever since America was discovered by Columbus in 1492, millions of people from Europe and from other parts of the world have dreamed the American dream. During the ensuing[1] Age of Discovery, utopias were often written about the New World. Religious persecution and social unrest in Europe drove masses of people to the shores of the land where—they had heard—they would be able to practice their religious faith freely.

For these persecuted[2] people, America represented their haven from political and social oppression, from the constraints[3] of class and serfdom[4], and from the resulting poverty and hunger. As a new land, one without principalities[5], archbishoprics or fiefdoms[6], America was a frontier eventually settled by individuals who believed that anything was possible with the help of ingenuity[7], hard work and the support of like-minded people.

As the frontier was conquered bit by bit, progress came to mean what was good for the individual. The early colonial politicians were aware this was a new type of man—freed from the chains of feudal Europe by the French Revolution, fostered[8] by a democratic feeling of brotherhood, supported by virtually inexhaustible[9] natural resources, and fed by the taste of freedom provided by their common dream.

As the 13 colonies grew, their economies and religious beliefs diversified. Some politicians thought it best to divide up into distinct confederacies or sovereignties. Most people, however, thought that if the colonies were divided, they would, as Alexander Hamilton wrote in the *Federalist Papers*, "have frequent and violent contests with each other" not to mention their vulnerability[10] at the hands of foreign powers.

So after declaring their independence from England and coming to terms with[11] their freedom and with the opportunities open to them on their relatively unexplored continent, the Americans established a system based on the prevailing political idealism. The Constitution, ratified in 1789, begins by stating its purpose and ideals:

[1] **to ensue** to follow – [2] **to persecute** *verfolgen* – [3] **constraint** limitation – [4] **serfdom** *Leibeigenschaft* – [5] **principality** *Fürstentum* – [6] **fiefdom** domain of a feudal lord – [7] **ingenuity** talent for solving problems in a clever way – [8] **to foster** to support – [9] **inexhaustible** *unerschöpflich* – [10] **vulnerability** that can be attacked easily – [11] **to come to terms with sth** to accept sth over a period of time

We the people of the United States, in order to form a more perfect union, establish justice, insure domestic tranquility[1], provide for the common defense, promote the general welfare, and secure the blessings of liberty to ourselves and our posterity[2], do ordain[3] and establish this Constitution for the United States of America.

In times of hardship and political unrest, the country's leaders have repeatedly tried to rally[4] the American people behind essential aspects of the American dream. During the First World War, President Wilson asked:

Just what is it America stands for? If she stands for one thing more than another, it is for the sovereignty of self-governing people.

When the Soviet Union sent their first sputnik[5] satellite into space in 1957, America saw herself challenged in the field of science and technology. Suddenly space was the new frontier and President Kennedy was quick to confront his countrymen with this image:

We stand today at the edge of a New Frontier—the frontier of the 1960s, a frontier of unknown opportunity and perils[6], a frontier of unfulfilled hopes and threats.

His goal of putting a man on the moon before the end of the decade was reached when Neil Armstrong walked out of the Apollo 11 spacecraft on July 20, 1969, and said, "This is one small step for [a] man, one giant leap for mankind." Kennedy, however, did not live to see this grand occasion because he was assassinated on Nov. 22, 1963, in Dallas, TX.

Black Americans at that time saw a more urgent problem, Martin Luther King Jr. also harked back to the discourse of the founding fathers by demanding the "riches of freedom and security of justice" that all Americans had been promised:

Every man has a right to life, and this means that he has also a right to make a comfortable living [...]. Our government, formal and informal, political and economic, owes to everyone an avenue[7] to possess himself of[8] a portion of that plenty[9] from our industrial society sufficient[10] for his needs, through his own work.

(Thomas) Woodrow Wilson, 28th President (1913–1921)

John Fitzgerald Kennedy, 35th President (1961–1963)

Dr. Martin Luther King Jr, (1929–1968) civil rights leader

[1] **tranquility** (Brit tranquillity) peace – [2] **posterity** later generations – [3] **ordain** *(Gesetz) festsetzen* – [4] **to rally sb behind sth** to come together to support sb/sth when there is danger, need, etc – [5] **sputnik** Soviet satellite (first launched October 4, 1957) – [6] **peril** danger – [7] **avenue** (*fig*) way – [8] **to possess oneself of sth** (*fml*) to own – [9] **plenty** adequate amount – [10] **sufficient** enough

James Earl Carter Jr, 39th President (1977–1981)

Ronald W. Reagan, 40th President (1981–1989)

George Herbert Walker Bush, 41st President (1989–1993)

Presidents often see it as their duty to show the Americans where they have come from and to point the direction in which their future lies. Often this path is paved with the promise of and the values inherent[1] in the American dream. In 1977 President Carter said:

I would hope that the nations of the world might say that we had built a lasting peace, based not on weapons of war but on international policies, which reflect our own most precious values. These are not just my goals, and they will not be my accomplishments[2], but the affirmation of our own nation's continuing moral strength and our belief in an undiminished[3], ever-expanding American dream.

President Reagan spoke of the power of the dream and of the individual in his 1981 Inaugural Address[4]:

And let us renew our faith and our hope. We have every right to dream heroic dreams [...]. Your dreams, your hopes, your goals are going to be the dreams of this administration, so help me God.

After the end of Reagan's eight-year term, his former Vice-president Bush promised to help America continue her course of prosperity at his inauguration on January 20, 1989:

I come before you and assume the presidency at a moment rich with promise. We live in a peaceful, prosperous time, but we can make it better. [...] A new breeze is blowing—and a nation refreshed by freedom stands ready to push on; there is new ground to be broken, and a new action to be taken [...]. America is never wholly herself unless she is engaged in high moral principle. We as a people have such a purpose today. It is to make kinder the face of the nation and gentler the face of the world.

Although Bush's presidency saw the end of the Cold War and a victory of sorts in Iraq, at home the American economy was crumbling[5]. Bill Clinton's optimistic talk got him elected twice and his leadership helped him rebuild the economy. Looking back at his eight years in office, President Clinton summarized his presidency during the State of the Union Address and looked at the road ahead:

Eight years ago, it was not so clear to most Americans there would be much to celebrate in the year 2000. Then our nation was gripped

[1] **inherent** existing as a natural or permanent feature or quality of sth/sb – [2] **accomplishment** achievement – [3] **undiminished** *unvermindert* – [4] **Inaugural Address** speech given by the new president to the nation on the day he takes office – [5] **to crumble** (*fig*) to fall apart

by economic distress, social decline, political gridlock[1]. The title of a best-selling book asked: America: What Went Wrong?

In the best traditions of our nation, Americans determined to set things right. We restored[2] the vital[3] center, replacing outmoded[4] ideologies with a new vision anchored in basic, enduring values: opportunity for all, responsibility from all, a community of all Americans. We reinvented government, transforming it into a catalyst[5] for new ideas that stress both opportunity and responsibility, and give our people the tools they need to solve their own problems. [...] But even more important, America again has the confidence to dream big dreams. But we must not let this confidence drift into complacency[6]. For we, all of us, will be judged by the dreams and deeds we pass on to our children. And on that score, we will be held to a high standard, indeed, because our chance to do good is so great.

William Jefferson Clinton, 42nd President (1993–2001)

After the eight-year presidency of democrat Bill Clinton, the new republican President portrayed in his Inaugural Address a nation that had been through hard times and was in need of reforms. In January 2001, President George W. Bush stressed the fact that everyone should be integrated into the American promise.

George W. Bush, 43rd President (since 2001)

We have a place, all of us, in a long story—a story we continue, but whose end we will not see. It is the story of a new world that became a friend and liberator of the old, a story of a slave-holding society that became a servant of freedom, the story of a power that went into the world to protect but not possess, to defend but not to conquer. It is the American story—a story of flawed[7] and fallible[8] people, united across the generations by grand and enduring ideals.

The grandest of these ideals is an unfolding[9] American promise that everyone belongs, that everyone deserves a chance, that no insignificant person was ever born.

Americans are called to enact this promise in our lives and in our laws. And though our nation has sometimes halted, and sometimes delayed[10], we must follow no other course.

Mapping out the relations

Pick out the key terms in the speeches above.
Make a mind map showing how the words relate to the American dream and to one another. ➪ Method kit, Mind map, p. 281

[1] **gridlock** *Stillstand* – [2] **to restore** to bring sth back to a former condition – [3] **vital** essential – [4] **outmoded** no longer in fashion; obsolete – [5] **catalyst** person or thing that causes change – [6] **complacency** *Selbstgefälligkeit* – [7] **flawed** imperfect – [8] **fallible** capable of making mistakes – [9] **to unfold** to open and spread out – [10] **to delay** to make late; to wait

Rhetoric

1. The Preamble to the Constitution shows good use of parallel constructions (in this case, verb plus direct object): "... establish justice, insure domestic tranquility, provide for the common defense, promote the general welfare, and secure the blessings of liberty ..." (ll. 35–37). Parallel grammatical structures are often used in speeches because they sound effective and are easy for listeners to follow. Look for other examples of parallelism in the other speeches.
2. Find the corresponding noun, adjective or verb for the following words:
   to persecute, constraint, ingenuity, mutual, vulnerability, tranquility, ordain, to possess, plenty, sufficient, accomplishment, vital, flawed.

Roger Rosenblatt

The Vanished, Banished, Beautiful American Loser

What stereotyped characters have you seen in movies recently?
Do the stereotypes differ depending on where the film was produced?

Stereotype: a fixed idea, image, etc that many people have of a particular type of person or thing, but which is often not true in reality.

For one brief, miserable moment, Michael Douglas, the novelist-professor hero of the new movie *Wonder Boys*, has it all. His wife has left him. His girlfriend, the chancellor of his university, who is married to his department chairman, is pregnant with Douglas' child. His second, never-to-be-finished novel has thickened to page 2.611, single-spaced. His gay editor is in town, hungry both for the new book and for Douglas' best student, a boy who has gunned down the department chairman's dog, who bit Douglas on the leg. The wound[1] has become infected. Douglas limps[2] through the slush[3] of a Pittsburgh winter, dressed in his former wife's pink chenille bathrobe. He hasn't shaved in three days. He drives around stoned, with the murdered dog in the trunk of a car, which he believes to be his but which was stolen from a man with a James Brown hairdo, who is out to get him.

A picture this lovely doesn't come along every day, but it used to. Until the greed-is-wonderful 1980s, the figure Douglas portrays was a regular in American culture—the beautiful loser, the shimmering failure, the mess who for all his stumbles in the slush still strove[4] for something honorable and was honored by the greater world in which he gloriously flopped.

[1] **wound** [wu:nd] – [2] **to limp** to walk with difficulty, esp when one foot or leg is hurt or stiff – [3] **slush** melting snow – [4] **to strive for sth** (strove or strived, striven) (*fml*) to try very hard or for a long time to obtain or achieve sth

He exists no longer, principally because failure in modern, NASDAQ times has no redeeming[1] social value. In its place sit rows and rows of gleaming successes. Last week on the same day that I saw *Wonder Boys*, I watched a different bunch of wonder boys (and women) strut[2] their stuff on a TV special called *Summit in Silicon Valley*. (*Bunch* is wrong for the collective noun. *Grin?*) I watched a grin of high-tech billionaires sunning themselves in national adoration, bright models of achievement for every double-breasted[3] hopeful yearning for a Lexus[4]. No one mentioned beautiful losers. The last shall be last.

Who wants to be a millionaire? In the song the answer was, "I don't." But that was in another country. Gone these days is the character who practically defined American heroism, epic and tragic—Huck and Holden; Charlie Chaplin, Charlie Brown. Nearly all of Hemingway's heroes are defeated in *Winner Take Nothing* and in the novels. In *To Have and Have Not*, Harry Morgan had not, The dark, antiheroes of a time as recent as the 1970s have disappeared too—De Niro, in *Taxi Driver*, Pacino in *Dog Day Afternoon*. Bruce Springsteen sang about his "town full of losers." In *Rocky 28*, our hero may finally knock out Adrian, but in his first fight (1976) he lost beautifully.

In some ways, it is easier to be an American winner than a loser, which had certain definite requirements:

1) The loser had to be blissfully[5] out of things; he walked around in a sort of self-assured[6] daze[7]. "Don't blame me, Lady," said the extravagantly out-of-it Oscar Levant in a movie of the 1940s. "I didn't make the world. I barely live on it."

2) He had to serve as an affront[8] to more purposeful lives. The most engaging character on the 1950s sitcom[9] *My Little Margie* was the boyfriend, Freddie, whose job consisted of spending the day looking at construction sites. My favorite scene in *Catcher in the Rye* occurs when Holden is in his public-speaking class. The teacher orders the students to yell out the word "digression[10]!" whenever a speech loses focus or direction. Holden is, of course, a living digression.

3) A loser's values had to be in the right place, but they also had to suggest that society's were in the wrong place. Muhammad Ali was stripped of his heavyweight title because he refused the draft[11], to protest the Vietnam War. He wasn't a hero to everyone, but people recognized the gesture[12].

4) He had no use for money(!). A hero in his character, if not in his cause, was Robert E. Lee[13], who after his considerable loss, was exhausted and without an income. An insurance company offered him $50,000 (easily a million today) to use

What is meant by 'NASDAQ times'?

An **antihero** is a main character in a dramatic or narrative work who is characterized by a lack of traditional heroic qualities, such as idealism or courage.

Tip: Willy Loman is the classic "American loser". Find out more about him!

[1]**to redeem** here: to compensate – [2]**to strut one's stuff** (*sl*) to show off – [3]**double breasted** *zweireihig (Sakko)* – [4]**Lexus** type of luxury car – [5]**bliss** extreme happiness; ecstasy – [6]**self-assured** having or showing confidence – [7]**daze** trance-like condition – [8]**affront** open insult – [9]**sitcom** situation comedy – [10]**digression** deviation from the main subject; *Abschweifung* – [11]**draft** *Einberufung* – [12]**gesture** ['dʒɛstʃə] – [13]**Robert E. Lee** Confederate General who led the losing forces during the US Civil War

his name. Lee said, "I cannot consent to receive pay for services I do not render," and eventually accepted the presidency of the small and impoverished Washington College which became Washington and Lee after his death. For what he told the insurance company, he could be put to death today.

Explain this exaggeration within the context of this piece.

The main requirement for the beautiful loser is that society must value him, must impute[1] virtue for no reason other than that he fails in a sincerely believed-in, preferably[2] noble cause[3]. When was the last time one saw that? Before the 1980s, there was a public shame attached to too much success. That attitude was useless and irrational but also sweet-natured and not unhealthy. The underlying idea was that failure was something potentially good for you and for everyone, that rejection and loss were not only personally inuring[4] but that losing was also a sign of high and admirable ambitions. To note how far the pendulum has swung, go see *Wonder Boys* and the *Silicon Summit* on the same day.

Even the makers of the Douglas movie could not bear to leave their hero a beautiful loser forever. At the end of the picture, there he is—clean-shaven, writing his new and tidy, novel, his new wife and child emerging[5] from his new car—all seen from a vast picture window in a new house so full of sunlight it makes one long for slush.

There is, sad to say, only one beautiful heroic mess of a man left in the land. It is Rodney Dangerfield[6], who claims to have received a sweepstakes letter that read, "You may already be a loser." Rodney also says that when he enters an elevator, the operator asks, "Down?" Looks like up to me.

Time, March 13, 2000, p. 64

Looking at losers

1. Explain the last line within the context of this author's opinion concerning losers in present-day American society.
2. Do loser characters appeal to you? Why (not)?
3. Which German movies that you have seen show characters who are losers?

... and winners

What does it take to be a 'winner' today in Germany? In America?

Irony

1. Why does the writer consider *bunch* wrong and *grin* (ll. 26) perhaps better? Look up the words in a dictionary. Find more expressions for "groups" of people or animals. Put them in a mind map.
   ➜ Method kit, Mind map, p. 281
2. Explain the irony in "The last shall be last."

[1] **impute** attribute sth to sb – [2] **preferably** ['----] – [3] **cause** here: goal or principle – [4] **to inure** [ɪ'njʊə] to make sb able to tolerate sth unpleasant – [5] **to emerge** (from sth) to come out of a place – [6] **Rodney Dangerfield** popular American comedian

Langston Hughes

Let America Be America Again

Langston Hughes (1902–1967) was an African-American author who wrote many poems about America, and especially about the injustices suffered by African-Americans as they, too, tried to take part in the American Dream.

What words do you need to talk about the American Dream? Collect them in small groups before reading this poem.

Let America be America again.
Let it be the dream it used to be.
Let it be the pioneer on the plain
Seeking a home where he himself is free.

(America never was America to me.)

Let America be the dream the dreamers dreamed—
Let it be that great strong land of love
Where never kings connive[1] nor tyrants scheme[2]
That any man be crushed by one above.

(It never was America to me.)

O, let my land be a land where Liberty
Is crowned with no false patriotic wreath[3],
But opportunity is real, and life is free.
Equality is in the air we breathe.

(There's never been equality for me,
Nor freedom in this "homeland of the free.")

Say, who are you that mumbles in the dark?
And who are you that draws your veil[4] across the stars?

I am the poor white, fooled and pushed apart,
I am the Negro bearing slavery's scars.
I am the red man driven from the land,
I am the immigrant clutching the hope I seek—
And finding only the same old stupid plan
Of dog eat dog[5], of mighty crush the weak.

I am the young man, full of strength and hope,
Tangled[6] in that ancient endless chain
Of profit, power, gain, of grab the land!
Of grab the gold! Of grab the ways of satisfying need!
Of work the men! Of take the pay!
Of owning everything for one's own greed!

Langston Hughes

[1] **to connive** [kə'naɪv] to conspire; *verschwören* – [2] **to scheme** to plan secretly sth to one's own advantage – [3] **wreath** [ri:θ] *Kranz* – [4] **veil** here: thing which conceals, covers or hides – [5] **dog eat dog** (*idm*) fierce competition – [6] **tangled** mixed up, confused, disordered

I am the farmer, bondsman[1] to the soil.
I am the worker sold to the machine.
I am the Negro, servant to you all.
I am the people, humble, hungry, mean—
Hungry yet[2] today despite the dream.
Beaten yet today—O, Pioneers!
I am the man who never got ahead,
The poorest worker bartered[3] through the years.

Yet I'm the one who dreamt our basic dream
In the Old World while still a serf[4] of kings,
Who dreamt a dream so strong, so brave, so true,
That even yet its mighty daring[5] sings
In every brick and stone, in every furrow turned
That's made America the land it has become.
O, I'm the man who sailed those early seas
In search of what I meant to be my home—
For I'm the one who left dark Ireland's shore,
And Poland's plain, and England's grassy lea[6],
And torn from Black Africa's strand[7] I came
To build a "homeland of the free."

The free?

Who said the free? Not me?
Surely not me? The millions on relief[8] today?
The millions shot down when we strike?
The millions who have nothing for our pay?
For all the dreams we've dreamed
And all the songs we've sung
And all the hopes we've held
And all the flags we've hung,
The millions who have nothing for our pay—
Except the dream that's almost dead today.

O, let America be America again—
The land that never has been yet—
And yet must be—the land where *every* man is free.
The land that's mine—the poor man's, Indian's, Negro's. ME—
Who made America,
Whose sweat and blood, whose faith and pain,
Whose hand at the foundry[9], whose plow in the rain,
Must bring back our mighty dream again.

[1] **bondsman** person in bondage, slave – [2] **yet** here: still – [3] **to barter** to trade (goods or services) without the exchange of money – [4] **serf** servant, slave – [5] **daring** boldness – [6] **lea** [liː] field where grass is grown temporarily – [7] **strand** (chiefly *poet*) region or land, esp a foreign country; also: shore of a lake, sea or river – [8] **relief** here: social welfare payments – [9] **foundry** factory where metal or glass is melted and moulded into various shapes or objects

Sure, call me any ugly name you choose—
The steel of freedom does not stain.
From those who live like leeches[1] on the people's lives.
We must take back our land again,
America!

O, yes,
I say it plain,
America never was America to me,
And yet I swear this oath—
America will be!

Out of the rack and ruin[2] of our gangster death,
The rape and rot of graft[3], and stealth[4], and lies,
We, the people, must redeem[5]
The land, the mines, the plants, the rivers.
The mountains and the endless plain—
All, all the stretch of these great green states—
And make America again!

Amending your lists

Add to your American Dream word list (from the pre-reading activity) those terms Hughes uses here to describe it in all its complexity. To what extent do negative words also belong on your lists?

Irony

Line 17 may remind Americans of the opening lines of their national anthem, "The Star Spangled Banner," which begins:
"Oh, say, can you see by the dawn's early light
What so proudly we hailed at the twilight's last gleaming."

Look at l. 17 and comment on the irony of this association.

Expanding your lists

"... the dream the dreamers dreamed—" (l. 6). Going back to your word list, expand it by finding other expressions related to the root of those words. Example: America, anti-American, to Americanize, Americanization, un-American, etc.

Describing a better future

Based on the speaker's description of the America he sees in front of him, describe the America he yearns for. For example, poor whites will be integrated into society and treated with respect, blacks will no longer suffer from slavery's destructive power, etc.

[1]**leech** *Blutegel* – [2]**rack and ruin** (*idm*) bad state, destruction – [3]**graft** use of illegal or unfair means to gain an advantage in business, politics, etc – [4]**stealth** *List, Tücke* – [5]**to redeem** to regain or recover

Does America Still Exist?

What would lead someone to ask such a question?

Harper's Magazine put this question to several prominent Americans, including Harold Livesay, the chairman of the history department at Virginia Polytechnic Institute and Louis L'Amour, whose 100 plus novels are still in print. Listen to these two texts and answer the questions at the end.

Analyzing the language in groups

Divide into two groups. One group listens for the metaphors used to explain America, and the other listens for examples of informal language in the first and formal language in the second selection.

Group 1: Share the metaphors you found in the first text. How helpful/harmful are they for our thinking about America?

Group 2: Compare the formal and informal language used in the two pieces. Listen for the use of clichés, colloquialisms, irony, and sentence structures.

Are women allowed to dream?

"Even a few women have started to believe [that the dream is still alive]," writes Harold Livesay ironically. Write a comment about the male-dominant image of the American Dream.

Interviewing

Question the two authors about the American Dream on the hot seat.

Immigration to America

Immigration to America

Info

Marc Chagall was born in Russia in 1887. After moving to Paris in 1923, he spent most of the rest of his life in France, where he died in 1985. During World War II, however, the Russian Jew sought refuge in New York, creating many important works of art in that city. This picture is an illustration for a story by André Malraux[1]. In 1926 it was first exhibited at the Art Expo in New York.

The first European immigrants in American history came from England and the Netherlands. Attracted by reports of great economic opportunities and religious and political freedom, immigrants from many other countries came to the United States in increasing numbers, the flow reaching a peak in the years 1892–1924. During the late 19th century, the government operated a special port of entry on Ellis Island; it was in operation from 1892 until 1954 and is now preserved as part of the Statue of Liberty National Monument. The Statue of Liberty, which was a gift from the people of France to the people of America in 1886, stands on an island in New York Harbor, near Ellis Island. Between 1820 and 1998, the United States admitted more than 64 million immigrants.
These words by the poet Emma Lazarus are etched[2] on a plaque[3] at Liberty's base:

> Give me your tired, your poor,
> Your huddled[4] masses yearning to breathe free,
> The wretched[5] refuse[6] of your teeming[7] shore.
> Send these, the homeless, tempest[8]-tossed to me,
> I lift my lamp beside the golden door!

[1] **André Malraux** (1901–1976) French writer and politician. A member of the French resistance during World War II, he served as minister of culture (1959–1969) under Charles de Gaulle. His written works include novels of adventure and political action, such as *Man's Fate* (1933), and books of art history. – [2] **to etch** to cut lines into a piece of glass, metal etc in order to make words or a picture – [3] **plaque** flat piece of stone, metal, etc, usually with a name and dates on, attached to a wall in memory of a person or an event – [4] **to huddle** (of people or animals) to gather closely together, usually because of cold or fear – [5] **wretched** ['rɜtʃɪd] making you feel sympathy or pity – [6] **refuse** ['rɜfju:s] (written) waste material that has been thrown away – [7] **teeming** present in large numbers – [8] **tempest** (*fml* or *lit*) a violent storm

The Statue of Prosperity

Brant Parker, Johnny Hart

Monarchy vs. Democracy The Kingdom of ID from this comic strip is ruled by the authoritarian king. How does he make sure his kingdom remains peaceful and prosperous?

Daphne Spain

How Healthy is Immigration?

Immigration to the United States has been so extensive during the past two decades that [the century ended] as it began, with healthy debates about how immigrants fit into the ideal US society.

Do we celebrate cultural differences or try to minimize them? Should ethnic and racial boundaries be erased through assimilation of immigrants by blurring[2] differences to achieve a melting pot, or should racial and ethnic differences be maintained to create a stronger pluralistic society?

What do you think?

There is a healthy degree of support for each point of view. A nationwide survey conducted by the National Opinion Research Center in 1994 included the following statement: "Some people say that it is better for America if different racial and ethnic groups maintain their distinct cultures. Others say it is better if groups change so that they blend[3] into the larger society as in the idea of a melting pot." People were asked to rank their opinions on a scale ranging from "maintaining distinct cultures" (pluralism) to "blending into the larger society" (assimilation). Roughly one-third of Americans thought pluralism was the best route, one-third endorsed assimilation, and one-third found themselves somewhere in between. […]

Regarding your society, where do you stand?

[1] **upscale** (US) at the higher end of the social scale – [2] **to blur** to make sth difficult to distinguish clearly – [3] **to blend** to join together so that one is not clearly separate from the others

Immigration is the "bookend[1]" demographic phenomenon of 20th-century United States history. Over one million immigrants arrived annually during the first decade of the century, and about one million have arrived annually in the last decade. (Relatively little immigration occurred between 1915 and 1965 due in part to the Depression of the late 1920s and 1930s and various forms of restrictive legislation.) Today, they hail[2] from different countries than the new arrivals of the 1900s, and proceed to a wider range of cities. Still, immigrants raise some of the same issues today that they did 100 years ago.

In *Immigration to the United States: Journey to an Uncertain Destination*, a 1994 report of the Population Reference Bureau, Philip Martin and Elizabeth Midgley identify three reasons that immigration has become a subject of debate in the 1990s. First, the number of immigrants is rising from its low point in the 1940s. Second, today's immigrants differ significantly in ethnicity, education and skills from native-born Americans. Third, no political consensus exists on whether immigrants are assets[3] or liabilities[4] to U.S. society. Although the 1994 General Social Survey revealed general tolerance for immigration, it also found that 60 percent of Americans believe immigration should be reduced from its current levels. Slightly more (about two-thirds) thought additional immigration would "make it harder to keep the country united." Americans think immigration is unlikely to contribute to higher economic growth, and over 80 percent think higher immigration would create higher unemployment (although they don't fear that immigrants affect their own job security).

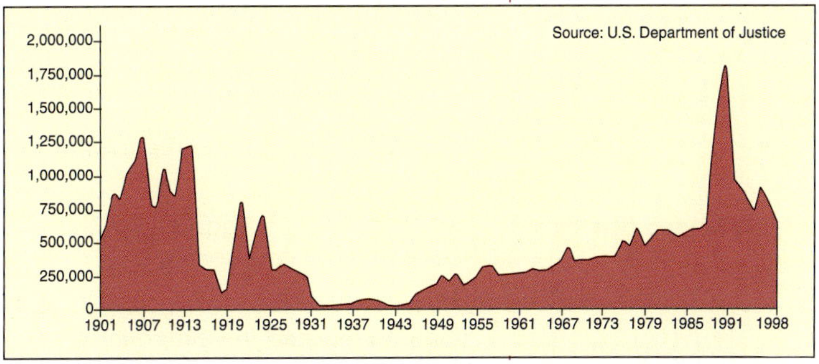

Legal immigration to the U.S. for the years 1901–1998

Headlining

Give each paragraph a short headline.

How healthy?

Answer the question posed in the title of this article.

Language

Explain the image of the "'bookend' demographic phenomenon of 20th-century United States history." (See the graph above.)

[1] **bookend** prop placed at the end of a row of books to keep them upright – [2] **to hail from** to come from – [3] **asset** advantage – [4] **liabilities** (*pl*) financial burden

Paraphrasing

Paraphrase the following expressions. Do not use the underlined words.

- Immigration to the United States has been so <u>extensive</u> during the <u>past two decades</u> (ll. 1f.)
- Should ethnic and racial <u>boundaries be erased</u> through assimilation (l. 5)
- one-third <u>endorsed</u> assimilation (ll. 18f.)
- various forms of <u>restrictive legislation</u> (ll. 25f.)
- Today, they <u>hail</u> from different countries (l. 26)
- no political <u>consensus</u> exists (l. 37)
- whether immigrants are <u>assets</u> or <u>liabilities</u> (l. 37)

Improve your vocabulary

Find the corresponding nouns:
extensive (l. 1), to minimize (l. 4), to conduct (l. 10), to include (l. 11), to maintain (l. 13), to endorse (l. 18), to occur (l. 24), to reveal (l. 38), to contribute (l. 43).

Taking a poll

In a double circle, take a poll amongst your classmates:

1. Do you think your society celebrates cultural differences or tries to minimize them? Explain.
2. Should immigration be reduced in your country? Why (not)?

Extended activities

1. Make a list or collage of ways in which cultural differences are celebrated in your society.
2. Make a short persuasive speech about why immigration should (not) be reduced in your country.

   ➪ Method kit, Comment and speech, p. 292

Checking up on immigration

1. How has the U.S. immigration policy changed since Sept. 11, 2001?
2. How have Americans' opinions concerning immigration changed since then? You may want to consult some of the following sources:
   - National Center for Policy Analysis – www.ncpa.org
   - U.S. Immigration and Naturalization Service – www.ins.usdoj.gov www.ins.gov/graphics/aboutins/history/teacher/resources.htm www.e-naturalization.net
   - The Great American Web Site – www.uncle-sam.com
   - American Immigration Center – www.us-immigration.com/news/newlaw.html
   - International Herald Tribune – www.iht.com
   - Christian Science Monitor – www.csmonitor.com
   - The Nando Times – www.nandotimes.com/opinions/
   - Yahoo message boards – www.yahoo.com

   ➪ Method kit, Internet research, p. 304

Sunita Jain

Fly the Friendly Skies

Born in 1941 in India, Sunita Jain received both her M.A. and her Ph.D. in the United States. Today she teaches English at the Indian Institute of Technology (ITT) in New Delhi.

It was again the hurry-home time—the time most difficult for an outsider or alien in a foreign country. The buildings belched[1] out men and women as if out of compulsion[2], and New York's Fifth Avenue, as were the other streets at that hour, was a veritable[3] escalator[4] of moving traffic. Arjun sat near the window inside the café and watched the Whites, Blacks and peoples of every description cluttering[5] the sidewalk in their simultaneous[6] onslaught[7].

He felt lonesome sitting by himself while all around him New York moved to get home. Arjun could not have moved even if he had wanted. All day he had window shopped, gazing gaga eyed[8] at the mannequins[9] in the windows, the automatic toys, the gadgets[10] galore[11]. He had no money to buy anything yet, and he was in no hurry to possess any of the wealth that littered[12] the shops. Instead he had felt extremely tired and alone. The excitement with which he had left India and reached New York three days ago, had disappeared.

A group of smartly dressed young women went past his window. *America is incredibly erotic. Too many legs make all these streets sexy …* Whose lines were these? Too many legs, but not erotic. Nothing stirred[13] in Arjun except the vague[14] evenings near Regal[15] or Junpath[16] and the sway[17] of some Indian girl's body baling out[18] the hypnotic scent of jasmine *gajaras*[19]. The girls outside his window were shadows on a screen and distant. He was too ignorant and unbearably scared.

➤ Scared of what exactly?

[1] **to belch out** here: to let out a lot at once – [2] **compulsion** feeling of being forced to do sth – [3] **veritable** here: looking like sth – [4] **escalator** moving staircase – [5] **to clutter** to fill a space with unnecessary things – [6] **simultaneous** [--ˈ---] at the same time – [7] **onslaught** [ˈɒnslɔːt] wild attack – [8] **gaga eyed** (*infml*) with great surprise – [9] **mannequin** *Schaufensterpuppe* – [10] **gadget** small, useful piece of machinery – [11] **galore** (*adj*) in great numbers – [12] **to litter** to be scattered around a place – [13] **to stir** here: to move, to excite – [14] **vague** [veɪg] unclear, difficult to formulate – [15] **Regal** part of New Delhi around a large cinema of that name – [16] **Junpath** popular main street in New Delhi – [17] **sway** motion of a rotating body – [18] **to bale out** here: to produce – [19] **gajara** (Indian) bracelet made of flowers

New York

The new world around him had expanded into the multitude[1] outside, and the sounds enveloping[2] him were unfamiliarly harsh. He understood now why his elder brother had not left the small 'village in Punjab[3] to which his family belonged. "What does a man need …" his brother had said in answer to Arjun's s pleading to shift to New Delhi, "what does a man need to live out his life happily except a small place he can belong to and a known face? I'll never belong to anything in your New Delhi …"

Nonsense. Arjun stiffened[4] himself. A small place stinks and stagnates—it chokes you by degrees. Even New Delhi got too small; there weren't any jobs anymore or decent houses within the reach of one's income. One had to, one must, enlarge one's world in order to fully unfold—Joyce[5] did it, and Henry James[6]…

It was getting dark outside, The shadows struggled with the glare of lights. He paid for his coffee and stepped out. "Don't loiter[7] in NY after seven … stay indoors. There is too much crime these days …," an old friend settled in Washington had advised him through letters. A close-cropped[8] young man ran swiftly past Arjun. His heart dropped a beat. "It's not healthy to be so scared," Arjun chastised[9] himself. "I am starting a new chapter of my life in America, the beautiful. I'll get used to it just as I got used to the IIT hostel life in Delhi."

The air grew slightly chilly. He walked close to the warmth of the walls that glowed with electric lights. He was ravenously[10] hungry. For three days now he had eaten more sweet dishes and fruits than at any other time in his life. The few vegetable and cheese preparations he tried had strange tastes, and were unable to satisfy his hunger. His stomach growled[11] for spicy food, for peas thick with large chunks of *panir*[12], for potatoes fried whole before they were curried, and for a plate of rich rice *pillao*[13] … The aroma of the food he hungered for assailed[14] his memory and he felt weak in the knees. The thought of sandwiches with milk for dinner revolted[15] him.

He stopped involuntarily outside the large show window of a shop which was now closed for business. Several Indian carpets rioted in[16] color behind the bright glass. Here and there a strategic-

[1] **multitude** large number of people or things – [2] **to envelop** [ɛn'vɛləp] – [3] **Punjab** state in India – [4] **to stiffen oneself** to become stronger – [5] **James Joyce** Irish writer (1882–1941), lived in France, Italy and Switzerland – [6] **Henry James** American writer (1843–1916), lived in France and England – [7] **to loiter** *sich herumtreiben, herumlungern* – [8] **close-cropped** with very short hair – [9] **to chastise** here: to criticize – [10] **ravenously hungry** extremely hungry – [11] **to growl** to make a low, rumbling sound – [12] **panir** (Indian) cheese – [13] **pillao** (Indian) meal made from rice and vegetables and/or meat – [14] **to assail** to attack violently – [15] **to revolt sb** to make sb feel horrible – [16] **to riot in** here: to display vividly

ally placed large brass[1] tabletop accented the flavor of the handknotted[2] Mirzapurs, Kashmirs, and Agras[3].

"Aren't they beautiful!" someone said to him, making him jolt[4] out of his reverie[5]. He turned around. An aged[6] white woman carrying a heavy grocery bag in the cradle of her left arm stood by the window. She too had stopped to look at the carpets.

"You know," she smiled, "I can't go past this window without slowing down. Tell me, how long does it take to make one of those?" She pointed to a sharp velvet[7] blue Kashmir. "I am told they are *actually* hand made …"

◀ Why does she ask him this?

He mumbled[8] a reply, for he himself did not know how long it takes to knot a Kashmir carpet, big or small. In just the few days away from home, Arjun had learned how little he knew about India, and how much he had taken for granted[9], or had never bothered to know the statistics of. Whenever people asked him *when* or *how* or *where* of something or an event—he uttered confused answers.

The two moved away from the window. The lady walked rather slowly as if her feet or legs hurt. He realized then that she was actually very old. She was telling him about how once when she was in high school she had wanted to go to India. The woman grew nostalgic and sentimental about her past. Her voice sounded glad to have an audience. She pointed out the names of buildings and places that could be of interest to a newcomer. Arjun's mind began to wander, looking for an excuse to excuse himself. The friend in Washington had written: you will meet a very large number of lonely elders in this country. Avoid cultivating their friendship even if you are lonesome, for you will end up hurting their feelings …

The two had drifted away from the business section, and he had a feeling he was lost. But somehow it did not bother him. Homesickness had made him reckless. "I'll hail[10] a taxi back to my hotel," he assured himself.

"I live in that building." The lady indicated one of the several red brick buildings sectioned into layers of apartments. "Have you had your supper?" she asked.

"Not yet." He tried to disengage himself[11]. A tall, dark Indian appeared on the other side of the street. "Excuse me, Ma'am, there's a friend I want to say hello to …" Waving a hurried goodbye, he crossed over to the other side.

◀ Why did he want to leave her?

Arjun was very eager to catch up with the Indian. He had seen other Indian men and women on the streets during the day; but

[1] **brass** *Messing* – [2] **handknotted** [-nɒtɪd] – [3] **Mirzapurs, Kashmirs, Agras** carpets named after the places where they were made – [4] **to jolt** to shock – [5] **reverie** here: daydream – [6] **aged** ['eɪdʒɪd] – [7] **velvet** *Samt* – [8] **to mumble** to speak unclearly and quietly – [9] **to take sth for granted** to accept sth without thinking about it – [10] **to hail** here: to signal to stop – [11] **to disengage oneself** to free oneself from sb/sth

right now he wanted to be able to talk to one. To have a chat[1] about *home* over a cup of tea!

"Hello …" His voice was as eager as his manner.

"Yes?" The man looked at him. The expression in the man's eye however made Arjun stammer suddenly.

"Are you from India?" he asked, but felt very foolish in asking it.

"Yes," the man answered.

"I am also from India."

"So?" The man stared at Arjun.

The lash[2] of the insult flushed his face. The man relented[3].

"Look, young man," he said to Arjun in a cryptic[4] voice, "you are probably new here, but you did not travel ten thousand miles to know another Indian, nor did I. Good-night."

Why does the man withdraw so abruptly?

The street light changed. The elderly woman had entered her apartment building. The revolving door swallowed her. In the distance the neon sign flashed rhythmically, fly the friendly skies— of United …

United we stand, divided we fall

United Airlines advertises its services with the jingle "Fly the friendly skies of United." Comment on the last sentence in light of this information.

Language

1. Find examples of personification in the text (e.g. l. 2, l. 34–35, l. 45, l. 66, l. 129).
2. Write down the word families for *alien* (l. 2), *alone* (l. 22), *to satisfy* (l. 65).

Substitutes

1. Find substitutes for the following adverbs; do not change the sentence structure:
   - a group of **smartly** dressed young women (l. 25)
   - America is **incredibly** erotic (l. 27)
   - too ignorant and **unbearably** scared (l. 32)
   - were **unfamiliarly** harsh (l. 35)
   - in order to **fully** unfold (l. 49 f.)
   - ran **swiftly** (l. 57)
   - was **ravenously** hungry (l. 62)
   - He stopped **involuntarily** (l. 71)
   - a **strategically** placed (l. 73)
   - they are **actually** hand made (l. 83)
   - the neon sign flashed **rhythmically** (l. 130)
2. The air *grew* slightly chilly … (l. 61); The woman *grew* nostalgic … (l. 94f.). Use a dictionary to find other expressions including the verb *to grow*.

[1] **chat** friendly conversation – [2] **lash** violent hit – [3] **to relent** to become less strict – [4] **cryptic** mysterious

Translation

Translate ll. 76–101 ("Aren't they ... their feelings ..."). Pay particular attention to verb tenses and indirect speech.

Home and its hold on us

1. Find the aspects of Arjun's image of home (e.g. as a word field) and compare them with your own.
2. Identify the various aspects of Arjun's homesickness.

Arjun's experiences

1. Write an interior monologue reflecting Arjun's thoughts as he sits at the café.
2. Write Arjun's diary entry for his first days in New York.
   → Method kit, Diary entry, p. 294
3. Imagine Arjun had joined the elderly lady in her apartment. Write their conversation.
4. Invent either the events leading up to this story or the continuation of the action.

Snow Anderson

I'm Not Borrowing History Anymore

Speak with your classmates about your history and theirs. How many times have you moved? Why did you move? Did you go through a long period of adjustment?

Snow Anderson

"I just can't get enough of her," I told a friend over dinner recently, describing the writer Bailey White. In addition to reading her essays, I had been listening to them on tape while driving.

White is a Southern writer who's lived her entire life in one place. She writes about eccentric relatives, quirky[1] neighbors and places she has known since she was a child.

"Borrowed history," my friend suggested, and I, to my surprise, burst into tears. Borrowing history. It's what I've been doing since my parents immigrated to the United States in December 1966, three weeks before my 11th birthday. It is as if during that transcontinental flight from Belgrade, Yugoslavia, to Chicago, Ill., my history was erased.

I left behind my eccentric neighbor "Crazy Drina," with her many cats, and her one-legged mother who scared us children with nothing more than her appearance. Gone were my friends, the books from which I learned the Cyrillic alphabet, my uncle who taught me how to tell time and my aunt who sewed clothes for me and my dolls.

[1] **quirky** eccentric

I would no longer spend summers in my grandmother's village, where day and night blended[1] into one and meals consisted of what we picked from her orchard[2]. My colorful childhood ceased[3] to exist. Everything in Chicago felt as gray as the color of the fire escape[4] on the apartment building that had become my home. The contrast made me yearn for every familiar street corner on the way from my house to the school in Belgrade, the aroma from the neighborhood bakery, the sound of my aunt's sewing machine, the grain bin and the oil lamp in my, grandmother's old house. These images embedded[5] themselves so deeply in my cellular[6] memory that three decades later I still feel a sense of loss.

Can you understand Snow's feeling of loss?

I love America with an immigrant's passion, but like everyone who has become an American citizen, I also live with a part of me missing. I search flea markets and antiques stores for objects that other families might have passed down to each other. I display an old, faded quilt[7] my son's great-grandmother made in Kentucky as if it were a priceless treasure. "Mammama," as her family called her, recently passed away[8] at the age of 104. Her grandson and I are divorced, but his Southern roots helped to give me more of a sense of belonging.

I never quite adapted to life in America until 11 years ago when I moved to New Mexico, a simple, rustic place with breathtaking beauty, not unlike my homeland. Here, in an old adobe[9] house with a wood floor in my bedroom, stained[10] pine laid simply over dirt, I feel at home. It's not the packed-dirt floor of my grandmother's house, but in its imperfection it comes close. My house does have electricity and running water, of course, but it also once had a well[11] like my grandmother's from which I drew water as a child.

Why does this house make her feel at home?

The house was last occupied by a much-loved schoolteacher. When the son of the local gas-station owner delivered my car one day, he asked if I saw a lot of butterflies on this property. Puzzled, I answered, "Yes, why do you ask?"

"Well, you know, the woman who used to live here was such a sweet old lady. They say butterflies come around to people like that."

My landlady, the old woman's daughter, seems to understand my need for history. She's given me some things that once belonged to her mother.

The granddaughter, who lives in Colorado and visits often, has become a friend. When we sit in this house where she played as a child or go for walks on land she knows so intimately, I vicariously[12] gain some more history.

My father doesn't understand my passion for old things. He's always been eager to shed[13] his past. His childhood memories are not

[1] **to blend** to join together so that one is not clearly separate from the others – [2] **orchard** piece of land, usually enclosed, in which fruit trees are grown – [3] **to cease** [si:s]to stop – [4] **fire escape** special staircase by which people can escape a burning building – [5] **to embed** to fix firmly – [6] **cellular** here: of the brain cells – [7] **quilt** padded bed cover (*Schlafdecke*) – [8] **to pass away** (*euph*) to die – [9] **adobe** [ə'dəʊb(ɪ)] house built of unburnt, sun-dried bricks – [10] **to stain** *beizen* – [11] **well** *Brunnen* – [12] **vicarious** experienced in the imagination through another person – [13] **to shed** to rid oneself of sth

as idyllic as mine. He was 11 when World War II made him head of the household. His home in Chicago, with its parquet floors, crystal chandeliers[1], hot tub[2] and fireplaces, is a monument to the American Dream. He has had to work very hard for his success, but he has also lived a life unencumbered[3] by the economic and spiritual constraints[4] of communism. In his heart he may sometimes wonder if we made the right choice coming to America, but to me he is a hero for making that choice and giving me the life I have today.

It has not been an easy thing, this business of becoming American. But there are times, like when I walk my dog in the country outside Santa Fe, when the sights and sounds of horses, roosters and donkeys so strongly evoke my childhood that I feel a deep sense of belonging. I've come to realize that by planting my roots here so firmly, I am no longer borrowing history. I am living and even creating it. Perhaps someday when I'm gone, someone will ask the person who lives in this house after me, "Do you see a lot of butterflies on this property?"

Newsweek, March 13, 2000, p. 68

◄ What does she mean by "this business of becoming an American"?

Creating history

1. What did the writer give up when she left her native Yugoslavia?
2. Why does she say she needs her history? In what way does this need of hers go against the American dream?

Your history

Compare your experiences of moving with those that the author presented here.

Opposites

Find the opposites: to borrow (l. 7), to erase (l. 12), eccentric (l. 13), loss (l. 28), to pass down (l. 32), priceless (l. 34), to adapt to (l. 38), rustic (l. 39), to shed (l. 60).

Matching expressions

Look through the text and find the corresponding English expressions for the following German ones:

- *schrullige Nachbarn*
- *Tag und Nacht verschmolzen/gingen ineinander über*
- *diese Dinge prägten sich so tief in mein Gedächtnis ein*
- *indirekt verschaffe ich mir noch mehr Geschichte*
- *ein von den wirtschaftlichen und geistigen Zwängen des Kommunismus unbelastetes Leben*
- *in Tränen ausbrechen*

[1] **chandelier** [ˌʃændəˈlɪə(r)] *Kronleuchter* – [2] **hot tub** very large tub made of ceramic, acrylic, wood, or another substance and filled with hot water in which one or more bathers may soak – [3] **unencumbered** free, not hindered – [4] **constraint** limitation

Multiculturalism in America

Rochelle L. Stanfield

The New Face in America

Imagine you want to sell a product (jeans, sports clothes, chocolate, etc). Whose face would work best to advertise your product?

To see the new face of the United States, go to a grocery store and look at a box of Betty Crocker-brand food products. Betty's portrait[1] is now in its eighth incarnation since the first composite painting debuted in 1936 with pale skin and blue eyes. Her new look is brown-eyed and dark-haired. She has a duskier[2] complexion than her seven predecessors, with features representing an amalgam[3] of white, Hispanic, Indian, African and Asian ancestry.

A computer created this new Betty in the mid-1990s by blending[4] photos of 75 diverse women. That process was relatively quick, General Mills Inc., spokesmen explain. But they acknowledge that it took quite a while to spread the new image to the whole range of Betty Crocker products.

1936

1955

1965

1968

1972

1980

1986

1996

[1] **portrait** ['pɔ:trɪt] – [2] **dusky** somewhat dark or black in colour – [3] **amalgam** [ə'malgəm] combination of various elements – [4] **to blend** to join together so that one is not clearly separate from the others

The slow pace of that process itself could be a metaphor for gradual racial and ethnic intermixing in this country. Indeed, it's taking a long time for the new blended American to surface in society's consciousness. Tiger Woods, the young golf great, publicized the trend by identifying himself as Cablinasian, a mixture of Caucasian, black, Native American and Asian.

In his attitude to race, Tiger Woods shows as superior ease as in his game

For the most part, the marketplace—not government—is leading the way in this evolution. Mixed-race models, particularly men, are in great demand, according to fashion industry experts. And multiracial child actors are now more likely to be tapped[1] for television advertisements.

The ad agencies that hire those models and actors "are not idealistic people," Wilkins said. "They are out to sell stuff, and they study trends very carefully. So, what they see is a big market out there that is reached by beautiful people who are not exactly white, or who are yearning for a melting pot America."

Tiger Woods

That serious scholars should be talking about a melting pot is itself a reversal[2]. As a metaphor for American diversity, the melting pot was first discredited after World War I, when the European immigrants streaming into American cities formed distinct ethnic and national enclaves that didn't melt together.

The timing was off, it turned out, and the metaphorical pot was in the wrong place. Interracial and multiethnic fusion started after World War II and happened in the suburbs. City folk moved from their Italian, Irish, Polish or Jewish urban neighborhoods into diffuse[3] suburban settings, then sent their kids to large public universities, throwing them together with youngsters from other ethnic backgrounds who, nonetheless, came from families with similar lifestyles. [...]

Ironically, the rise in immigration and the trend toward multiculturalism that so many analysts view as major factors leading to divisiveness[4] actually contribute to this blending of races and ethnic groups. "Once you fragment ... the society into so many different ethnic origins, you make it mathematically less and less likely to meet somebody of your own ethnicity," said Ben J. Wattenberg, a senior fellow at the American Enterprise Institute for Public Policy Research (AEI) in Washington.

National Journal, September 13, 1997

The melting pot is a term expressing the view that immigrants to the US have been fused or melted into a single people. The term was taken from a 1908 play written by the English writer Israel Zangwill (1864–1926).

[1] **to tap** here: to nominate – [2] **reversal** act of moving backward – [3] **diffuse** [dɪˈfjuːs] widespread – [4] **divisiveness** [dɪˈvaɪsɪvnəs] creating disagreement

Germany's old and new faces

1. What faces in German advertising have been slow to change? Why?
2. What would the "new face" of Germany look like? Consider the typical faces you see in different types of advertisements and TV shows, movies and in the news. Draw a picture of it or make a collage.

Anna Kuchment

Ethnic Education

What elements of your ethnic background do you consider worthy of teaching to others?

Ethnic: of or relating to groups of people sharing a common and distinctive racial, national, religious, linguistic, or cultural heritage.

As America welcomes its largest influx[1] of immigrants since 1910, it is seeing the rise of an alternative kind of educational institution—the culture school. From California to Connecticut, more and more such programs, also known as cram[2] schools or ethnic-heritage schools, are opening to help preserve children's native culture and language. In some cases they also aim to compensate for shortcomings[3] in the American education system. […]

Almost every ethnic group now has a cultural program of its own, from Latvians and Nigerians to Chinese, Korean and Japanese immigrants, who have some of the oldest and best-established schools in the United States. Though there are no national statistics encompassing[4] all schools, some individual ethnic groups keep track[5]: the number of Polish-language schools on the East Coast, for instance, has more than doubled since 1990; the number of Korean schools nationwide has boomed from 490 in 1990 to 890 today; and the number of students enrolled in Chinese-heritage programs nationwide has grown by more than 25 per cent since 1995, topping 100,000.

Marcela Maryniak goes to Polish school on Saturdays.

Along with language, culture and history instruction, many of the schools also instill[6] ethnic customs and values. Kin Sheung Wong, principal of the New York Chinese School in Chinatown, the largest such school in North America with more than 3,000 students, says he is still shocked by the degree of freedom bestowed[7]

[1] **influx** mass arrival or incoming – [2] **to cram** (*infml*) *pauken* – [3] **shortcoming** a lack of – [4] **to encompass** to constitute or include – [5] **to keep track** to maintain a record – [6] **to instill** to introduce by gradual efforts – [7] **to bestow** [bɪ'stəʊ] (*fml*) to present as a gift or honour

on American teenagers and the lack of respect they show their elders. After a younger faculty member enters his office, bows and extends a party invitation to him, holding it in both hands, he demonstrates how an unmannered youngster would do it. "In America, this," he says, lightly tossing the paper across his desk with one hand. […]

Many youngsters pass seamlessly[1] between their American world and their ethnic one. Fifteen-year-old Marcela Maryniak, who emigrated from Poland with her parents when she was 5, has been attending a Polish Saturday school virtually since she arrived in Brooklyn. "I guess I'm more American now," she muses. "But there are so many good things about being Polish." For one thing, the food is good, she says. Also, she and her friend Gabriella can gossip in their native language without fear of being understood by their English-speaking peers[2]. But isn't there something ever-so-slightly uncool about sitting in a classroom, discussing Polish Renaissance literature while your friends are out shopping? Not at all, says Marcela. Many of her friends do the same thing on weekends: one goes to Chinese school and another attends Hebrew school. […]

In many places, ethnic heritage schools are becoming increasingly visible. Some are beginning to organize themselves into national networks and to seek connections with public schools. In Montgomery County, Maryland, for instance, Chinese schools have begun accepting non-Asian students for language-immersion[3] programs that are accredited[4] by public schools. Select public schools in other parts of the country have begun experimenting with public schools in other parts of the country with dual-language immersion programs—putting native English speakers in classes with native Spanish speakers, for instance—and teaching a mixed group of kids in one language at a time. Ethnic-heritage schools will never replace American schools for immigrants. But they may forever change them—just as immigrants have permanently transformed America itself.

Newsweek, April 2, 2001, pp. 74–75

Culture classes ...

Why do some foreign pupils attend culture schools in the US?

... near you

Find out about similar programs offered in your city. Report about them to your class. ➜ Method kit, Presentation, p. 309

Translation

Translate ll. 36–63 ("Many youngsters … America itself."). Pay attention to the verb tenses and indirect speech. First work alone, then compare with your partner.

[1]**seamless** *nahtlos* – [2]**peer** sb equal in age and standing – [3]**language-immersion program** course in which the student hears only the target language – [4]**accredited** officially recognized

Kris Axtman

African-Americans Give Houston Top Marks

Brett Grace was torn. Rising fast in Houston's banking scene, he knew his next career move was New York, the financial capital of the world. He was set to leave until his father and mother—executives at Compaq and Texaco—talked some sense into him.

"I would have been stupid to leave. The opportunities in Houston are booming ... It's definitely the place to be," says Mr. Grace, a loan officer at Washington Mutual. "I'm gonna ride this little crest[1] as long as I can."

Dressed smartly in a gray suit and pale orange shirt, Grace is one of hundreds of thousands of African-Americans living—and prospering[2]—in Houston. While many US cities are struggling under old hurts and new prejudices, this bayou[3] city is known for embracing diversity and fostering[4] success—regardless of race.

In fact, a recent survey of online readers of "Black Enterprise" placed Houston as the No. 1 US city for African-Americans to live, work, and play. [...]

"We sometimes look at New York and Los Angeles as the cultural epicenters of America, but they are just too big and expensive for many people," says Derek Dingle, the magazine's executive editor. "Houston is an accessible[5], dynamic city with a low cost of living, affordable housing, and amazing job opportunities. African-Americans look at all that and think, 'I can make a name for myself here.'"

While educators see the survey, like most Internet surveys, as unscientific, it backs up a perception held here in Houston by many in the black community: With a bit of effort, anybody can succeed.

In fact, ever since the Allen brothers floated[6] up the mosquito-infested Buffalo Bayou in 1836 and deemed[7] the swamp[8] land livable, Houston's creed[9] has been business first, ideology second.

"Business first, ideology second"—how is that put into practice in Houston?

That's not to say that Houston wasn't racist in many ways. It was part of the Confederacy, after all, Segregation was enforced in restaurants and other public facilities, not by law but by custom.

In more recent decades, the city has faced charges of police brutality, a steady exodus of whites to the suburbs, and only now has its first black mayor. But its entrepreneurial[10] spirit has helped the city make steady, if still incomplete, progress on racial matters.

[1] **crest** (of a wave) (*idm*) point of greatest success, happiness, etc – [2] **to prosper** to be successful, esp financially – [3] **bayou** (US) ['bʌɪu] in the southern States, part of a river away from the main stream that moves slowly and contains many water plants – [4] **to foster** to support – [5] **accessible** able to be reached – [6] **to float** to move slowly on the surface of the water – [7] **to deem** announce; decide – [8] **swamp** *Sumpf* – [9] **creed** belief – [10] **entrepreneur** ['ɒntrəprə'nɜ:] businessman

Examples include quiet moves by the city's ruling elite to desegregate lunch counters[1] in 1960, and an early shift toward community policing in the 1980s. […]

The city has enjoyed almost constant economic growth since the Civil War. Its worst downturn occurred, not during the Great Depression as in most other parts of America, but during the oil bust of the 1980s.

"With an expanding economy and plentiful jobs, some of the worst elements of prejudice, racism, discrimination were held at bay[2]. Everybody was too busy." says Cary Wintz, a historian at Texas Southern University here.

As Houston has prospered, doubling its population every 20 years, African-Americans have been the city's cornerstone. Whites have fled[3] and Hispanics and Asians have poured in[4], but the black population has remained solid at roughly 25 percent since 1850.

As the city grew, so too did the housing stock[5], and the city did not impose discriminatory zoning laws.

"African-Americans in Houston weren't forced to live in inferior housing, in ghettos with severe overcrowding," Dr. Wintz says.

◄ Do you know examples of black ghettos?

All this meant that blacks around the turn of the century were better off in Houston than in many cities, enjoying higher homeownership rates than elsewhere. Today, their homeownership rate here is 43 percent, one of the highest in the US for blacks.

"Homeownership is a very important indicator," says Mr. Dingle of Black Enterprise. "It is a symbol of the American dream."

◄ Why is homeownership a symbol of the American dream?

"Our city has been blessed to avoid some of the racial strife[6] experienced in other cities in recent years," says Al Calloway, president of the Houston Citizens Chamber of Commerce[7], which represents the city's black business community. "Sure, there are issues, but our leadership has been up front about[8] recognizing those problems and getting to them soon."

In the civil rights era, for example, with sit-ins[9] sweeping[10] across the South, the city's elite worked with black leaders to come up with a plan. They were determined to integrate the city peacefully and quietly.

The plan was to integrate 70 lunch counters across the city during the last week of August 1960. The local news media, including both the *Houston Chronicle* and *Houston Post*, agreed to a total news blackout. Wire services sent out reports of the lunch-counter integration and the press cover-up, leaving the Austin-based *Texas Observer* to

[1] **lunch counter** flat surface in a restaurant where food is served – [2] **to hold sth/sb at bay** to keep at a distance – [3] **to flee** (fled, fled) to leave quickly – [4] **to pour in** (*fig*) to enter quickly – [5] **stock** supply or amount of sth available for use – [6] **strife** trouble, difficulties – [7] **Chamber of Commerce** *Handelskammer* – [8] **to be up front about sth** open and willing to discuss sth – [9] **sit-in** demonstration, etc, in which people occupy a workplace, public building, etc – [10] **to sweep** to move suddenly and with force over an area

conclude that "Texans everywhere but Houston read about lunch-counter integration."

And so it was that Houston emerged[1] as the only major US city not to have a race riot[2]—a distinction it still holds today.

What effect does umemployment have on racial relations?

Chamber president Mr. Calloway concedes[3] that conflict is easier to avoid in the current era of abundant[4] jobs. [...]

Top US cities for blacks

1. Houston, TX
2. Washington, DC
3. Atlanta, GA
4. Charlotte, NC
5. Memphis, TN
6. Detroit, MI
7. Baltimore, MD
8. Dallas, TX
9. Chicago, IL
10. Philadelphia, PA

The Christian Science Monitor, June 18, 2001, p. 5

America in depth

Give a brief report on one of the following topics, all of which are significant for an understanding of America:

- segregation
- lunch counter integration
- the Great Depression
- zoning laws
- sit-ins
- Confederacy

➩ Method kit, Presentation, p. 309

Antonyms

Find the antonyms of the following words, keeping in mind their specific meaning within the context you find them here:
to rise (l. 1), to leave (l. 3), stupid (l. 5), crest (l. 7), diversity (l. 14), online (l. 16), expensive (l. 21), dynamic (l. 23), to float (l. 31), bust (l. 51), plentiful (l. 53), inferior (l. 64), avoid (l. 72), elite (l. 79).

Internet research

Find out about Houston's recent population growth, taking into consideration the increases in the numbers of Blacks, Whites, Hispanics and Asians. What trends do you notice and how might you explain these? How do Houston's demographics compare to those of the USA in general?
www.census.gov/prod/2001pubs/statab/sec01.pdf

➩ Method kit, Internet research, p. 304

	Percentage of the population in Houston		Percentage of the population in the USA	
	1990	2000	1990	2000
Blacks			12.3	12.8
Whites			83.9	82.2
Hispanics			9.0	11.8
Asians			3.0	4.1

[1] **to emerge** (as sth) to develop and become noticeable, important or prominent – [2] **riot** violent demonstration – [3] **to concede** to admit to be true – [4] **abundant** plentiful

Ralph Linton

One Hundred Percent American

Write down a list of items which you believe to be—or at least which you consider—100% American.

There can be no question about the average American's Americanism or his desire to preserve this precious heritage at all costs. Nevertheless, some insidious[1] foreign ideas have already wormed their way into his civilization without his realizing what was going on. Thus dawn finds the unsuspecting patriot garbed[2] in pajamas, a garment[3] of East Indian origin; and lying in a bed built on a pattern which originated in either Persia or Asia Minor. He is muffled[4] to the ears in un-American materials: cotton, first domesticated in India; linen, domesticated in the Near East; wool from an animal native to Asia Minor; or silk whose uses were first discovered by the Chinese. All these substances have been transformed into cloth by methods invented in Southwestern Asia. If the weather is cold enough he may even be sleeping under an eiderdown quilt invented in Scandinavia.

On awakening he glances at the clock, a medieval[5] European invention, uses one potent Latin word in abbreviated form, rises in haste, and goes to the bathroom. Here, if he stops to think about it, he must feel himself in the presence of a great American institution; he will have heard stories of both the quality and frequency of foreign plumbing[6] and will know that in no other country does the average man perform his ablutions[7] in the midst of such splendor[8]. But the insidious foreign influence pursues him even here. Glass was invented by the ancient Egyptians, the use of glazed tiles for floors and walls in the Near East, porcelain in China, and the art of enameling[9] on metal by Mediterranean artisans of the Bronze Age. Even his bathtub and toilet are but slightly modified copies of Roman originals. The only purely American contribution to the ensemble is the steam radiator[10], against which our patriot very briefly and unintentionally places his posterior[11].

◄ What might the word be?

◄ What stories?

In this bathroom the American washes with soap invented by the ancient Gauls. Next he cleans his teeth, a subversive European practice which did not invade America until the latter part of the eighteenth century. He then shaves, a masochistic rite first developed by the heathen[12] priests of ancient Egypt and Sumer[13]. The process is made less of a penance by the fact that his razor is of steel, an iron-carbon alloy[14] discovered in either India or Turkestan. Lastly, he dries himself on a Turkish towel.

◄ Why 'subversive'?

Returning to the bedroom …

American Mercury, 40 (1937), pp. 427–429

[1] **insidious** working harmfully – [2] **to garb** to clothe – [3] **garment** piece of clothing – [4] **to muffle** here: to wrap up tightly – [5] **medieval** [medɪ'i:vəl] from the Middle Ages – [6] **plumbing** *Wasserleitungen* – [7] **ablution** act of washing clean – [8] **splendor** brilliance – [9] **enamel** [-'--] *Email* – [10] **radiator** heating device – [11] **posterior** backside – [12] **heathen** ['hi:ðn] *heidnisch* – [13] **Sumer** ['--] – [14] **alloy** *Legierung*

Discussing the text

Discuss the article in groups.
Designate one member of your group as scribe/reporter. He or she will take notes on your discussion and present your collective response to the class. Formulate at least three statements indicating your group's response to the article.

Continuation

Continue the daily routine in the same style based on information you find, e.g. in an encyclopedia.

Primary Colours

The new census[1] figures show America absorbing the most profound change in its racial and cultural make-up in a century, but barriers still exist.

White, black, red, yellow, brown or a mix of them all, every colour of American is thriving[2]. That was the Census Bureau's message this week as it released details on race from last year's national headcount. Every racial or ethnic group, including the white majority, is growing larger.

Last year's snapshot shows 281.4 million people inside America's borders, whether legally or not: 13% more than a decade earlier. Some 211 million of them say they are white, a rise of 12 million, but a slightly lower share of the total than last time. The white share is

How have these two factors affected the share of whites?

[1] **census** ['sensəs] official count of a country's total population – [2] **to thrive** to develop well and healthy

dipping as other groups grow faster, thanks to immigration and to higher birth rates.

Latinos have made most gains. That group has soared[1] to 35.3 million people, and for the first time is larger than the black total. Although no one doubted blacks would eventually lose their spot as America's top minority, few thought it would happen quite so soon.

◄ What effect might this have on America?

Some blacks have reacted defensively. The growth, they say, is explained by a re-ordering of questions on the census form that put the Latino choice higher up. The Latino trend will be less pronounced[2] next time, because this census caught many people who were missed in the past. Most important, the powers that decided that the term Latino is not racial, but ethnic. So anybody who chose to put down "Hispanic or Latino," also had to pick a race. Half chose white; most of the rest chose a category called "some other race." (One price of this absurd piece of political correctness is that very few of the figures in the Census add up.)

The black population saw a hefty[3] increase in numbers, partly because of a campaign by minority groups to get more people to send back their census forms. An estimated 3.3 million people were still missed, most of them from minority groups. But the Census Bureau and the government have failed to find a satisfactory method to make good the "undercount."

◄ How might minority groups achieve this?

Other, smaller groups appear to have grown even more. The total for native Americans rose by more than a quarter, Asians by nearly a half and "other races" by more than a half. Add in the 7 million (2.4 % of the total) people who were allowed for the first time to identify with two or more racial groups (for example both Asian and white), and the increases are even more striking.

This new option was taken up most eagerly by young people, who are more likely to have parents of mixed race and are more likely to be relaxed about admitting it. They may also be swung by the "Dances with Wolves" phenomenon: aspiring to have some interesting warrior ancestors.

The Census Bureau predicts[4] that there will be many more mixed-race people in the future. "These small but significant numbers point to where we are going," says Gregory Rodriguez of the New America Foundation in Washington, DC. "Those born now will be farther away from the time of segregation; kids will feel less bound by ethnicities. America is diversifying." As generations pass through mixed colleges and marry across racial lines, black and white America may give way to a blend[5] of browns.

What does this melting pot amount to? Well, a lot—if you set modern multicultural America down alongside either Europe, which seems to be running out of people, or the 1960s "Guess who's coming to dinner?" America, which was basically a black-and-

[1] **to soar** to go upward esp far or fast – [2] **pronounced** here: *deutlich* – [3] **hefty** of considerable size or amount – [4] **to predict** to see or describe a future happening – [5] **blend** the joining of elements so that one is not clearly separate from the others

What countries are at dis-/advantages concerning human capital?

white affair. A possible 63 combinations of race (rising to 126 permutations[1] if you add in the Latino option) were available on the census form, up from just six in the past. If you believe that competitive advantage is wrapped up in human capital, then the change in America's people will surely affect its future far more than a mere device[2] such as the Internet.

On the other hand, it is possible to exaggerate just how quickly the melting pot is cooking this stew. William Frey, a demographer at the University of Michigan, applauds as democratic the fact that Americans can "write down who they think they are," but he insists that separation between races remains the norm. The census seems to back him up: 97 % of Americans still describe themselves as belonging to just one race.

The Economist, March 17, 2001, pp. 53–54

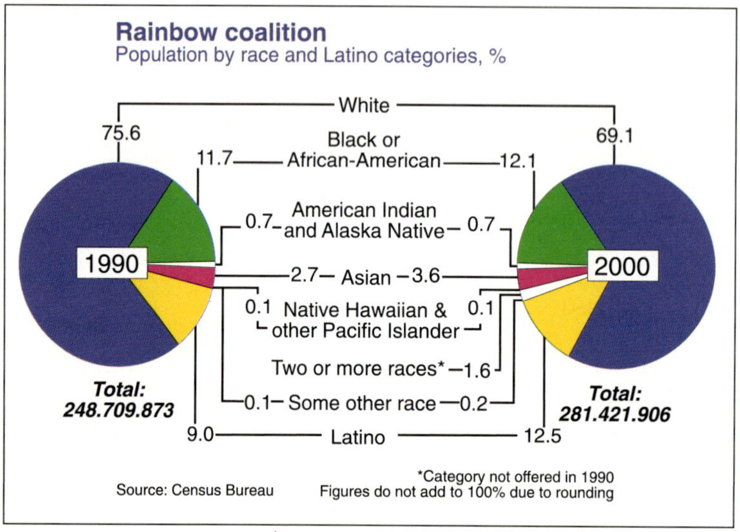

Language of demographics

Collect words and phrases that are useful for talking or writing about demographics.

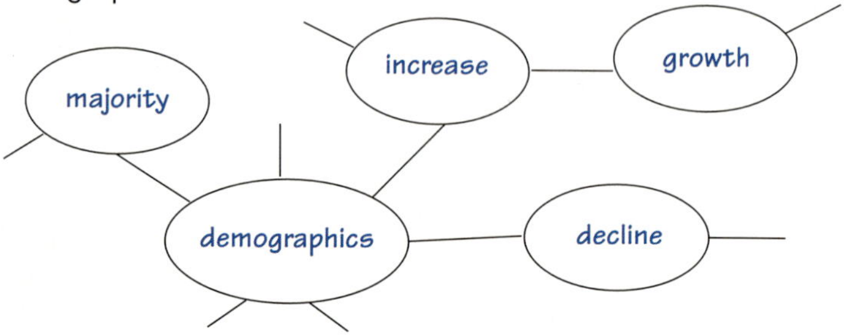

Comment

Comment on the fact that young people are more relaxed about admitting that they have parents of mixed race. Why might this be the case? How may it affect future generations?

[1] **permutation** here: different ways of combination – [2] **device** instrument

Certain Inalienable Rights … and Wrongs

Martin Luther King Jr.

Letter From a Birmingham Jail

What do you know about King's work within the civil rights movement in America?

In April 1963, Martin Luther King, Jr. was taken to prison after a confrontation with Public Safety Commissioner "Bull" Connor and other Birmingham city authorities. Connor's police force used beatings, fire hoses[1], and vicious[2] dogs in an effort to keep blacks from demonstrating in what otherwise may have been peaceful parades in downtown Birmingham. Because King had been criticized by a group of white clergymen who blamed him for starting the violence, he wrote the following letter of reply to his colleagues, smuggling it out of jail on scraps of toilet tissue and in the margins of newspapers. This document shows King in a state of despair, yet it is an eloquent declaration of the intense moral concern for oppressed humanity which was King's legacy[3] to his fellow Americans. This letter was the genesis[4] of his third book, called *Why We Can't Wait.*

King is arrested during a lunch counter sit-in.

We know through painful experience that freedom is never given by the oppressor … For years now I have heard the word "Wait!" It rings in the ear of every Negro with piercing[5] familiarity. This "Wait" has almost always meant "Never."

We have waited for more than 340 years for our constitutional and God-given rights. The nations of Asia and Africa are moving with jet-like speed toward the goal of political independence, and we still creep[6] at horse-and-buggy pace[7] toward the gaining of a cup of coffee at a lunch counter[8]. I guess it is easy for those who have never felt the stinging[9] darts of segregation to say, "Wait."

But when you have seen vicious mobs[10] lynch your mothers and fathers at will[11] and drown[12] your sisters and brothers at whim[13];

What strikes you about the syntax in this paragraph?

[1] **fire hose** *Feuerwehrschlauch* – [2] **vicious** ['viʃəs] aggressive, savage – [3] **legacy** *Vermächtnis* – [4] **genesis** beginning, origin – [5] **to pierce** to go in and through sth – [6] **to creep** to move or proceed very slowly – [7] **pace** rate of speed – [8] **lunch counter** flat surface in a restaurant where food is served – [9] **to sting** to cause to suffer keenly in the mind or feelings – [10] **mob** large noisy crowd often using violence – [11] **to do sth at will** to do sth as or when one wishes – [12] **to drown** to kill sb by holding him/her under water – [13] **to do sth at whim** to act impulsively

when you have seen hatefilled policemen curse, kick, brutalize and even kill your black brothers and sisters; when you suddenly find your tongue twisted and your speech stammering[1] as you seek to explain to your six-year-old daughter why she can't go to the public amusement park[2] that has just been advertised on television, and see tears welling up[3] in her eyes when she is told that "Funtown" is closed to colored children, and see the depressing cloud of inferiority begin to form in her little mental sky, and see her begin to distort[4] her little personality by unconsciously developing a bitterness toward white people; when you are humiliated day in and day out by nagging[5] signs reading "white" and "colored," when your first name becomes "nigger" and your middle name becomes "boy" (however old you are) and your last name becomes "John," and when your wife and mother are never given the respected title "Mrs."; when you are harried[6] by day and haunted by night by the fact that you are a Negro, living constantly at tiptoe[7] stance[8], never quite knowing what to expect next, and plagued with inner fears and outer resentments; when you are forever fighting a degenerating[9] sense of "nobodyness"; then you will understand why we find it difficult to wait. I hope you can understand our legitimate impatience.

What does King ➤ want to convey with this coining?

In no sense do I advocate[10] evading[11] or defying[12] the law as the rabid[13] segregationist would do. This would lead to anarchy. One who breaks an unjust law must do so openly, lovingly … with a willingness to accept the penalty. I submit that an individual who breaks a law that conscience tells him is unjust, and willingly accepts the penalty by staying in jail to arouse the conscience of the community over its injustice, is expressing the highest respect for law. […]

The question is not whether we will be extremists but what kind of extremist will we be. Will we be extremists for hate or will we be extremists for love? Will we be extremists for the preservation[14] of injustice—or will we be extremists for the cause of justice? In that dramatic scene on Calvary's hill[15], three men were crucified for the same crime—the crime of extremism. Two were extremists for immorality, and thus fell below their environment. So, after all, maybe the South, the nation and the world are in dire[16] need of creative extremists.

Before the Pilgrims landed at Plymouth, we were here. Before the pen of Jefferson etched[17] across the pages of history the majestic words of the Declaration of Independence, we were here. For more than two centuries, our foreparents labored[18] in this country without wages; they made cotton "king," and they built the homes of

What strikes ➤ you about the word *foreparents*?

[1] **to stammer** to speak with sudden pauses – [2] **amusement park** an open area with swings, rides, etc – [3] **to well up** to rise to the surface, ready to flow – [4] **to distort** to twist or pull sth out of its normal shape – [5] **to nag** to annoy, to worry – [6] **harry** to disturb or annoy sb with repeated attacks – [7] **tiptoe** (*adj*) cautious – [8] **stance** attitude or position – [9] **to degenerate** to pass into a worse state than one which is considered normal or desirable – [10] **to advocate** to speak in favour of – [11] **to evade** to avoid – [12] **to defy** to disobey, to resist – [13] **rabid** (*adj*) *tollwütig* – [14] **preservation** the action of keeping sth in its original state or in good condition – [15] **Calvary's hill** hill outside ancient Jerusalem where Jesus was crucified – [16] **dire** here: extreme – [17] **to etch** to imprint clearly – [18] **to labor** (Brit labour) to work

their masters in the midst of brutal injustice and shameful humiliation, and yet out of a bottomless[1] vitality[2], they continued to thrive[3] and develop. If the inexpressible cruelties of slavery could not stop us, the opposition we now face will surely fail. We will win our freedom because the sacred[4] heritage[5] of our nation and the eternal will of God are embodied[6] in our echoing demands.

Rhetoric

1. Identify examples of King's mastery of rhetorical devices (parallelism, metaphor, simile, alliteration, allusion, antithesis, etc).
   ➩ Language kit, p. 316 ff.
2. Identify the *-ing* forms in ll. 4, 8, 10, 17, 20, 23, 30, 35, 40, 62. Substitute or paraphrase each one in its context. For example: with **piercing** familiarity (*present participle*) → with **painful** familiarity
3. Noun prefixes like *in-* (independence, injustice) and *im-* (impatience, immorality) are highly productive. Work with your dictionary and find five further words beginning with *in-* and five beginning with *im-*. Find the corresponding adjectives.

noun with *in-* or *im-*	corresponding adjective(s)
independence injustice impatience immorality	independent injust (unjust) impatient immoral

4. Find the related adjective(s), verb(s) or noun(s) of the following words:
   vicious (l. 13), to curse, (l. 15) to distort (l. 22), to humiliate (l. 24), resentment (ll. 31f.), to evade (l. 35), to defy (l. 35), unjust (l. 37), eternal (l. 62), to embody (l. 62).
   An example:

noun	verb	adjective
relation, relative, relationship, etc	to relate	relative, relational, etc

5. Explain the word order in l. 35 "In no sense do I advocate …".

[1] **bottomless** limitless – [2] **vitality** physical or intellectual energy – [3] **to thrive** to make steady progress; prosper – [4] **sacred** [seɪkrɪd] worthy of respect – [5] **heritage** something that is passed down from earlier generations – [6] **to embody** to include or contain

Translation

Translate ll. 6–34 ("We have waited ... impatience.") in groups. Pay particular attention to the syntax and the idioms. Exchange your translations and discuss the other ones' German texts in your group.

Creating understanding

1. Trying to understand their "legitimate impatience": Write the response that King's white brethren might have given. Before you write, decide whether or not they understand his situation.
2. Create a pamphlet, seeking support for the blacks' struggle for justice by using phrases from the text.

Rudolph Kizerman

Martians[1]

Hey, Brother Soul,
suppose
you woke up
one morning
and heard on the radio
that the Martians had landed,
and they were Black
but were a little bit rough[2]
on the other brothers on earth,
because they're white.
Would you go out to meet them
on a mission of arbitration[3]?

The dialogue Who is talking to whom?

Dealing with the message

1. What kind of scenario is being portrayed here?
2. Answer the question posed in the poem.

[1] **martian** *Marsianer* – [2] **to be rough on sb** to be violent, not gentle with sb – [3] **arbitration** peace negotiation

The Electoral System and the Voting Citizen

Info

Growing up in the US, Americans receive little theoretical information about the electoral system in school and no practical information from official sources. That means when they turn 18 and are first allowed to vote, they are often unaware of the official procedure involved. Americans have to register with the local authorities so that their names appear on the list on election day. In most states, the initiative usually must be taken by the individual citizen to become a registered voter. Partly for this reason registration figures have often been proportionately lower in the United States than in western Europe or even in Australia, where citizens are fined for not voting. Another reason is the relatively high number of mobile Americans who are temporarily disqualified by residence or other legal requirements.
In former times in some backward parts of the US, literacy tests or poll taxes[1] imposed by county governments intentionally kept certain groups of people from voting. The Voting Rights Act of 1965 took the registration process out of the hands of local election officials in many counties, providing instead for federal registrars. The rural[2] population was often underrepresented because a trip to the nearest courthouse meant a day they could not spend working. Today the majority of states allow workers to take off several hours on election day (officially, the first Tuesday after the first Monday in November) to cast their votes.

The Electoral College

The president and the vice president are the only elected federal officials not chosen by direct vote of the people. They are elected by the members of the Electoral College, an institution provided for in the Constitution. The Electoral College system protects the interests of less populous states by setting the number of electoral votes in each state equal to the number of members of congress and senators representing that state in Washington. Thus, a state with only one representative has at least three electoral votes. In addition to protecting the rights of the smaller states, the Founding Fathers[3] were also perhaps not totally at ease with turning over the election process to the masses. In the end, the system leaves the election of the president and vice president to the 538 more or less elite members that make up the Electoral College.
The rest of the world became familiar with this system during the 2000 presidential elections. The media reported on how an absolute majority of 270 electoral votes is needed to elect the president and vice president.
As the 2000 election for the world's most powerful leader came down to Florida's 25 electoral votes, however, people began asking who exactly these electors are. In most cases, they are political party members nominated by their party at their respective state conventions. With nothing more than long-established custom dictating whom they vote for, the world was wondering if any of these party

[1] **poll tax** tax that must be paid at the same rate by every person or every adult in a particular area – [2] **rural** *ländlich* – [3] **Founding Father** member of the convention that wrote the U.S. Constitution in 1787

Info

An absolute majority of 270 electoral votes is needed to elect the president and vice president.

members might ultimately cast his or her vote for the opposing party's candidate, thus changing the final result of the election. While it is possible that an elector could ignore the results of the popular vote, that occurs very rarely.
As it turned out George W. Bush lost the popular vote to Al Gore (50,455,156 to 50,992,335) yet won the electoral vote (271 to 266). This seemingly undemocratic phenomenon had occurred in the elections of 1876 and 1888 as well. When the 2000 election was finally decided by the 537 votes in Florida that tipped the scales[1], throwing all 25 of Florida's electoral votes into the hands of the Republicans, people around the world began wondering how easily it might have gone the other way. As the election process dragged on[2] for 35 days, the foreign media grinned at the problems this technologically advanced country was having to count its votes properly.

[1]**scales** instrument for weighing – [2]**drag on** to go too long so that sth becomes boring

America counts

Did the problem result from low voter turnout (51%), spoiled ballots, or were there other irregularities? These fundamental questions were raised after the election and officials, including former presidents Jimmy Carter and Gerald Ford, led a study on election reform for the seemingly troubled system.

The first problem lay in counting the votes correctly. Every election has its share of spoiled ballots, including "overvotes" (more than one candidate is selected), "undervotes" (no selection is made for an office), and punch cards with "hanging" or "dimpled[1]" chads[2]. Although this last group was particularly problematic in Florida during the 2000 presidential election, nearly 180,000 spoiled ballots were thrown out of the final count across the country that year.

Literacy[3] discrimination, ineligible[4] absentee[5] ballots, inaccurate registration lists, illegal voting, media influence, racial discrimination, and confusing ballots were cited as some of the irregularities during the 2000 presidential election. And yet others pointed once again to the Electoral College, calling it elitist and undemocratic, and claiming it should be changed. In more than 200 years, 700 proposals by Congress to change the Electoral College have been made as potential constitutional amendments—more than about any other issue. Moreover, in most polls, Americans favour abolishing the Electoral College.

[1]**dimple** slight depression or indentation in a surface – [2]**chad** small piece of paper generated by punching a hole in a data card – [3]**literacy** ability to read and write – [4]**ineligible** legally or officially disqualified – [5]**absentee** here: person who lives away from his or her home

Voices on Votes

Timothy J. Pearson, a high school student in Middleport, NY, said, "I can remember how surprised my US History class was when we were taught about the Electoral College. We could hardly believe that many of the things we believed to be undemocratic were used in our own presidential voting system. Learning about the Electoral College can be enough for most people to lose faith in presidential elections in this country. The drop in the number of young voters can be attributed to our lack of faith in the system that we are being asked to partake in." On the other hand, local elections often see as few as 20% of the registered voters going to the polls.

Emily C. Talmage, a student of environmental education, believes voter apathy among young adults is a result of another phenomenon. "Most of us are wrapped up in our daily lives, and the political process is something far away from us. My generation has not experienced hardship, in the form of a war or a food shortage. We assume that we will always be provided for because our country is so affluent. As long as our beef comes from the supermarket, we don't have to think about the rainforest destruction or the water pollution caused by factory farming. We don't see this, and are not held accountable[1] by anyone for the choices we make as consumers, which have political effects. The United States likes to hide ugliness, so most of us do not see the havoc we wreak[2] on the natural world or on other cultures. If we were ever to experience the ramifications[3] of our actions, we might take a little more interest in the political process."

Class project

1. Divide into groups and investigate various aspects of the US election process, using the following Internet addresses. Before you do the research, decide on a few specific questions you hope to answer during your research. Report to the class about your findings.

How the Electoral College works	www.fec.gov/pages/eeworks.htm
A brief history of the Electoral College	www.fec.gov/pdf/eleccoll.pdf
US Constitution voting provisions	www.fec.gov/votregis/constitutionalprovisio.htm
FAQ about voter registration	www.fec.gov/pages/Faqvoterreg.htm
2000 Presidential election results	http://fecweb1.fec.gov/pubrec/2000presgeresults.htm

2. Again working in groups, analyse the following suggestions for improving the US electoral system. Based on what you have learned about this system, which of the following suggestions do you think might really work? Discuss your results with the whole class.

[1] **to hold sb accountable for sth** to hold sb responsible for sth – [2] **to wreak** [ri:k] **havoc on sth** to cause destruction – [3] **ramification** any of a large number of complex or unexpected results that follow an action or a decision; *Auswirkungen*

Suggestions for Improving the Electoral System

Some of the ideas concerning election reform that were reported in *Newsweek's* "Participation in Government Newsletter: Election Reform" in the wake of the 2000 election included the following:

- Increase the accuracy of voter registration lists by using a central database maintained at the state level.
- Require all students, before graduating from high school, to successfully complete a civics[1] course or participate in a Voter Registration and Education program.
- Publish sample ballots that look exactly the same as the one that voters will receive at the polls.
- Eliminate punch-card ballots.
- Make Election Day a national holiday.
- Allow voting to continue over a two-day period.
- Hold elections on a weekend.
- Establish a uniform closing time for all polling places in the country.
- Simplify the application process for absentee voting.
- Establish a uniform voting system throughout the state.
- Require poll workers to hand-inspect each ballot for errors before the voter puts it in a box to be counted.
- In order to encourage third-party participation, allow the voter to make a first and a second choice for president. If the first-choice candidate does not receive a specific percentage of the vote, then the ballots will be immediately recounted, using the voter's second choice.
- Adopt a formula for distributing state electoral votes proportionate to the popular vote in that state.
- Establish consistent standards and time frames for recounts.
- Prohibit exit polling, which is when a sample of voters are asked whom they voted for as they leave a polling place. This is used especially to predict the outcome of an election or to determine the opinions and characteristics of the candidates' supporters.

During election 2000 every punch card in certain areas of Florida was examined carefully by a group of officials.

[1] **civics** branch of political science that deals with civic affairs and the rights and duties of citizens

Info

The Supreme Court and Capital Punishment

Nearly as important as the Constitution for the functioning of the United States' legal system are the landmark[1] decisions made by the Supreme Court. These are interpretations of the law by the nine justices of the nation's most powerful court. They are called on to hear cases involving, for instance: the Constitution, including Americans' basic rights; laws and treaties of the United States; cases affecting foreign dignitaries[2]; controversies in which the US government is involved; and controversies between states (or their citizens) and foreign nations (or their citizens).

Their decisions have often involved the definition—and sometimes re-definition—of terms such as *citizen* [Dred Scott v. Sanford 1857], *equal* [Plessy v. Ferguson 1896 and Brown v. Board of Education 1954], *freedom of speech and press* [Schenck v. U.S. 1919], *guarantee of personal liberty* [Bolling v. Sharpe 1954], *obscene* [Roth v. U.S. 1957] and *general standards of decency* [NEA v. Finley 1998], *average person* and *local community* [Miller v. California 1973], *malice*[3] [New York Times Co. v. Sullivan 1964], *personal privacy* [Griswold v. Connecticut 1965], *person* [Roe v. Wade 1973], *cruel and unusual punishment* [Gregg v. Georgia 1976], and *executive privilege of immunity* [Clinton v. Jones 1997].

When the country was founded, full citizens' rights were not automatically extended to everybody. Women could not vote, for example; and slaves were considered property, being counted as only three-fifths of a person in determining the number of congressmen each state could elect to the House of Representatives in the early days.

The death penalty was reinstated[4] in 1976 after the justices of the Supreme Court decided that death, as a punishment for persons convicted of first degree murder, did not necessarily constitute "cruel and unusual punishment," something American citizens are protected from by the Eighth Amendment. However, the Court ruled that the sentencing[5] judge and jury must consider the individual character of the offender and the circumstances of the particular case, which was supposed to rule out sending the "wrong people" to the electric chair.

[1] **landmark** event marking an important stage of development or a turning point in history – [2] **dignitary** person of high rank or position – [3] **malice** (*law*) *böse Absicht* – [4] **to reinstate** to restore sb or sth to his or its previous position – [5] **to sentence** to state that sb is to have a certain punishment

The Case of the Oklahoma City Bombing

Until September 11, 2001, the most infamous case of terrorism in the United States was the bombing of the Murrah Federal Building in Oklahoma City in 1995 in which 168 people were killed. In this case, Timothy McVeigh was found guilty of the bombing and executed in Terre Haute, IN, for that crime in June 2001. As the date of his execution drew closer, McVeigh accepted the fact that the President was not going to commute[1] his death sentence to life imprisonment and that he was going to be put to death. The former Gulf War veteran had become the criminal most deserving of the death penalty, according to its proponents[2]. He was not repentant about his deed; he confessed to the crime; there was no racial bias involved in his case; and he had a good attorney. Although Americans' voices had begun to turn against the death penalty in general (see Figure 1), one relative of an Oklahoma City bombing victim put it this way: "I don't want him to be able to do anyone else any more harm ever again." Looking back in anger at the government that he no longer respected, he claimed: "In the end the score will be Timothy McVeigh: 168, US Government: 1."

Figure 1: Americans' support for the death penalty changes with time.

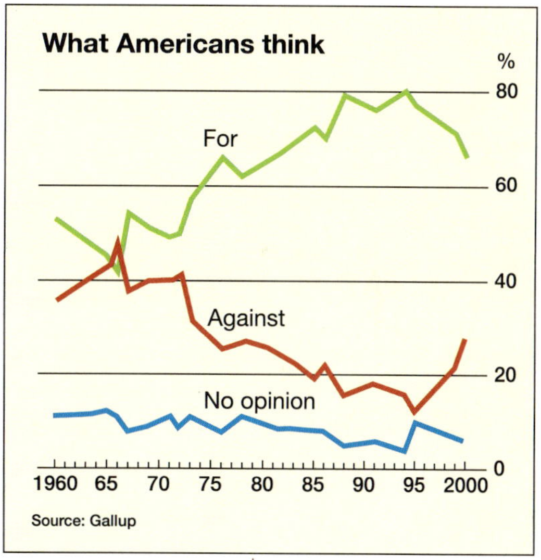

While over 700 individuals have been executed by the states in the past 40 years, his was the first federal execution since 1963. Thirty-eight states permit death penalty sentences (see Figure 2, p. 164), although only 31 have actually carried one out since reinstatement of the death penalty in 1976. Similar to gun control and the abortion issue, which can also be seen as an issue of one person making a choice concerning the life of another, the death penalty is one of the most hotly discussed topics in America. Support for the death penalty rests on two pillars[3]: the desire for retribution, which runs deep in the fundamentally religious United States, and the belief among the public that execution can act as a deterrent[4].

On the other hand, an increasing number of organizations oppose the death penalty. The Murder Victims' Families for Reconciliation[5], a national organization of people who have lost a family member to homicide[6] and oppose the death penalty, made the following statement before Timothy McVeigh's execution: "Our hearts know that pain for which there are no

[1] **to commute** here: to make substitution or exchange – [2] **proponent** (*fml*) person who supports an idea or course of action – [3] **pillar** (*fig*) basic part or feature of a system, organization, belief, etc; *Säule* – [4] **deterrent** thing that makes sb less likely to do sth – [5] **reconciliation** an end to a disagreement and the start of a good relationship again; *Versöhnung* – [6] **homicide** crime of killing sb deliberately

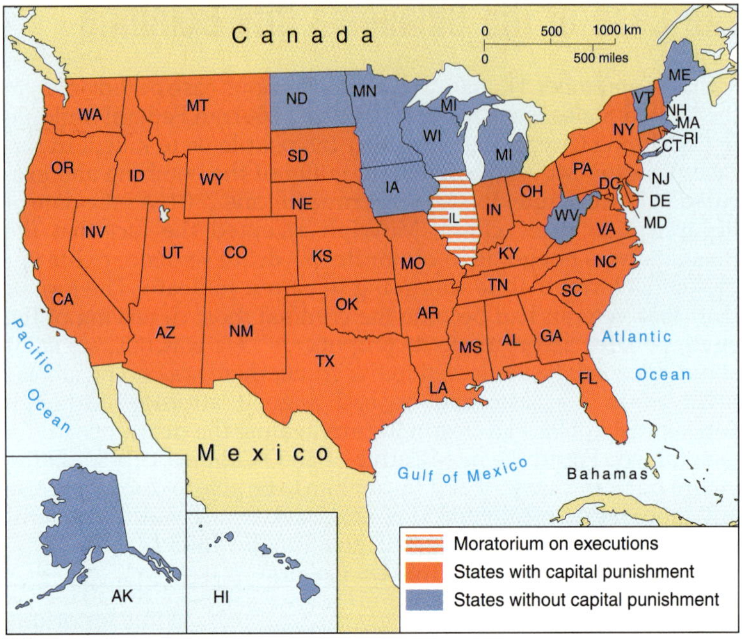

Figure 2: The death penalty is legal in 38 states.

words. With the surviving family members of those killed in the Oklahoma City bombing, we share lives that involve a continual healing process. Empty chairs at holidays, disbelief and anger at unexpected times, and moments of quiet tears are part of our reality as victims. And as victims, we oppose the death penalty … The ritual of executions damages all of us in society and creates another grieving[1] family. With the focus on putting someone to death, capital punishment makes anti-heroes out of murderers, while the lives of victims are forgotten and the needs of survivors are often ignored. Everyone knows the name of the bomber; few know the names of the 168 who died."

In a country where the national mottos are "In God We Trust" and "*E pluribus unum*" (out of many, one), there are still numerous issues on which many voices have not yet become united. Capital punishment is but one of these. Over 60% of those Americans polled still consider the death penalty fitting punishment for violent crimes; however, public support for it drops to around 50% when voters are offered the alternative of life without parole[2]. Increasing pressure from some of the 108 countries that have so far abolished the death

[1] **to grieve** to feel very sad, esp because sb has died – [2] **parole** *Entlassung auf Bewährung*

penalty may convince more Americans to change their attitudes toward it. Others will patiently wait for the Supreme Court to rule it unconstitutional. Some people point out that more important issues need solving first. The annual execution of 100 criminals, some say, or the mental agony[1] of the nearly 4000 death row[2] inmates[3] wondering when they will be executed is hardly as important as working to solve bigger problems, such as terrorism, immigration and environmental issues, inadequacies in education and health care, poverty, drugs or child abuse.

Unfortunately, the Constitution says very little about how to solve these specific problems, so what shall be our guide?

What shall be your guide?

Discuss the question at the end of the text with your classmates.

Landmark decisions

1. Study one or two cases of "landmark decisions" (see Info-text: The Supreme Court and Capital Punishment) on the Internet:
   - www.uscourts.gov

   ➜ Method kit, Internet research, p. 304
2. Present your case as a short summary to your class.

   ➜ Method kit, Presentation, p. 309

Death penalty

Gather information about the death penalty:

www.fireball.de (insert "death penalty" and click "weltweit")

or browse the popular newspapers on the Internet. You will find addresses here:

➜ Method kit, Internet research, p. 304

Dead Man Walking

Dead Man Walking is a film about capital punishment. Touching such universal themes as revenge and redemption, crime and punishment, and fear and salvation, the movie explores the relationship between Matthew Poncelet, a convicted rapist/murderer on death row, and his spiritual advisor, Sister Helen Prejean.

➜ Method kit, Film analysis, p. 306

[1] **agony** extreme mental or physical suffering – [2] **death row** a group of prison cells for prisoners condemned to death – [3] **inmate** any of a number of people living together e.g. in a prison

America's Global Role

There is no country on earth that is not touched by America, for we have become the motive force for freedom and democracy in the world. And there is no country in the world that does not touch us. We are a country of countries with a citizen in our ranks from every land. We are attached by a thousand cords to the world at large, to its teeming[1] cities, to its remotest[2] regions, to its oldest civilizations, to its newest cries for freedom. This means that we have an interest in every place on this Earth, that we need to lead, to guide, to help in every country that has a desire to be free, open and prosperous.

Colin L. Powell, Secretary of State (from an official statement, 2000)

Challenges, Opportunities, Choices

On September 11, 2001, terror struck at the heart of the United States, destroying the World Trade Center, scarring[3] the Pentagon and leaving thousands dead. Yet Americans in their grief stood together, unbowed[4], as a new kind of war began.
Page one newspaper headlines from the days following the attacks show international responses and trace how the mystery slowly unfolded:

[1] **to teem** to be full of people, animals, etc, moving around – [2] **remote** far away – [3] **to scar** to leave a scar (*Narbe*) – [4] **to bow** [baʊ] *beugen*

Day 1 Sept. 12	For Washington, a Modern Pearl Harbor World Air Traffic Turns Chaotic Germans Express Solidarity With U.S. After Terrorist Attack Europeans Worry They May Be Hit
Day 2 Sept. 13	Early Clues Point to bin Laden Striking Back: Harsh New Tactics?
Day 3 Sept. 14	Bush Vows[1] to 'Lead World to Victory' FBI Pursues 'Thousands' of Leads[2] in Investigation
Day 4 Sept. 15–16	A Global Outpouring[3] of Grief and Solidarity CIA's Headache: How to Find bin Laden Suspects Lived Openly, Hiding a Deadly Secret
Day 5 Sept. 18	U.S. Stocks Fall Sharply Despite Rate Cuts Bush Says: He Wants bin Laden Brought to Justice 'Dead or Alive' Pakistan Fails to Sway[4] Taliban

Following the trail

On the Internet, find headlines from later stages in the conflict. How do they portray the changing attitudes among the various countries? ➜ Method kit, Internet research, p. 304

Reinterpreting a statement

How does Secretary of State Powell's statement take on a different meaning after the terrorist attacks?

A New Global Popular Culture?

Ask other pupils in your class how affected they are by American popular culture.

America's main export is not found in manufacturing, agriculture, pharmaceuticals, or high technology. It is popular culture. More than two-thirds of movie ticket sales in Western Europe are for U.S. films. The songs of pop stars like Bruce Springsteen and Michael Jackson are anthems[5] for youth around the world. Hamburgers and U.S. soft drinks are consumed in nearly every major city worldwide.

Is the spread of pop culture good for the United States and the rest of the world?

Todd Gitlin, professor of sociology, University of California, Berkeley: "American popular culture is the closest approximation[6] there is today to a global lingua franca[7] […].

[1] **vow** solemn promise – [2] **lead** piece of information that may help to find out the truth or facts about a situation, esp a crime – [3] **outpouring** strong and sudden expression of feeling; *Erguss* – [4] **to sway** to change sb's mind – [5] **anthem** ['ænθəm] *Hymne* – [6] **approximation** a thing that is similar to sth but is not exactly the same – [7] **lingua franca** language used for communication between the people of an area in which several languages are spoken

"The emergence[1] of a global semiculture coexists with local cultures and sensibilities more than it replaces them. As the Norwegian researcher Helge Ronning suggests, global, largely American, popular culture has become, or is in the process of becoming, everyone's second culture. It activates a certain bilingualism.

"Why does American popular culture succeed? Economies of scale[2] are a part of the explanation. The United States can simply undersell other suppliers, but no one is forcing the Danes, for example, to watch Dallas on TV. The dominance of American popular culture is a soft dominance—[... it] has been driven by a single overriding[3] purpose: to entertain. For this reason, [...] it is easy to see why American goods have outdone[4] the competition—British goods were developed in large part for high-culture elevation[5], Soviet goods for didactic purposes."

James Boman, American editor, the (London) *Times Literary Supplement*[6]: "Throughout history, there have been official and unofficial cultures. Young people have gravitated[7] to the open, unstructured unofficial culture. What we're calling the American popular culture is increasingly not American. It is an international, youth culture."

Pico Iyer, columnist *Time* magazine: "Pop culture makes the world go 'round, and America makes the best pop culture. By now, indeed, such products represent the largest single source of America's export earnings, even as America remains the single most popular destination[8] for immigrant visas. The more straitened[9] or shut off a culture, the more urgent its hunger for all the qualities it associates with America: freedom and wealth and modernity."

George Gerbner, professor of communications, University of Pennsylvania: "A child today is born into a home in which a television set is turned on an average of seven hours a day. Most of the stories today are told not by the parent, not by the school, not by the church, and in many places not by the native country or by America, but by a handful of transnational conglomerates[10] that have something to sell on TV. Here the chances of exploitation[11] or manipulation are much greater. So we do not have a direct expression of American values. What we have is a global marketing operation. It profoundly affects the way children grow up, and the way we think about citizenship."

Karlyn Keene, editor, *The American Enterprise* magazine: "If American culture is corrupting, why is it that 78 percent of secondary school students in a recent poll say that having a good marriage is extremely important to them, that 68 percent say they and their

[1] **emergence** cf. to emerge: to develop and become noticeable – [2] **of scale** the relative size of sth – [3] **overriding** more important than any other considerations – [4] **outdone** cf. to outdo – [5] **elevation** cf. to elevate: to raise sth to a higher place or rank – [6] **supplement** book or section of a book that treats a special subject – [7] **to gravitate** to move towards sth gradually but steadily – [8] **destination** place to which sb is going or being sent – [9] **straitened** in a difficult situation – [10] **conglomerate** [kən'glɒm(ə)rət] large corporation formed by joining together different companies – [11] **exploitation** use of sth in an unfair and selfish manner for one's own advantage or profit

friends are working hard, and that a majority say that they regularly go to church? Why is it that 86 percent of young people say that premarital[1] sex for teens is always or almost always wrong? And if a movie like *The Doors* glorifies drug use, why is it that only a quarter of young people today, in contrast to a near-majority of my generation in the late 1960s, say that marijuana should be legalized?"

Jack Valenti, president, Motion Picture Association of America: "The question to me always is who draws the line? The only arbiter[2] of anybody's culture and tastes ought to be the people who inhabit that land. I don't understand why anybody would want to insert his or her judgments in this area. Audiences are also voters: they're readers, they're critics[3], they're parents, and they're teachers.

When people say, 'why don't you make movies the way you used to,' I always say, 'why isn't the society the way it used to be?' We live in a changing world. When people say, 'I don't like that kind of film,' I say, 'you have the most effective weapon known to man—don't go to see it.'"

The American Studies Newsletter, Special Issue 1983–1993, pp. 53–59

Talking about the text

1. How is 'popular culture' defined in this text?
2. What are the advantages and disadvantages of a global popular culture?
3. Through what different methods does American popular culture dominate?
4. Does American television clearly reflect that country's culture? Explain.
5. Rephrase Karlyn Keene's argument for American culture. Use only two sentences.

Finding opposites

Find opposites for the following underlined words:

l. 2 – popular culture
l. 5 – for youth around the world
l. 12 – global semiculture
l. 17 – culture succeed
l. 30 – increasingly not American
l. 52 – culture is corrupting
l. 58 – glorifies drug use
l. 60 – should be legalized
ll. 64f. – insert his or her judgments
l. 69 – a changing world

Translation

Translate ll. 27–39 ("Throughout history ... modernity."). Pay particular attention to the verb tenses.

[1] **premarital** before marriage – [2] **arbiter** ['ɑ:bɪtə] person who has power or influence over what will be done in a particular area of activity – [3] **critic** ['--] person who judges the quality of sth

Jonathan Freedland

Time to Just Say 'No'

This editorial was written by a British journalist. Before you read it, jot[1] down any manifestations of anti-Americanism you have observed in Germany.

The old, crude anti-Americanism is fading. With the cold war over, the left has felt able to drop its Vietnam-era obligation to side against Uncle Sam. Now center-left governments from London to Rome to Jerusalem wear their American influence with pride. I welcome this shift[2]. But it would be a mistake to trade the previous blanket[3] condemnation[4] of the United States for an equally undiscriminating embrace of it. For there are some aspects of American conduct that we have every right to abhor[5]. In the globalized 21st century, we have more than a right; we have a duty to turn to America every now and again and just say no[6].

In the past, anti-Americans saved their bile[7] for two separate areas of US misconduct. They were appalled[8], first, by America's antics[9] abroad. They were disgusted, second, by the way Americans behaved inside their own country. Intellectuals would inveigh against[10] a society apparently riddled[11] with crime, riven[12] by race and obsessed[13] with money. Now, thanks to globalization, the two older forms of hostility have converged: America's external and internal conduct have become one and the same thing. Now it's not nuclear warheads or the CIA that anti-Americans fear, but what the United States does to itself. For, in today's world, that affects people far beyond America's shores.

How does it affect other people?

If America cultivates genetically modified foods, then green activists in Australia will be justifiably concerned: the risk to the environment is disrespectful of borders. And if Americans' cultural habits change, then so do ours: what "they" watch in Kansas is what "we" watch in Kazakhstan. The old anti-Americanism, which had foreigners sneering at the Yanks, must give way to a subtler[14] form of dissent[15]. The rest of the world now has a legitimate stake[16] in faulting[17] the way Americans live their own lives. For in the new century, what happens in the United States happens to all of us.

Newsweek, January 31, 2000, p. 22

[1] **to jot sth down** to write sth quickly – [2] **shift** change – [3] **blanket** here: applying to all cases – [4] **to condemn** to express strong disapproval – [5] **to abhor** to feel hatred and disgust for sb/sth – [6] **just say no** First Lady Nancy Reagan's popular antidrug campaign slogan – [7] **bile** bad temper – [8] **to appall** (US), **appal** (Brit) [ə'pɔ:l] to shock sb deeply – [9] **antics** (*pl*) behaviour which is ridiculous or dangerous – [10] **to inveigh against sb/sth** [ɪn'veɪ] (*fml*) to attack sb/sth violently with words – [11] **to be riddled with** to be full of sth esp sth bad or undesirable – [12] **to rive** (rived, riven) to tear apart – [13] **to be obsessed with** having one's mind filled with sth continually so that one can think of nothing else – [14] **subtle** fine – [15] **dissent** holding opinions which differ from common or officially held ones – [16] **to have a stake in** to have a special interest or right in – [17] **to fault** to discover a fault in sb or sth

In your own words

Describe the differences between the old and new forms of anti-Americanism.

Collecting changes

Which changes have taken place that have apparently given the rest of the world not only the right but also the duty to say no to America now and then?

Listing America's effects

Consider the last sentence of this article. Make a list of ways in which the United States affects you. Compare your ideas with those of others in your class.

Turning the tables

Imagine someone wrote a similar article about Germany's global role. What might be some of the main points? How would you respond to them?

Your thematic vocabulary

Who wants to be an American?

1. Go through the chapter and collect those words, which are important for talking or writing about "The American Way: From Dream to Reality."

2. Using this vocabulary, make up questions similar in form to those used on TV quiz shows.

3. Gather all the questions and play the game in class. The person being questioned should be able to give the reason for his or her choice of answer. Here are two examples:

   Which of the following is **not** a branch of the U.S. federal government?

   a) judicial
   b) legislative
   c) executive
   d) political

   What structure of power in the federal government keeps potential excesses in check?

   a) system of separate and distinct branches
   b) system of checks and balances
   c) system of power and excesses
   d) system of specific powers

Living and Working in

Evolution of man ...

Cathy

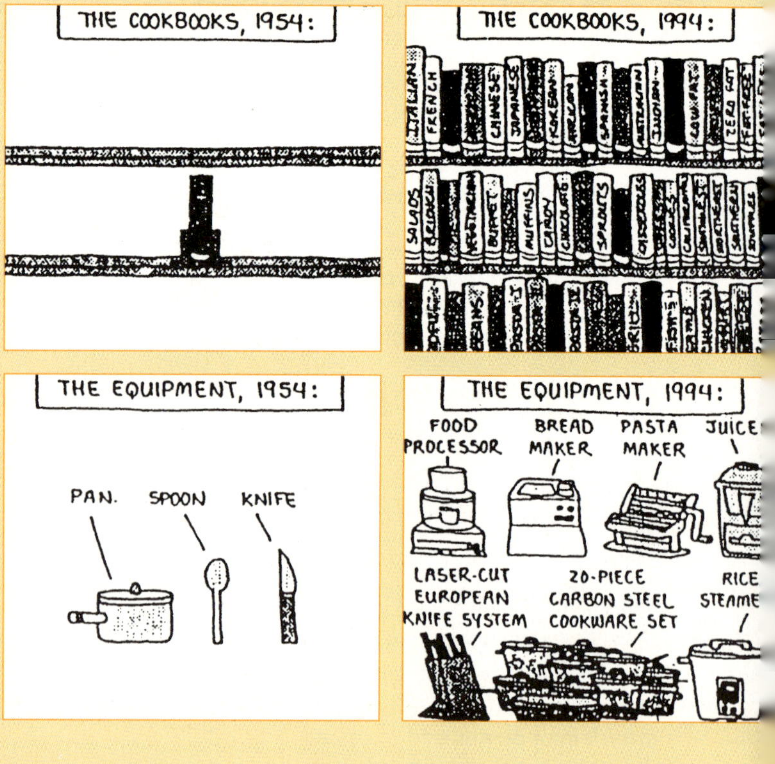

Cathy Guisewite

a Changing World

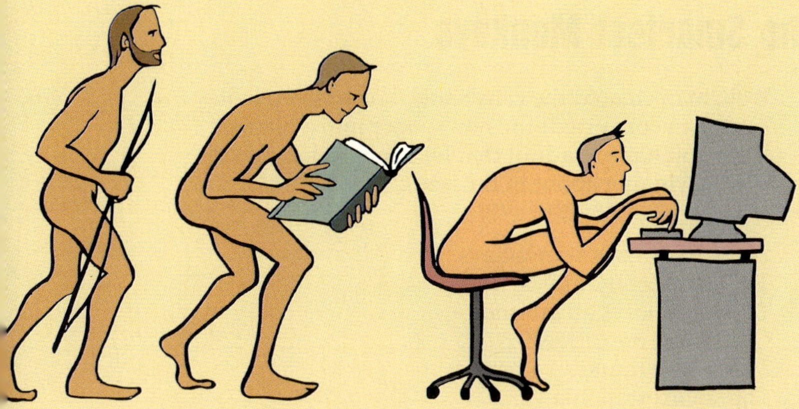

Do you agree with the message of the cartoon? Draw the next picture.

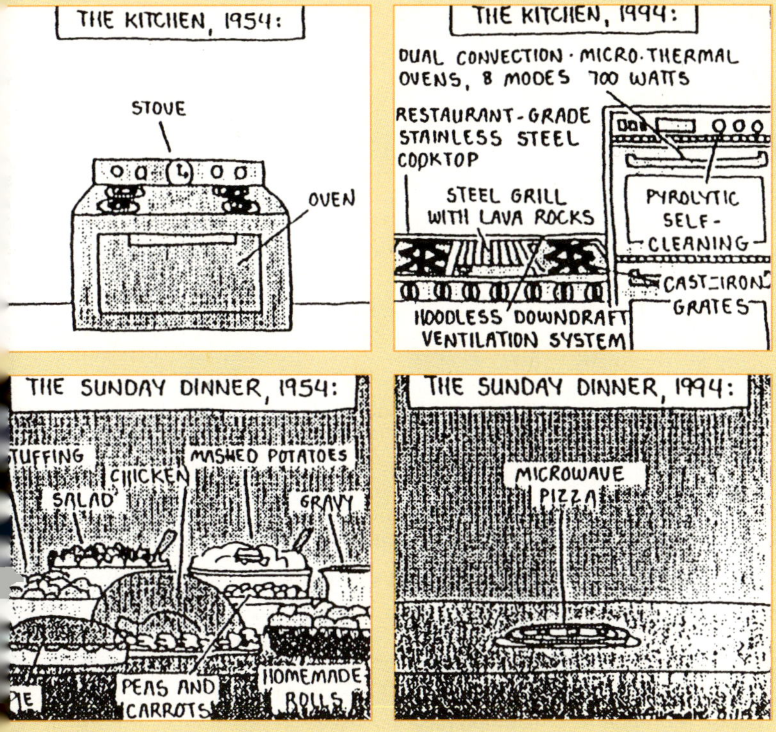

What will cooking be like in 2054?

Generation @

Colin Moulding

The Smartest Monkeys

Well, man created the cardboard[1] box to sleep in it.
And man converted[2] the newspaper into a blanket.
Well, you have to admit that he's come a long way
Since swinging about in the trees.

(refrain)
We're the smartest monkeys.
The smartest monkeys.
The evidence is all around
Our brains are bigger.
This we've found.
The smartest monkeys.

Well, man discovered the park bench can make a transition.
And the rubbish tip[3] makes a valid form of nutrition.[4]
With discoveries like these
Civilisation agrees
To give itself a pat on the back.

We're the smartest monkeys.
The smartest monkeys.
The evolution's plain to see.
We're the dominant of the species.
The smartest monkeys.

We brought the caveman from the stoneage
To the subways of the modern world.
How they pack so many in.
Quick call the Guinness Book of Records.
Well, you have to admit …

(refrain)

(EMI Virgin Music Ltd.,
EMI Virgin Musik Publishing Germany GmbH, Hamburg)

The lyrics

1. Listen to the song. What comparisons and images are used by the songwriter to catch the listener's attention?
2. What idea about the evolution does the songwriter express? Do you agree with his opinion?

[1]**cardboard** thick type of paper used for making boxes – [2]**to convert** change from one form/use to another – [3]**tip** (Brit) place where rubbish is brought to – [4]**nutrition** food, nourishment

Life's What You Make of It

Choose one of the depicted persons and write a short biography. Think about their family, job, interests and changes they have lived through in the course of time. Compare your results in class.

Writing a biography

Douglas Coupland

A Day in the Life of danielu@microsoft.com

In his book *Microserfs* the Canadian author Douglas Coupland gives some insights into the lives of a group of young Americans who work at Microsoft headquarters near Seattle, Washington. Although their jobs are well paid, they are struggling to find their place in a high-speed high-tech environment. The following excerpt is taken from the very beginning of the protagonist's fictionalised diary introducing the readers to his way of life.

Give the definition of a "serf" and then speculate on the title of Coupland's book.

Friday
Early Fall, 1993

This morning, just after 11:00, Michael locked himself up in his office and he won't come out. Bill (Bill!) sent Michael this totally wicked[1] flame-mail[2] from hell on the e-mail system—and he just wailed on[3] a chunk[4] of code[5] Michael had written. Using the *Bloom County*-cartoons-tape-on-the-door index[6], Michael is certainly the most sensitive coder in Building Seven—not the type to take criticism easily. Exactly why Bill would choose Michael of all people[7] to wail on is confusing. We figured it must have been a random[8] quality check to keep the troops in line. Bill's so smart.

Bill is wise.
Bill is kind.
Bill is benevolent.[9]
Bill, Be My Friend ... *Please!*

Bill Gates

Actually, nobody on our floor has ever been flamed by Bill personally. The episode was tinged[10] with glamour and we were somewhat jealous. I tried to tell Michael this, but he was crushed[11]. Shortly before lunch he stood like a lump[12] outside my office. His skin was pale like rising bread dough, and his Toppy's cut[13] was dripping sweat, leaving little damp[14] marks on the oyster-gray-with-plum highlights of the Microsoft carpeting. He handed me a printout of Bill's memo and then galumphed[15] into his office, where he's been burrowed[16] ever since.

He won't answer his phone, respond to e-mail, or open his door. On his doorknob he placed a "Do Not Disturb" thingy stolen from

[1]**wicked** (*infml*) ['wɪkɪd] very good; *affengeil* – [2]**flame-mail** reprimanding mail; *Rüge per Mail* – [3]**to wail on** here: *heruntermachen, zur Sau machen* – [4]**chunk** (*infml*) very large amount of – [5]**code** set of instructions for programming a computer – [6]**Bloom County cartoons- ... index** daily cartoon strip similar to *Calvin and Hobbes*, indicating what mood Michael is in – [7]**(he) of all people** *ausgerechnet (er)* – [8]**random** chosen without method – [9]**benevolent** kind, friendly – [10]**tinged** slightly coloured or affected with – [11]**to crush** to press or squeeze hard – [12]**lump** (*infml*) heavy, clumsy or stupid person – [13]**Toppy's cut** short haircut; *Igelfrisur* – [14]**damp** slightly wet – [15]**to galumph** to walk or run noisily or clumsily – [16]**burrowed** *eingegraben, eingebuddelt*

the Boston Radisson[1] during last years's Macworld Expo. Todd and I walked out onto the side lawn to try to peek[2] in his window, but his venetian blinds[3] were closed and a gardener with a leaf blower chased us away with a spray of grass clippings[4]. They mow the lawn every ten minutes at Microsoft. It looks like green Lego pads. […]

There was a mist floating on the ground above the soccer fields outside the central buildings. I thought about the e-mail and Bill and all of that, and I had this weird feeling—of how the presence of Bill floats about the Campus, semi-visible, at all times, kind of like the dead grandfather in the *Family Circus* cartoons[5].

Bill is a moral force, a spectral[6] force, a force that shapes, a force that molds[7]. A force with thick, thick glasses.

I am danielu@microsoft.com.

What strikes you about the protagonist's name?

I am a tester—a bug[8] checker in Building Seven. I worked my way up the ladder from Product Support Services (PSS) where I spent six months in phone purgatory[9] in 1991 helping little old ladies format their Christmas mailing lists on Microsoft Works.

Like most Microsoft employees, I consider myself too well adjusted to be working here, even though I am 26 and my universe consists of home, Microsoft, and Costco[10]. I am originally from Bellingham, up just near the border, but my parents live in Palo Alto now. I live in a group house with five other Microsoft employees: Todd, Susan, Bug Barbecue, Michael, and Abe. We call ourselves "The Channel Three News Team."

I am single, I think partly this is because Microsoft is not conducive[11] to relationships. Last year down at the Apple Worldwide Developer's Conference in San Jose, I met a girl who works not too far away, at Hewlett-Packard on Interstate 90, but it never went anywhere. Sometimes I'll sort of get something going, but then work takes over my life and I bail out of[12] all my commitments[13] and things fizzle.[14]

Lately I've been unable to sleep. That's why I've begun writing this journal[15] late at night, to try to see the patterns of my life. From this I hope to establish what my problem is—and then, hopefully, solve it. I'm trying to feel more well adjusted than I really am, which is, I guess, the human condition. My life is lived day to day, one line of bug-free code at a time.

The house: Growing up, I used to build split-level[16] ranch type homes out of Legos. This is pretty much the house I live in now, but its ambiance[17] is anything but sterilized lego-clean. It was built

[1] **Radisson** name of a hotel chain – [2] **to peek** to look quickly and often secretly – [3] **venetian blind** [vəˈniːʃn blaɪnd] *Jalousie* – [4] **clippings** cut-off pieces – [5] **Family Circus cartoons** American comic strip – [6] **spectral** *gespenstisch* – [7] **to mold** (US); **to mould** (Brit) to shape sth or sb into a particular form – [8] **bug** (*infml*) defect in a machine, esp in a computer – [9] **purgatory** *Fegefeuer* – [10] **Costco** supermarket chain – [11] **conducive** [kənˈdjuːsɪv] *förderlich, dienlich* – [12] **to bail out of sth** here: to escape from – [13] **commitment** being dedicated or devoted to – [14] **to fizzle** to end or fail in a weak or disappointing way – [15] **journal** (US) diary (Brit) – [16] **split-level** *mit versetzten Geschossen* – [17] **ambiance** [ˈæmbɪəns] atmosphere of a place

Why does he point out the ambiance?

about twenty years ago, maybe before Microsoft was even in the dream stage and this part of Redmond had a lost, alpine ski-feel.

Instead of a green plastic pad with little nubblies[1], our house sits on a thickly-treed lot beside a park on a cul-de-sac[2] at the top of a steep hill. It's only a seven-minute drive from Campus. There are two other Microsoft group houses just down the hill. Karla, actually, lives in the house three down from us across the street.

People end up living in group houses either by e-mail or by word-of-mouth[3]. Living in a group house is a little bit like admitting you're deficient[4] in the having-a-life department, but at work, you spend your entire life crunching[5] code and testing for bugs, and what else are you supposed to do? Work, sleep, work, sleep, work, sleep. I know a few Microsoft employees who try to fake[6] having a life—many a Redmond garage contains a never-used kayak collecting dust. You ask these people what they do in their spare time and they say, "*Uhh*—kayaking. That's right. I kayak in my spare time." You can tell they're faking it.

Why do people 'fake' their spare time?

I don't even do many sports anymore and my relationship with my body has gone all weird. I used to play soccer three times a week and now I feel like a boss in charge of an underachiever[7]. I feel like my body is a station wagon in which I drive my brain around, like a suburban mother taking the kids to hockey practice.

A day on the job

1. What does Daniel's way of life look like? What effect does his job at Microsoft have on it? Comment on the fact that he is writing a diary in our time.
2. Describe the relationship between Bill and his employees as it is given in the text. Do you think this description is realistic?
3. If you had the opportunity to work at such a successful company, would you take it? What are the pros and cons of a job at a major company?

Keeping a diary

1. Why does Daniel keep a diary? What other reasons might there be to keep one?
2. Write a diary entry taking the perspective of Karla, the young woman he is going to fall in love with or his ex-girlfriend working at HP. → Method kit, Diary entry, p. 294

American English

In groups, collect words and expressions from the text, which are characteristic of American English and compare your findings.

[1] **nubblies** round parts on top of Legos – [2] **cul-de-sac** street open at one end only – [3] **by word-of-mouth** *durch mündliche Überlieferung* – [4] **deficient** [dɪˈfɪʃnt] lacking in sth – [5] **to crunch** here: *Zahlen verarbeiten* – [6] **to fake** (*infml*) to pretend – [7] **underachiever** sb who does worse than expected

Melinda Ligos

Traps for Young Job-Hunters

Imagine you were applying for your dream job. What should you pay special attention to?

The interview was over five minutes after it began.

Ron Donoho, executive editor of San Diego magazine, had barely ushered[1] a job prospect[2] into his office to discuss an internship[3] when he stumped[4] her with what he thought was an easy question. "All I did was ask her what she could offer the magazine," Mr. Donoho recalled. But the woman, a recent college graduate, froze. "All she could say was, 'Hmmmmm, that's a toughie[5],'" he said. "Then she added, 'I was more wanting to hear what you could do for me.'" A few hours later, in an apparent attempt to redeem[6] herself, Mr. Donoho said, the candidate sent him an e-mail message on her qualifications for the news reporting post. The note began: "Besides the occasional hangover, here's what else I could bring into the office," and proceeded to list attributes she seemed to feel would make her more desirable, including her sense of fashion. She did not get the job.

▲ Why didn't she get the job?

Experts say that such candidates are becoming increasingly common. Many young workers who entered the marketplace in the recent boom years never learned the traditional rules of hunting for a job, from showing up for an interview in a suit to following up with a thank-you note. Now that the job market has tightened, though, more and more job hunters are scrambling[7] to master these basic skills.

◄ Can you think of any traditional rules?

For the most part, "Twenty-somethings[8] have never had to compete for jobs" in such a climate, said Allison Hemming, president of the Hired Guns, a temporary-staffing agency based in New York. She founded the Pink Slip Party, a Manhattan club for people who have been laid off[9] from dot-com jobs[10]. "They're used to being pursued[11], not being the pursuer." Certainly, the job market was much different for those who entered the employment world in the mid-1990s. For instance, the U.S. Conference Board's index of help-wanted ad-

[1]**to usher** to lead sb in a specified direction – [2]**job prospect** here: job applicant – [3]**internship** ['ɪntɜ:nʃɪp] *Praktikum* – [4]**to stump** to puzzle – [5]**toughie** (*infml*) difficult question – [6]**to redeem oneself** to make up for faults – [7]**to scramble** to struggle – [8]**twenty-something** person in his or her twenties – [9]**to lay sb off** to dismiss workers (for a short time) – [10]**dot-com jobs** jobs in the Internet business – [11]**to pursue** to follow sb or sth

vertising fell from 82 in July 1995 to 58 last month. Young job candidates who find they have to sell themselves, Ms. Hemming said, often do not even know where to look for their next job.

"These guys have relied strictly on the Internet and headhunters in the past," she said. "Now, headhunters aren't as interested in this age group, and so a lot of these people have no clue how to go at it on their own." Employers say candidates who manage to land interviews are increasingly unprepared—sometimes woefully[1] so—for the interviewing process. "Many can't provide details to probing[2] questions," said Paige Soltano, a hiring director for Bozell Group, a New York advertising agency. "If they tell you they completed a successful project at their old job, and you ask them why it was successful, they aren't able to give any details."

But the biggest difference that Ms. Soltano has noticed recently is the attire[3]. Although she is used to interviewing candidates in their twenties, Ms. Soltano said recent applicants had "reached a new low" in dressing for interviews. "I see young women all the time who wear little sun dresses with bra straps showing, along with fancy flip-flops[4], " she said. "This winter, I had guys coming in T-shirts and Army boots. It's as if no one ever taught them how to look for a job."

Should you learn ➤ this at school?

Mrs. Hemming said she had even had to counsel[5] members of her Pink Slip club on their hair for interviews, recently urging one young Web designer to dye[6] his orange hair back to brown. Larry Engelgau, president of Management Recruiters of Portland in Oregon, said that while most of the young people he saw were relatively polished, many were less than enthusiastic or even realistic. "Folks in their twenties are still coming in expecting to get six-figure jobs right off the bat[7], and they seem put off when you tell them they might have to work their way up to that figure", he said.

From "Young Job-Hunters Grapple With Formal New World",
New York Times, August 9, 2001

Applying for a job

1. Compare your strategy of applying properly with the examples mentioned in the text. Comment on the "mistakes" the applicants made. Find reasons for their behaviour.
2. Write a list of do's and don'ts in a job interview.
3. Act out a job interview with your classmates. Prepared role-cards and a look at your do's and don'ts-list might help you. After that decide who gets the job.
4. Write a C.V. for the job you would like to apply for.
➜ Method kit, Letter of application and curriculum vitae, p. 296

[1]**woeful** sad, regrettable – [2]**probing** searching, intended to discover the truth – [3]**attire** clothes – [4]**flip-flops** type of open sandal – [5]**to counsel sb** to give professional advice to sb – [6]**to dye** *färben* – [7]**right off the bat** at the beginning

Reported speech

Collect all the sentences containing direct speech and put them into reported speech. Pay special attention to the various tenses.

Translation

Translate ll. 32–54 ("Certainly ... dressing for interviews."). Be careful with the *-ing* forms.

Anonymous

Life Before the Computer

Do you know any special terms used in the field of computers? Collect as many as possible and jot them down in a mind map.

➜ Method kit, Mind map, p. 281

An application was for employment
A program was a TV show
A cursor used profanity
A keyboard was a piano!

Memory was something that you lost with age
A CD was a bank account
And if you had $3\,^1/_2$ inch floppy
You hoped nobody found out!

Compress was something you did to garbage
Not something you did to a file
And if you unzipped anything in public
You'd be in jail for a while!

Log on was adding wood to a fire
Hard drive was a long trip on the road
A mouse pad was where a mouse lived
And a backup happened to your commode!

Cut—you did it with your pocket knife
Paste you did with glue
A web was a spider's home
And a virus was the flu!

I guess I'll stick to my pad and paper
And the memory in my head
I hear nobody's been killed in a computer crash
But when it happens they wish they were dead!

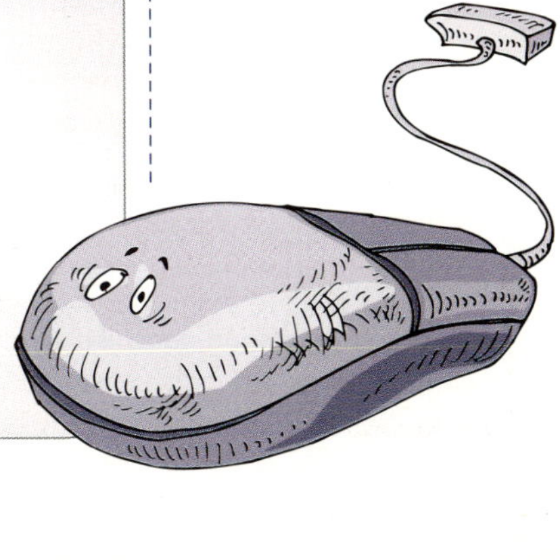

Working with a dictionary

1. Go through the poem and note down words whose meanings have been expanded.
2. Take a look at a dictionary and find out about their meaning before and after the invention of the computer. Add your findings to the list.
3. Write a further verse to this poem, using either the words you have collected or similar ones.

Translation

1. Translate the poem in groups. Pay special attention to the translation of the words you looked up.
2. Can you find out why certain words were used to signify special parts or functions of a computer?

Robert J. Samuelson

The Internet and Gutenberg

Make a list of mankind's five most important inventions and rank them according to their importance. Give reasons for your rankings and compare your results in class.

In our self-absorbed[1] age, everything is the newest New Thing or the biggest Big Thing. This spirit inevitably invests[2] the Internet with transcendental[3] significance. Steve Case of America Online already calls the new century "the Internet Century," and some authorities whisper that the Internet rivals the importance of Gutenberg's invention of the printing press in the 15th century. We suffer from historical amnesia[4].

Suppose you were born in 1900. You wouldn't yet watch movies, let alone[5] imagine global TV. The airplane hadn't been invented, and Henry Ford wouldn't produce the first Model T[6] until 1908. Fewer than 10 per cent of US homes had phones, and fewer than 8 per cent had electricity. Antibiotics[7] hadn't been discovered. As yet the Internet isn't in the same league with these developments.

How did the car change American communities?

Each changed lifestyles and popular beliefs. The automobile suburbanized[8] America and inaugurated mass travel. Antibiotics, vaccines[9] and public-health advances helped raise life expectancy from 47 in 1900 to 77 today. The explosion of prosperity—a conse-

[1] **self-absorbed** only interested in oneself – [2] **to invest sth with sth** (*fml*) to cause sth to have a particular quality – [3] **transcendental** going beyond the limits of human knowledge – [4] **amnesia** loss of memory – [5] **let alone** *ganz zu schweigen von* – [6] **Model T** first mass-produced car – [7] **antibiotics** [ˌæntɪbaɪˈɒtɪks] – [8] **to surburbanize** to bring about the emergence of suburbs – [9] **vaccine** [vækˈsiːn] *Impfstoff*

quence of electricity, other technologies and modern management—shortened working hours and expanded leisure. Movies and TV transformed popular culture.

In what way has pop culture changed?

The Internet is too young for anyone to foretell[1] its ultimate significance—and time might vindicate[2] the brashest[3] prophecies. But some present claims aren't true. It is not true that no major innovation has spread so quickly.

Lauren Uram: Johannes Gutenberg (1395–1468)

In 1990 only a handful of computer buffs[4] used the Internet; by 1999 perhaps 38 per cent of all households were connected. [...] This roughly matches[5] the adoption of the radio (which went from 0 to about 46 per cent of households in the 1920s) and lags[6] TV (which went from 9 per cent of households in 1950 to 87 per cent in 1960). [...]

Technologies acquire historical weight by reshaping the human condition. Gutenberg's press led to mass literacy, fostered[7] the Protestant Reformation and, through the easy exchange of information, enabled the scientific revolution. In the 19th century railroads created a truly national American market that favored mass production and the consumer society. To join this league, the Internet must be more than e-mail or a marketing platform. If you buy a book or a car on the Net, the critical part of the transaction is still the book or car. Especially in business-to-business commerce, the Internet may improve efficiency through more price competition and supplier[8] choice. But these changes are of degree, not kind.

What is meant by 'critical part of the transaction'?

Thoughtful Internet enthusiasts offer plausible speculations about its greater meaning. [...] Kevin Kelly of Wired magazine, author of "New Rules for the New Economy", argues that the "Internet is actually being under-hyped[9]. Of all the people online in

[1] **to foretell** to predict – [2] **to vindicate** to prove the truth of sth that has been disputed – [3] **brash** loud, showy – [4] **computer buff** computer expert – [5] **to match** to be equal to – [6] **to lag** to fail to keep pace with – [7] **to foster** to promote – [8] **supplier** here: *Anbieter* – [9] **under-hyped** not fully used concerning its potential

10 years, only a tenth are online today." This could accelerate global commerce and weaken (for good or for ill) national governments.

All the large issues remain unsettled[1]. Will the Net enhance[2] individual autonomy—or infringe[3] on privacy? Will it increase people's economic independence—or expand corporate[4] power? Before answers become clear, the Internet will have to attain[5] economic viability[6]. Though booming, it is now largely a capitalist charity. Almost everything on it is being given away or sold at a loss. [...]

The great Internet fortunes arise mainly from stock speculation or building the infrastructure—supplying computers, software and fiber optics[7]. Sooner or later, the investment must pay a return, or it will stop. Even if the Internet flourishes, it may remain smaller than early Big Things. Our historical amnesia could benefit from the words of a Tennessee farmer at a church meeting in the 1940s. "Brothers and sisters, I want to tell you this," he said. "The greatest thing on earth is to have the love of God in your heart, and the next great thing is to have electricity in your home." Can the Internet really top that?

Newsweek, January 24, 2000, p. 2

[1] **unsettled** unsolved, open to further discussion – [2] **to enhance** to increase (the good qualities of sth/sb) – [3] **to infringe on** to limit – [4] **corporate** of or relating to a business – [5] **to attain** to succeed in getting, to achieve – [6] **viability** [vaɪəˈbɪləti] practicability – [7] **fiber optics** *Glasfasertechnik*

Are we living in "The Internet Century"?

1. Compare your list with the inventions mentioned in the text.
2. Which problems do you see in connection with the use of the Internet? What opportunities does it offer? How has it affected your life?
3. What areas of life will have to be improved?

Time travel

1. Imagine that Johannes Gutenberg met Bill Gates. They are discussing the (dis-)advantages of book vs. computer. Write an account (dialogue, short story, newspaper article, etc) of this meeting. ➪ Method kit, Newspaper article, p. 298
2. What will the future of information technology look like? Take into consideration what role it may play for people who haven't got access or the technical expertise to use it.

Translation

Form three groups and translate ll. 14–20 ("Each ... popular culture."), ll. 21–35 ("The Internet ... in 1960") and ll. 36–57 ("Technologies ... not kind."). Pay special attention to idiomatic expressions. Then exchange your translations and correct them if necessary.

Diagramming

Transform the statistical information in the text into pie charts or bar charts (e.g. "The use of media in US households" or "Life expectancy in the US 1900–2000"). Find the current numbers and draw them in.

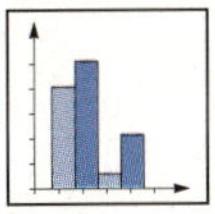
Bar chart

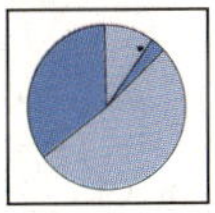
Pie chart

Project Internet

Check out Project Gutenberg at http://www.gutenberg.net. What is its goal? Do you find it useful?

Lillian E. Carlton

TV or Not TV—A Modern Soliloquy

Check your TV viewing habits in class.

- Who spends most/least time in front of the telly? What kind of programmes do you prefer?
- When would you talk of an "addiction to the screen"?

Sounds familiar— do you recognize the original?

TV or not TV: that is the question:
Whether 'tis smarter in the head to suffer
The sound and fury of the one-eyed monster,
Or to rise up against outrageous[1] programs
And by a dial-twist end them. To rest; to sleep;
No more; and by that sleep to say we end
The eyestrain[2] and the thousand silly shows
That we're exposed to. 'Tis a consummation[3]
Devoutly[4] to be wished. To sleep; to dream;
Ay, there's the rub[5]; for in that sodden[6] sleep
What dreams may come? What visions of delights
We'll never get to see on any chance,
Must give us pause. There's respect
That makes such fools of those who'd seek their pillows.
For who would bear to watch the hoary[7] westerns,
... who Bonanza ... who Walt Disney,
When he himself might his quietus[8] make
With a swift Nytol[9]? ...
... the hope of better things to come,
Great undiscovered glories, stays the hand,
And makes us rather bear the shows we have
Than dream of others we may never see.
Thus wishing does make viewers of us all,
And thus the honest need to go to bed
Is vanquished by the will-o'-wisp[10] of promise,
And keeps us staring at the boob-tube[11].

Each elite has its special signs to be recognized by.

The world of perception

1. Make a list of all the images taken from the field of mental/visual perception.
2. Why is "sleep" mentioned so often?

[1]**outrageous** [aʊt'reɪdʒəs] very shocking and unacceptable – [2]**eye strain** a tired condition of the eyes caused e.g. by a long period of reading or looking at a computer screen – [3]**consummation** the action or moment of completing, making perfect, or fulfilling sth – [4]**devoutly** [dɪ'vaʊtlɪ] *inbrünstig* – [5]**there's the rub** that's the problem – [6]**sodden** completely wet as a result of absorbing a lot of liquid – [7]**hoary** very old and well-known or familiar – [8]**quietus** 1. the end of one's life; 2. (*fig*) come-uppance – [9]**Nytol** name of a sleeping tablet – [10]**will-o'-the-wisp** *Irrlicht, Täuschung* – [11]**boob-tube** (*infml*) TV screen; boob = fool

1. Compare the text to its original (p. 234f.). How much is left of it?
2. Concerning the "sleep" metaphor, what meaning did sleep have for the Elizabethans? Is it the same today?

The original

Make an advertising poster for attracting people to read the old classics like Shakespeare. Work with the professional tricks of manipulation and address as many senses as possible.

Advertising for a good read

Metaphor ['metəfə(r)] the imaginative use of a word or phrase to describe sb or sth with another object in order to show that they have the same qualities and to make the description more forceful, e.g. 'She has a heart of stone'.

William Underhill

The SMS Generation

Over 100 billion SMS messages are sent every day. Have you ever sent an SMS? What is special about them?

The following text introduces you to the success of SMS and gives reasons for its popularity especially among teenagers.

The downfall of Philippine President Joseph Estrada is an example of what the people can do when they're well armed—in this case, with mobile phones that deliver short, simple text messages. Opposition organizers used this powerful new medium to broadcast details of upcoming rallies[1], reaching 100 supporters at a time. And this is no isolated case. On Valentine's Day lovesick Thais crashed the country's largest mobile-phone network by sending 100,000 messages in less than an hour. In Finland, the average teenager is now thought to tap out[2] 100 messages a month. A Danish medical clinic recently admitted its first texting addict, a chauffeur who sent up to 200 messages a day.

The word **handy** is a German creation. It is not used by English people. They either say mobile (phone) or cell(ular) phone.

Why do people get addicted in such a way?

[1] **rally** large gathering of people with a common purpose – [2] **to tap out** to knock gently on sth

Something strange has happened to the mobile phone. In defiance of[1] all industry forecasts, today's user seems to want to *write*, not chat. SMS, Short Message Service, has been around for a decade, but in recent years it began spreading like a virus throughout the globe. [...] This phenomenon has surprised everybody. The telecom industry adopted SMS as a standard technology in 1991 as a way to sop up[2] extra network capacity, just in case somebody might find it useful.

Unlike e-mail, text messages arrive almost instantaneously, so that two people can have a text-based conversation as though they were in an Internet chat room. At first, subscribers[3] were able to send messages only within their own networks. The service was neither advertised nor promoted. Phone manufacturers were no more ambitious: telephone keyboards are optimized for numbers, not letters. On many handsets, it still takes plenty of scrolling[4] just to find the menu options for texting.

A year or two ago, teenagers and twenty-somethings spotted potential. Here was an efficient way of communicating that had the powerful charm of novelty. Numbers rose rapidly, especially in the tech-friendly[5] countries of the Far East and Scandinavia, where the mobile-phone boom took off among young consumers. "This was the accidental[6] revolution," says Simon Buckingham of the mobile Lifestreams consultancy. "Consumers just adopted SMS as their own medium. Every generation needs its own way of expressing itself, this is the text generation."

Devotees[7] say the charms of texting go far beyond novelty. The service has all the immediacy[8] of a phone call—as well as extra privacy and just a hint of the subversive. "My dad overhears[9] me on the phone all the time, but I don't have to worry about that with text messages," says Chika Saito, a high-school junior in Japan who sends about 10 messages a day." I can punch the buttons real quick using just one hand, and my dad says it drives him crazy just seeing me do it." Background noise is no problem—ever tried talking on a mobile phone from a crowded bar?—and reception isn't an issue. [...] Best of all, the text habit[10] doesn't strain[11] even modest student budgets. A brief message—the technology allows the maximum length of just 160 characters—won't usually cost more than 15 cents. "It's cheap, it's quick and it's international", says 21year-old Paris student Lara Bourji. "I can send a message anywhere in the world for one franc." These budget rates encourage constant, informal text conversation. Says 15-year-old Christina Jensen from

Why are parents so upset? ➤

How much does it cost you? ➤

[1] **in defiance of** in spite of – [2] **to sop up** to take up liquid with a sponge or cloth – [3] **subscribers** here: *Teilnehmer* – [4] **to scroll** to move gradually up and down – [5] **tech-friendly** technology friendly – [6] **accidental** happening by chance – [7] **devotee** enthusiast – [8] **immediacy** closeness or reality of sth, so that one feels directly involved or has to deal with it at once – [9] **to overhear** (overheard, overheard) to hear sth without the knowledge of the speaker – [10] **habit** thing a person does often and almost without thinking – [11] **to strain** to weaken (esp a part of the body) by stretching too much

Copenhagen: "I send and receive between five and 10 a day, mostly things like 'sleep well', 'how's it going' or 'see you tomorrow." Popularity now seems to be spreading across the generation gap. "It's better than any answering service," says 45-year-old Rome housewife Annamaria Lovari, who lives without e-mail or a fixed-line phone. "My sons always let me know when they have arrived at their destination[1] with a text message instead of a call."

◀ How many SMS' do you send a day?

For many texting aficionados[2] the practical difficulty is just part of the fun. Spelling out a message with a thumb's edge takes more time than most teenagers or young adults can afford. So users have developed their own highspeed vocabulary, a mix of all the available icons, snappy acronyms[3] and phonetic shorthand[4]. Although adults may be foxed[5], youngsters will know just what's meant by CUL8R (see you later) or QL (cool). Guides are available for the uninitiated[6]. In Britain, three of the top 10 best-selling books are English-to-text dictionaries. […] But the language is evolving[7] quicker than publishers can keep up. "The whole point is that everyone can invent it; it's just a visual translation of the spoken word," says Gabrielle Mander, who compiled "Wan2Tlk? Ltl Bk of Txt Msgs."

◀ Read this aloud.

Having gotten over their initial surprise, network operators are now sharing in the thrill of text messaging. Since text takes up only a thin sliver of handwidth, messages whiz around[8] effortlessly even on the most congested[9] networks. This makes it a high-margin business[10] and a welcome relief from the highly competitive market for voice calls, where profits are being squeezed. Some European telcos[11] now derive up to 20 per cent of revenues[12] from the "thumb culture." Others are luring[13] subscribers with package deals that include free messaging. […]

Emoticons

:) happy
:(sad
;) making a joke
:] grinning
:[groggy
:* kissing

Where fashion leads, commerce follows. For the marketers and admen[14], SMS has some rare and valuable qualities. Sometimes subscribers will be offered a special service—say, news or weather reports—in return for receiving occasional ads. […] Already ads for everything from condoms to airlines have begun reaching subscribers through their handsets. Other SMS services range from news and traffic warnings to fertility advice and directions to the hottest beach parties on Ibiza, Europe's clubbing mecca. […]

The mobile-phone firms hope that the success of SMS may help answer one big question about the future of wireless: what (if anything) are customers likely to want from Internet-linked smart phones[15], which will hit Europe and Asia in the next year or so? Phone companies have spent $ 100 billion on the third-generation

◀ What would you want?

[1] **destination** place sb is going to – [2] **aficionado** person who is very enthusiastic about sports or a pastime, fan – [3] **acronym** word formed from the initial letters of a group of words, e.g. UNESCO – [4] **shorthand** method of writing rapidly, using special quickly-written symbols – [5] **foxed** confused, baffled – [6] **uninitiated** not introduced to sth – [7] **to evolve** to develop gradually – [8] **to whiz around** to move very fast – [9] **congested** overcrowded – [10] **high-margin business** *Geschäft mit hoher Gewinnspanne* – [11] **telcos** telecommunication companies – [12] **revenues** income – [13] **to lure sb** to attract or tempt sb with sth – [14] **adman** person who produces commercial advertisements – [15] **smart phones** multifunctional phones that you can mail with

technology that will allow these phones to send and receive vast amounts of data. What's the point of this fancy[1] technology if customers really just want to send short text messages? Now engineers are scrambling[2] to develop so-called multimedia messaging services, in which users would send text messages enriched with still or video images[3] or sound clips—a sort of voice e-mail. Only when the third generation hits the market will they know for sure whether it's GR8 (great) or NAGI (not a good idea).

From "The Text Generation", *Newsweek*, April 2, 2001, pp. 58–59

QL ??s 4 U

1. Write a response to this text in the form of a short SMS using up to 160 characters (spaces count as characters).
2. Sum up the (dis-)advantages of using the mobile phone to send messages instead of writing letters or e-mails.
3. "Every generation needs its own way of expressing itself." (ll. 36f.) Comment on that statement.

Active and passive voice

1. Transform the following passages into the active voice:
   "… the average teenager is now thought to tap out …" (l. 8f.)
   "The service was neither advertised nor promoted." (ll. 24f.)
   "Sometimes subscribers will be offered a special service … (ll. 84f.)
2. Transform the following passages into the passive voice:
   "Opposition organizers used this powerful new medium to broadcast details of upcoming rallies …" (ll. 4f.)
   "At first, subscribers were able to send messages only within their own networks …" (ll. 22–24)
   "… it still takes plenty of scrolling just to find the menu options for texting." (l. 27f.)
   "Consumers just adopted SMS as their own medium." (ll. 35f.)
   "So users have developed their own high-speed vocabulary …" (ll. 63f.)
   "… network operators are now sharing in the thrill of text messaging." (ll. 74f.)
   "Others are luring subscribers with package deals that include free messaging." (ll. 81f.)
   "Phone companies have spent $ 100 billion on the third-generation technology that will allow these phones to send and receive vast amounts of data." (ll.95–97)

[1] **fancy** extravagant, exaggerated – [2] **to scramble** to struggle with, to compete with others – [3] **still images** *Standfotos*

Maia Szalawitz

Can We Become Caught in the Web?

Ask your classmates how often they use the Internet and what they use it for. Make five similar questions about computer use and habits. Do that in a double circle.

I've lived and worked on the Internet for nine years now. At first, the online world threatened to engulf[1] me. But now it has made possible a life I love and couldn't sustain[2] any other way.

I have an intense relationship with the Net. Because my boyfriend lives in England, it is our primary means of communicating. And since I work as a freelance journalist[3], I spend much of my time doing research on the Web and communicating with editors by e-mail. I'm online at least half of my day.

When I began my wired life, the Web hadn't been invented. A friend founded a "bulletin board[4]" in New York City in 1990 called Echo, and invited me to help start the conversation. I was immediately hooked[5] by a world where what you write—not how you look or sound—is what you are. It had definite appeal to someone who has always found socializing difficult. And as a writer, I even had an advantage. My style online is conveyed[6] by my sentences and syntax, not my fashion sense or physical appearance.

But there are some serious problems with an online existence. If you aren't careful to limit yourself, you can start to find human contact frightening—even phonecalls become scary. Computers do what you want for the most part, but life outside is noisy, unpredictable[7] and crowded. Seeing friends comes to seem a chore[8]; getting groceries an unwanted adventure.

The repetitive nature of online tasks—checking e-mails, searching for data, sending replies—has a soothing[9], ritualistic quality, somewhat like preparing and using drugs. The Net also offers druglike distractions: engaging in flame-fest-arguments[10] with people who you will never meet, discussing topics you love but rarely get a chance to share in real life. You write, but don't feel isolated as your words generate near-instant responses. The sense of connection—whether true or false—is compellingly[11] attractive.

Why is the Internet compared to drugs?

Still, I wouldn't call my Internet use an addiction[12]. As a former heroin and cocaine addict, I know that experience all too well. Addiction inherently[13] moves you away from love and work. My relationship to the Internet is far more complex. While heroin and cocaine failed to deliver what I thought they'd promised, the Internet

[1] **to engulf** to swallow up – [2] **to sustain** to maintain, to keep – [3] **freelance journalist** writer who earns his living by selling work to several employers – [4] **bulletin board** (US) here: e-board; *Anschlagtafel* – [5] **hooked** (*sl*) totally committed to – [6] **to convey sth** to make (ideas, feelings) known to another person – [7] **unpredictable** *unvorhersehbar* – [8] **chore** unpleasant task – [9] **soothing** calming – [10] **flame-fest-arguments** arguments carried out by extensive use of flame-mails – [11] **compelling** undeniable – [12] **addiction** condition of taking drugs habitually without being able to stop – [13] **inherent** essential

lived up to its billing[1]. For one, I don't know how people sustain[2] long-distance relationships without it. My boyfriend and I use a chat program that allows us to see what the other is writing as we type. We usually spend at least an hour a day communicating this way.

Many couples who live together don't spend that much time "listening" to each other. In today's mobile world, the Net also provides community that geography sometimes can't. While many pundits[3] claimed that the Web helped push the Columbine High School shooters[4] to the edge, I figure that it may have prevented many other such situations. After all, outcast[5] teens can now find friends online—without fear of ridicule[6] or attack. I wish I'd had the net when I felt there was no one in the world who understood me. [...]

How can compulsive Internet-use be harmful?

Like anything else that is pleasurable, the Net can be misused. My boyfriend's first few years on the Net included a lot of 18-hour days online. Such compulsive[7] use can be harmful—but it is probably less so than many other distractions. People can and do use everything from methamphetamine[8] to mountaineering to avoid doing what they should. If you can't face the world, you'll always find somewhere to hide. And even my boyfriend's Net overdose wasn't entirely negative: he now knows UNIX[9], Linux[10] and other programs I can't even name and has started a Net-related business.

I think psychologists looking to treat "Internet addiction" and fear-mongering[11] pundits hype[12] the bad side of the Net for their own purposes: profits and ratings[13]. What you find in the vast chaos of the Web is mainly what you choose to look for. If you don't look for trouble, chances are, you won't find it.

Newsweek, December 20, 1999, p. 17

"You have seven phone messages telling you to check your e-mail, and thirteen e-mails telling you to answer your phone."

The pros and cons of the Internet

1. Sum up the author's arguments in favour of or against the use of the Internet. Can you find some more?
2. To what extent are these arguments convincing?
3. "The Internet is a drug." Discuss this issue in a fish bowl and take notes. Then discuss your findings.

[1]**billing** promise – [2]**to sustain** to keep sth/sb alive or in existence – [3]**pundit** expert – [4]**Columbine High School shooters** teenagers who shot 15 schoolmates and a teacher near Denver, CO, in 1999 – [5]**outcast** sb who is driven away from home, friends, society etc. – [6]**ridicule** making sb appear foolish – [7]**compulsive** caused by an obsession; *exzessiv* – [8]**methamphetamine** type of synthetic drug used esp as a stimulant – [9]**UNIX** operating system – [10]**Linux** popular operating system based on UNIX – [11]**fear-mongering** [fɪə(r)'mʌŋgə(r)ɪŋ] *Angst schürend* – [12]**to hype** to publicize sth in a wildly exaggerated way – [13]**rating** popularity

Globalisation

Info

Many changes are spinning through our world, which has never before seen such extreme transformations. We are facing alterations[1] in communication, economy, technology, transport etc. Economic mergers[2] between influential international companies have strengthened economic ties across the globe. We are living in a world where anything can be produced and sold anywhere. Time and space don't seem to be serious barriers any longer on a planet where new opportunities as well as unpredictable[3] risks are linked with one trend—the phenomenon[4] of globalisation.

What is meant by the term 'globalisation'?

Globalisation is a process that has spread across the world as one of the most important developments in contemporary[5] history. It is a distinctive and important development; a process that cannot be stopped. Supporters and critics believe that the current growth of globalisation is as significant as the spread of printing presses 500 years ago or the invention of writing 5,000 years ago.

The buzzword[6] itself captures all major changes that have been taking place in the world in the 19th and 20th century. Since the 1960s—when the expression first appeared in a dictionary—this development has unfolded[7] with such unprecedented[8] speed and extent, that almost every person in today's world has been touched by it. The vision of a Malaysian living in the Netherlands with his Brazilian wife, doing business in Canada and selling Russian goods is not just a dream, but a reality faced by a growing number of people.

Which developments brought about globalisation?

If you take a look at the driving forces of globalisation, you will find various causes, especially in the field of economy. Consumers get goods faster, cheaper and better than ever before, because new economic developments have helped to minimize production costs. Technological innovation (e.g. air transport, electronic communication, digital information processing[9]) has also played an important role: With the

[1] **alteration** act or result of changing – [2] **merger** (act of) joining together (esp two commercial companies); *Fusion* – [3] **unpredictable** changeable – [4] **phenomenon** [fə'nɒmɪnən] – [5] **contemporary** belonging to the same time – [6] **buzzword** specialist or technical word or phrase that becomes fashionable and popular – [7] **to unfold** to (cause sth to) be revealed or made known – [8] **unprecedented** never having happened, been done or been known before – [9] **processing** performance of operations (on sth) in a computer

help of high-tech and multi-media, business transactions from a great distance have become possible, increasing free capital flow around the world. At the beginning of the 21st century, more and more companies have become interlinked and interdependent, judging the process of globalisation positively, with unlimited prospects for prosperity.
With developments like this, is the world becoming the much talked-about 'global village'? To some extent, this statement is certainly true. In most parts of the world, young people develop some sense of belonging together in one global culture, by listening to the same music, watching the same TV programs, playing the same video games, wearing similar clothes and communicating across national boundaries. One should, however, bear in mind that a remarkable number of people has not been included in this game. Apparently, globalisation has mostly spread in the Northern part of the globe, in urban centres rather than in rural areas, and among younger generations rather than traditional societies.

The consequences of globalisation

Considering that the process of globalisation is not inherently[1] good or bad, it is hard to decide whether its beneficial[2] or harmful potential is predominant. Without doubt, there are positive consequences of globalisation, e.g.:

- higher range of available products
- improved communication systems
- increased economic efficiency
- positive influences on culture (intermingling of cultures)
- rising living standards and major increase in international investment (building roads etc) in less developed countries.

There is, however, a growing number of critics who point out the negative effects of globalisation. These negative influences are not only felt in the economic sector, but also on a political and social scale. Everything seems to be changing too fast without time to understand everything that is going on. With regard to increasing ecological problems, persistent[3] poverty, worse working conditions, growing inequalities between the developing countries and the industrial nations, the influences of global changes are painful for a high number of people. In times of crisis, multinational companies are affected more easily with the steady capital flow. The Internet and other technologies have not only increased the pace, but also the stress to remain competitive.
As the new global economy keeps restructuring, social conditions get worse not only for non-skilled workers who might have to face lower wages or the risk of being "out-

[1] **inherently** *von Natur aus* – [2] **beneficial** having a helpful or useful effect – [3] **persistent** continuing without interruption

sourced". With the welfare state on retreat, social problems (drugs, unemployment, poverty, crime, the breakdown of relationships) have nurtured[1] fears of an uncertain future—even in countries that have profited from globalisation.

One of the most problematic effects of globalisation is the growing loss of identity. This in turn has reinforced already existing problems like xenophobia[2], fundamentalism, racial and religious problems in all parts of the world. Recent years have shown an increasing awareness about the risks of globalisation, culminating[3] in peaceful and violent demonstrations of its various opponents. In 2001, a sad climax was reached with the death of a young Italian protester in Genoa after street-fights between the police and rioters on various occasions (Seattle 1999, Stockholm 2001) had led to a deteriorating relationship between the authorities and enemies of globalisation.

Likewise, the terrorist attacks on the World Trade Center on 11th September 2001 must be seen in the light of "what went wrong with globalisation." Since this event, the Western World has had to face the fact that even after the Cold War a considerable amount of people doesn't want to take part in a process that is interpreted as a clash of cultures rather than becoming One World. As a consequence, globalisation will certainly have an important (both positive and negative) impact on global human security: military, ecologically, economically, culturally and psychologically. Whether these problems will be tackled[4] in the 21st century, remains to be seen. The biggest challenge of globalisation remains, that its fruits will be shared by all people on this planet.

Demonstration against the World Trade Organization. Seattle, December 1999

[1] **to nurture** to nourish, to support – [2] **xenophobia** [zenə'fəʊbɪə] intense dislike or fear of foreigners or strangers – [3] **to culminate in** to have the specified final conclusion or result; *gipfeln in* – [4] **to tackle** to deal with or overcome sth difficult

Facets of a Changing Society

Fighting for the Environment—Actions From All Over the World

Wangari Maathai (*1940)
In the late 1970s Wangari Maathai began a small treeplanting operation in Nairobi for Kenya's poor who were running out of firewood. Her Green Belt Movement, composed largely of women, quickly spread throughout Kenya and beyond. Maathai turned to politics and fought successfully against the construction of an office tower in Uhuru (Freedom) Park, a vital public space.

Chico Mendes (1944–1988)
Mendes was Brasil's environmental conscience: he organized a rural workers' union and formed them into human barriers whenever chain saws and bulldozers threatened the rainforest that was their livelihood. Mendes' Ghandi-like tactics brought him global acclaim[7] and enemies: in 1988 he was shot by ranchers.

George Schaller (*1933)
The German-born biologist's first rule is: "Don't study animals along the barrel[1] of a gun!" With just notebook and camera, he has followed lions, wild sheep and giant pandas in different parts of the world. His findings are important: he has explained, for example why you can't save animals without saving habitat[2].

Barry Commoner (*1917)
Brooklyn-born biologist Barry Commoner was one of the first scientists to worry about a deteriorating[8] environment. He established a pioneering ecological center at Washington University in 1966. Despite his age, he remains an active warrior for the environment.

Ken Saro-Wiwa (1941–1995)
Ken Saro-Wiwa was a famous Nigerian man of letters and a well-known figure on TV. But in the 90s, he quit his TV career to lead a campaign against oil drilling that was devastating[3] his tribe[4]. His crusade[5] ran into trouble. Despite his pleas[6] of innocence and international support he was accused of killing four pro-government chiefs and was hanged for murder.

Medha Patkar (*1954)
Medha Patkar is fighting the Indian government's plans to harness[9] Narmada River by dams. Huge amounts of land would be swamped[10], half a million villagers displaced and a fertile river basin ruined. Up to this moment Patkar has been successful but the Indian government persists with this project. Will she be able to resist the pressure?

[1] **barrel** *Gewehrlauf* – [2] **habitat** the natural home of a plant or an animal – [3] **to devastate** to cause damage – [4] **tribe** *Stamm* – [5] **crusade** *Kreuzzug* – [6] **plea** urgent request – [7] **acclaim** praise for a person or their achievements – [8] **to deteriorate** to become worse in quality or condition – [9] **to harness** *nutzbar machen* – [10] **to swamp** *überschwemmen*

Imagine you had the chance of meeting one of these persons or a member of his/her family. Prepare questions about environmental issues you'd like to ask this person. Ask these questions in class.

Getting closer

Bill Clinton

Saving the Environment—A Global Challenge

On the occasion of the Earth Day 2000, Bill Clinton, former president of the United States of America, reflects on the role of the globalised world in matters of ecology.

As we enter the 21st century, a new global economy draws nations even closer. But our growing interdependence hinges[1] on much more than technology and trade. For we are linked intrinsically[2] by the physical and biological webs that sustain[3] life on our planet—and, increasingly, by the threat of their unravelling[4]. Indeed, unless we reach across borders and face this threat together, the next century may dawn on an Earth in ecological crisis, with half of all species gone, and our grandchildren enduring deadly floods, drought and disease brought on by global warming. When

Earth Day: During the 1960s a growing number of people became increasingly concerned with environmental issues, but government didn't care. Therefore, Senator Gaylord Nelson tried to thrust this topic into the political mainstream: he organized nationwide protests on behalf of the environment. It was a tremendous success. Since 1970 Earth Day is celebrated every year on April 22 with people organizing very many different activities.

[1]**to hinge on** to depend on – [2]**intrinsic** being part of the nature or character of sb or sth – [3]**to sustain** to make sth continue to exist – [4]**to unravel** to become separated

millions across America celebrated the first Earth Day 30 years ago, our focus understandably was our own backyard. Our rivers were catching on fire, and our skylines were disappearing behind a veil of smog. […] But we must look well beyond our own cities and countryside, make environment a core[1] foreign policy objective […]. And without question, we must do more to counter[2] a threat that shows more clearly than any other how closely our nations' fates are linked: the threat of global warming. As the world's largest emitter of greenhouse gases, the U.S. has a special responsibility to lead this effort. Despite mounting evidence, too many in Congress continue to deny the problem. Instead, we must see—and seize—the opportunities in its solution. Promising new technologies, and others just over the horizon, can power our homes, factories and cars with cleaner, more efficient energy—cutting emissions while strengthening our economy.

We must ensure also that this global challenge is met with a global solution, for the heat-trapping gases warming the earth pose the same risk whether they come from the U.S. or from China. An agreement forged in 1997 in Kyoto, Japan, […] calls for strong action by industrialized nations. But developing countries must join us. […]

Ultimately, our best hope may be that even where governments lag[3], their people understand both the stakes[4] and the urgent need for action. […] For the sake of our children, and our planet.

From "A Global Challenge for the New Century", *Time*, Special edition: Earth Day 2000, April/May 2000, p. 25

Clinton's view

1. Which threats does Clinton see for the environment?
2. What does he propose to improve the situation?

Getting active

1. What are your personal ideas about how to act in favour of the environment? Report about projects known to you.
2. Design a leaflet calling for action.
3. Deliver a persuasive speech to protect the environment.
   → Method kit, Comment and speech, p. 292

Translation

Translate ll. 9–29 ("When millions … must join us.") into German. Pay special attention to the collocations.

[1] **core** central part – [2] **to counter** to oppose – [3] **to lag** to move or develop more slowly than others – [4] **stake** risk

Phil Collins

Another Day in Paradise

A day in paradise—what would it be like for you?

She calls out to the man on the street
"Sir, can you help me?"
"It's cold, and I've nowhere to sleep,
is there somewhere you can tell me?"

He walks on, doesn't look back,
He pretends he can't hear her,
Starts to whistle as he crosses the street,
Seems embarrassed to be there.
Oh, think twice, it's another day for
You and me in paradise.
Oh, think twice, it's just another day for you,
You and me in paradise.

She calls out to the man on the street.
He can see she's been crying.
She's got blisters[1] on the soles of her feet.
Can't walk, but she's trying.

Oh, think twice, it's another day for
You and me in paradise.
Oh, think twice, it's just another day for you,
You and me in paradise.

Oh Lord, is there nothing more anybody can do?
Oh Lord, there must be something you can say.

You can tell from the lines on her face.
You can see that she's been there.
Probably been moved on from every place
'Cos she didn't fit in there.

Oh, think twice, it's another day for
You and me in paradise.
Oh, think twice, it's just another day for you,
You and me in paradise.

"He" and "she"

1. What is "her" situation like?
2. What is "his" attitude towards "her"?

[1] **blister** swelling on the skin containing liquid

"Us"

1. "Think twice"—why?
   What problems do you think about when you listen to the song?
2. Imagine "he" and "she" start a conversation in the street. Work with your partner, make it up and act it out.

Lucas Cranach d. Ä.: Paradise (1530)

Pieter Bruegel d. Ä.: Land of Cockaigne (1567)

Imagine paradise

Have a close look at the pictures and describe them. How have the artists' representations of paradise changed over the centuries? Why?

Pablo Picasso: Peace (1952)

Jan Bruegel d. Ä.: Paradise

John Michell: Garden of Allah

John Berger

An Old Woman with a Pram

"Home, sweet home" and "My home is my castle." These are well-known English sayings. Explain what they mean. What does the idea of "home" mean to you? Give explanations starting with "Home is ..."

What effect does this sentence structure have on you?

Near Oxford Circus, London. In the nineties. Difficult to judge her age, probably around forty-five. Her belongings were in a shopping chariot, lifted from a supermarket. She wheeled it along the pavement, her face slightly inclined, as if it were a pram and she were looking for a baby. Her belongings in the chariot were in plastic bags. She wore a scarf around her head and a fur hat—what the Russians call a chapka. Much of its fur had fallen out. She also wore trousers, a padded[1] jacket and an imitation-fur coat, the colour of dust. From a distance you might think she was clothed like an Eskimo. Except for her feet. She was wearing a pair of American style sneakers. She found them in a dustbin on New Cavendish Street, which is near Hallam Street where my mother once lived when she was alive.

In the London underground stations a number of platform benches have recently been replaced by a new piece of public furniture. A kind of perch[2]—which allows waiting passengers to take the weight off their feet and thus lean back a little. Its notable advantage is that no tramp can lie down on it to sleep. At night when the woman with the chapka lies down on a piece of cardboard which she places on the station asphalt, she doesn't take off her white shoes but just loosens the laces so they don't pinch[3] her feet, which swell up at night like my mother's did. Now it is midday and she is walking towards a pedestrian precinct[4] behind Oxford Circus where hundreds of pigeons gather. As soon as the pigeons perceive the woman with the chapka they waddle on their feet, or fly over the paving stones towards her. From her chariot she takes a black plastic bag of stale[5] bread, thrown out by a restaurant in Mortimer Street, and breaking up the bread with her hands, she flings fistfuls of breadcrumbs into the air.

[1] **padded** filled or covered with soft material – [2] **perch** kind of branch – [3] **to pinch** to hurt by being too tight – [4] **pedestrian precinct** area of a town where people can walk and cars are not allowed – [5] **stale** no longer fresh or good

Several pigeons perch[1] on her arms, a few hang, fluttering, in the air above her head, but most wait on the ground to peck up the crumbs as they fall. From time to time, absent-mindedly, the woman puts a scrap of bread[2] into her own mouth.

During my childhood we had a stone birdbath in the back garden of our house and during one hard hard winter my mother—who must have been about the age of this woman at that time—strode every morning through the deep snow between the silver birch trees to put out toast on the frozen water. Like Maeterlinck[3], my mother believed birds carried messages from the dead. The tramp woman, holding a bird in her hands, is shooing[4] the others away by tossing her head and prodding[5] with her elbows into the air. The bird held against her breast has lost some of its feathers and its round head, a little smaller than a ping-pong ball, is half bald. It has refused the bread she offered. Still holding the pigeon against her coat, she searches in another one of her plastic bags and finds a baby's bottle and a little milk in it. She expresses a few drops into the pigeon's beak, which she manages to hold open.

Each day, before coming to Oxford Circus, she prepares the bald pigeon's bottle and each day, after feeding the rest of the flock, she gives the bald one its milk.

Talking about the woman

1. Read the text up to l. 57. What will happen to the woman? Write a possible continuation in a few sentences.
2. The end of the story isn't really surprising. Find clues in the text that foreshadow this ending.
3. Give an outline of how the woman spends her day.

Meeting the woman

One day, a reporter, a social worker and a priest meet the woman and ask her questions about her previous life. Work in groups: one pupil is the reporter, the other is the women, the third is the social worker, the fourth is the priest. Think of the conversation they could have.

[1]**to perch** to sit on top of – [2]**scrap of bread** piece of bread – [3]**Maurice Maeterlinck** [metaliŋk] Belgian poet and dramatist (1862–1949) – [4]**to shoo** to drive away by making this cry – [5]**to prod** to push with sth pointed

Info

Recent Trends in British Society

The Office for National Statistics (ONS) suggests that Britain is experiencing trends that have not been seen since the boom of the 1980s. It reveals important information on the degree of social deprivation[1] in Britain.
In fact, during the Conservative Government, prosperity[2] was growing and there were expectations that society would be less divided by class in the 90s. Yet, under the New Labour, the class divide is growing. Poverty increased during the first year of the Labour government; regional differences have to be taken into consideration and correlate with the unemployment rate in the respective[3] area:

The Rowntree report, the most comprehensive[4] and scientifically rigorous survey of this type ever undertaken, is alarming. It is based on interviews with individuals drawing a list of items that a majority considered "necessities[5]." These were defined as those things that everyone should be able to afford and which they shouldn't have to go without. The survey claims that poverty is in sharp rise: in 1983, 14% of households lacked three or more necessities because they couldn't afford them. That proportion had increased to 21% in 1990 and to over 24% by 1999. By the end of 1999 a quarter (26%) of the British population were living in poverty.
Over 90 per cent of the people questioned defined necessities as a bed, heating, a damp-free[6] home, two meals a day and medical prescriptions. Less than 10 per cent of those questioned considered dishwashers, mobile phones and Internet access or satellite television to be necessities.

The study produces some terrifying statistics:

- Some four million do not eat adequately by today's standards, i.e. they cannot afford to eat fresh fruit and vegetables, or two meals a day.
- Around 9.5 million people cannot afford to keep their homes adequately heated, free from damp or in a decent state of decoration.
- Some eight million people cannot afford one or more essential household items such as a refrigerator or carpets for the living area of their homes.
- Almost 6.5 million adults go without essential clothing due to lack of money.
- Nearly 7.5 million people are too poor to engage in social activities considered necessary, such as visiting friends and family, attending weddings and funerals or having celebrations on special occasions.

[1] **deprivation** lack of sth you need – [2] **prosperity** having money and everything that is needed for a good life – [3] **respective** *jeweilig* – [4] **comprehensive** including all the necessary facts that need to be dealt with – [5] **necessity** sth you need to have – [6] **damp** slightly wet

The impact[1] of such deprivation on children was also laid bare by the study. It found that more than two million children go without two or more necessities and around four million (34 per cent) lack at least one essential item, including such things as adequate clothing, a healthy diet, items to help their educational development, an annual week's holiday away from home or social activities.
Recently the Organisation for Economic Cooperation and Development published a study of international comparisons of poverty. It examined the years 1991 and 1996; one result is that 20 % of the British population on average experienced poverty for the years studied. Another information is that during the six years studied 38 % of the British population experienced poverty for at least a year. Britain possesses the worst record on long-term poverty of all countries studied. The United Nations define this state as severe deprivation of basic human needs.

Aaron Medres

I'm Still a Man

What is your idea of a "real man"?

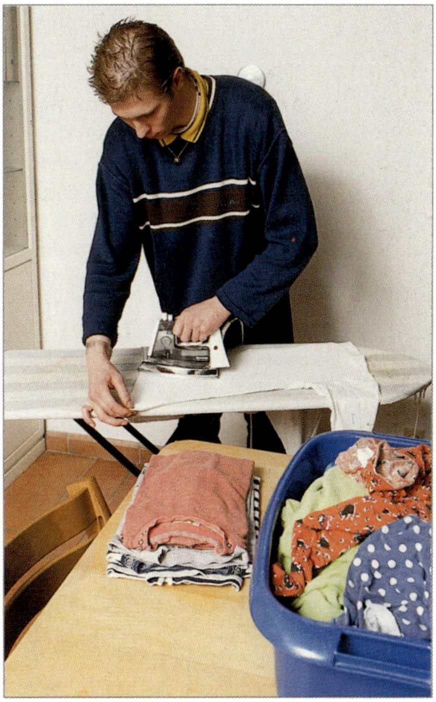

Here I sit once again another long night. I think a lot of what to do with my life. I stay busy doing a lot of different things. I got laid off work 4 weeks ago. So, since then, I have done a few things, tried watching TV (but I can't sit that long). So you go through things like the ones I wanted to do when I was working and didn't have the time to do them. You might say "What about another job? Get off and get a job!" What a concept! The guilt sets in right away. Isn't it the guilt that makes us do a lot of things? What would my family say? I just can't face my friends. How about the friends you haven't seen for a while. "What are you doing?" they say. "Well," you say, "I saw that talk show. Oh, no, you didn't, you were at work." So, nothing to talk about.

Terry, she is my wife, says, "Take time off, enjoy, relax. Do what you want for a while, then go back to work." Well, at least I got the o.k. She knows I know what to do. I'm redoing now the drop-leaf table, stripping[2] it down to bare wood, staining[3] it and putting a new shiny coat[4] on it. I clean the house every day, dust, wash clothes, vacuum, prepare dinner, if she wants it. She calls me from work to let me know about dinner. [...] She comes home and says: "I could get used to this." Does she think I'm never going back to work? Isn't it

[1] **impact** effect, influence – [2] **to strip** to remove paint, varnish from a surface, furniture – [3] **to stain** *beizen* – [4] **coat** *Schicht*

A slot-machine

funny when you are unemployed, no matter what you do, it never feels as if you had accomplished something. The first unemployment cheque! I get on the phone and call her to tell her it came. Excitement fills the air, we hang up. I have to cash[1] this money. I have to cash it at the bank I have been cashing my work cheques at. The bank where everyone knows you by name. The same thing every week for years. Now I walk in the bank in the middle of the afternoon with unemployment stamped on my cheque and forehead. "Ok," I say to myself, hold your head up high, "you are still a man. No job, but still a man." Of course, the teller says he wished he had time off; that makes it worse for me.

The day I got laid off I decided to go to Las Vegas. My wife had looked at me as if I were nuts[2]. Two days later I was in Las Vegas gambling. I blame it all on the shock. I wasn't thinking straight. I'll hit the big one! I flew back with $ 4 in my pocket. I got home and showed it to my wife and it was actually three pennies and a dime, So, I could have had two more pulls on the nickel slot-machine[3]. Now I know with everything in me that those two pulls I would have hit it big!

I watch television, there is a traffic report. I wish I were in it. Off to work! In reality, I hate traffic and everything about it, but I wish I were in it going to any job. Depression tries to come in and I yell[4] "I don't allow you to come in, I'm stronger than that." Now, I'm getting depressed. Nobody cares. Sometimes, people who like me call to see how I'm doing, they can't come over because they work. The table, ok. Why not start my own business, then I won't have to worry about being laid off. So, I make it through another day. I can think of a business to start. Yes, I'm a man.

Protagonist: a major character in a drama; the main person in a story or real event

No job ...

1. Outline the protagonist's feelings while he is unemployed.
2. What role does his wife play in his new situation?

... but still a man

There are self-help groups for unemployed people. Find out how they work and report about them in class.

1. Make a list of terms related to "unemployment".
   Method kit, Mind map, p. 281
2. Transform this text into a newspaper report.
   Method kit, Newspaper article, p. 298

[1] **to cash** to obtain money for – [2] **nuts** (*infml*) crazy – [3] **slot-machine** machine for gambling, activated by placing a coin in – [4] **to yell** to shout, to scream

One year later

We meet the man again after a year. Continue his narration (200 to 300 words) or conduct an interview with him. Work with your partner: write the interview down and present it in class.
➡ Method kit, Interview, p. 308

Simon Trump

A Single Mum Struggles to Keep Her Family out of the Underclass

What might life be like in this building?

In 1989, Denise Cronin was a young housewife. Her husband was in the army and they had a happy, healthy family. Today, she is a single mother; so is one of her daughters, another is living with a boyfriend and Cronin is struggling to raise three more children on one of Britain's most notorious housing estates. Things fell apart after her husband left the forces[1]. He was unemployed for a long period, and their marriage collapsed after the birth of their youngest children, the twins Natalie and Nicole.

Now 38, Cronin has spent the past nine years bringing up her five daughters alone. They have lived an itinerant[2] life, moving from council property to council property around the Cardiff area, never staying anywhere more than three years.

[1] **the forces** here: the army – [2] **itinerant** [aɪ'tɪnərənt] travelling from place to place

Cronin's present home is one of the infamous[1] St Mellons estate, where the high prevailing[2] of single mothers was highlighted recently. On the northeastern fringes[3] of the Welsh capital, it is a grim complex of run-down local authority housing.

Her eldest daughter, Sherry, 19, has fallen into the same trap. She had her first child, Junior, a year ago and her second is due in the next fortnight. She lives in a council flat.

Sherry said: "I was only 11 when Dad walked out and I had to help Mum bring up my sisters. I always loved doing that and I was studying a childcare course when I got pregnant. I suppose I thought I might as well look after my own as someone else's."

Cronin added: "In some ways I was sad when Sherry got pregnant. I was happy to be a granny but it wasn't what I wanted for her. I didn't want her making the same mistakes I had, but she has chosen her path. I will give her all the support I can."

Cronin's second eldest, Claire, 17, is living with her boyfriend in a flat on the St Mellons estate. She said: "I hope I'll get married, but I'm not having any children yet. No way. I've got other things I want to do first."

It was the same message once voiced by Sherry, says Cronin, who still has Sarah, 12, as well as Nathalie and Nicole, now 9, with her.

They live in a clean, tidy, three-bedroom house with few house comforts. "I can't afford any," said Cronin. She receives £122.90 family credit, £33.60 child benefit and £4 housing benefit a week. Her outgoings are £10 to a loan company that paid for furniture for the house, £10 gas, £10 electricity, £2.50 clothing catalogue, £4 television licence, £10 on basic frozen foods such as burgers and chips and £5 on packed lunches.

Could you and your family manage living on that money?

She is sometimes left with as little as £10 a day for essentials such as bread and milk and any other costs for the children. She also smokes.

"It is hard to make ends meet[4]," she says. "It has always been. I think it probably always will be. What's most important is bringing the kids up the best I can. When they leave home the benefits will stop and I'll have to find work. That's not easy when you've never really worked for 30 years, which it will be by then."

Cronin, the daughter of a soldier, was born in Anglesey and moved to Cardiff when she was six. When she was 15, her mother died and Cronin dropped out of school to look after her brother who was 7. At 16, she met her husband in a nightclub in the seaside resort of Penarth. Within 6 months she was married and Sherry was born a year later. Cronin said: "He was a waste of space. He was never faithful and when he came out of the army nobody wanted him. I gave him an ultimatum. I told him he had to face up to his responsibilities and get a job to look after us. Instead, he took the easy way out and walked away."

[1] **infamous** ['ɪnfəməs] well known for being bad or morally evil – [2] **to prevail** [prɪ'veɪl] to be widespread – [3] **fringe** here: borderline – [4] **to make ends meet** to get just enough money for one's needs

Life in the Cronin family

1. Denise Cronin has had a hard life. Write a short biographical sketch. Use all the information given in the text.
2. Considering their difficult economic situation, what will a day in the life of the Cronin family be like?
3. Find out about the situation of children in single-parent families in Germany. Ask people you know and scan your newspaper.
   → Method kit, Skimming and scanning, p. 278

Just imagine

1. Denise Cronin has quite a negative attitude towards her ex-husband. One day, she decides to write him a letter about her and her daughters' situation and the share he has got in it. Write this letter.
2. Imagine you and your classmates have decided to start a campaign in order to help kids in need. What could you do?

Anne Fine

Madame Doubtfire

Daniel Hillard (Robin Williams) loves his children deeply, but divorce proceedings reduce his interaction with them to one day a week only, which, as far as he's concerned, isn't enough. When his ex-wife Miranda (Sally Field) decides to hire a housekeeper, Daniel sees his chance, unorthodox as it may be. He gets his make-up artist brother Frank to turn him into a woman, and he arrives at his old house as the redoubtable Scottish widow Mrs. Doubtfire, who rapidly becomes an indispensable fixture. Here is the scene where Daniel learns about Miranda's intention to get a nanny for the children.

At six o'clock, Daniel realised he could no longer pretend he was waiting for the right moment to tell them his news.

"I have some news. I've got a job. Down at the Art College. Four mornings and two evenings a week," Daniel went on: "It's not exactly a proper acting job, but it's not badly paid, not badly paid at all, considering …"

"Mum says she doubts it. She says you won't earn very much anyway."

"Less in a week than our cleaning lady."

Daniel looked puzzled.

"But you don't have a cleaning lady."

"Not yet," Lydia conceded. "But we are getting one."

"What for? Why does your mother need a cleaning lady? Cleaning things is her hobby. Her

Robin Williams as Mrs. Doubtfire

house is spotless, flawless, perfect. It actually gleams at people when they walk in. It hurts their eyes. Surfaces keep winking[1] and sparkling[2], like in the Babycham adverts."

He paused, remembering ancient battles, and added a little wistfully[3] after a moment:

"Still, that was the way she always liked it, wasn't it? Personally, I always found a little bit of clutter[4] more comfortable."

He waved his arms about expansively, inviting them to enjoy all the comfortable clutter. The bookshelf in the corner that fell down at one end eight months before unfortunately caught his eye. So did the grubby[5] paper lantern hanging in tatters[6] from the lamp fitting. And the waste paper basket that hadn't been emptied of apple cores, orange peel and banana skins for so many weeks that it had formed the delusion that it was a little indoor compost heap, and had begun fermenting gently. Daniel's proud and proprietorial air gradually dwindled into a look of deepening unease. Thick layers of dust prevented any of his surfaces from even aspiring to gleam, let alone sparkle. The furniture was ill-assorted[7] and ill-arranged. The blind[8] hung awry[9]. Discarded[10] reading matter littered the room to such an extent that when, earlier, he'd ordered Christopher to keep his mess of wood shavings and glue on newspaper, his son had simply slid from the table on to the sea of colour supplements all over the floor, and carried on.

The room, Daniel was forced to admit, was not far short of a hopelessly lost cause. Even Hetty had withdrawn cooperation from all attempts at natty[11] housekeeping, and kicked most of her stale[12] food and soiled[13] bedding out through the cage bars on to the floor.

For the first time since he became entirely responsible for his own domestic arrangements, Daniel felt a mild wave of depression sweep over him.

"This place could do with a bit of spring clean," he admitted. "I should get down to it."

Merely the passing thought of all the hours of drudgery[14] it would entail[15] appalled[16] him.

[1] **to wink** to shine with a light that flashes on and off – [2] **to sparkle** to shine in small flashes – [3] **wistful** sad – [4] **clutter** things lying in disorder, mess – [5] **grubby** fairly dirty – [6] **in tatters** ruined, badly damaged – [7] **ill-assorted** not seeming to belong together – [8] **blind** *Jalousie* – [9] **awry** [ə'rai] not in the correct position – [10] **discarded** thrown out or away, put aside – [11] **natty** (*infml*) neat – [12] **stale** no longer fresh or good – [13] **soiled** here: laying on the ground – [14] **drudgery** ['drʌdʒəri] hard boring work – [15] **to entail** to make necessary – [16] **to appal** to fill with fear

Daniel and his apartment

What parallels do you see between Daniel's life and his apartment?

Daniel and his family

Daniel's ex-wife comes to fetch the children. When she sees how Daniel is living, she starts to scold him. Imagine this scene, then act it out. Form different groups where he assumes different roles: obedient, disobedient, demanding, resigned, etc.

Reported speech

Lydia reports this incident to her mother. Put ll. 3–22 ("I have some news ... more comfortable.") into reported speech.

Nick Hornby

About a Boy

Nick Hornby was born in 1957. After graduating from Cambridge University, he first worked in a petrol station, then he became a teacher, a job he quickly gave up. Now, he is a bestselling author of *Fever Pitch* (1992), *High Fidelity* (1995), *About a Boy* (1999) and *How to be Good* (2001). In 1999 he was awarded the *E.M. Forster Award* by the *American Academy of Arts and Letters*.

For most people a happy childhood is something very special. What do you associate with "happy childhood"?

What does his mother look like?

When he got home his mother was lying on the floor with a coat draped over her, watching children's cartoons. She didn't look up.

"Didn't you go to work today?"

"This morning. I took the afternoon off sick."

"What kind of sick?"

No answer.

What are Marcus's ideas about being a kid?

This wasn't right. He was only a kid. He'd been thinking that more and more recently, as he got older and older. He didn't know why. Maybe it was because, when he really was only a kid, he wasn't capable of recognizing it—you had to be of a certain age before you realized that you were actually quite young. Or maybe when he was little there was nothing to worry about—five or six years ago his mum never spent half the day shivering under a coat watching stupid cartoons, and even if she had he might not have thought it was anything out of the ordinary.

But something was going to have to give. He was having a shit time at school and a shit time at home, and as home and school was all there was to it, just about, that meant he was having a shit time all the time, apart from when he was asleep. Someone was going to have to do something about it, because he couldn't do anything about it himself, and he couldn't see who else there was, apart from the woman under the coat.

She was funny, his mum. She was all for talking. She was always on at him to talk and tell her things, but he was sure she didn't really mean it. She was fine on the little things, but he knew that if he went for the big stuff then there'd be trouble, especially now, when she cried and cried about nothing. But at the moment he couldn't see any way of avoiding it. He was only a kid, and she was his mum, and if he felt bad it was her job to stop him feeling bad, simple as that. Even if she didn't want to, even if it meant that she'd end up feeling worse. Tough. Too bad. He was angry enough to talk to her now.

"What are you watching this for? It's rubbish. You're always telling me."

"I thought you liked cartoons."

"I do. I just don't like this one. It's terrible."

Why does Marcus insist?

They both stared at the screen without speaking. This weird[1] dog-type thing was trying to get at a boy who could turn himself into a kind of flying saucer.

"What sort of sick?" He asked the question roughly, the way a teacher would ask someone like Paul Cox whether he'd done his homework.

No answer again.

"Mum, what sort of sick?"

"Oh, Marcus, it's not the sort of sick that—"

[1] **weird** [wɪəd] strange, unusual

"Don't treat me like an idiot, Mum."

She started crying again, long, low sobs that terrified him. "You've got to stop this."

"I can't."

"You've got to. If you can't look after me properly then you'll have to find someone who can. "

She rolled over on to her stomach and looked at him. "How can you say I don't look after you?"

"Because you don't. All you do is make my meals and I could do that. The rest of the time you just cry. That's … that's no good. That's no good to me."

She cried even harder then, and he let her. He went upstairs to his room and played NBA Basketball with the earphones on, even though he wasn't supposed to on school nights. But when he came downstairs she was up and the duvet[1] had been put away. She was spooning pasta and sauce on to plates, and she seemed OK. He knew she wasn't OK—he may have been just a kid, but he was old enough to know that people didn't stop being nuts[2] (and that, he was beginning to realize, was what sort of sick it was) just because you told them to stop—but he didn't care, as long as she was OK in front of him.

What kind of illness does his mother probably suffer from?

"You're going to a picnic on Saturday," she said out of the blue[3].

"A picnic?"

"Yes. In Regent's Park."

"Who with?"

"Suzie."

"Not that SPAT[4] lot."

"Yes, that SPAT lot."

"I hate them." Fiona had taken Marcus to a SPAT summer party in someone's garden when they first moved to London, but she hadn't been back since; Marcus had been to more meetings than she had, because Suzie had taken him on one of their outings.

"Tant pis."

What did she have to say things like that for? He knew it was French for "tough shit", but why couldn't she just say "tough shit"? No wonder he was a weirdo[5]. He put loads and loads of cheese on his pasta and stirred it around.

"Are you going?"

"No."

[1]**duvet** [du:vei/dju:vei] bed quilt used in place of blankets – [2]**nuts** crazy – [3]**out of the blue** (*infml*) unexpectedly – [4]**SPAT** abbreviation for an organization called *Single Parents Alone Together* – [5]**weirdo** (*infml*) sb who behaves strangely

"So why do I have to?"

"Because I'm having a rest."

"I can keep out of your way."

"I'm doing what you said. I'm getting someone else to look after you. Suzie's much more capable than I am."

Suzie was her best friend; they'd known each other since school days. She was nice; Marcus liked her a lot. But he still didn't want to go on a picnic with her and all those horrible little kids from SPAT. He was ten years older than most of them, and every time he'd done anything with them before, he'd hated it. The last time, when they all went to the zoo, he'd come home and told his mum he wanted a vasectomy[1]. That made her laugh a lot, but he'd meant it. He knew for a fact that he was never going to have children, so why not get it over and done with now?

Why has he made up his mind never to have children of his own?

"I could do anything. I could sit in my room all day playing games. You wouldn't even know I was in the house."

"I want you to get out. Do something normal. It's too intense here."

"What do you mean?"

"I mean … Oh, I don't know what I mean. I just know that we're not doing each other any good."

Hold on a moment. They didn't do *each other* any good? For the first time since his mother had started crying, he wanted to cry too. He knew she wasn't doing him any good, but he had no idea it worked both ways. What had he done to her? He couldn't think of a single thing. One day he'd ask her what she was on about, but not today, not now. He wasn't sure he'd like the answer.

Reality and …

1. Describe Marcus's present situation.
2. What condition is his mother currently in? What could have caused it?
3. Find out about Marcus's relationship to his mother.

… dream

1. "He was having a shit time all the time." What could set an end to this situation?
2. Marcus is looking for a new dad. He writes an ad for his mum and himself. Write this ad.

[1] **vasectomy** medical operation to make a man sterile

Caryl Churchill

Top Girls

At the beginning of her career, Caryl Churchill wrote stage plays for students and radio plays for the BBC. In 1972, she began her transition to the professional stage and served as resident dramatist at the Royal Court Theatre.
The following excerpt is taken from the play *Top Girls*, Act 2, Scene 3, first published in 1982.

MRS KIDD *comes in*.

MRS KIDD: Excuse me.

MARLENE: Yes.

MRS KIDD: Excuse me.

MARLENE: Can I help you?

MRS KIDD: Excuse me bursting[1] in on you like this but I have to talk to you.

MARLENE: I am engaged at the moment. If you could go to reception—

MRS KIDD: I'm Rosemary Kidd, Howard's wife, you don't recognize me but we did meet, I remember you of course but you wouldn't—

MARLENE: Yes of course, Mrs Kidd, I'm sorry, we did meet. Howard's about somewhere I expect, have you looked in his office?

MRS KIDD: Howard's not about, no. I'm afraid it's you I've come to see if I could have a minute or two.

MARLENE: I do have an appointment in five minutes.

MRS KIDD: This won't take five minutes. I'm very sorry. It is a matter of some urgency.

MARLENE: Well of course. What can I do for you?

MRS KIDD: I just wanted a chat, an informal chat. It's not something I can simply—I'm sorry if I'm interrupting your work. I know office work isn't like housework which is all interruptions.

MARLENE: No, no, this is my niece. Angie. Mrs Kidd.

MRS KIDD: Very pleased to meet you.

[1] **to burst** (burst, burst) **in on sb** to interrupt suddenly and noisily

ANGIE: Very well thank you.
MRS KIDD: Howard's not in today.
MARLENE: Isn't he?
MRS KIDD: He's feeling poorly.
MARLENE: I didn't know. I'm sorry to hear that.
MRS KIDD: The fact is he's in a state of shock. About what's happened.
MARLENE: What has happened?
MRS KIDD: You should know if anyone. I'm referring to you being appointed managing director instead of Howard. He hasn't been at all well all weekend. He hasn't slept for three nights. I haven't slept.

What's wrong with Howard?

MARLENE: I'm sorry to hear that, Mrs Kidd. Has he thought of taking sleeping pills?
MRS KIDD: It's very hard when someone has worked all these years.
MARLENE: Business life is full of little setbacks[1]. I'm sure Howard knows that. He'll bounce back[2] in a day or two. We all bounce back.
MRS KIDD: If you could see him you'd know what I'm talking about. What's it going to do to him working for a woman? I think if it was a man he'd get over it as something normal.
MARLENE: I think he's going to have to get over it.
MRS KIDD: It's me that bears the brunt[3]. I'm not the one that's been promoted. I put him first every inch of the way. And now what do I get? You women this, you women that. It's not my fault. You're going to have to be very careful how you handle him. He's very hurt.

What is the relationship between Mrs Kidd and her husband like?

MARLENE: Naturally I'll be tactful and pleasant to him, you don't start pushing someone round. I'll consult him over any decisions affecting his department. But that's no different, Mrs Kidd, from any of my other colleagues.
MRS KIDD: I think it is different, because he's a man.
MARLENE: I'm not quite sure why you came to see me.
MRS KIDD: I had to do something.
MARLENE: Well you've done it, you've seen me. I think that's probably all we've time for. I'm sorry he's been taking it out on[4] you. He really is a shit, Howard.
MRS KIDD: But he's got a family to support. He's got three children. It's only fair.
MARLENE: Are you suggesting I give up the job to him then?
MRS KIDD: It had crossed my mind if you were unavailable after all for some reason, he would be the natural second choice I think, don't you? I'm not asking.
MARLENE: Good.
MRS KIDD: You mustn't tell him I came. He's very proud.

[1] **setback** here: defeat, disappointment – [2] **to bounce back** to feel better quickly or become successful again – [3] **to bear the brunt of sth** to receive the worst part of an attack – [4] **to take it out on sb** to make sb suffer because you are feeling angry, tired etc

MARLENE: If he doesn't like what's happening here he can go and work somewhere else.
MRS KIDD: Is that a threat?
MARLENE: I'm sorry but I do have some work to do.
MRS KIDD: It's not that easy, a man of Howard's age. You don't care. I thought he was going too far but he's right. You're one of these ballbreakers that's what you are. You'll end up—
MARLENE: I'm sorry but I do have some work to do.
MRS KIDD: miserable and lonely. You're not natural.
MARLENE: Could you please piss off?
MRS KIDD: I thought if I saw you at least I'd be doing something.
MRS KIDD *goes.*
MARLENE: I've got to go and do some work now. Will you come back later?
ANGIE: I think you were wonderful.
MARLENE: I've got to go and do some work now.
ANGIE: You told her to piss off—
MARLENE: Will you come back later?
ANGIE: Can't I stay here?
MARLENE: Don't you want to go sightseeing?
ANGIE: I'd rather stay here.
MARLENE: You can stay here I suppose, if it's not boring.
ANGIE: It's where I most want to be in the world.
MARLENE: I'll see you later then.
MARLENE *goes.*
ANGIE: *sits at desk.*

Why is Angie so pleased?

Talking about the women

Here are 50 adjectives to characterize Marlene, Mrs Kidd and Angie. Find out which adjectives go with which woman. If you don't know the words, look them up in a dictionary.

arrogant, timid, old-fashioned, self-confident, courageous, offensive, outspoken, impressive, intimidating, obedient, rebellious, coward, mousy, patient, polite, indulging, imposing, submissive, attentive, self-absorbed, serene, modest, obliging, impertinent, resolute, stubborn, headstrong, disrespectful, coy, rude, considerate, well-behaved, lofty, self-possessed, determined, restrained, superior, candid, commanding, disdainful, proud, liberal, generous, selfish, dynamic, torpid, rigorous, mean, open-minded, condescending

Talking it over again

1. Work in groups. After the meeting, Mrs Kidd talks on the phone to a friend of hers about the meeting she has just had with Marlene. Perform this dialogue. At the same time, Marlene is chatting with a friend of hers. Write this dialogue.
2. Angie, Marlene's niece, has just witnessed the encounter between these two very different women. Sitting over her diary, she reflects on her own future and the kind of woman she wants to be and why. Write the diary entry for Angie.
   → Method kit, Diary entry, p. 294

Acting it out!

Knowing Mrs Kidd and Marlene quite well now, act out this scene. One group takes over the work of the director, one group is responsible for the stage props.

Virginia Woolf

Shakespeare's Sister

The following excerpt is taken from *A Room of One's Own*, written in 1929. This essay soon became a feminist classic, in which Virginia Woolf (1882–1941) points out the necessity of independence and privacy for any writer, either male or female.

Do you have a room or place of your own? What does it mean to you?

I am asking why women did not write poetry in the Elizabethan Age, and I am not sure how they were educated; whether they were taught to write; whether they had sitting rooms to themselves, children before they were twenty-one; what, in short, they did from eight in the morning till eight at night. They had no money evidently; according to a historian they were married whether they liked it or not before they were out of the nursery, at fifteen or sixteen very likely. It would have been extremely odd had one of them written the plays of Shakespeare. I thought of that old gentleman, who is dead now, but was a bishop, who declared that it was impossible for any woman past, present, or to come, to have the genius of Shakespeare.

Women cannot write the plays of Shakespeare, I couldn't help thinking as I looked at the works of Shakespeare on the shelf, that the bishop was right at least in this: it would have been impossible, completely and entirely, for any woman to have written the plays of Shakespeare in the age of Shakespeare. Let me imagine, since facts are so hard to come by[1], what would have happened had Shakespeare had a wonderfully gifted sister, called Judith, let us say. Shakespeare himself went, very probably,—his mother was an heiress—to the grammar school, where he may have learnt Latin—Ovid, Virgil and Horace[2]—and the elements of grammar and logic. He was, it is well known, a wild boy who poached[3] rabbits, perhaps shot a deer, and had, rather sooner than he should have done, to marry a woman in the neighbourhood, who bore him a child rather quicker than was right. That escapade sent him to seek fortune in London. He had, it seemed, a taste for the theatre; he began by holding horses at the stage door. Very soon he got work in the theatre, became a successful actor, and lived at the hub[4] of the universe, meeting everybody, knowing everybody, practising his art on the boards[5], exercising his wits in the streets, and even getting access to the palace of the queen.

Virginia Woolf

▲ What kind of boy was Shakespeare?
▼ What kind of girl was Judith?

Meanwhile his extraordinarily gifted sister, let us suppose, remained at home. She was as adventurous, as imaginative, as agog[6] to see the world as he was. But she was not sent to school. She had no chance of learning grammar and logic, let alone of reading Horace and Virgil. She picked up a book now and then, one of her brother's perhaps, and read a few pages. But then her parents came in and told her to mend the stockings or mind the stew and not moon[7] about with books and papers. They would have spoken sharply but kindly, for they were substantial people who knew the conditions of life for a woman and loved their daughter—indeed, more likely than not she was the apple of her father's eye. Perhaps she scribbled some pages up in an apple loft on the sly[8], but was careful to hide them or set fire to them. Soon, however, before she was out of her teens, she was to be betrothed[9] to the son of a neighbouring woolstapler. She cried out that marriage was hateful to her, and for that she was severely beaten by her father. Then he ceased to scold her. He begged her instead not to hurt him, not to shame him in this matter of her marriage. He would give her a chain of

[1] **to come by** here: to obtain – [2] **Ovid, Virgil, Horace** Roman poets – [3] **to poach animals** to catch or shoot animals illegally – [4] **hub** central point of activity, interest or importance – [5] **on the board** (*dated* or *joc*) as a professional actor – [6] **to be agog** to be eager – [7] **to moon about** (*infml*) to spend one's time lazily – [8] **on the sly** secretly – [9] **betrothed** (old formal use) engaged to be married

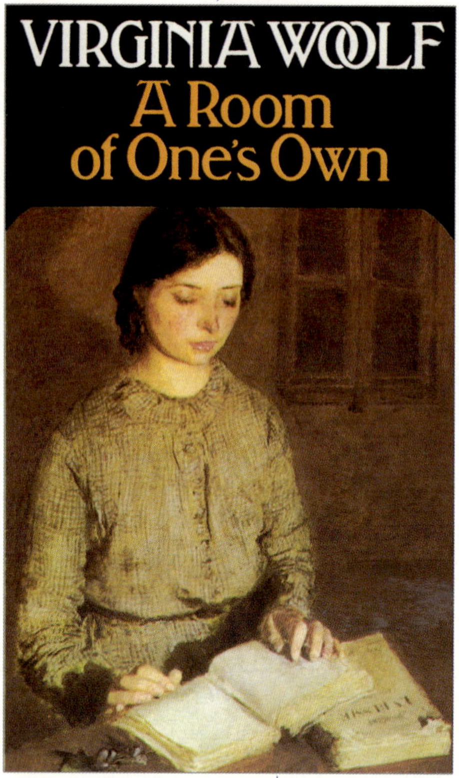

beads or a fine petticoat, he said; and there were tears in his eyes. How could she disobey him? How could she break his heart? The force of her own gift alone drove her to it. She made up a small parcel of her belongings, let herself down by a rope one summer's night and took the road to London. She was not seventeen. The birds that sang in the hedge were not more musical than she was. She had the quickest fancy[1], a gift like her brother's, for the tune of words. Like him, she had a taste for the theatre. She stood at the stage door; she wanted to act, she said. Men laughed in her face. The manager—a fat, loose-lipped man—guffawed[2]. He bellowed something about poodles dancing and women acting—no woman, he said, could possibly be an actress. He hinted—you can imagine what. She could get no training in her craft[3]. Could she even seek her dinner in a tavern or roam[4] the streets at midnight? Yet her genius was for fiction and lusted[5] to feed abundantly upon the lives of men and women and the study of their ways. At last—for she was very young, oddly like Shakespeare the poet in her face, with the same grey eyes and rounded brows—at last Nick Greene the actor-manager took pity on her, she found herself with child by that gentleman and so—who shall measure the heat and violence of the poet's heart when caught and tangled in a woman's body?—killed herself one winter's night and lies buried at some crossroads where the omnibuses now stop.

How do you feel about the manager?

That, more or less, is how the story would run, I think, if a woman in Shakespeare's day had had Shakespeare's genius.

Shakespeare and his sister

1. Summarize in a few words the life of Shakespeare and of his imaginary sister Judith. Compare these two lifestyles.
2. Describe the relationship between Judith and the men mentioned in the text (her father, her brother, the manager, Nick Greene). What does this tell us about women's position in the Elizabethan Age? To what extent is it different today?

[1] **fancy** mind – [2] **to guffaw** to laugh loudly – [3] **craft** skill – [4] **to roam** to walk or travel with no clear purpose or direction – [5] **to lust** to want sth very much

Judith

1. Judith's father wants to marry her off to a man she doesn't love; she rebels against his decision and has a serious quarrel with her father. Enact this quarrel with your partner, then perform it in class. Pay attention to gestures, facial expressions and language.
2. Before leaving home, Judith writes a farewell letter to her family commenting on her life. Write this letter.
3. After her death, there is a trial in which all the persons having influenced her life in one way or the other have to justify themselves. Act out this trial.

Translation

Translate ll. 13–34 ("Women cannot ... palace of the Queen.") into German. Pay special attention to the differences in the syntax between English and German.

Your thematic vocabulary

Collect the words connected with life and work in a changing world from the texts you have read and assemble them in two mind maps. Pay special attention to globalisation and problems in society. Include nouns, verbs and adjectives.

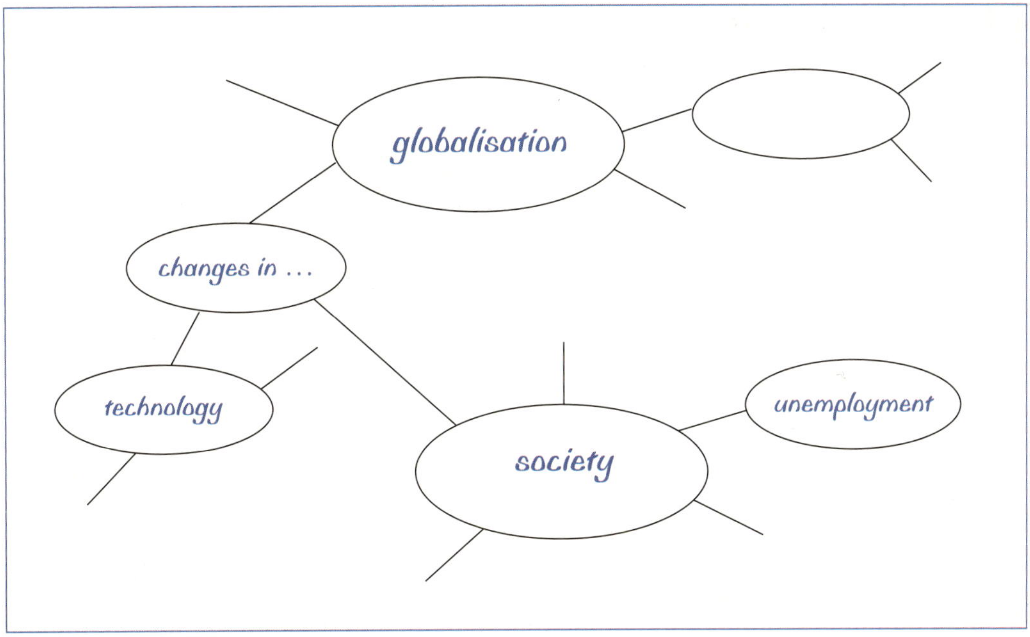

William Shakespeare—

"He made films, he was in a lot of films. I think he wrote Swan Lake about swans dying. It was always on TV. Most of his plays were about dancing."
Peter Weston, student

"He was a famous playwright. Everyone used to like him. He wrote mostly about romance. There was a love potion and the first person who woke up and drank it fell in love. We've got a book about it at home. Shakespeare used words like hath and yea."
Tracy Hennessey, student

"Shakespeare wrote sonnets to his love. Now a couple of lines over the mobile will do the job just as well."
Lycos UK

"I don't read Shakespeare. I think it's dull as ditchwater," *Carol Vorderman*, stumbling over Sir Toby Belch, a character in Shakespeare's *Twelfth Night* in the special charity edition of *Who wants to be a millionaire, April 2001*. She caused an official debate on the necessity of the classics in the school curriculum.

Who Can Beat the Bard?

"He opened a few theatres. He wrote a lot of plays, some funny. They were about jesters. He wouldn't allow women to act. I think he went to college and travelled to America. The plays were written in a very complicated language. I think it was Latin."
Alan Coughlan, student

"If the day ever comes when Shakespeare is no longer acted, read and studied, quoted and loved, western man will be near his end."
J.B. Priestley, social commentator, broadcaster and man of letters (1894–1984)

ITV's top quiz show *Who Wants To Be a Millionaire?* turned up its first £ 1 million winner, who knew her Shakespeare well.
The Guardian, November 20, 2000

"Murder, intrigue, lust, and men in tights—they are all in *The Bard.*" *The Tabloid Shakespeare by Nick Page*

Who was William Shakespeare?

- Four different portraits—four different men?
- What do you know about the Bard?

Compare your ideas to the statements—what strikes you as being odd?

The Enigma—Who Was William Shakespeare?

An Investigation

Edward de Vere, 17th Earl of Oxford (1550–1604)

Four centuries after his first dramas were presented, William Shakespeare remains the most admired and most performed playwright in the world. However, very little is known about the man himself. No one even knows what he really looked like. The shortage of facts has encouraged claims that someone else wrote the plays—perhaps Sir Francis Bacon[1], or even Queen Elizabeth I herself. The theory of choice, lately, has claimed that Edward de Vere, 17th Earl of Oxford, an Elizabethan courtier poet-soldier, wrote the plays.

In the past, Christopher Marlowe was said to have used the pseudonym "Shakespeare" for some of his works. This may have been on account of his biography. He lived a risky life and was fascinated by extremes: he was driven by ambition, boundless desire, a restless, reckless[2] willingness to go beyond limits, be it in the worlds of spies, blackmailers[3], or the equally unstable world of actors and playwrights. He was under official investigation for atheism and treason[4]. On May 30, 1593, Christopher Marlowe, at twenty-nine years old perhaps England's most famous playwright and poet, went to a tavern in London. There, an argument about the bill arose in the course of which Marlowe drew his knife and lunged at one of the man, Ingram Frizer, sitting at the table. In the scuffle that followed, Marlowe's knife ended up stuck in his own head, just above his eye, fatally wounding him. Frizer was briefly[5] held, but then released[6] without punishment. The case was closed. The murder of Marlowe was seen as a manifest sign of God's judgement.

Christopher Marlowe, English dramatist and poet (1564–1593)

[1] **Sir Francis Bacon** (1561–1626) English philosopher, statesman, and essayist – [2] **reckless** without thinking or caring about the consequences or the danger involved – [3] **blackmailer** a person demanding money from sb in return for not revealing secret or unpleasant information about them – [4] **treason** the crime of betraying one's country, e.g. by helping its enemies during a war, or of trying to kill its ruler – [5] **briefly** for a short time – [6] **to release** to set sb or sth free

Max Beerbohm (1872–1956): *William Shakespeare, His Method of Work*

Who wrote Shakespeare?

1. Investigating the cartoon: Sir Francis Bacon stands behind Shakespeare. How do you interpret the situation?
2. Investigating Christopher Marlowe:
   - Find reasons for and against the thesis that Marlowe might have been the author of what is known as Shakespeare's work. For information on the authorship debate go to: www.bardweb.net → Method kit, Internet research, p. 304
   - In the film *Shakespeare in Love,* Will meets Marlowe at the tavern. Have a look at that scene. What is the relationship like between the two? → Method kit, Film analysis, p. 306

www.shakespeare—A Computer Project

"Oh my God,
such ado 'bout my thing!"

Finding Shakespeare on the Internet

Find out about Shakespeare yourself. Work in teams. Use the following links for collecting information from the Internet.
The Method kit will help you organize your group (➜ Method kit, Group activities, p. 314), the Internet research (➜ Method kit, Internet research, p. 304) and a very impressive presentation (➜ Method kit, Presentation; p. 309).

- www.Shakespeare-online.com
- www.stratford-upon-avon.co.uk
- http://daphne.palomar.edu/Shakespeare
- www.Shakespeare.com
- www.luminarium.org/renlit/eliza.htm

Here are your Internet research tasks:

1. Shakespeare—Biography

- When and where was Shakespeare born?
- Where and how did he live?
- What did he write? (Give names and dates of his most important works and find out about the gist of at least three of them.)
- Is there anything new about the Bard?

2. Shakespeare's Time—The Elizabethan Age

- Who was Elizabeth I?
- Did she know Shakespeare?
- What was it like to be a playwright in that era?
- What was theatre like then?

Elizabeth I

The Wheel
of Fortune

3. Shakespeare's World—The Elizabethan World View

The effect of Shakespeare's plays is mostly based on the philosophical, religious and mythical ideas of his time. People believed in the chain of being, the wheel of fortune etc, and they were superstitious about supernatural appearances as might occur in a thunderstorm, magical tricks or dreams.

- Why did people see life as a chain of being?
- What is the "wheel of fortune" and what function did it have for the common man?
- What knowledge did the Elizabethans have about the function of the body and the influence of nature on it (idea of humours, dreams)?

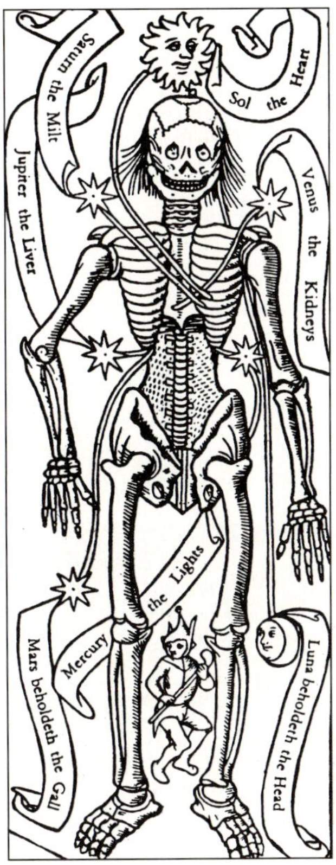

Man and the influence of the stars

The estates

Using a search engine

To find more information on these subjects, you should use a search engine, e.g. www.google.com.

Method Kit, Internet research, p. 304

Now—go for 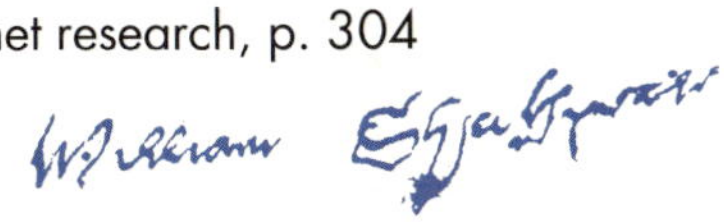

Shakespeare's Language

Info

What Do You Read, My Lord?— Words, Words, Words (*Hamlet* II.2.165–166)

Every spoken language changes. Remember the slang meanings like "shocking" or "cool"? Words come and they go. Shakespeare's people seem to talk funny: lots of *thee*'s and *thou*'s, *hence*'s and *whence's* and then—the rhymes.

Reading Shakespeare, we are confronted with the early modern period of English. His language was not that fixed as to grammar and spelling. The Anglo-Saxon vocabulary of Old English was immensely increased with loanwords from Latin and French. So around 1600 there were many synonyms for one and the same thing:

Anglo-Saxon	**Latin/French**
playhouse	theatre
writer	poet
playgoers	audience
manhood	masculinity

Shakespeare was able to draw on his education at *King Edward VI Grammar School for Boyes* where Latin and Greek were given particular emphasis. Equipped with the knowledge of the ancient classics and historical chronicles, e.g. the *Holinshed Chronicles,* he made good use of that treasure of stories for his own work. Moreover, he profited from the verbal inventiveness and structural flexibility of the Elizabethan language. There was almost no limit to creating new words or playing with double meanings.

Shakespeare was also aware of his audience. The playgoers were people from all walks of life, all levels of education. What made Shakespeare popular with them was that he spoke their language.

A room at the Grammar School (Stratford upon Avon, 16th century)

Witty and sophisticated[1] conversation intermingled with puns and not seldom some smutty[2] joke guaranteed amusement as in this dialogue:

SPEED: Why then, how stands the matter with them?
LAUNCE: Marry, thus: when it stands well with him, it stands well with her.
SPEED: What an ass art thou, I understand thee not.
LAUNCE: What a block art thou, that canst not! My staff understands me.
SPEED: What thou say'st?
LAUNCE: Ay, and what I do too: look thee, I'll but lean, and my staff understands me.
SPEED: It stands under thee indeed.
LAUNCE: Why, stand under and understand is all one.

The Two Gentlemen of Verona II.5.19–29

"Shall I compare thee to a summer's day ?"

Pun: the humorous use of a word that has two meanings, or of different words that sound the same; a play on words.

Special Language Features

• The personal pronoun *you*

One of the striking differences between Shakespearean English and modern English is the use of three different ways to say *you*. For the Elizabethans the use of either *thou* or *you* was an indicator for the closeness or distance between people and their relationship.

- **Thou** [θaʊ] is informal. It was used only among family members, among friends, and to address children or servants. It was also the way one addressed God. You can still find that form in the Bible and in prayers. **Thee** [θi:] is the object form: *dost thou know who speaks to thee?* **Thy** [θaɪ] was used before consonants, and **thine** [θaɪn] was used before vowels for the possessive forms of **thou** [like *your, yours*]. **Thou** was regarded as a means of offence, especially when used with persons of higher rank or authority.
- **You** is formal. Strangers or persons of a higher station were addressed that way and shown respect. Lovers would address their lady with **you**, unless they were an intimate couple; then they would switch to the more private **thou**.
- **Ye** [ji:] is the plural form and also a synonym for *you*.

A Midsummernight's Dream

[1] **sophisticated** *raffiniert* – [2] **smutty** (*infml, derog*) (of talk, pictures, stories, etc) dealing with sex in an offensive way

Info

• The verb

When creating his verses and getting his rhymes right, Shakespeare also took advantage of the verb conjugations that were still used in his time. So we find forms like *thou art, thou dost, thou hast, thou canst* as second-person verb forms. A typical feature of his age was the ending *-th* used in the third-person singular form: *he hath, she knoweth, he wanteth*. Since the modern forms gradually appeared in Shakespeare's time, he could mix them, if necessary, to fit the metre:

The quality of mercy is not strain'd.[1]
It **droppeth** as the gentle rain from heaven
Upon the place beneath: it is twice **blest**,
It **blesseth** him that **gives**, and him that **takes**,
'Tis mightiest in the mightiest, it **becomes**
The throned monarch better than his crown.

Portia in *The Merchant of Venice* IV.1.182–187

Another common stylistic device, which makes reading hard for modern readers, is the use of contractions:

How far is't called to Forres? What are these,
So withered and so wild in their attire[2],
That look not like th' inhabitants o' th' earth,
And yet are on't?—Live you, or are you aught[3]
That man may question? You seem to understand me,
By each at once her choppy[4] finger laying
Upon her skinny lips; you should be women
And yet your beards forbid me to interpret
That you are so.

Banquo in *Macbeth* I.3.37–44

is't = is it
th' inhabitants = the inhabitants
o'th'earth = of the earth
on't = on it

Why did Shakespeare use verse?

There are two reasons why he used verse in his drama. It was a long tradition and it was good for memorization. Sometimes to achieve a certain effect, he used prose. For the actors, though, it was easier to learn a lot of lines in a short time, if they rhymed. Some lines, however, challenged the actors' skills. Shakespeare often exercised his poetic license to fit words into the scheme, especially those with more than two syllables (glorious: 3 syl. – read: ['glɒrjəs]: 2 syl.). Or, on the other hand, he extracted words that were too short (bruised: 1 syl. – read: ['bru:zɪd]: 2 syl.).

[1] **strain(e)d** to take or use sth to or beyond the limit of what is acceptable or possible – [2] **attire** (*fml* or *rhet*) clothes; dress – [3] **aught** [ɔ:t] (*arch*) something – [4] **choppy** slightly rough

Info

His lines often had a song-like even nursery rhyme-like quality with a rather regular stress:

Two households both alike in dignity
(In fair Verona, where we lay our scene)
From ancient grudge[1] break to new mutiny[2],
Where civil blood makes civil hands unclean.
From forth the fatal loins[3] of these two foes[4]
A pair of star-cross'd lovers take their life,
Whose misadventur'd piteous[5] overthrows
Doth with their death bury their parents' strife.
The fearful passage of their death-mark'd love
And the continuance of their parents' rage,
Which, but their children's end, nought[6] could remove,
Is now the two hours' traffic of our stage;
The which, if you with patient ears attend,
What here shall miss, our toil[7] shall strive to mend[8].

Romeo and Juliet, Prologue. 1–14

Crispin de Passe: *Lovers Making Music.*
In Shakespeare's world music was a symbol for harmony that was disturbed and had to be reconstructed again.

Reading rhythm

Start by reading the prologue aloud to your partner. Then let him or her read it to you.

1. Can you find the stress pattern?
2. What does it sound like? Try beating the rhythm.

Reading rhyme

How does the rhyme scheme work? What special kind of structure does the prologue have?

[1] **grudge** (*fml* or *rhet*) feeling of dislike, ill will, envy or resentment – [2] **mutiny** refusal to obey the proper authorities, esp by soldiers or sailors – [3] **loins** the place where a person's legs, or trouser legs, join – [4] **foe** enemy – [5] **piteous** deserving or causing pity – [6] **nought** [nɔːt] (*arch*) nothing – [7] **toil** work that is hard and makes one very tired – [8] **to mend** to repair, to make sth better; to improve sth; to return to health; to heal

Two Sonnets

Sonnet 130

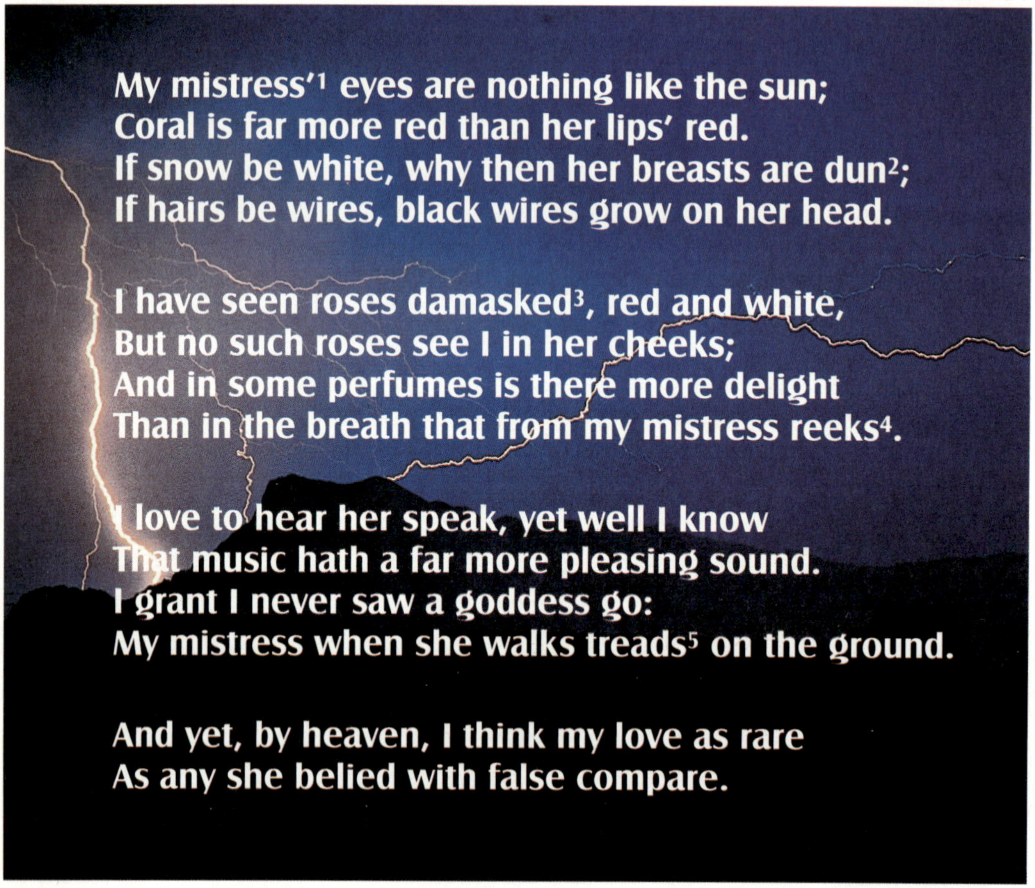

My mistress'[1] eyes are nothing like the sun;
Coral is far more red than her lips' red.
If snow be white, why then her breasts are dun[2];
If hairs be wires, black wires grow on her head.

I have seen roses damasked[3], red and white,
But no such roses see I in her cheeks;
And in some perfumes is there more delight
Than in the breath that from my mistress reeks[4].

I love to hear her speak, yet well I know
That music hath a far more pleasing sound.
I grant I never saw a goddess go:
My mistress when she walks treads[5] on the ground.

And yet, by heaven, I think my love as rare
As any she belied with false compare.

The mistress

1. Shakespeare did not give titles to his sonnets. Later they were numbered. What title would you give this poem?
2. Paraphrase each line in modern English. What does Shakespeare really say about the woman?
3. What might the mistress look like? Draw a picture of her.

[1] **mistress** beloved woman – [2] **dun** *fahl* – [3] **damasked** ['dæməskt] *rosig, zweifarbig* – [4] **to reek** to smell very strongly of sth – [5] **to tread** [tred] (trod, trodden *or* trod) to set one's foot down; to walk or step

Sonnet 18

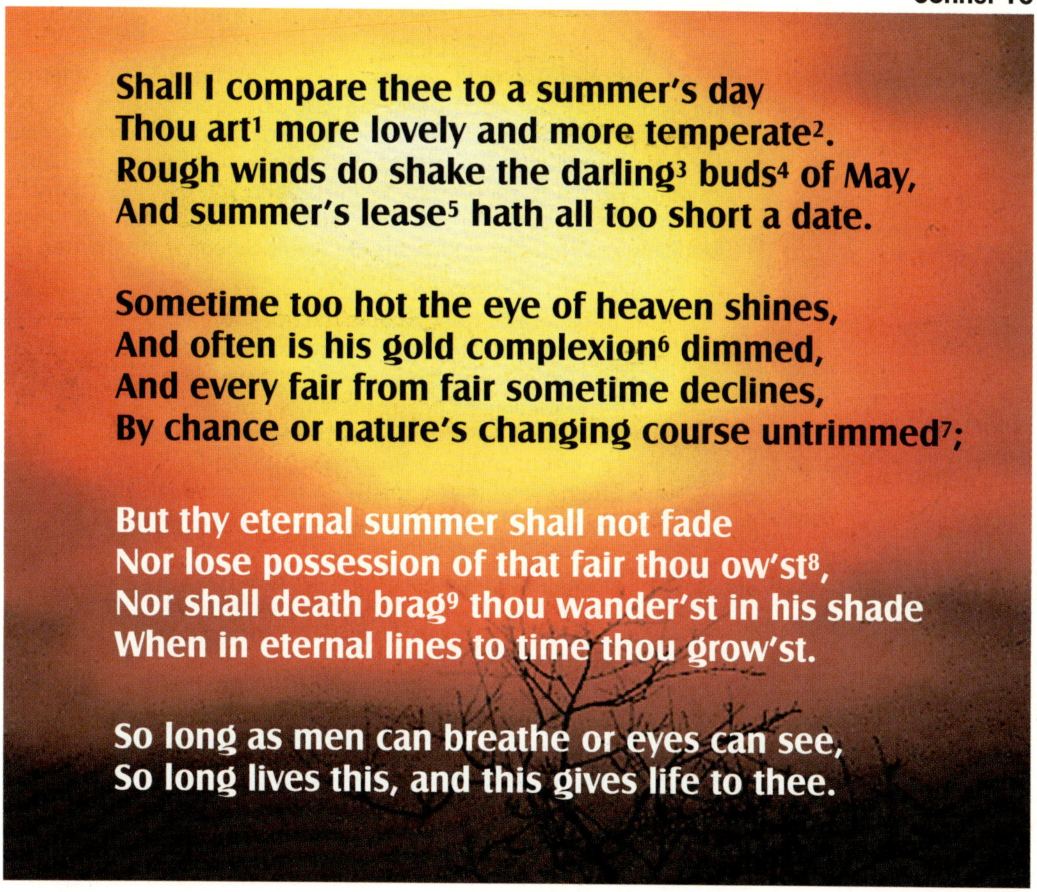

Shall I compare thee to a summer's day
Thou art[1] more lovely and more temperate[2].
Rough winds do shake the darling[3] buds[4] of May,
And summer's lease[5] hath all too short a date.

Sometime too hot the eye of heaven shines,
And often is his gold complexion[6] dimmed,
And every fair from fair sometime declines,
By chance or nature's changing course untrimmed[7];

But thy eternal summer shall not fade
Nor lose possession of that fair thou ow'st[8],
Nor shall death brag[9] thou wander'st in his shade
When in eternal lines to time thou grow'st.

So long as men can breathe or eyes can see,
So long lives this, and this gives life to thee.

Comparing the sonnets

1. Who might the addressees of these sonnets be?
2. Which images does Shakespeare use to praise beauty?
3. What formal aspects do the sonnets have in common?

Your sonnet

Write your own (mock) sonnet. What or whom do you want to praise?
➪ Language kit, Sonnet, p. 319

[1] **thou art** you are – [2] **temperate** mild – [3] **darling** lovely – [4] **bud** *Knospe* – [5] **lease** time – [6] **complexion** face – [7] **untrimmed** the decorations of beauty taken away – [8] **thou ow'st** you own – [9] **to brag** to show off

Hesitation and Conscience: Two Famous Soliloquies

Soliloquy [-'---]: a speech of a protagonist to himself and to the audience taking them inside his mind thus revealing his thoughts and feelings.

Hamlet, Prince of Denmark, wonders if he might have been better off if he had simply not been born. He also considers suicide, but his Christian belief forbids it and honour demands action. Haunted by the ghost of his late father, he is supposed to take revenge on his Uncle Claudius, who has succeeded to the throne after killing Hamlet's father and marrying his mother Gertrude. Yet he hesitates. He wants Claudius's soul to suffer and plans the re-enactment of the murder.

A student's performance of Hamlet's soliloquy

To be, or not to be, that is the question:
Whether 'tis nobler in the mind to suffer
The slings and arrows of outrageous[1] fortune,
Or to take arms against a sea of troubles
And by opposing end them. To die— to sleep,
No more; and by a sleep to say we end
The heartache and the thousand natural shocks
That flesh is heir to: 'tis a consummation[2]
Devoutly[3] to be wish'd. To die, to sleep;
To sleep, perchance to dream— ay, there's the rub[4]:
For in that sleep of death what dreams may come
When we have shuffled off[5] this mortal coil[6],
Must give us pause—there's the respect
That makes calamity[7] of so long life.
For who would bear[8] the whips[9] and scorns[10] of time,
Th' oppressor's wrong, the proud man's contumely[11],
The pangs of dispriz'd love, the law's delay,
The insolence[12] of office, and the spurns[13]
That patient merit of th' unworthy takes,
When he himself might his quietus[14] make
With a bare bodkin[15]? Who would these fardels[16] bear,
To grunt and sweat under a weary[17] life,
But that the dread[18] of something after death,
The undiscover'd country from whose bourn[19]
No traveller returns, puzzles the will,
And makes us rather bear those ills we have

Hamlet

[1] **outrageous** [aʊt'reɪdʒəs] very shocking and unacceptable – [2] **consummation** final ending – [3] **devoutly** [dɪ'vaʊtlɪ] *inbrünstig* – [4] **there's the rub** that's the problem – [5] **to shuffle off** to get rid of sth – [6] **coil** chaos, disorder – [7] **calamity** disaster – [8] **to bear** [beər] (bore, borne) to accept sth unpleasant without complaining; to stand sth – [9] **whip** *Peitschenhieb* – [10] **scorn** offence, contempt – [11] **contumely** (*fml*) derision, scorn – [12] **insolence** extremely rude behaviour showing a lack of respect – [13] **spurn** *Fußtritt* – [14] **quietus** 1. the end of one's life; 2. (*fig*) come-uppance – [15] **bodkin** (*arch*) short sword – [16] **fardel** (*arch*) burden – [17] **weary** ['wɪərɪ] no longer interested in or enthusiastic about sth; tired of sth – [18] **dread** [dred] fear – [19] **bourn** border

Than fly to others that we know not of?
Thus conscience does make cowards of us all,
And thus the native hue[1] of resolution
Is sicklied o'er[2] with the pale cast[3] of thought,
And enterprises of great pitch[4] and moment
With this regard their currents[5] turn awry[6],
And lose the name of action. Soft you now,
The fair Ophelia! Nymph, in thy orisons[7]
Be all my sins remember'd.

Hamlet, III.1.56–90

Macbeth is on the verge of killing his king, Duncan. Duncan sleeps soundly in Macbeth's castle, where he feels safe since Macbeth has been his loyal soldier and as his host has to care for the well-being of his guest and keep him from any harm. Supported by his ambitious wife and driven by the prophecies of witches, he has planned to murder Duncan and become his successor to the throne. Before the deed, he sees an imaginary dagger[8] leading the way to his victim. Hesitantly, he turns the dreadful business over and over in his mind until he overcomes his scruples.

"Come, let me clutch thee." Sir Laurence Olivier in a 1955 London theatre production

Is this a dagger which I see before me,
The handle toward my hand? Come, let me clutch[9] thee:
I have thee not, and yet I see thee still.
Art thou not, fatal vision, sensible
To feeling as to sight? Or art thou but
A dagger of the mind, a false creation
Proceeding from[10] the heat-oppressèd[11] brain?
I see thee yet, in form as palpable[12]
As this which now I draw.
Thou marshall'st[13] me the way that I was going,
And such an instrument I was to use.

[1] **hue** [hju:] complexion, shade of colour – [2] **to sickly over** (*arch, fig*) to cover with a colour of sickness – [3] **cast** shade of colour, hue – [4] **pitch** (*arch*) *Höhe* – [5] **current** movement of water flowing in a certain direction through a larger body of water – [6] **awry** [ə'raɪ] (*adj*) wrong; not as expected – [7] **orison** (*arch*) prayer

Macbeth
[8] **dagger** *Dolch* – [9] **to clutch** to seize sb or sth eagerly – [10] **to proceed from** to be caused by or originate from sth – [11] **heat-oppressèd** ['--ˌ--] feverish – [12] **palpable** ['---] touchable – [13] **to marshall** to guide

Mine eyes are made the fools o' th' other senses,
Or else worth all the rest. I see thee still
And on thy blade and dudgeon[1] gouts[2] of blood,
Which was not so before. There's no such thing:
It is the bloody business which informs
Thus to mine eyes. Now o'er the one half-world
Nature seems dead, and wicked dreams abuse
The curtained sleep. Witchcraft celebrates
Pale Hecate's[3] off'rings, and withered murder[4],
Alarumed by his sentinel[5], the wolf,
Whose howl's his watch, thus with his stealthy pace[6],
With Tarquin's ravishing[7] strides[8], towards his design[9]
Moves like a ghost. Thou sure and firm-set earth,
Hear not my steps, which way they walk, for fear
Thy very stones prate[10] of my whereabout,
And take the present horror from the time,
Which now suits with it. Whiles I threat, he lives;
Words to the heat of deeds too cold breath gives.
A bell rings
I go, and it is done. The bell invites me.
Hear it not, Duncan, for it is a knell[11]
That summons[12] thee to heaven or to hell.

Macbeth, II.1.33–64

Tarquin: a Roman king who raped and mutilated his friend's wife, Lucrece. To Elizabethans, he was a symbol of betrayal and cruelty.

What do they say?

Make a copy of one of the speeches. Cut it out and stick it in the middle of a larger piece of paper. Use the space around it to add your comments and thoughts about it. Keep it for discussing your ideas with your classmates.

Bare bones

1. Reduce Macbeth's speech to the most important keywords or phrases. Connect them with the fewest possible words. Your text should not be longer than ten lines but understandable for anyone who doesn't know it.
2. Compare your version to your partner's. What is the essence of the speech?
3. What has been lost by cutting it down to the "bare bones"? What about the dramatic effect? Compare it again with the original.

[1]**dudgeon** handle – [2]**gout** drop – [3]**Hecate** ['hɛkətɪ] goddess of witchcraft – [4]**withered murder** (*fig*) death coming as a murderer – [5]**sentinel** watchman – [6]**pace** *Schritt* – [7]**to ravish** to rape, to violate – [8]**stride** one long step – [9]**design** purpose – [10]**to prate** (*dated, derog*) to talk – [11]**knell** [nel] funeral bell – [12]**to summon** to order a group of people to attend a meeting, etc

Double talking

Work in pairs. Present one of these two soliloquies in dialogue form (e.g. as good angel—bad angel). You might use two voices to represent opposing viewpoints, or develop the meaning of the passage by having each voice contribute an idea in turn; sometimes you might speak together, sometimes your exchange may be in a whisper or in vigorous assertions.

Writing to a soulmate

Imagine Hamlet has a good friend. He writes him about what is worrying him and asks him for advice. Write that letter using Hamlet's thoughts but "translate" them into modern English.

Robert Dudley: *The Assassination of King Duncan* (19th century)

Supernatural Forces

The Weird Sisters

Would you go to a fortune-teller to be told about your future? Ask your classmates. How many are there who would do so? How many believe in horoscopes or superstitions?

This is Macbeth's second encounter[1] with the witches. At the beginning of the play he met them by chance—so it seems. Now he seeks them out on purpose. He wants greater certainty about what they had indicated[2] to him with the sing-song of "fair is foul and foul is fair". This odd mixture of double meanings will prove to be the motto of the whole story. Everything turns out to be a fatal machination[3] of appearances, lies and intrigues. Macbeth, though, does not doubt the predictions. He wants the fulfilment of the expected glory and power so badly that he demands the witches to show him more of his future and possible obstacles in his way to the throne of Scotland. He has already killed the king and eliminated his best friend Banquo, whom he feared as a possible rival because he had also heard the witches and was prophesied to become the father of future kings.

The Weird Sisters conjure[4] up three apparitions[5] for him who seem to assure him of his invincibility. But a show of spirits and the ghost of Banquo remind him of the prediction that his friend's sons will be kings. Indeed Fleance, Banquo's son, had escaped the assassination and could be a threat. More violence will be necessary and now he is willing to use it pitilessly. So as he learns that Macduff, another brave Scottish thane, could be harmful, he decides to murder Macduff's family while he is away.

Art nouveau theatre poster, early 20th century

[1]**encounter** meeting – [2]**to indicate** to suggest that sth is possible or likely – [3]**machination** secret plot or scheme – [4]**to conjure** to ask a spirit or ghost to appear, esp by using a magic ceremony – [5]**apparition** person or thing that appears strange or not real

Thunder. Enter the three Witches (with a cauldron[1])

FIRST WITCH Thrice[2] the brindled[3] cat hath mewed.

SECOND WITCH Thrice and once the hedge-pig[4] whined.

THIRD WITCH Harpier[5] cries, 'Tis time. Tis time.'

FIRST WITCH Round about the cauldron go
In the poisoned entrails[6] throw.
Toad[7], that under cold stone
Days and nights has thirty-one
Sweltered venom[8] sleeping got,
Boil thou first i' th' charméd[9] pot.

ALL Double, double toil[10] and trouble:
Fire burn, and cauldron bubble.

SECOND WITCH Fillet of a fenny snake,
In the cauldron boil and bake:
Eye of newt[11], and tongue of dog,
Adder's[12] fork- and blind-worm's[13] sting,
Lizard's[14] leg, and howlet's[15] wing,
For a charm[16] of powerful trouble,
Like a hell-broth, boil and bubble.

ALL Double, double toil and trouble,
Fire burn, and cauldron bubble,

THIRD WITCH Scale[17] of dragon, tooth of wolf,
Witches' mummy, maw and gulf
Of the ravined salt-sea shark[18],
Root of hemlock[19], digged i' th' dark;
Liver of blaspheming Jew,
Slivered in the moon's eclipse;
Nose of Turk, and Tartar's lips,
Finger of birth-strangled babe.
Ditch-delivered by a drab[20],
Make the gruel[21] thick and slab[22].
Add thereto a tiger's chawdron[23]
For th' ingredience of our cauldron.

ALL Double, double toil and trouble
Fire burn, and cauldron bubble.

Where else in literature do you find the number 3 to have magic significance? How often does it occur in this scene and what other number is of importance?

An image from Ulric Molitor's *De Lamiis et phitonicis mulieribus* (1489): Witches insert a cock and a snake into a cauldron, invoking thunder and rain.

Why would an Elizabethan audience think that Jews, Turks and Tartars are appropriate ingredients for a 'hellish' stew?

[1] **cauldron** a large deep pot for boiling liquids or cooking food – [2] **thrice** three times – [3] **brindled** (esp of dogs and cats) brown with markings of another colour – [4] **hedge-pig** hedge-hog; *Igel* – [5] **Harpier** a spirit – [6] **entrails** internal organs of a person or an animal, esp the intestines – [7] **toad** *Kröte* – [8] **sweltered venom** sweated poison – [9] **charmed** under a magic spell – [10] **toil** work that is hard and makes one very tired – [11] **newt** [nju:t] *Molch* – [12] **adder** *Viper* – [13] **blind-worm** *Blindschleiche* – [14] **lizard** *Eidechse* – [15] **howlet** *Käuzchen* – [16] **charm** magic spell – [17] **scale** *Schuppe* – [18] **maw and gulf … shark** *Magen und Schlund des vollgefressnen Meereshais* – [19] **hemlock** *Schierling* – [20] **ditch delivered … drab** born in the gutter by a whore – [21] **gruel** [grʊəl] *Brei* – [22] **slab** thick, sticky – [23] **chawdron** (*arch*) entrails

Hecate, the chief witch

SECOND WITCH Cool it with a baboon's[1] blood,
Then the charm is firm and good.

(Enter Hecate and the other three Witches)

HECATE O, well done! I commend your pains[2],
And everyone shall share i' th' gains.
And now about the cauldron sing
Like elves and fairies in a ring,
Enchanting all that you put in.

(Music and a song, "Black spirit", etc. Exeunt Hecate and the other three witches)

What kind of music would be suitable for this scene?

SECOND WITCH By the pricking of my thumbs,
Something wicked this way comes.

(Knock within)

Open, locks, whoever knocks.

(Enter Macbeth)

MACBETH How now, you secret, black, and midnight hags[3],
What is 't you do?

ALL THE WITCHES A deed without a name.

MACBETH I conjure you by that which you profess,
Howe'er you come to know it, answer me.
Though you untie the winds and let them fight
Against the churches, though the yeasty waves
Confound and swallow navigation up.

[1] **baboon** *Pavian* – [2] **pains** efforts – [3] **hag** (*derog*) ugly or evil old woman

Though bladed corn be lodged[1] and trees blown down,
Though castles topple on their warders' heads,
Though palaces and pyramids do slope
Their heads to their foundations, though the treasure
Of nature's germens[2] tumble all together
Even till destruction sicken, answer me
To what I ask you.

FIRST WITCH Speak.

SECOND WITCH Demand.

THIRD WITCH We'll answer.

FIRST WITCH Say if thou'dst rather hear it from our mouths
Or from our masters.

MACBETH Call 'em, let me see 'em.

FIRST WITCH Pour in sow's blood that hath eaten
Her nine farrow[3]; grease that's sweaten
From the murderer's gibbet[4] throw
Into the flame.

ALL THE WITCHES Come high or low.
Thyself and office[5] deftly[6] show.

(Thunder. First Apparition: an armed[7] head)

MACBETH Tell me, thou unknown power –

FIRST WITCH He knows thy thought.
Hear his speech, but say thou naught.

FIRST APPARITION Macbeth, Macbeth, Macbeth, beware Macduff,
Beware the Thane of Fife. Dismiss[8] me. Enough.

(Apparition descends)

MACBETH Whate'er thou art, for thy good caution[9] thanks.
Thou hast harped[10] my fear aright. But one word more –

FIRST WITCH He will not be commanded. Here's another;
More potent[11] than the first.

(Thunder. Second Apparition: a bloody child)

SECOND APPARITION Macbeth, Macbeth, Macbeth.

MACBETH Had I three ears I'd hear thee.

SECOND APPARITION Be bloody, bold, and resolute. Laugh to scorn
The power of man, for none of woman born
Shall harm Macbeth.

(Apparition descends)

▲ What impression does Macbeth's enumeration of the witches' powers and his demand for answers make on you?

▼ How do the witches react?

◄ This will be Macbeth's fatal error. In the end he will be beheaded by Macduff in a duel. But isn't Macduff "of woman born"?

[1] **bladed corn be lodged** the corn is blown down and thus spoilt for harvesting – [2] **nature's germens** the seeds of life – [3] **farrow** piglets – [4] **gibbet** gallow – [5] **office** (*arch*) intention, purpose – [6] **deftly** quickly – [7] **armed** here: with a helmet – [8] **to dismiss** to send sb away; to allow sb to leave – [9] **caution** warning – [10] **to harp** (*arch*) to guess – [11] **potent** powerful

MACBETH Then live. Macduff—what need I fear of thee?
But yet I'll make assurance double sure,
And take a bond of fate thou shalt not live,
That I may tell pale-hearted fear it lies,
And sleep in spite of thunder.

(Thunder. Third Apparition: a child crowned, with a tree in his hand)

What is this
That rises like the issue[1] of a king,
And wears upon his baby-brow the round
And top of sovereignty?

ALL THE WITCHES Listen, but speak not to 't.

Another warning with a hidden truth: Macbeth will see the wood move against him in the final stage of his tyrannical rulership when the king's sons come upon his castle with troops to take revenge. Can you imagine how that can happen?

THIRD APPARITION Be lion-mettled[2], proud, and take no care
Who chafes, who frets[3], or where conspirers[4] are.
Macbeth shall never vanquished[5] be until
Great Birnam Wood to high Dunsinane Hill
Shall come against him.

(Apparition descends)

MACBETH That will never be.
Who can impress the forest, bid the tree
Unfix his earth-bound root? Sweet bodements[6], good!
Rebellious dead, rise never till the wood
Of Birnam rise, and on 's high place Macbeth
Shall live the lease of nature[7], pay his breath
To time and mortal custom. Yet my heart
Throbs to know one thing. Tell me, if your art
Can tell so much, shall Banquo's issue ever
Reign in this kingdom?

ALL THE WITCHES Seek to know no more.

Why does he become so furious?

MACBETH I will be satisfied. Deny me this,
And an eternal curse fall on you! Let me know.

(The cauldron sinks. Hautboys[8])

Why sinks that cauldron? And what noise is this?

FIRST WITCH Show.

SECOND WITCH Show.

THIRD WITCH Show.

ALL THE WITCHES Show his eyes and grieve[9] his heart.
Come like shadows, so depart.

(A show of eight kings, the last with a glass[10] in his hand)

[1] **issue** child – [2] **lion-mettled** lion-hearted – [3] **who chafes, who frets** who is dissatisfied with your rule – [4] **conspirer** *Verschwörer* – [5] **vanquished** defeated – [6] **bodements** messages, prophecies – [7] **lease of nature** the natural length of life – [8] **hautboy** oboe – [9] **to grieve** to cause pain to – [10] **glass** crystal ball or mirror

MACBETH Thou art too like the spirit of Banquo. Down!
Thy crown does sear[1] mine eyeballs. And thy hair.
Thou other gold-bound brow, is like the first.
A third is like the former. Filthy hags,
Why do you show me this?—A fourth? Start, eyes!
What, will the line stretch out to th' crack of doom?
Another yet? A seventh? I'll see no more—
And yet the eighth appears, who bears a glass
Which shows me many more; and some I see
That twofold balls and treble sceptres carry.
Horrible sight! Now I see 'tis true,
For the blood-boltered[2] Banquo smiles upon me,
And points at them for his.

(Exeunt kings and Banquo)

What, is this so?

HECATE Ay, sir, all this is so. But why
Stands Macbeth thus amazedly?
Come, sisters, cheer we up his sprites[3],
And show the best of our delights.
I'll charm the air to give a sound
While you perform your antic round,
That this great king may kindly say
Our duties did his welcome pay.

What does he realize by the marching-in of the identical spirits?

Did the witches give Macbeth what he wanted?

Cauldron scene—students in action

[1] **to sear** to burn – [2] **blood-boltered** with a crust of blood – [3] **sprite** spirit

What should the music and dance be like? Slow, fast, crazy, graceful, noisy, etc?

(Music. The Witches dance, and vanish)

MACBETH Where are they? Gone? Let this pernicious[1] hour
Stand aye[2] accursed in the calendar.
Come in, without there.

(Enter Lennox)

LENNOX What's your grace's[3] will?

MACBETH Saw you the weird sisters?

LENNOX No, my lord.

MACBETH Came they not by you?

Why did the others not see the witches?

LENNOX No, indeed, my lord.

MACBETH Infected be the air whereon they ride,
And damned all those that trust them. I did hear
The galloping of horse. Who was 't came by?

LENNOX 'Tis two or three, my lord, that bring you word
Macduff is fled to England.

Macbeth VI.1.1–154

From a 1976 Royal Shakespeare Company Production

[1] **pernicious** having a very harmful effect on sb or sth – [3] **aye** here: always, forever – [3] **your grace** *Euer Gnaden*

Demonic cookery

There are many unfamiliar words in the first forty lines of the scene, but you probably got the idea: What the witches are using as ingredients for their stew are the most disgusting or frightening bits of the most disgusting or frightening animals.

1. See which animals or body parts you can identify. Which are most disgusting? Why?
2. Do you know any stories or myths in folklore in which these animals appear? What is their function and meaning in these stories?
3. Invent a recipe of your own. What would you use as ingredients for a strong potion? What do you want to use it for? Rewrite the witches' verses.

Macbeth and the apparitions

Take a closer look at the apparitions.

1. How many are there and what shapes do they take? What signs do they additionally have and what for?
2. What meaning does Macbeth give to them?
3. What is paradoxical about their predictions?

An eavesdropper

Lennox and the others say that they haven't seen or heard a thing. Imagine that this is not the truth and that someone accompanying Macbeth has overheard the strange conversation among the witches, Macbeth and the apparitions. Write the eavesdropper's report in the form of a letter to Macduff.

Act out the witches' brewing

1. Each one in your class takes a sentence or sense unit. You should repeat your part to yourself to learn it by heart if you can. Try whispering it, shouting it, or singing it. After feeling confident about your line/s reassemble in a circle in the order the lines occur (ll. 1–44).
2. You can enhance your performance by first scattering to the edges of the room and moving in to an imaginary cauldron in the centre to drop in your ingredient as your line comes. Once in the centre, you can take up a kneeling or sitting position suggestive of witchcraft.

The witches

In many Elizabethan plays we find supernatural figures, such as devils and demons, ghosts and gods.

1. Do you think it is difficult for a modern audience to accept the witches?
2. How is the supernatural presented on TV or in movies that are popular today?
3. Find more information about witchcraft and superstition at the time Shakespeare was writing his plays, and see how the lines of this scene reflect such practices.
   www.askjeeves.com or use a search engine,
   e.g. www.google.com (enter *witchcraft Shakespeare*)
   → Method kit, Internet research, p. 304

Madness and Love

Ophelia—Beauty and Honesty

Hamlet, Prince of Denmark, is deep in thought ("To be, or not to be, ...") when Ophelia enters. He is pondering a plan to avenge the murder of his father. In order to gain time, Hamlet has recently shown signs of madness. Ophelia's father Polonius thinks he knows the root of the Prince's strange behaviour: it must be his love for Ophelia.
So he and the king make ready to observe the two young people. They hide behind an arras[1] and watch as Ophelia tests the Prince's love for her. When Hamlet notices Ophelia, a flood of affection seems to come over him. But then he remembers that he has promised to free his mind of all its preoccupations, including Ophelia, to fulfill the oath[2] he has sworn to his father's ghost. The situation makes it even easier for him. A movement behind the arras makes him realize that Ophelia is not alone and that he is being observed. He is suddenly overcome by disgust for all womankind, which his mother's behaviour originally inspired in him. For she has married Claudius, her brother-in-law and murderer of her husband, only some weeks after his father's burial[3].
Now here is Ophelia, whom he trusted, lending herself as a tool and a spy to trap him for the king. From this point on he does nothing but insult her, mocking her virtue and her beauty and advising her to enter a convent[4]. Ophelia, who has only naively obeyed her father's and the king's orders, now believes him to be genuinely insane and is broken-hearted. What she does not know is that he had been acting for the eavesdroppers behind the arras.

Hamlet hasn't seen Ophelia for quite a long time. How is his greeting?

OPHELIA Good my lord,
How does your honour for this many a day?

HAMLET I humbly thank you, well, well, well.

OPHELIA My lord. I have remembrances[5] of yours
That I have longèd[6] long to re-deliver.
I pray you now receive them.

HAMLET No, no, I never gave you aught[7].

OPHELIA My honoured lord, you know right well you did,
And with them words of so sweet breath composed
As made the things more rich. Their perfume lost,

[1]**arras** *italienischer Wandteppich* – [2]**oath** solemn promise to do sth – [3]**burial** *Beerdigung* – [4]**convent** building in which a community of nuns live – [5]**remembrance** souvenir, present – [6]**to long** to want sth very much – [7]**aught** [ɔ:t] (*arch*) anything

Take these again; for to the noble mind
Rich gifts wax poor when givers prove unkind.
There, my lord.

(Proffers[1] some jewels)

▲ Why does Ophelia return the Prince's presents?

▼ Why does Hamlet start arguing about beauty and honesty here?

HAMLET Ha, ha? Are you honest?

OPHELIA My lord.

HAMLET Are you fair?

OPHELIA What means your lordship?

HAMLET That if you be honest and fair, your honesty should admit no discourse[2] to your beauty.

OPHELIA Could beauty, my lord, have better commerce[3] than with honesty?

HAMLET Ay, truly, for the power of beauty will sooner transform honesty from what it is to a bawd[4] than the force of honesty can translate[5] beauty into his likeness. This was sometime a paradox, but now the time gives it proof. I did love you once.

OPHELIA Indeed, my lord, you made me believe so.

HAMLET You should not have believed me, for virtue cannot so inoculate[6] our old stock[7] but we shall relish[8] of it. I loved you not.

OPHELIA I was the more deceived.

HAMLET Get thee to a nunnery[9]. Why wouldst thou be a breeder of sinners? I am myself indifferent[10] honest, but yet I could accuse me of such things that it were better my mother had not borne me. I am very proud, revengeful, ambitious, with more offences at my beck[11] than I have thoughts to put them in, imagination to give them shape, or time to act them in. What should such fellows as I do crawling between heaven and earth? We are arrant[12] knaves[13], all. Believe none of us. Go thy ways to a nunnery. Where's your father?

Film scene with Kenneth Brannagh and Kate Winslet (*Hamlet*, 1996)

In Kenneth Branagh's *Hamlet* (1996) this conversation is acted out as a struggle between the two. Hamlet tosses Ophelia around and in the end presses her against a mirror. He pours his disgust with himself and men out on her. Finally he sends her away from him and advises her to go to a nunnery. He does not care for love anymore.

[1] **to proffer** to offer sth to sb – [2] **discourse** here: *Umgang* – [3] **commerce** *Umgang* – [4] **bawd** *Kupplerin* – [5] **to translate** here: to transfer into – [6] **to inoculate** *impfen* – [7] **stock** stem of a tree; here *fig* – [8] **to relish** to enjoy – [9] **nunnery** 1. convent; 2. (*derog, arch*) brothel – [10] **indifferent** indifferently – [11] **at sb's beck** always ready to obey sb's orders immediately – [12] **arrant** (*derog*) (of a bad person or thing) to the greatest extent – [13] **knave** (*arch*) a dishonest man

Why does she lie?

OPHELIA At home, my lord.

HAMLET Let the doors be shut upon him, that he may play the fool nowhere but in 's own house. Farewell.

(Turns to go)

Who is she talking to and why does she want help for him?

OPHELIA O help him, you sweet heavens!

HAMLET If thou dost marry, I'll give thee this plague[1] for thy dowry[2] be thou as chaste[3] as ice, as pure as snow, thou shalt not escape calumny[4]. Get thee to a nunnery, go, farewell. *(Turns to go)* Or if thou wilt needs[5] marry, marry a fool; for wise men know well enough what monsters[6] you make of them. To a nunnery, go, and quickly, too. Farewell. *(Turns to go)*

OPHELIA O heavenly powers, restore[7] him!

HAMLET I have heard of your paintings[8], too, well enough. God hath given you one face, and you make yourselves another. You jig[9], you amble[10], and you lisp, and nickname God's creatures, and make your wantonness[11] your ignorance. Go to, I'll no more on 't. It hath made me mad. I say we will have no more marriages. Those that are married already—all but one[12]—shall live. The rest shall keep as they are. To a nunnery, go.

Why does he advise her to go to a nunnery and why is he so mad about the institution of marriage?

(Exit)

OPHELIA O what a noble mind is here o' erthrown!
The courtier's[13], soldier's, scholar's eye, tongue, sword,
Th' expectancy[14] and rose of the fair state,
The glass of fashion and the mould of form[15],

[1] **plague** here: curse – [2] **dowry** *Mitgift* – [3] **chaste** (dated) not having had sex with anyone – [4] **calumny** a false statement about sb, made to damage their reputation – [5] **needs** *unbedingt* – [6] **monster** (*arch*) cuckold, fooled husband – [7] **to restore** to bring sb or sth back to a former condition – [8] **your paintings** women's make-up – [9] **to jig** dance – [10] **to amble** to stroll, walk at a slow pace – [11] **wantonness** sexual lust, delight – [12] **all but one** (he means the king) – [13] **courtier** companion or adviser of a king or queen at court – [14] **expectancy** hope – [15] **mould of form** example of courtly behaviour

Th' observed[1] of all observers. quite, quite, down!
And I, of ladies most deject[2] and wretched[3],
That sucked the honey of his music vows[4],
That unmatched[5] form and feature of blown youth[6]
Blasted[7] with ecstasy[8]. O woe[9] is me,
T' have seen what I have seen, see what I see!

Re-enter king and Polonius [...]

Hamlet III.1.64–132

What does Ophelia lament?

After Hamlet's fierce words and obvious loss of mental health, Ophelia will have even more pain to suffer: her father Polonius is killed by Hamlet, who mistakes him for the king hiding behind an arras in his mother's bedroom while they are having a serious conversation. Her brother Laertes, whom she loves dearly, cannot help her since he has left for Paris again. She has also witnessed some of the machinations[10] at Court and is appalled[11] by the adulterous[12] marriage of the queen. Hamlet's rejection, her grief at her father's death and all the other factors lead her to madness. The queen and Claudius send Horatio, Hamlet's and Ophelia's friend, to call Ophelia in to see what is wrong with her and why.

(Enter Queen Gertrude and Horatio)

QUEEN GERTRUDE I will not speak with her.

HORATIO She is importunate[13],
Indeed distraught[14]. Her mood will needs be pitied.

QUEEN GERTRUDE What would she have?

HORATIO She speaks much of her father, says she hears
There's tricks i' th' world, and hems[15], and beats her heart,
Spurns[16] enviously[17] at straws, speaks things in doubt
That carry but half sense. Her speech is nothing,
Yet the unshapèd use of it doth move
The hearers to collection[18]. They aim at it[19],
And botch[20] the words up fit to their own thoughts,
Which, as her winks and nods and gestures yield[21] them,
Indeed would make one think there might be thought,
Though nothing sure, yet much unhappily.

[1]**observed** respected – [2]**deject** (*adj*) sad – [3]**wretched** ['--] miserable – [4]**vow** a solemn promise, esp a religious one – [5]**unmatched** unprecedented – [6]**feature of blown youth** *Ebenbild blühender Jugend* – [7]**blasted** destroyed in an explosion – [8]**ecstasy** here: madness – [9]**woe** great sorrow or distress – [10]**machination** *Machenschaft* – [11]**appalled** terrified – [12]**adulterous** *ehebrecherisch* – [13]**importunate** stubborn – [14]**distraught** distracted – [15]**to hem** *sich räuspern* – [16]**to spurn at** to kick at – [17]**enviously** here: with bad intention – [18]**collection** here: conclusion – [19]**to aim at sth** (*arch*) to have suspicions – [20]**to botch sth up** *zusammenschustern* – [21]**to yield** to reveal

A student's performance

Why does Gertrude suddenly change her mind?

QUEEN GERTRUDE 'T were good she were spoken with, for she may strew
Dangerous conjectures[1] in ill-breeding minds.
Let her come in.

(Horatio withdraws to admit Ophelia) [...]
(Enter Ophelia mad, her hair down, with a lute)

OPHELIA Where is the beauteous[2] majesty of Denmark?

QUEEN GERTRUDE How now, Ophelia?

OPHELIA *(sings)* How should I your true love know
From another one?—
By his cockle hat and staff,
And his sandal shoon[3].

QUEEN GERTRUDE Alas, sweet lady, what imports this song?

OPHELIA Say you?[4] Nay, pray you, mark[5].
(Sings) He is dead and gone, lady,
He is dead and gone.
At his head a grass-green turf,
At his heels a stone.

QUEEN GERTRUDE Nay, but Ophelia—

[1] **conjecture** guess – [2] **beauteous** beautiful – [3] **cockle hat and staff and his sandal shoon** *Kleidung eines Pilgers auf dem Weg zu St. Jakob von Compostela (Nordspanien)* – [4] **say you?** what do you say? – [5] **pray you, mark** please listen

OPHELIA Pray you, mark.
(Sings) White his shroud[1] as the mountain snow—

(Enter King Claudius)

QUEEN GERTRUDE Alas, look here, my lord.

OPHELIA *(sings)* Larded[2] with sweet flowers,
Which bewept to the grave did—not—go
With true-love showers.

KING CLAUDIUS How do ye, pretty lady?

OPHELIA Well, God 'ield you[3]. They say the owl was a baker's daughter. Lord, we know what we are, but know not what we may be. God be at your table!

KING CLAUDIUS *(to Gertrude)* Conceit[4] upon her father.

OPHELIA Pray you, let's have no words of this, but when they ask you what it means, say you this.
(Sings) Tomorrow is Saint Valentine's day,
All in the morning betime[5],
And I a maid[6] at your window
To be your Valentine.
Then up he rose, and donned[7] his clothes,
And dupped[8] the chamber door;
Let in the maid, that out a maid
Never departed more.

KING CLAUDIUS Pretty Ophelia—

OPHELIA Indeed, la? Without an oath, I'll make an and on't.
(Sings) By Gis[9], and by Saint Charity,
Alack[10], and fie[11] for shame!
Young men will do 't if they come to't,
By Cock[12], they are to blame.
Quoth she[13] "Before you tumbled me[14],
You promised me to wed."
So would I 'a' done, by yonder[15] sun,
An[16] thou hadst not come to my bed.

KING CLAUDIUS *(to Gertrude)* How long hath she been thus?

OPHELIA I hope all will be well. We must be patient. But I cannot choose but weep to think they should lay him i' th' cold ground. My brother shall know of it. And so I thank you for your good counsel. Come, my coach! Good night, ladies, good night, sweet ladies, good night, good night. *(Exit)*

K. J. Makowskij: *Ophelia* (1881)

[1] **shroud** *Leichentuch* – [2] **to lard** *spicken* – [3] **God 'ield you** *Gott vergelt's* – [4] **conceit** excessive pride in oneself or in one's powers, abilities, etc – [5] **betime** early – [6] **maid** virgin – [7] **to don** (to do on) to wear – [8] **to dup** (to do up) to open – [9] **Gis** [ʒɪs] Jesus – [10] **alack** *oh weh* – [11] **fie** *pfui* – [12] **cock** 1. male chicken, 2. penis, 3. (corrupted) God – [13] **quoth she** she said – [14] **to tumble** to make fall; to have sexual intercourse – [15] **yonder** (*arch* or dialect) that is or that can be seen over there – [16] **an** if

What does he suspect?

KING CLAUDIUS *(to Horatio)*
Follow her close. Give her good watch, I pray you.

(Exit Horatio)

O, this is the poison of deep grief! It springs
All from her father's death. O Gertrude, Gertrude,
When sorrows come they come not single spies[1],
But in battalions. First, her father slain[2];
Next, your son gone, and he most violent author
Of his own just remove[3]; the people muddied[4],
Thick and unwholesome in their thoughts and whispers
For good Polonius' death; and we have done but greenly
In hugger-mugger[5] to inter[6] him; poor Ophelia
Divided from herself and her fair judgement,
Without the which we are pictures or mere beasts;

Hamlet, IV.4.1–65

What does Claudius reveal about himself and his contribution to all the sorrows?

Ophelia is carried along the river. She is said to have drowned herself. With a song on her lips she was floating in the water waiting for the weight of her soaked clothes to draw her under water and away from the world's cruel surface. John Everett Millais (1829–1896)

[1] **spy** *Späher* – [2] **slain** (slay, slew, slain) (dated or *fml* or US) to kill sb or sth in a violent way – [3] **remove** distance – [4] **muddied** here: confused – [5] **in hugger-mugger** clandestinely, done in secret – [6] **to inter** to bury a dead body

For the following class activities mind this advice:

When you have been given a line, repeat it a number of times to yourself in different tones of voice. Try to learn your piece by heart. Try to capture the mood and effect of the scene. The point is to get the feel of the dialogue and the emotions underlying it. Discuss your presentation.

The language of madness

1. After a read through the dialogue between Ophelia and Hamlet, divide the class into two groups: one is to be Ophelia, one Hamlet. Take ll. 1–30.
2. Within the group decide on the lines you want to deliver. It doesn't matter if two or more of you have the same lines.
3. Having practiced a bit on your lines for yourself or with a partner, get ready to alternately present the dialogue.

"Go get thee to a nunnery"

1. One of you plays Ophelia, who is kneeling. Take ll. 30–60. All the rest of the class will circle Ophelia and speak the words of Hamlet in turn.
   Try out different ways of delivering the lines and movements, effects that will bring out the conflict between Ophelia and Hamlet. Rehearse a few times until you are satisfied with your performance. Answer the following questions with your enactment:
2. What has made Hamlet so aggressive towards the innocent girl he seemed to have once loved?
3. How is Ophelia feeling, knowing as she does that her father and Claudius are listening nearby?

Listeners behind the curtain

What will Polonius and Claudius discuss after their eavesdropping of the scene where they hid behind the arras? Work out a short dialogue in pairs. Then present it to the class. You may sit with your partner in the middle surrounded by the others. After your conversation let them ask questions or give comments on what they think of your secret listening, use of Ophelia, further actions etc.

Comparing mad talk

1. Compare the form of Hamlet's and Ophelia's speech as to metre, rhyme etc. How does Shakespeare express Hamlet's "absent-mindedness"? Then compare it to Ophelia's performance in Act IV.4. How does her language show the signs of madness?
2. Where do you find signs or traces in Ophelia's words that show the impact of the events on her and that will probably lead her to commit suicide? Collect the terms of madness in a mind map and add expressions by consulting a dictionary.

Case conference

Improvise a role-play and discuss the case of Ophelia's suicide between a psychiatrist, a doctor and the interested parties: her brother Laertes, Hamlet, Horatio, Gertrude and the King.

Fair Ophelia's death

1. Write an obituary for Ophelia.
2. Put Hamlet on the hot seat.

Hamlet on Screen

The latest release of a rather individual interpretation is Michael Almereyda's production with Ethan Hawke playing a freaky Hamlet.

The Australian actor Mel Gibson starred as Hamlet in Zefirelli's 1990 Hollywood Shakespeare.

Sir Laurence Olivier directed, produced and acted in this 1948 version. To date, he is the only actor ever to direct *himself* and earn an acting Oscar with this film.

Kenneth Branagh produced and acted in a monumental four-hour film in 1996 with Titanic star Kate Winslet as Ophelia.

A poster show

1. These are posters of famous Hamlet films. What do they tell you about the probable way of staging the story? Think of the characters, their time and the usual genre they are known for. Are they typical Shakespearian actors? What could be the reasons for them to be playing the Prince of Denmark?
2. Which one do you like best?

Hamlet and Ophelia

If you can get hold of at least two of the films, compare the scene of Hamlet and Ophelia's encounter that ends in their parting from each other. Hamlet is left to his plan of revenge; Ophelia is left alone in grief about Hamlet's seeming madness and contempt for her (*Hamlet* III.1.64–132).

- Concentrate on textual cuts, visual elements such as costumes, scenery, and lighting.
- How is space used? How do the camera angles frame the actors in performance space?
- What interpretation of the situation does the film suggest?

➩ Method kit, Film analysis, p. 306

Come Not Between the Dragon and His Wrath

King Lear rules Britain in a mythical past. He feels old and worn and therefore has made up his mind to divide his kingdom and possession among his three daughters. He wants to abdicate[1] and live under the care of his children till death. We meet him and his children right at his announcement.

(Enter King Lear, the Dukes of Cornwall and Albany, Goneril, Regan, Cordelia, and attendants)

LEAR Attend[2] the lords of France and Burgundy, Gloucester.

GLOUCESTER I shall, my lord.

(Exit)

LEAR Meantime we shall express our darker purpose[3].
Give me the map there. Know that we have divided
In three our kingdom and 'tis our fast[4] intent
To shake all cares and business from our age,
Conferring them on younger strengths while we
Unburdened crawl toward death. Our son of Cornwall,
And you, our no less loving son of Albany.
We have this hour a constant will[5] to publish
Our daughters' several dowers[6], that future strife[7]
May be prevented now. The princes France and Burgundy—
Great rivals in our youngest daughter's love—
Long in our court have made their amorous[8] sojourn[9],
And here are to be answered. Tell me, my daughters—
Since now we will divest[10] us both of rule,

▲ How does he explain his intention to give up the throne?

[1] **to abdicate** to resign from being king, etc – [2] **to attend** to care for, to accompany – [3] **darker purpose** secret intention – [4] **fast** fixed, unalterable – [5] **constant will** fixed purpose – [6] **dowers** dowery; *Mitgift* – [7] **strife** quarrel – [8] **amorous** openly showing or feeling love – [9] **sojourn** temporary stay in a place away from one's home – [10] **to divest** to take away power, rights, authority, etc from sb or sth

What does he want from his daughters?

Interest of territory, cares of state—
Which of you shall we say doth love us most,
That we our largest bounty[1] may extend
Where nature doth with merit challenge[2]? Goneril,
Our eldest born, speak first.

GONERIL Sir, I love you more than words can wield[3] the matter;
Dearer than eyesight, space, and liberty;
Beyond[4] what can be valued, rich or rare,
No less than life: with grace, health, beauty, honour;
As much as child e'er loved or father found;
A love that makes breath poor and speech unable.
Beyond all manner of so much I love you.

Why does Cordelia speak as an aside and what does she fear?

CORDELIA *(aside)* What shall Cordelia speak? Love and be silent.

LEAR *(to Goneril)* Of all these bounds[5] even from this line to this,
With shadowy forests and with champaigns[6] riched,
With plenteous rivers and wide-skirted meads[7].
We make thee lady. To thine and Albany's issues[8]
Be this perpetual[9]—What says our second daughter?
Our dearest Regan, wife of Cornwall?

REGAN I am made of that self mettle[10] as my, sister,
And prize me at her worth. In my true heart
I find she names my very deed of love –
Only she comes too short, that I profess[11]
Myself an enemy to all other joys
Which the most precious square of sense possesses[12]?
And find I am alone felicitate[13]
In your dear highness' love.

Why does Cordelia increasingly lose heart?

CORDELIA *(aside)* Then poor Cordelia—
And yet not so, since I am sure my love's
More ponderous[14] than my tongue.

LEAR *(to Regan)* To thee and thine hereditary[15] ever
Remain this ample[16] third of our fair kingdom,
No less in space, validity[17]. and pleasure
Than that conferred on Goneril.

What does Lear expect from Cordelia?

(To Cordelia) Now our joy,
Although our last and least, to whose young love
The vines of France and milk of Burgundy
Strive to be interessed: what can you say to draw
A third more opulent than your sisters? Speak.

[1]**bounty** (dated) money, etc given generously as a gift or a reward; generous acts – [2]**where nature … challenge** where it is demanded by the right of birth and merit – [3]**wield** to hold sth and use it as a weapon, tool, etc – [4]**beyond** at or to the further side; further on – [5]**bounds** boundaries – [6]**champaigns** *Gefilde* – [7]**mead** *Aue* – [8]**issues** here: children – [9]**perpetual** without interruption; continuous – [10]**mettle** ability to endure difficulties and to face opposition, here: the same material – [11]**to profess** to state openly that one has a belief, feeling, etc – [12]**which the most precious … possesses** which appeal delicately to all senses – [13]**felicitate** [-'--'-] (*arch*) happy – [14]**ponderous** slow and awkward because of great weight – [15]**hereditary** passed on from parent to child, or from one generation to following generations – [16]**ample** enough or more than enough – [17]**validity** here: value

CORDELIA Nothing, my lord.

LEAR Nothing?

CORDELIA Nothing.

LEAR Nothing will come of nothing. Speak again.

CORDELIA Unhappy that I am, I cannot heave[1]
My heart into my mouth. I love your majesty
According to my bond, no more nor less.

LEAR How, how, Cordelia? Mend[2] your speech a little
Lest you may mar[3] your fortunes.

CORDELIA Good my lord,
You have begot me, bred me, loved me.
I return those duties back as are right fit—
Obey you, love you, and most honour you.
Why have my sisters husbands if they say
They love you all? Haply[4] when I shall wed
That lord whose hand must take my plight[5] shall carry
Half my love with him, half my care and duty.
Sure, I shall never marry like my sisters.

LEAR But goes thy heart with this?

CORDELIA Ay, my good lord.

LEAR So young and so untender?

CORDELIA So young, my lord, and true.

LEAR Let it be so. Thy truth then be thy dower:
For by the sacred radiance of the sun,
The mysteries of Hecate[6] and the night,
By all the operation of the orbs[7]
From whom we do exist and cease[8] to be,
Here I disclaim[9] all my paternal care,
Propinquity[10] and property of blood,
And as a stranger to my heart and me
Hold thee from this for ever. The barbarous Scythian[11],
Or he that makes his generation messes[12]
To gorge[13] his appetite, shall to my bosom
Be as well neighboured, pitied, and relieved[14]
As thou, my sometime daughter.

KENT Good my liege[15]—

Why does she say "nothing"?

Why does Lear react so aggressively?

[1] **to heave** to lift or drag sb or oneself or sth heavy with great effort – [2] **to mend** to improve – [3] **to mar** to damage or spoil sth – [4] **haply** if it should happen – [5] **plight** a promise, esp to marry sb – [6] **Hecate** goddess of witchcraft – [7] **operations of the orbs** movement of the planetary orbits – [8] **to cease** [si:s] to come to or bring sth to an end; to stop – [9] **to disclaim** to say that one does not have sth, to deny – [10] **propinquity** close family relationship – [11] **Scythian** Scottish people said to be cannibals – [12] **messes** meals – [13] **to gorge** to eat a lot in a greedy way, to fill oneself – [14] **to relieve** to ease or remove pain, distress or anxiety – [15] **good my liege** *O edler König*

LEAR Peace[1], Kent.
Come not between the dragon and his wrath[2].
I loved her most, and thought to set my rest
On her kind nursery[3].
(*To Cordelia*) Hence, and avoid my sight! –
So be my grave my peace as here I give
Her father's heart from her. Call France. Who stirs[4]?
Call Burgundy.
[…]

King Lear, I.1.1–98

Graham Arnold: King Lear

How the story continues: After this unexpected clash, Cordelia is banned from Lear's court. Although she is disinherited, the King of France thinks Cordelia "most rich being poor" and marries her. While Cordelia is away from England, Lear is alone. He has dismissed his close adviser and friend, the Earl of Kent. Lear had counted on Goneril and Regan and the deal he had made with them: they received the kingdom and in exchange for Lear being able to live for

[1] **peace** silence – [2] **wrath** fury, anger – [3] **nursery** care – [4] **to stir** to move

one month at a time with one of them attended by 100 knights. The daughters are not delighted because the arrangement means stress for them and unnecessary expenditure. They do not know why Lear needs courtiers since he is no longer king. In the end Lear is deprived of everything. Having realized his foolishness in banishing Cordelia and handing over all his power, he and his Fool flee onto the heath in a stormy night. The family tragedy ends with Cordelia being hanged. She and the troops of France cannot help her father regain his rule. Both she and Lear, are imprisoned by the sisters; Regan is poisoned by Goneril because she wants to have it all with her lover Edmund, a villain in his own right; Goneril kills herself when she sees Edmund severely wounded and her guilt revealed. Lear dies under the piles of grief. England's rule is turned over to Kent, a true and loyal king's man. He does not keep the crown for himself but gives it to his son Edgar, who was treated badly by his half-brother Edmund and had disguised himself as "poor Tom" playing a madman in the company of the storm-wandering Lear. With families like these, who needs enemies?

Father and daughters

1. Cordelia is a fool—do you agree?
2. Why is the "nothing" Cordelia answers more than anything the other two sisters said? Compare their speeches.
3. Why does Lear not grasp the deeper sense of Cordelia's words?
4. Why does Lear react so vehemently that even his counsellor Kent, who wants to calm him, is admonished to keep quiet?
5. Is Cordelia a tragic figure? Discuss on the basis of the meaning of tragedy.

Tragedy: serious play with a sad ending, originally with the death of a king, later the death of the main character or a similar catastrophe.

The love test

Work in groups of five. Read the conversation in roles. Work out "shadow thoughts" the speakers might have. For example, when Lear says, "Meantime we shall express our darker purpose. Give me the map," he could be thinking, "Today I'm going to make my daughters happy. I'm really excited to hear what Cordelia, my favourite one, will say."

- After 20 minutes: One group should volunteer. The others gather in a semi-circle around the actors. The actors speak their lines with the interjections of their thoughts. Those outside the circle should take notes or keep in mind what they say.
- After the performance discuss if you agree with the shadow thoughts or if you have done it differently in your group.

Cordelia

How does Cordelia feel after that event? Write down her feelings and thoughts in form of a diary entry. Method kit, Diary entry, p.294

Act it out

Imagine the situation in a modern family. Write down the conversation of a wealthy father who has decided to distribute his inheritance to his children. Where do you put the setting, what could be the trigger for conflict? Act it out with partners.

Shakespeare on Stage

Sam Wanamaker with the model of his new playhouse on the Thames

Lyn Gardner

The Globe Theatre

It took an American actor, Sam Wanamaker (1919–1993), to found the Shakespeare Globe Trust in 1970 and lead the effort to build a replica of the Globe Theatre near the location of the original. His performances in Shakespeare's plays were famous in the United States and the United Kingdom. He was disappointed that he could not find a suitable memorial to England's greatest playwright, so he arranged to have one built himself. His efforts were greatly enhanced in 1989 when construction workers accidentally discovered the foundation of the original Globe Theatres. There were two of them. Shakespeare used the first one, of which he was one of the shareholders. It burned down in 1613. Wanamaker died before he could see the final fruition of his dream. In 1997, the New Globe Theatre opened.

- Read the questions below, then listen to the text.
- While listening, jot down the information you find suitable for answering the questions.
- Listen to the text again to check what you have understood.

The real Globe feeling

1. Director Rylance is called a visionary as Wanamaker was. What criticism did he have to stand firm against?
2. When did Rylance himself find a purpose in the reconstruction?
3. Why does the Globe change both the actors' and audiences' preconceptions of theatre?
4. What makes Rylance feel happy and blessed in his job?
5. Why is the American woman "transformed" after the play?

Going beyond listening

1. What is the most important matter for Rylance? He says: "What is the point of a theatre that has room for the Ariels but none for the Calibans?" Both names come from a play by Shakespeare. Find out about it.
2. In the beginning, Wanamaker is compared to Fitzcarraldo. Who was he? Present a short biographical sketch on him to your class. → Method kit, Presentation, p. 309

Elizabethan theatre

Find out more about the theatre in Shakespeare's time:

1. What other theatres were there for the Elizabethans in London?
2. Who were the actors?
3. Who was the audience?

You can get the information in your library or:
www.shakespeare-globe.org
www.angband.demon.co.uk/Globe

➔ Method kit, Internet research, p. 304

The Globe Playhouse, 1599-1613. A conjectural reconstruction

Key

- AA Main entrance
- B The Yard
- CC Entrances to lowest gallery
- D Entrances to staircase and upper galleries
- E Corridor serving the different sections of the middle gallery
- F Middle gallery ('Twopenny Rooms')
- G 'Gentlemen's Rooms' or 'Lords' Rooms'
- H The stage
- J The hanging being put up round the stage
- K The 'Hell' under the stage
- L The stage trap, leading down to the Hell
- MM Stage doors
- N Curtained 'place behind the stage'
- O Gallery above the stage, used as required sometimes by musicians, sometimes by spectators, and often as part of the play
- P Back-stage area (the tiring-house)
- Q Tiring-house door
- R Dressing-rooms
- S Wardrobe and storage
- T The hut housing the machine for lowering enthroned gods, etc, to the stage
- U The 'Heavens'
- W Hoisting the playhouse flag

The world's a stage

The illustration on page 261 is a historian's guess at what Shakespeare's Globe may have looked like.

1. Make yourself familiar with the building using the annotations.
2. Speculate on the organization and preparation that must have gone on behind the stage while the actors were performing, e.g. the cauldron-scene (*Macbeth*) or the balcony-scene (*Romeo and Juliet*). How was the scenery related to the audience? What about day and night scenes?

Mickey-Mouse Shakespeare

The New Globe in London has been criticized as a "museum piece" offering "Mickey-Mouse Shakespeare."

1. Why do you think the critics call it "Mickey-Mouse Shakespeare"?
2. What do you think of the idea to reconstruct a theatre that burnt down about 400 years ago, only to present the plays of a playwright who has been dead for almost 400 years? Discuss.

For comparison:

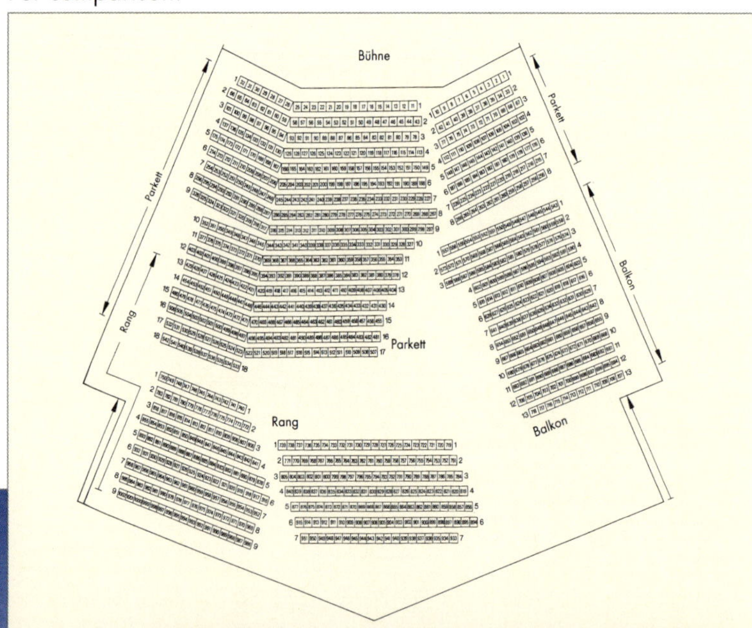

This is the "Badisches Staatstheater Karlsruhe". The "Großes Haus" accommodates 1002 persons, the "Kleines Haus" has 396 seats.

Your local theatre

What about your local theatre? Do research and write a newspaper article on it:

1. Get the facts: How big is it? How do you get there? What kind of stage is there? Where does the audience sit?
2. Is there a play by Shakespeare on? Has Shakespeare been performed there before?
3. Compare it to the Globe. To get the real "Globe feeling" you could go to London. But there is also the possibility to visit imitations of the Globe. Find out where they are. What do you think about a German Globe reconstruction?

→ Method kit, Newspaper article, p. 298

Shakespeare on Screen

The balcony of Shakespeare's famous couple in Verona, Italy

The following texts are modern adaptations of the famous balcony scene from Shakespeare's *Romeo and Juliet* (Act 2, scene 2). Baz Luhrmann's film is another "rediscovery" of the Shakespearian material. The setting is 20th century Verona Beach, California. The families are Mafia-like organisations.

Shakespeare in Love is a creation of bits of Shakespeare's biography interwoven with themes from his plays.

Baz Luhrmann: Romeo and Juliet (1996)

The musical *West Side Story* sets the ageless tale against the background of New York City gang warfare in the late 1950s. The Jets are white American youngsters who fight against the Puerto Ricans, who call themselves the Sharks. Tony, one of the Jets, falls in love with Maria. But their love does not stand a chance since she is the sister of the leader of the Sharks, Bernardo. In the end Bernardo and Tony are killed in a fight between the Jets and the Sharks.

A film project

1. Compare the original version of *Romeo and Juliet* (Act 2, scene 2) with the extracts from *Shakespeare in Love* and *West Side Story*. Where are the differences and what has been kept? Pay attention to the settings as well as to the situations and the language.
2. Compare the balcony scenes in the films concentrating on the effects created by camera movements, lighting, music, etc.

➩ Method kit, Film analysis, p. 306

Marc Norman, Tom Stoppard

Shakespeare in Love

Viola's Balcony. Night. There is a lighted window on the balcony. Viola, dressed for bed, and the nurse pass across the lighted space. Will is in the garden. He sees her, the light in the room is extinguished. Will sighs, then Viola comes out onto the balcony in the moonlight, Will gasps. He watches her. Viola sighs dreamily.

Viola: Romeo, Romeo ... a young man of Verona. A comedy. By William Shakespeare.

Will reckons that's a good enough cue. He comes out of hiding, and approaches the balcony.

Will *(whispers)*: My lady!

Viola *(gasps)*: Who is there?

Will: Will Shakespeare!

The Nurse calls "Madam!" from inside the room.

Viola: Anon, good nurse. Anon. *(To Will)* Master Shakespeare?!

Will: The same, alas.

Viola: Oh but why "alas"?

Will: A lowly player.

Viola: Alas indeed, for I thought you the highest poet of my esteem and a writer of plays that capture my heart.

Will: Oh—I am him too!

The Nurse calls again.

Viola *(To Nurse)*: Anon, anon! *(To Will)* I will come again.

She goes inside for a moment.

Will *(To himself)*: Oh. I am fortune's fool. I will be punished for this!

Viola returns. Will comes forward again.

Will *(Cont'd)*: Oh my lady, my love!

Viola: If they find you here they will kill you.

Will: You can bring them with a word.

Viola: Oh, not for the world!

The Nurse calls her again: "Madam!"

Viola *(Cont'd)*: Anon, nurse!

But she goes inside. Will looks around and sees that there is, as ever, a convenient tree. He starts to climb up towards the balcony. When his head is nearly level, a soft figure comes once more onto the balcony. Will pops his head over the parapet and is face to face with the Nurse. The Nurse gives a yell. Will falls out of the tree.

Marc Norman and Tom Stoppard (1998) won seven Academy Awards with *Shakespeare in Love*.

Arthur Laurents, Leonard Bernstein, Stephen Sondheim

West Side Story—The Musical

Jerome Robbins, Arthur Laurents, Leonard Bernstein and Stephen Sondheim (1956) worked on this colourful musical.

11:00 p.m. A back alley. A suggestion of buildings; a fire escape climbing to the rear window of an unseen flat. As Tony sings, he looks for where Maria lives, wishing for her. And she does appear, at the window above him, which opens on to the fire escape. Music stays beneath most of the scene.

(TONY *sings*) Maria Maria …

MARIA: Ssh!

TONY: Maria!!

MARIA: Quiet!

TONY: Come down.

MARIA: No.

TONY: Maria …

MARIA: Please, If Bernardo—

TONY: He's at the dance. Come down.

MARIA: He will soon bring Anita home.

TONY: Just for a minute.

MARIA *(smiles)*: A minute is not enough.

TONY *(smiles)*: For an hour, then.

MARIA: I cannot.

TONY: Forever!

MARIA: Ssh!

TONY: Then I'm coming up.

WOMAN'S VOICE *(from the offstage apartment)*: Maria!

MARIA: *Momentito*, Mama ...

TONY *(climbing up)*: Maria, Maria—

MARIA: *Cállate! (Reaching her hand out to stop him.)* Ssh!

TONY *(grabbing her hand)*: Ssh'

MARIA: It is dangerous.

TONY: I'm not 'one of them'.

MARIA: You are; but to me, you are not. Just as I am one of them—

(She gestures towards the apartment.)

TONY: To me, you are all the—

(She covers his mouth with her hand)

MAN'S VOICE *(from unseen apartment)* Maruca!

MARIA: *Si, va vengo*, Papa.

TONY: Maruca?

MARIA: His pet name for me.

TONY: I like him. He will like me.

MARIA: No. He is like Bernardo: afraid. *(Suddenly laughing.)* Imagine being afraid of you! [...] *They sing.*

(MARIA) All the world is only you and me!

(And now the buildings, the world fade away, leaving them suspended in space.)

Tonight, tonight,
it all began tonight,
I saw you and the world went away.
Tonight, tonight [...]

MAN'S VOICE (*offstage*): Maruca!

MARIA: Wait for me!

Songs like "America," "Maria" and "Tonight" composed by Leonard Bernstein have become evergreens.

(She goes inside as the buildings begin to come back into place.)

(TONY *sings.*)

Tonight, tonight,
It all began tonight,
I saw you and the world went away.

MARIA *(returning)*: I cannot stay.
Go quickly!

TONY: I am not afraid.

MARIA: They are strict with me. Please.

TONY *(kissing her)*: Good night.

MARIA: *Buenas noches.*

[…]

TONY: I love you […]

West Side Story I.5

Shakespeare Without the Boring Bits

Humphrey Carpenter

Macbeth—Told by Macbeth

This is the tragedy of Macbeth told in somewhat different language and style—so what? It's the thrill of the story that matters.

Call me Mac.

It was the kind of day when you can do your washing without taking your clothes off. That's to say, damp. Banquo and I were damp all night. And not just from the rain. We'd been beating the hell out of a bunch of rebels and Norwegians. And I'm not talking about tennis.

Scotland's a big place, and we had most of it to cross to get home. A lot of the scenery looks as though someone backstage is having a joke, and this bit was no exception. They called it a blasted[1] heath[2]. It looked as if whoever drew it had been trying to rub it out ever since. Kind of weird[3].

But not as weird as the three dames we ran into. I mean, I've seen all kinds of broads[4], but this trio made me realize I had to redefine the species. If Helen of Troy had a face that launched[5] a thousand ships, this lot would have sent any fleet into a mudbank.

"Hail!" yelled out the youngest of them, and she wouldn't see ninety-five again. I looked up into the sky. Well, I thought she was talking about the weather!

"All hail, Macbeth!" screamed the second, who'd passed her sell-by date a couple of centuries ago. "Hail, Thane of Cawdor."

"You got the wrong guy, ladies," I told them. But they hadn't finished their little production number.

[1] **blasted** (*infml*) very annoying – [2] **heath** [hi:θ] *Heide* – [3] **weird** [wɪəd] mad, crazy – [4] **broad** (US *sl, derog*) woman – [5] **to launch** to put sth or sb into action; to start sth

"All hail, Macbeth, who'll be king one day!" screamed the third, who made the other two look like winners in a beautiful baby contest.

Now, I'm the last guy to mind a compliment from an older woman, but this was ridiculous. No one gets to be king unless he's got royal blood in his veins. Or unless he drains[1] a bucketful of the stuff out of its rightful owners.

"What about me, ladies?" snaps out Banquo. "Don't I get nothing?"

"No throne for you, big boy," says the third crone[2], the one who looks like she's just taking five minutes off from being dead. "But your kids'll be sitting on it all right."

"Ladies, talk sense," I told them but suddenly they were nowhere to be seen. I was just wondering whether it was something I ate, when up come a couple of guys with a message from the king. They told me he liked the way I'd recycled those rebels into crow food. In fact, he liked it so much he was going to make me Thane of Cawdor.

I called my wife, told her the news. If that close-harmony trio had got it right about me being Thane of Cawdor, chances were the king bit might be on the line too. I told her that.

She liked it. And when I got home she had news for me. The king was checking in for the night into our guest bedroom. "See to it that he doesn't get any breakfast," my wife told me. And it wasn't his diet she had in mind. Round about the cocktail hour, the king steps on to our front porch. "I like the view here, folks," he tells everyone. Enjoy it, king. It's the last you're ever gonna see.

I wasn't feeling so good about what I had to do. As kings go, he was a good one. And now he'd really gotta go. "I ain't doin' it," I told my wife.

She had a few things to say to me about that. Like how she was gonna give me a new name. Coward was the name she had in mind. And a lot more like that. "Ok," I told her, "I'm doin' it."

What a broad. And she had a plan. The king had the usual crowd with him, bodyguards, hair-dressers, you know the stuff. She served them up a nightcap with a kick like the acceleration of a getaway car. Besides the liquor, there was a certain little white powder in it. Those guys weren't gonna wake till morning. Not if you'd tickled the soles of their feet with a dentist's drill.

By this time, I was strung up to such a pitch I was seeing daggers before my eyes. And they weren't pointing to the exit doors.

A few minutes later, there was a lot of blood about the place. The king's blood and most of it was all over me. I could see my wife didn't think the colour red suited me. Nor was she too keen that I was carrying a handful of daggers. "Get back in there," she hissed, "and make it look as if his servants did it."

[1]**to drain** to empty a glass, etc by drinking everything in it – [2]**crone** (usually *derog*) ugly old woman

"Lady," I said, "I'm not going back in there." Quite apart from the king looking like someone had been trying to turn him into several orders of steak tartare, I'd been hearing this voice, saying I wouldn't be sleeping no more. Not for the rest of my born days. Which wasn't exactly the king's problem. Just then, someone knocked at our front door. I wished they could have woken the king. But he'd dropped off into the big sleep.

The guy beating a drum-break on the door was a fella named Macduff. He had an appointment with the king. An early one. He was a spot late for it though. He went into the king's bedroom and came out looking as if he'd just bet twelve million dollars on a horse. And lost.

"He's dead," he snapped out.

"You don't say?" I said, acting as hard as if I were in line for an Academy Award.

Just at that moment, the king's sons, who were staying at our place with the rest of the crowd, wandered along to see what had happened. When they realized daddy wouldn't be tucking them up[1] at night no more, they took one look at me, packed their bags, and got out of the place with the speed of an express elevator.

A couple of days later, I was sitting around in my crown, thinking how swell[2] it was to be king, when I recalled what those geriatric[3] chorus-girls had told Banquo about his descendants becoming king after me. That didn't sound so good, so I called up a couple of guys I knew.

Swell guys, these. So tough they made Al Capone look like Minnie Mouse. "Hi, fella," I greeted them. "I got a guy called Banquo and his kid son coming over for a meal. See he gets a knuckle sandwich[4] instead."

"Just that, boss?" they grunted.

"Not just that. I'd like some local undertaker[5] to be making enough dough[6] today to take his wife and kiddies to the seaside." I'm such a soft-hearted individual.

"We get you, boss," they said. And sure enough, a couple of hours later, Banquo was being measured for a wooden overcoat. But not his kid, who'd run off when the fat hit the fire.

Just because Banquo was dead, it didn't mean we shouldn't lay a place for him at table. A lot of the smart set[7] were coming to dinner and it doesn't do to let on you've just introduced one of your guests to the grim reaper[8]. So there was Banquo's knife and fork.

And jeez[9], there was Banquo looking like he'd just been through somebody's office shredder. And he was the colour of the day-before-yesterday milk (apart from the blood which was all over him and was the usual red). "Get the hell out of here!" I snapped at him. "Don't you know you're dead?"

[1]**to tuck up** *mit der Bettdecke zudecken* – [2]**swell** (dated US *infml*) excellent, very good, nice – [3]**geriatric** here: *altersschwach* – [4]**to give sb a knuckle sandwich** (*infml*) *jemandem eine in die Fresse hauen* – [5]**undertaker** person whose business is to prepare dead people for burial and arrange funerals – [6]**dough** [dəʊ] *Knete* (money; dough = *Teig*) – [7]**set** (sometimes *derog*) group of people who spend a lot of time together socially or have similar interests, etc – [8]**grim reaper** (*fig*) death – [9]**jeez** (*euph*) Jesus

Seems he agreed with me, because he just vanished[1], the way those sweet old ladies had done. Talking of them I reckoned it was time I paid them another visit.

As blasted heaths go, this one was looking more blasted than ever. And my lady friends were brewing up a bit of lunch. You know the sort of menu, eye of newt[2], tongue of dog, leg of lizard[3]. The kind of things you can get at any witches' lunchcounter. "How's the future looking?" I asked them. So they told me. Or rather, they laid on a show.

You've heard of special guest appearances? Well, these were special ghost appearances. And I just sat there listening, and freaked out. A case of spook when you're spooken to.

"Beware Macduff!" snapped out the first ghost, but the second one said I didn't need to fuss myself about any guy who'd been born of a woman. Which I reckoned meant I had nothing to fear from one hundred per cent of the population.

Then up comes another of these freaks, this time to tell me I wouldn't bite the dust till Birnam Wood marched up Dunsinane Hill. Suited me, since most woods I know like to stay put. But what about Banquo's descendants, I asked them. Was there any truth in the nasty little rumour[4] that they, and not my kids, if I had any, would become king after me?

For an answer, who should pop up but Banquo again, showing me his family photo album. And sure enough, all the kids were wearing crowns.

That was all I needed to make my day. And no sooner was I back home than some guy tells me Macduff has fled to England, and is getting a lot of guys together to pay a visit to me. Not the friendliest of visits.

Well, two can play at that game. He'd made a little mistake, had Macduff. He'd left his family behind. So I got those guys who'd done such a nice job on Banquo to pay a call on the Macduffs. Next day, there weren't no Macduffs left to call on.

Things were starting to get hot for me. You've heard of rats leaving a sinking ship? Well, let's just say the vermin[5] count at my place was going down by the hour.

Then there was my wife. She'd taken to washing her hands.

Approximately ninety-seven times an hour! To get the blood off, she said though there wasn't any blood that I could see.

Yes, the poor dame was losing her mind. And I thought my own had decided to say goodbye to me when I looked out of the window and saw a lot of trees on the march. Sure enough, it was Birnam Wood, come to see how things were doing on Dunsinane Hill.

[1] **to vanish** to disappear – [2] **newt** *Molch* – [3] **lizard** *Eidechse* – [4] **rumour** story that is spread by being talked about but may not be true – [5] **vermin** *Ungeziefer*

Now, the habits of trees don't greatly concern me, but after a while it struck me that all this travelling timber[1] was just a load of camouflage. I mean, real trees don't carry swords.

Yeah, they'd come to get me, and just as my wife had decided it was time she tried out her grave for size. I was rattled[2], I admit, but if it was curtains for me, I was gonna take a hell of a lot of guys with me.

Sure enough, in a few minutes, my sword had managed to investigate quite a few sets of guts[3]. Then who should come up for a personal encounter but Macduff. "Save your strength," I told him. "No one who was born of a woman can harm me. Which just about rules out the whole of homo sapiens."

"Sorry to disappoint you," smirks[4] Macduff. "Ever heard of a Caesarean[5]? My ma was gonna have a difficult labour, so they cut me out. Geddit?" I got it, all right. And I got his sword too. Right where it hurts most. If I ever meet those three weird sisters in the next world, I've got a bone to pick with them.

Macduff with a 'shorter' Macbeth

Macbeth, the villain

1. Re-tell the story as a mini-saga. Do not write more than 50 words.
2. Macbeth is a "hell-hound", but what makes him sympathetic to you in this narration?

The boring bits

1. Perhaps you've become interested in the real thing, now. You can, of course, read the original or watch one of the movies, e.g. by Roman Polanski.
2. Check some of the passages with the original, e.g. the dagger-monologue (pp. 235–237) and the witches (pp. 238–244). Compare the language.

Macbeth before hell's gate

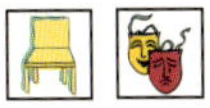

Put Macbeth on trial. He has not the slightest chance to escape the fires of hell. But he can try to defend himself at the entrance. Act out this situation. One of you is Macbeth. The others stand around him and accuse him of his dreadful deeds. If it's too hard to do for one person, use two or three Macbeths, who then should speak in turn to the judges.

[1] **timber** wood prepared for use in building or carpentry – [2] **to rattle** (*infml*) (esp passive) to make sb nervous, worried or frightened – [3] **guts** stomach and the internal organs around it; here pars pro toto for soldiers – [4] **to smirk** *grinsen* – [5] **Caesarean** [sɪˈzeəriən] *Kaiserschnitt*

All the World's a Stage

Brainstorm about the manifold ways of describing life metaphorically. What images for comparison come to your mind?

All the world's a stage,
And all the men and women merely players;
They have their exits and their entrances;
And one man in his time plays many parts.
His acts being seven ages. At first the infant,
Mewling[1] and puking[2] in the nurse's arms.
Then the whining school-boy, with his satchel[3],
And shining morning face, creeping like snail
Unwillingly to school. And then the lover,
Sighing like furnace[4], with a woeful ballad
Made to his mistress' eyebrow. Then a soldier,
Full of a strange oaths[5], and bearded like the pard[6],
Jealous in honour, sudden and quick in quarrel,
Seeking the bubble reputation[7]
Even in the cannon's mouth. And then the justice,
In fair round belly, with good capon[8] lin'd,
With eyes severe and beard of formal cut,
Full of wise saws[9] and modern instances[10];
And so he plays his part. The sixth age shifts
Into the lean and slipper'd pantaloon[11],
With spectacles on nose and pouch[12] on side,
His youthful hose, well sav'd a world too wide
For his shrunk shank[13]; and his big manly voice,
Turning again toward childish treble, pipes
And whistles in his sound. Last scene of all,
That ends this strange eventful history,
Is second childishness and more oblivion[14];
Sans teeth, sans eyes, sans taste, sans everything.

As You Like It II.7.139ff.

The Seven Ages of Man

[1] **mewling** crying (like a cat) – [2] **to puke** to vomit – [3] **satchel** *Ranzen* – [4] **furnace** an enclosed fireplace for heating the water used to heat a building by means of pipes – [5] **oath** solemn promise to do sth or a solemn declaration that sth is true – [6] **pard** leopard – [7] **bubble reputation** reputation as fragile as a bubble, i.e. not lasting long – [8] **capon** (*arch*) chicken – [9] **wise saws** proverbs – [10] **modern instances** dull examples – [11] **pantaloon** here: silly old man – [12] **pouch** purse – [13] **shrunk shank** thin leg – [14] **oblivion** the state of being forgotten, esp by the public

Your thematic vocabulary

Go through the chapter again and collect words to add to the following word map. You can share the texts in groups. Do not forget to put in vocabulary from your Internet research on the background of William Shakespeare's life and world. Expand it with as many words you think are useful to talk about the Bard, his time and his work.

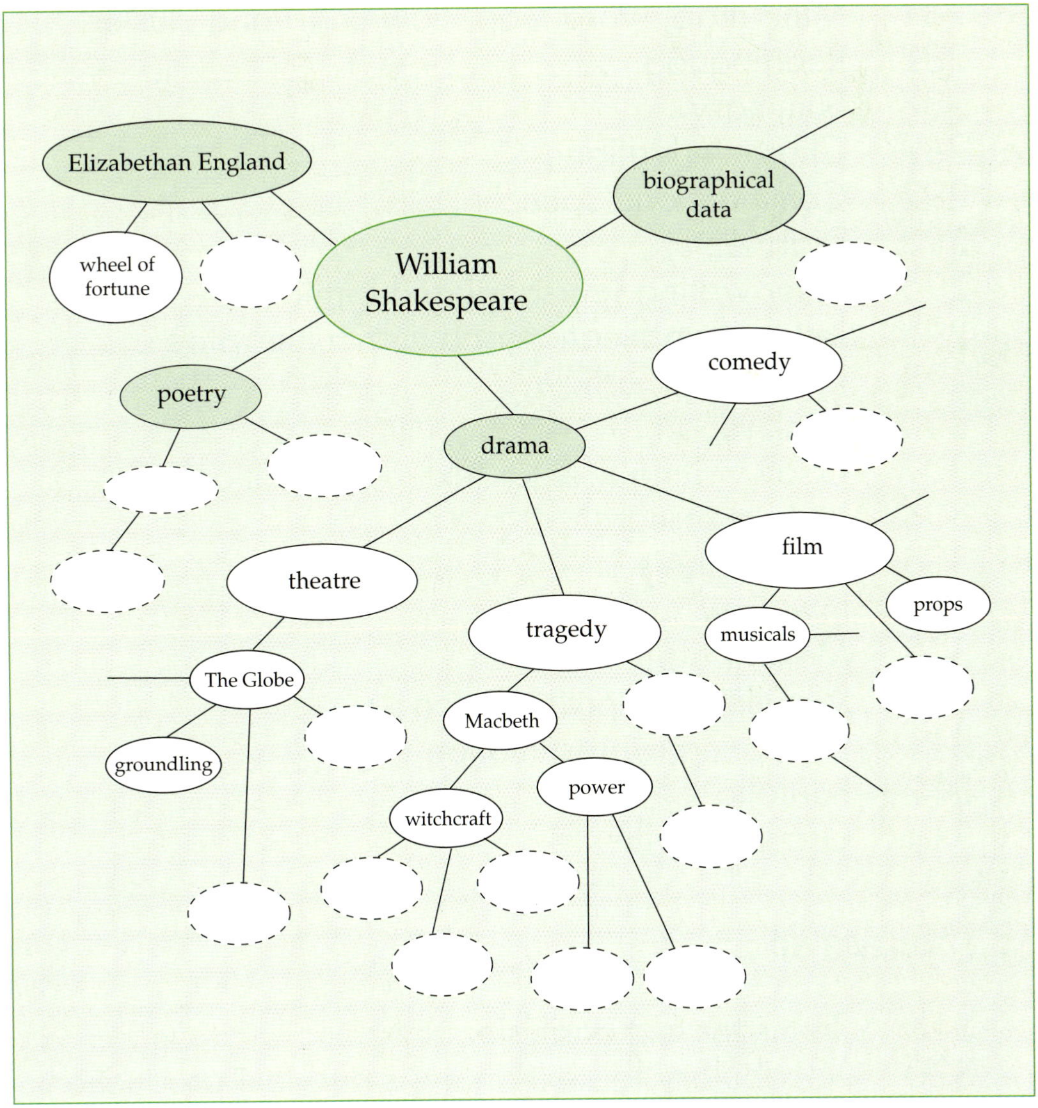

Appendix: Contents

Method kit

Language kit

Method kit

Words within text and context—using a dictionary

If you come across a word you do not know, you can either guess its meaning from the **context** or look it up in a **dictionary**.

Using the context

What to do

The context, i.e. the words and sentences that come before and after the unknown word, helps you guess the meaning of the word.

Examples

1. We sat at a table by the window watching the rain **slap** against the glass. (Guess, how rain can **hit** the window pane.)
2. The rain slowed by late afternoon. The girls went back to their side of the camp to change into their **outdoor gear**. (Guess what they changed into before walking **outdoors.**)

Using an English dictionary

What to do

1. Check which word class the word you are looking for belongs to (e.g. noun, verb etc).
2. Look for the correct meaning of the word. Different meanings are indicated by numbers.

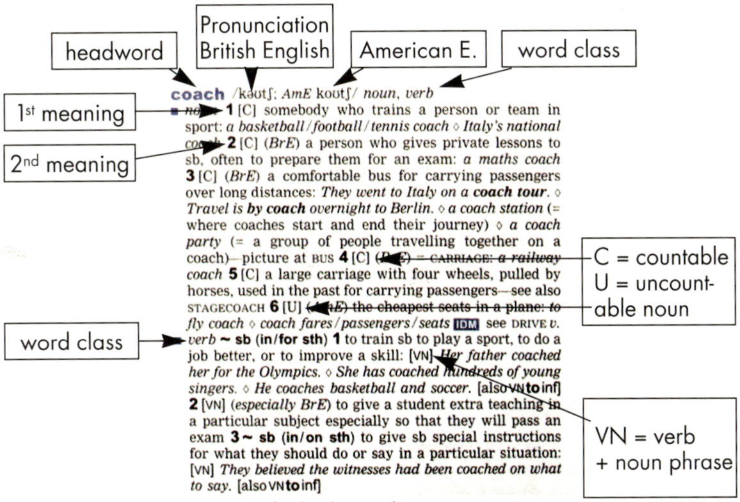

coach /kəʊtʃ; *AmE* koʊtʃ/ *noun, verb*
■ *noun* **1** [C] somebody who trains a person or team in sport: *a basketball/football/tennis coach* ◇ *Italy's national coach* **2** [C] (*BrE*) a person who gives private lessons to sb, often to prepare them for an exam: *a maths coach* **3** [C] (*BrE*) a comfortable bus for carrying passengers over long distances: *They went to Italy on a* ***coach tour***. ◇ *Travel is* ***by coach*** *overnight to Berlin.* ◇ *a coach station* (= where coaches start and end their journey) ◇ *a coach party* (= a group of people travelling together on a coach)—picture at BUS **4** [C] (*BrE*) = CARRIAGE: *a railway coach* **5** [C] a large carriage with four wheels, pulled by horses, used in the past for carrying passengers—see also STAGECOACH **6** [U] (*AmE*) the cheapest seats in a plane: *to fly coach* ◇ *coach fares/passengers/seats* IDM see DRIVE *v.*
■ *verb* **~ sb (in/for sth) 1** to train sb to play a sport, to do a job better, or to improve a skill: [VN] *Her father coached her for the Olympics.* ◇ *She has coached hundreds of young singers.* ◇ *He coaches basketball and soccer.* [also VN **to** inf] **2** [VN] (*especially BrE*) to give a student extra teaching in a particular subject especially so that they will pass an exam **3 ~ sb (in/on sth)** to give sb special instructions for what they should do or say in a particular situation: [VN] *They believed the witnesses had been coached on what to say.* [also VN **to** inf]

Oxford Advanced Learner's Dictionary

◀ Which is which?

1. John: "I'll sit in the third **coach** from the front of the train."
2. The teacher **coached** his pupils in arithmetic.

1. coach, noun, 4; 2. coach, verb, 2

Skimming and scanning—extensive reading

When you want to get information from a text but you do not have a lot of time for intensive reading in detail, you can apply **extensive reading techniques**.

- **Skimming** through or over a text means reading it quickly to get a general impression of it.
- **Scanning** a text means reading it quickly to find information about special points.

What to do

1. Skim the following text to get the main idea of what it is about.
2. Scan the text for information about caning in private schools.

Example

Corporal Punishment in British Schools

Although corporal punishment has been banned in state schools for more than 10 years, it still remains legal in private schools, although very few establishments use the cane *(Stock)*. 1

Don Foster, Liberal Democrat education spokesman, has tabled an amendment *(Zusatzartikel)* to the Schools Bill which would extend the ban to private schools. The Government has promised a free vote when it is debated later this month. 2

Government sources said they were confident that the measure would be carried out although it is likely to face substantial opposition from Tory and Ulster Unionist MPs.

Mr Foster said the ban was necessary to end what he called a breach of fundamental human rights and which others have likened to child abuse.

He added that Britain remained the only country in the European Union that still allowed corporal punishment in any of its schools and that it was time to bring the independent sector into line with state schools.

The ban is unlikely to attract much opposition from the private schools themselves. The Independent School Council said it welcomed the move because it reflects opinion and practice in the schools. 2

David Woodhead, national director of the Independent Schools Information Service, said the 1,300 schools in the council accounted for 80 per cent of the children educated in the private sector and none used corporal punishment. All the major public schools have abandoned the use of the cane.

There are around 1,000 private schools outside the council and some of them still use corporal punishment. Of the small minority that have retained (*kept*) the right, the best known is St. James, a boys' school in Twickenham, Middlesex, where staff and pupils practise meditation. 3

1. Skimming result: The text is about caning in private schools
2. Scanning results:
(1) Caning is still legal but not practised everywhere.
(2) Attempts to ban caning in private schools.
(3) A small minority still has the right to cane pupils.

! These techniques are based on the rapid movement of your eyes over a text. You can improve the speed of spotting keywords or key phrases by training with other texts. You should fix a period of time and work with a stop watch. Repeat collecting basic information by skimming and scanning until you are content with your results.

Note-taking

Note-taking can help you in many ways. By filtering a text for the most important information, keywords or key phrases, you get a clearer idea of what it is about. There are three types of note-taking that can be applied to either written or spoken texts:
You can write down from what you read or hear

- as many details as possible,
- the main points, or
- certain aspects.

What to do

While reading

- Underline or mark the information you need for your task.
- Use different colours for details, main points or special aspects.
- Use the → skimming technique for finding keywords and main points.
- Use the → scanning technique for finding as many details as possible.
- Put your findings in a logical order e.g. a list or a grid (see below).

Example

This is the beginning of George Orwell's short story (→ p. 59ff.). If you want to, you can go on practicing the note-taking technique with the complete story. Here the main information is highlighted. See the arrangement of facts below:

A Hanging

It was in Burma, a sodden morning of the rains. A sickly light, like yellow tinfoil, was slanting over the high walls into the jail yard. We were waiting outside the condemned cells, a row of sheds fronted with double bars, like small animal cages. Each cell measured about ten feet by ten and was quite bare within except for a plank bed and a pot of drinking water. In some of them brown silent men were squatting at the inner bars, with their blankets draped round them. These were the condemned men, due to be hanged within the next week or two.

↺ (look up Burma: geographical and cultural information needed later on!)

! topic

One prisoner had been brought out of his cell. He was a Hindu, a puny wisp of a man, with a shaven head and vague liquid eyes. He had a thick, sprouting moustache, absurdly too big for his body, rather like the moustache of a comic man on the films. Six tall Indian warders were guarding him and getting him ready for the gallows. Two of them stood by with rifles and fixed bayonets, while the others handcuffed him, passed a chain through his handcuffs and fixed it to their belts, and lashed his arms tight to his sides. They crowded very close about him, with their hands always on him in a careful, caressing grip, as though all the while feeling him to make sure he was there. It was like men handling a fish which is still alive and may jump back into the water. But he stood quite unresisting, yielding his arms limply to the ropes, as though he hardly noticed what was happening. […]

the condemned man

the procedure of the hanging starts here

man's reaction

Writing down ➤ the topic	A prisoner is being prepared for his execution.		
Writing down ➤ the main points	place/setting: prison in Burma	the prisoner	the procedure of the preparation for the gallows
Writing down ➤ as many details as possible	nasty, rainy day prison cells like animal cages	the man who is taken out of the cell is a Hindu his reaction: he does not resist the handcuffing, he stays calm as if he didn't know what was going to happen to him	six Indian warders are busy with him they guard him with bayonets they handcuff him clumsily
Writing down ➤ particular points	the prison and the prisoners the men have brown faces they will be hanged within the next week or two the cells are bare except for plain bed and pot of water	he is small, bald he looks comical because his moustache is too big	

! These techniques also work for making **excerpts** of longer texts. When you go through texts, you should not only mark or underline important facts. You should also have a system for marking passages:

- Which words do you have to look up?
- Where do you need the teacher's help for understanding a passage?
- Which phrases or passages do you want to use for your essay?
- Here are some signs, you could put in the margin for
  - consulting the dictionary: ↺
  - good idea: ☺
  - asking someone for an explanation: ?
  - important, interesting: !
  - did not understand: ☹

Mind map, word map, flow chart and cluster

Word maps and **mind maps** are net-like groupings of words and ideas. They both start off with a main idea. Then appropriate words are put down along or at the end of lines which branch off from the original idea. Typical of **word maps** are free associations of words whereas the hierarchic and systematic linking of pieces of information is the distinguishing feature of **mind maps, flow charts** or **net diagrams**, and **clusters**.

Flow chart

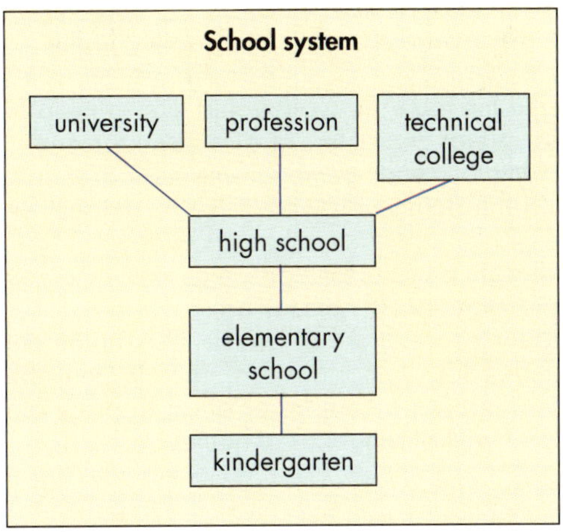

Cluster

Characterizing a hobo			
hair	**clothes**	**face**	**behaviour**
fair	ragged	smile	decent
uncombed	coat	blue eyes	polite
reaches over collar	holes in shoes	dirty	begging
needs a haircut	worn-out jeans	looks cheerful	slightly tipsy
needs washing	second-hand pullover	thin	doesn't like to be asked about himself

Word map

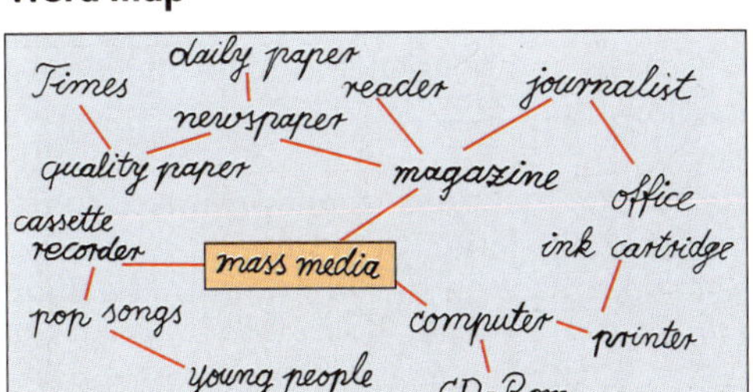

Mind map

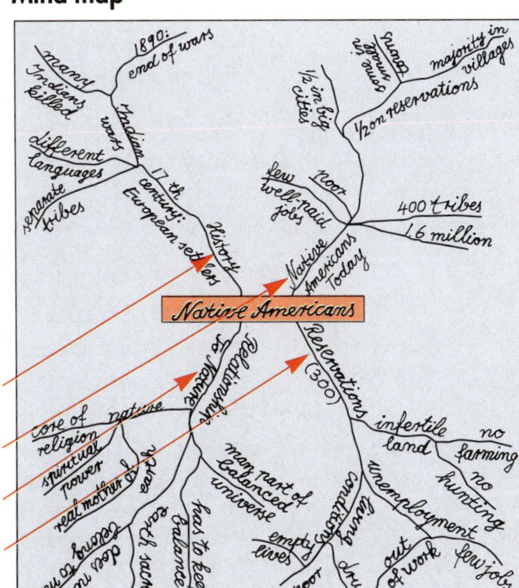

First level in the hierarchy:

History

Native Americans today

Relationship to nature

Reservations

Reading log

A **reading log** is a record of a reader's thoughts while reading a longer fictional text such as a novel or a drama. It contains entries about setting and action but especially reflects the reader's experiences with the text, the "dialogue" with the literary text.

What to do

Preparing a reading log

- You will need a special notebook (an exercise book or folder will do) for your entries.
- Divide it into two big columns (*Spalten*).

Keeping a reading log

- Use the left-hand column for facts that you would like to keep in mind for later discussions (e.g. characters or plot development).
- Use the right-hand column for your personal impression of and reaction to the text and the points you would like to suggest for later discussions in class.
- A small column in the margin is useful for signs, e.g. to remind you to look up a word in a dictionary (➔ note-taking).
- You can write complete sentences or use keywords. Use a different colour for a different kind of note: important (red), idea (green) etc.
- Make your entries after finishing a chapter or at an appropriate moment while reading the text at school or at home.

Example

Toni Morrison's novel *Song of Solomon* begins with a dream-like scene showing a man on a roof about to fly. Actually, that is the setting of the protagonist's birth. He undergoes a complicated process of maturing in the course of the story.

The passages that are highlighted and annotated appear in the student's reading log on the following pages.

topic/setting

The North Carolina Mutual Life Insurance agent promised to fly from Mercy to the other side of Lake Superior at three o'clock. Two days before the event was to take place he tacked a note on the door of his little yellow house:

"own wings"/ farewell note

> *At 3:00 p.m. on Wednesday the 18th of February, 1931, I will take off from Mercy and fly away on my own wings. Please forgive me. I loved you all.*
>
> *Robert Smith, Ins. agent*

Mr Smith/indication of time

everyday life

Mr Smith didn't draw as big a crowd as Lindbergh had four years earlier—not more than forty or fifty people showed up—because it was already eleven o'clock in the morning, on the very Wednesday he had chosen for his flight, before anybody read the note. At that time of day, during the middle of the week, word-of-mouth news just lumbered along. Children were in school; men were at work;

and most of the women were fastening their corsets and getting ready to go see what tails or entrails the butcher might be giving away. Only the unemployed, the self-employed, and the very young were available—deliberately available because they'd heard about it; or accidentally available because they happened to be walking at that exact moment in the shore end of Not Doctor Street, a name the post office did not recognize.

"Not Doctor Street"/story of the name

Town maps registered the street as Mains Avenue, but the only colored doctor in the city had lived and died on that street, and when he moved there in 1896 his patients took to calling the street, which none of them lived in or near, Doctor Street. Later, when other Negroes moved there, and the postal service became a popular means of transferring messages among them, envelopes from Louisiana, Virginia, Alabama, and Georgia began to arrive addressed to people at house numbers on Doctor Street. The post office workers returned these envelopes or passed them on to the Dead Letter Office.

Then in 1918, when colored men were being drafted, a few gave their address at the recruitment office as Doctor Street. In that way, the name acquired a quasi-official status. But not for long. Some of the city legislators, whose concern for appropriate names and the maintenance of the city's landmarks was the principal part of their political life, saw to it that "Doctor Street" was never used in any official capacity. And since they knew that only Southside residents kept it up, they had notices posted in the stores, barbershops, and restaurants in that part of the city saying that the avenue running northerly and southerly from Shore Road fronting the lake to the junction of routes 6 and 2 leading to Pennsylvania, and also running parallel to and between Rutherford Avenue and Broadway, had always been and would always be known as Mains Avenue and not Doctor Street.

It was a genuinely clarifying public notice because it gave Southside residents a way to keep their memories alive and please the city legislators as well. They called it Not Doctor Street, and were inclined to call the charity hospital at its northern end No Mercy Hospital since it was 1931, and the day following Mr. Smith's leap from its cupola, before the first colored expectant mother was allowed to give birth inside its wards and not on its steps. The reason for the hospital's generosity to that particular woman was not the fact that she was the only child of this Negro doctor, for during his entire professional life he had never been granted hospital privileges and only two of his patients were ever admitted to Mercy, both white. Besides, the doctor had been dead a long time by 1931. It must have been Mr. Smith's leap from the roof over their heads that made them admit her. In any case, whether or not the little insurance agent's conviction that he could fly contributed to the place of her delivery, it certainly contributed to its time.

the residents' reaction/the No Mercy Hospital

the doctor's daughter

When the dead doctor's daughter saw Mr. Smith emerge as promptly as he had promised from behind the cupola, his wide blue silk wings curved forward around his chest, she dropped her covered peck basket, spilling red velvet rose petals. The wind blew them about, up, down, and into small mounds of snow. Her half-grown daughters scrambled about trying to catch them, while their

velvet rose petals/ the doctor's daughter and her children

mother moaned and held the underside of her stomach. The rose-petal scramble got a lot of attention, but the pregnant lady's moans did not. Everyone knew the girls had spent hour after hour tracing, cutting, and stitching the costly velvet, and that Gerhardt's Department Store would be quick to reject any that were soiled.

real reason for the artificial flowers

It was nice and gay there for a while. The men joined in trying to collect the scraps before the snow soaked through them—snatching them from a gust of wind or plucking them delicately from the snow. And the very young children couldn't make up their minds whether to watch the man circled in blue on the roof or the bits of red flashing around the ground. Their dilemma was solved when a woman suddenly burst into song. […]

action like a colourful show/a woman sings the "Sugarman" song

O Sugarman done fly away
Sugarman done gone
Sugarman cut across the sky
Sugarman gone home …

the on-lookers

A few of the half a hundred or so people gathered there nudged each other and sniggered. Others listened as though it were the helpful and defining piano music in a silent movie. They stood this way for some time, none of them crying out to Mr. Smith, all of them preoccupied with one or the other of the minor events about them, until the hospital people came.

the hospital staff

They had been watching from the windows—at first with mild curiosity, then, as the crowd seemed to swell to the very walls of the hospital, they watched with apprehension. They wondered if one of those things that racial-uplift groups were always organizing was taking place. But when they saw neither placards nor speakers, they ventured outside into the cold: white-coated surgeons, dark-jacketed business and personnel clerks, and three nurses in starched jumpers.

The sight of Mr. Smith and his wide blue wings transfixed them for a few seconds, as did the woman's singing and the roses strewn about. Some of them thought briefly that this was probably some form of worship. Philadelphia, where Father Divine reigned, wasn't all that far away. Perhaps the young girls holding baskets of flowers were two of his virgins. But the laughter of a gold-toothed man brought them back to their senses. They stopped daydreaming and swiftly got down to business, giving orders. […]

rescue comes too late

Downtown the firemen pulled on their greatcoats, but when they arrived at Mercy, Mr. Smith had seen the rose petals, heard the music, and leaped on into the air.

the birth of the first coloured baby inside "No Mercy Hospital"/ foreshadowings of the protagonist's fate

The next day a colored baby was born inside Mercy for the first time. Mr. Smith's blue silk wings must have left their mark, because when the little boy discovered, at four, the same thing Mr. Smith had learned earlier—that only birds and airplanes could fly—he lost all interest in himself. […]

Example

My Reading Log
Song of Solomon by Toni Morrison

Important facts [quoted from the text]	Personal impressions— ideas—notes	
(p. 9) The North Carolina Mutual Life Insurance agent promised to fly from Mercy to the other side of Lake Superior at three o'clock.	Strange idea **to fly with self-made wings**. He must be crazy. Perhaps he wanted to commit suicide: the note he fixes to his door seems to be a farewell-note. As if he knew he was going to die. Or why else should he do that?	→ discuss in class
Mr Smith didn't draw as big a crowd as Lindbergh had four years earlier.	Lindbergh: found a stamp in my Dad's collection! 	↻ Lindbergh? encyclopaedia or google.com! → show class!
(p.10) Not Doctor Street, a name the post office did not recognize. […] the only colored doctor in the city had lived and died on that street […] Then in 1918, when colored men were being drafted, a few gave their address at the recruitment office as Doctor Street. In that way, the name acquired a quasi-official status. But not for long. […] they had notices […] saying that the avenue […] had always been and would always be known as Mains Avenue and not Doctor Street […] They called it Not Doctor Street […]	**The story of the street is amazing.** But it shows the cleverness of the black people and on the other hand the stupid bureaucracy of the whites. They only tolerated the blacks when they risked their lives for them in the war. **That is not fair.** Pure segregation … !→ reminds me of Martin Luther King and all that … That is **irony** at its best or was it satire? The blacks simply took the notice literally and made a joke of the public order.	idea: ! Civil Rights Movement ↻ when? → ask in class ↻ definition of satire
[…] and were inclined to call the charity hospital at its northern end No Mercy Hospital since it was 1931, and the day following Mr. Smith's leap from its cupola, before the first colored expectant mother was allowed to give birth inside its wards and not on its steps. (p. 11) The rose-petal scramble got a lot of attention, but the pregnant lady's moans did not. […] And the very young children couldn't make up their minds whether to	The name fits the hospital, I think, now Mr Smith's leap seems to have something to do with his experiences of injustice against blacks. **But the following scene with the pregnant mother is a strange scenario— guess I have to ask the teacher about:** the velvet rose petals → what are they for: window decoration or dress decoration (it is said that Gerhardt's Department Store wouldn't buy them if they were dirty)??	? → ask in class if they got that with the petals

watch the man circled in blue on the roof or the bits of red flashing around the ground. Their dilemma was solved when a woman suddenly burst into song. […]	**That is really colourful imagery!** blue and red—there must be some meaning to the colours: blue—? red—blood, birth, violence, but blue …	The colours: do they have meanings?
Sugarman, done fly away […] (p. 12)	**The song** surely has more to it. Why does she call the "flyer" sugarman?	Sugarman?
They wondered if one of those things that racial-uplift groups were always organizing was taking place. […] Some of them thought briefly that this was probably some form of worship.	**The hospital staff:** Why do they not react more quickly? The firemen are too late. I would have tried to get him off the roof if I had been one of the staff there. Explanation of the late reaction of the on-lookers: curiosity, not believing their eyes, trance (?), whites: no interest in black's crazy performance or death, prejudices	➔ compare with the others in class
(p. 15) The next day a colored baby was born inside Mercy for the first time. Mr. Smith's blue silk wings must have left their mark, because when the little boy discovered, at four, the same thing Mr. Smith had learned earlier—that only birds and airplanes could fly—he lost all interest in himself.	Finally the protagonist appears—but his birth takes place in a **very unreal scenario** and the text foreshadows no good future—I don't understand the last sentence at all!!!	☹!! need help!!

The following questions and hints might help you with your entries:

- Is there anything that puzzles you?
- Jot down (*notieren*) phrases from the text that strike you as important, odd, etc.
- Have you read or seen (on TV, cinema) anything that is similar to the story?
- Can you identify with the protagonists/one of the persons/none of them? Write down your reasons.
- Do you like/dislike any of the characters? State why, using the information given in the text.
- Stop once in a while and guess how the story might develop. Your prediction can be based on the knowledge you already have about the author, the type of story (horror, love, science fiction, etc), or the characters and their relationships in the story. After your reading: have you come close to guessing the real ending?
- Add some pictures, map of locations, sketches on the setting, or anything that comes to mind.
- Sort out your feelings—do you always agree with the author's intention? Write down any feelings and associations that you have with the story or drama.

Summary

A **summary** is a short version of a text. It only includes the facts that a reader needs to know to get a general idea of what the original text is about.

What to do

Before writing

- Read the original text carefully to find out what is important (→ skimming, scanning).
- Find the main ideas in the text and mark them or take notes (→ note-taking). Leave out information which is not essential, e.g. statistics, anecdotes, quotations, detailed descriptions, etc.
- Make a topic outline (see below).

While writing

- Use the notes as the basis for your summary, i.e. not your interpretation.
- Mind the tense. Use the present simple when summarizing literary texts.
- Write the summary from the author's point of view.
- Try to use your own words as much as possible.
- When necessary, change direct speech into reported speech (mind the backshift rules).
- Do not add new material such as your own opinion or interpretation.

After writing

- Re-read your summary. Have you covered the essential points?
- Check if you have observed the rules above.
- Will your summary be clear to somebody who does not know the original text?

Example

See: Reading log sample text *Song of Solomon*, p. 282

Topic outline:

1. A life insurance agent wants to fly from Mercy (Hospital) to the other side of Lake Superior.
2. He leaves a note on the door: at 3 p.m. on Wednesday the 18th of February 1931; Robert Smith.
3. It is a normal weekday. Some people who have time go there.
4. Not Doctor Street is not the real name of the place, but the black residents called it this after some quarrelling with the officials in honour of their dead doctor.
5. They also re-named the charity hospital No Mercy Hospital because it didn't admit blacks.
6. Only that day the first black woman ever to give birth in the clinic is the daughter of the dead doctor. It is certainly due to the sensation Mr Smith caused with his leap.

7. Before the pregnant woman is taken inside, she spreads velvet rose petals with her other children where Mr Smith is going to jump off the hospital roof.
8. A woman starts singing.
9. The hospital staff wonders about Mr Smith. He could be a protester against racial discrimination or a religious fanatic.
10. The firemen are alarmed but arrive too late.
11. The baby is born in Mercy.

Summary:

In the beginning of Toni Morrison's novel *Song of Solomon*, there is Mr Robert Smith, a Life Insurance agent, who is going to fly from the roof of the Mercy Hospital to the other side of Lake Superior with wings he has made himself. He fixed a note to his door, announcing that this was going to take place on Wednesday 18th February 1931 at 3 p.m. It is a normal weekday, but some people have time to go to Not Doctor Street and wait for the event. The street has a story of its own. After some quarrels with the legislators, the black residents kept calling the street Not Doctor Street and additionally called the hospital No Mercy Hospital. It is a charity hospital, which does not admit colored people. That does not change until the day Mr Smith draws attention to himself and a young pregnant woman. She is the dead doctor's daughter and while Mr Smith stands on the roof-top, she spreads out handmade velvet rose petals on the street with her other children. A woman starts singing. After some time the hospital people come out and wonder why the man on the roof might be acting as he is. They believe him to be a protester against racial discrimination or a religious fanatic. The firemen are called at last, but the rescue comes too late. Mr. Smith has already jumped. At the same time the doctor's daughter is taken inside the hospital and the next day the first coloured baby is born at Mercy Hospital.

Characterization

People's (or—in fictional texts—characters') social position, their situation as well as their outward appearance, behaviour, words and thoughts, feelings and attitudes are aspects of a **characterization**. They are all connected with each other in order to give readers or audiences a full and complex idea of the character. The reactions of other people (or other characters in the text) also add to the characterization.

What to do

Before writing

- Read the text carefully. Mark the words or sentences or write down the lines that give you information about the character(s).
- Draw a chart that includes columns like "outward appearance", "situation/position", etc.

Name of character: --------------------	Chapter 1/ paragraph1/ lines xx–xx	Chapter 2/ paragraph2/ lines xx–xx	Chapter 3/ paragraph3/ lines xx–xx	Chapter x/ paragraph x/ lines xx–xx
outward appearance				
situation/ position				
etc				

- Ask yourself if the character(s) change(s) during the development of the text and if so, how.
- Number your notes and group them according to importance.

While writing

- Write a short introduction in which you present the character(s) and his or her (their) situation.
- Organize your notes in paragraphs. Every paragraph should deal with one characteristic feature (*Eigenschaft*). Present the evidence (*Beleg*) taken from the text and comment on it. Don't forget to refer to or quote the text.
- Try to show how the different characteristic features relate to one another.
- Write a conclusion that sums up the results of your detailed analysis.

After writing

- Does your introduction lead to the detailed analysis of one or more characters?
- Does your characterization take into consideration all the notes that you made before starting to write?
- Have you linked up the different aspects in a logical way?
- Have you referred to or quoted the text enough to support your description?
- Does your conclusion offer a convincing summary of what you have found?

Example **See text: *An Old Woman with a Pram*, p. 202**

Chart of notes

an old woman	**lines 1–2**	**lines 2–14**	**lines 15–40**	**lines 41–end**
outward appearance	age: probably around 45 1	scarf around her head; fur-hat; Russian chapka, much of fur fallen out; trousers; padded jacket; imitation-fur coat: colour of dust; looks like an Eskimo; a pair of American-style sneakers 2	her feet swell up at night 2	
situation/position	Oxford Circus, London 1	belongings in plastic bags in a shopping chariot lifted from a supermarket; lives out of dustbins 3	at night she sleeps on cardboard on the station asphalt 4	she is a tramp 1
behaviour		her face slightly inclined as if it were a pram and she were looking for a baby 5	at midday she walks to the pedestrian precinct where she feeds the pigeons; she puts a piece of bread into her mouth absent-mindedly 6	she takes special care of a sick, bald pigeon; she nurses the animal with a specially prepared baby milk bottle every day 6
feelings/attitudes				she doesn't care about the curious crowd and feels as if she were living in a garden with the pigeons 8
others' reactions				a crowd of shoppers watch the woman 7

1 outward appearance The old woman in the story is a tramp woman of about 45 years of age living in London near Oxford Circus. She wears a collection of clothes that make her look like an Eskimo. Around her head she has a scarf and wears a Russian-style fur-hat, called a chapka. She also wears trousers and a padded jacket with an imitation-fur coat. Her feet, that tend to swell up at
2 situation night, are in a pair of American-style sneakers. All her belongings fit in some plastic bags that she carries
3/4 around in a chariot stolen from a supermarket. That chariot is like a pram for her. She seems to be looking at a baby inside. At night she sleeps on a piece of card-
5 board on the station asphalt. She lives out of dustbins. It is her everyday routine to prepare a baby bottle of milk to nurse a weak, bald pigeon along with the
behaviour other pigeons she feeds in the pedestrian precinct.
6 Sometimes she seems absent-minded. The shoppers
others' reactions that watch her do not bother her much. She considers
7 them to be voyeurs and from what she says to her pigeons we learn that she feels as if she were living in
attitude 8 a garden and those curious people were shut out by a wall.

conclusion The old woman seems to be living in a world of her own. She seems to be content with her poor and desolate living conditions and does not show any interest in communication with the so-called normal people around her. To them she is a social failure, a tramp, a weird old mad-woman. They gaze at her but only as if she were some alien creature from outer space. That seems alright with her. She lives a free life in harmony with the pigeons, which have become substitute children for her. She is a kind of island unto herself.

Comment and speech

We can write or talk about our opinions on a topic. We distinguish between short, mostly spoken **comments** and written, longer forms of expressing **opinions**. The written form and a **speech** usually have the following parts:

a) presentation of the topic
b) statement of opinions
c) support for your opinions
d) conclusion

What to do

Before talking or writing

- Brainstorm on the topic. Develop an opinion.
- Write down your opinion of the problem or describe the situation.
- Find facts, examples, etc to support your opinion (e.g. in form of a → mind map).
- Put in a logical order the information which you have found.
- If you are dealing with a controversial subject, think about the opposite position and find arguments to reject it.
- Find a good conclusion.

While talking or writing

- Begin your statement with an introduction to the problem, e.g. in form of a summary of your understanding of the subject.
- Give your opinion.
- Support your opinion with the facts you have found.
- Sum up the problem and your opinion and bring your statement to a conclusion.

Example

George Orwell: Serious Sport is War Minus the Shooting

topic: author argues against the idea that sport creates goodwill between the nations

I am always amazed when I hear people saying that sport creates goodwill between the nations, and that if only the common people of the world could meet one another at football or cricket, they would have no inclination to meet on the battlefield. Even if one didn't know from concrete examples that international sporting contests lead to orgies of hatred, one could deduce it from general principles.

opinion: international sporting contests lead to orgies of hatred

Nearly all the sports practised nowadays are competitive. You play to win, and the game has little meaning unless you do your utmost to win. On the village green, where no feeling of local patriotism is involved, it is possible to play simply for the fun and exercise: but as soon as the question of prestige arises, as soon as you feel that you and some larger unit will be disgraced if you lose, the most savage combative instincts are aroused. Anyone who has played even in a school football match knows this.

support of opionion example 1

At the international level sport is frankly mimic warfare. But the significant thing is not the behaviour of the players but the attitude of the spectators; and, behind the spectators, of the nations who work themselves into furies over these absurd contests, and seriously believe—at any rate for short periods—that running, jumping and kicking a ball are tests of national virtue.

As soon as strong feelings of rivalry are aroused, the notion of playing the game according to the rules always vanishes. People want to see one side on top and the other side humiliated and they forget that victory gained through cheating or through the intervention of the crowd is meaningless. Even when the spectators don't intervene physically they try to influence the game by cheering their own side and "rattling" opposing players with hatred, jealousy, boastfulness, disregard of all rules and sadistic pleasure in witnessing violence: in other words it is war minus the shooting.

example 2

example 3

example 4

conclusion

Special features of a speech

- Address the audience with a note of welcome ("Good morning, Ms/Mr X, good morning fellow students ...").
- Then organize your speech according to the structure of a comment (see above).

Mind some rhetorical rules:

- Do not speak too long (20 minutes is the longest your listeners can concentrate well).
- Speak clearly and neither too quickly nor too slowly.
- Try to speak rather freely without being fixed on your paper. Look into the audience at least once in a while, if you cannot do without reading from your script.
- Have a well-structured plan; otherwise, you will confuse your listeners.

Make your speech interesting—try to avoid boredom ...

- by emphasizing phrases or passages.
- by using a mixture of mostly short and only a few long sentences.
- by using stylistic devices (metaphors, alliteration etc).
- by bringing in jokes or anecdotes, examples from your own life, etc, to make a dry subject more pleasant (but be careful with appropriateness and decency).
- by modulating your voice (change your volume and speed of speaking where it is appropriate).
- Do not forget to say "Thank you for your attention" at the end.

Diary entry

Keeping a **diary** can help you sort out your feelings about people or events around you. Kept regularly, it can serve as a memory-book for anything that is on your mind. It is a kind of "silent friend" you can talk to when there is no one around.

What to do

Writing a diary entry

- Each entry is headed by the date, sometimes additionally by the time of writing.
- When you are supposed to write a diary entry for a fictional person, e.g. Lady Macbeth (see example), you should try to slip into the role. The following questions may help you to find the right tone, style and ideas to write about and connect with the situation:
  - What is the person's character like? (well-liked, hated, aggressive ...)
  - What is the situation like at the moment of writing?
  - What is the reason for writing?
  - What do you know about the events right before/after the diary entry?
  - What do you know about the person's past/family/job/friends/...?
  - What will be the person's hopes/fears/dreams/next actions?
- The style of the entry depends on the person's character. But usually a diary is a "stream-of-consciousness", a loose collection of thoughts, ideas and plans.

Example

Here is a page of Lady Macbeth's diary. She has taken down some notes after she received a letter by Macbeth announcing his coming and the strange encounter with the witches.

Friday, 13th (midnight)

I am so excited! At last he is going to return safely from the battlefield. Now I can calm down. There is an end to all the tormenting questions whether he was alive or wounded. No way, he is announcing his coming and I will do my best to give him a warm welcome. Tomorrow I'll order his favourite wine and a sow to be roasted. We will feast on his great success. Thane of Cawdor – I can hardly believe it. And what was that about the weird old women or creatures he met in the heath?
Oh dear – I know, they are around. Hecate is up to no good – I know she must be around with her likes. My maid has reported about the strange behaviour of the dogs and last night twice the horses in their stables were going half mad with panic no one could account for. The moon is full and it is the time for the sisters to do their mysterious work. So they told him his fortune – oh, what glory and happiness if it came true: he – the king of Scotland and me – the queen! But I have to keep cool and be his clever adviser. Too often is he hesitating just because of his ideal of decency and moral – pah – I will make him strong and forget about remorse. But first I'll strengthen myself with the powers of the ghosts that are around. I'll call them to make me ready for the bloody deed that has to be done – and then the throne will be ours. But now – to bed and sleep in sweet dreams of the bright future to come. All hail, Macbeth!

Letter writing (personal and formal)

Letters are usually divided into two main types: **personal letters** (e.g. to a friend) and **formal letters** (e.g. a business letter or a job application). There are no standard rules for informal or personal letters, whereas formal letters follow strict rules (e.g. avoidance of "I," polite phrases and special use of "would", etc). There is also a difference in register. A letter usually consists of four parts: a) address and date, b) salutation, c) body of letter, d) closing and name.

A personal letter

24 Lynford Avenue
Hants SO22 GBN

14 August 200_

Dear John,

I was very sorry to hear that your grandmother died last week. You have my heartfelt sympathy.
I know you were very fond of her. I only met her once but she seemed a very kind and friendly person. I'm sure you will miss her very much.
Please give my regards to your parents and tell them that I'm thinking of you all.

Love,
Peter

A formal letter

A formal letter	Examples
24 Lynford Avenue Hants. S022 GBN 14 August 200_	Writer's address and date
Mr Richard Miller Riverside Rd. London	Recipient's name and address
Dear Sir,	Salutation
It was with deep regret that we learnt of the death of the chairman of your company last week. Please convey our condolences to the Board of Directors. We have enjoyed a professional relationship with your firm for more than 20 years, and we greatly appreciate what his loss must mean to you all.	Body of letter
Yours sincerely, S.T. Johnson.	Closing

Letter of application and curriculum vitae

If you want to apply for a job, a scholarship or a position as a nanny, you have to write a **letter of application** together with a **curriculum vitae**. The letter is written in the formal style while the CV is a typed table.

Letter of application

Sonnenstraße 20
20001 Sonnenhausen
Germany

1 May 200_

Earlington Hotel
20 Lester Road
London WC2 7NN
Great Britain

Dear Sir or Madam,

I am writing to apply for the position of assistant hotel manager advertised in the Herald Tribune of 28 April. Find enclosed a copy of my CV.
In autumn I am going to finish my studies and I would like to become a hotel manager. I have worked for the Hilton Hotel in Mexico City, and since then I have wished to develop my career in that direction. I am very interested in English and would welcome the chance to work in a creative team where I could make a significant contribution while developing my professional and language skills.

I look forward to hearing from you soon.
Yours sincerely

Susanne Summit

Susanne Summit

Curriculum vitae

Susanne Summit

Sonnenstraße 20 ~ 20001 Sonnenhausen ~ Germany
Tel. +49(0)44 44/55 55 55
E-mail: susummit@mail.de

◆ PERSONAL INFORMATION

Birthdate: July 4, 1976
Birthplace: Villingen, Germany
Nationality: German

◆ EDUCATION

Sep. 1986–July 1995 Anne-Frank-Gymnasium (Grammar School), Abitur (A-levels)

Sep. 1996–present Pädagogische Hochschule Freiburg (University of Education), Subjects: English, physical education and technical engineering

◆ PROFESSIONAL EXPERIENCE

June–Oct. 1998 *Night manager, Hilton Hotel, Mexico City.* Worked for nearly four months as night manager for Mexico's largest hotel chain. My duties included registering late-arrivals and taking care of guests' requests at all times. Due to my successful teamwork, the hotel manager has invited me to work for him again next summer as well.

Feb.–Apr. 1997 *Student teaching, Karlschule (Elementary and Comprehensive School), Freiburg.*
Taught my three major subjects in the 7th and 8th grades as part of my first four-week practical training course. Final grade: 1.5 (A-).

◆ LANGUAGE ABILITIES

- Native speaker of German.
- Nine years of English in school, including *Leistungskurs* (advanced course); one year in England.
- Cambridge Proficiency Certificate.
- Five years of French in school; three summers spent travelling through France.
- Three-month intensive course in Spanish; four months working in Mexico.

◆ COMPUTER LITERACY

- Windows XP; Word 2000; WordPerfect 7; various graphic programs, including QuarkXpress and Freehand; Internet Explorer.
- Three years' experience working with these programs on a weekly, if not daily, basis.

◆ HOBBIES AND INTERESTS

- Triathlon (two first-prizes, three second-prizes in regional competitions)
- Cross-country skiing (instructor)
- Cabinet-making (second-prize in local craft show for a chair I made)
- I have tutored several school children in my neighborhood in English, French and math for six years.

Newspaper article

A **newspaper article** (esp a report) informs the reader about what happened somewhere. It gives answers to the five "W's" and an "H" ("*Who* did *what, when, where, why* and *how*?"). Reports have to be objective, but there are other articles that only want to entertain the reader.

What to do

Before writing

- Decide whether you are going to write an article to inform or to entertain the reader and think about how you can make it either objective or entertaining and sensational.
- Write down notes about the "who", "what", "when", "where", and, if possible, the "why" and "how" of the event. Decide on the sequence of the different points (e.g. to create suspense).

While writing

- Begin your article with an introduction to the event.
- Use your notes while writing the article.
- Divide your article into paragraphs.
- Include adjectives, adverbs, etc to create a vivid impression and, if possible, quote what other people said about the event.
- Write a catchy headline when you have finished.

After writing

- Does your article contain enough detailed information or can you add some more?
- Is the article interesting and easy to understand?
- Is the headline attractive?
- How have you connected your ideas and sentences?

Front-page of a British quality paper

THE INDEPENDENT

EUROPEAN EDITION

PLUS HOME NEWS 2-8, WORLD NEWS 9-11, BUSINESS 12, SPORT 20-24, CROSSWORD 24

Byers in new storm over air traffic crisis

Banks seek millions to prevent collapse of system

The man who would testify against Sharon is blown up. Was this another targeted killing?

'Long trolley waits' frequent at hospital in NHS dispute

INSIDE

Example

Teenager attacked on way home from disco

A 16-year-old girl was attacked and robbed on her way home from a disco last night. She was taken to hospital, but released soon afterwards with minor injuries.

Jane Jackson spent the evening at a local disco not far from her home. She left before her friends because she had promised not to be home late. As she was walking through a park she was attacked by a man she later described as darkhaired and in his early thirties. The man took her money and her watch. Luckily a car was just passing by when the attack happened. The driver stopped and went to help the girl while the thief ran off.

The police have often warned teenagers not to walk through the park alone after dark. "Jane Jackson had a narrow escape, but it might be worse next time", a police officer told our reporter.

headline

introduction:
a short summary of the story answering the *who, what, where* and *when* questions

the story in detail:
the *why* and *how* questions

ending:
summary, comment or quotation from somebody

Quality papers:
The Times (UK; independent)
The Guardian (UK; Liberal/Labour)
Daily Telegraph (UK; Conservative)
The New York Times (USA)
Washington Post (USA)

Magazines:
Newsweek (USA)
Time (USA)

Tabloids/yellow press:
The Sun (UK; independent)
Daily Mirror (UK; Labour)

"Headlinese" is the name for the English speciality of creating headlines that cannot be understood at once, they seem rather to be "Chinese" (headline + Chinese = Headlinese). The headlines often consist of incomplete sentences, provocative questions or simply of a row of similar sounding words (→ onomatopoeia) or → puns like: Rising England Soccer Star Dropped for Drink-Driving (*The Times*, Sept. 3, 1997).

Book report

A **book report** or a review is a summary and a critical evaluation. Its purpose is to inform the readers about what to expect and to give an idea of the wider context. A good report should have the specific reader in mind whom the author is trying to address. The formal aspects of the report are shown below.

What to do

Time-management organization

You usually get some instructions as to how many pages your report should cover (e.g. 2–5 typed DIN A4 pages) and how much time you have to work on it (e.g. over a holiday; 3–4 weeks, etc). Keep these conditions in mind and arrange a realistic schedule for yourself (make a time-table, e.g. "I'm going to read and excerpt one/two chapter(s) a day").

Before writing

- Of course you have to read the book first. Since the length of the book is a challenge to your ability of understanding and time-management, your reading time should be organized from the start.
- Prepare a notebook for excerpts, notes, quotations etc (➔ note-taking).
- Before reading the book, look at the blurb *(Klappentext)* to get an idea of what to expect.
- After reading the book once, ➔ skim each chapter again. Then write down headlines for the chapters or larger sections to reduce the contents to the most important facts.
- You can take these notes in form of a ➔ reading log. Having covered the whole book that way, you can start formulating your notes into a report.

Writing the book report

Bibliographical data

- Give the author's name, the title of the book, place and date of its publication, and the publisher's name.

Here are the two main standards of how to present biographical data:

1. If you **cite** *(zitieren)* **a book**,
   - give the author's or editor's name, then the title either in italics *(kursiv)* or underlined,
   - the city in which the book was printed,
   - the publisher,
   - the year of publication, e.g.:

   Smith, Zadie. *White Teeth*. Harmondsworth: Penguin Books, 2000.

2. If you **cite a story, a poem or an article taken** from a collection of texts, e.g. an anthology of short stories, which has an editor:
   - give the author's name,
   - put the title of the article or story in inverted commas,
   - give the title of the anthology either in italics *(kursiv)* or underlined,
   - the editor's name,
   - the city in which the book was printed,
   - the publisher,
   - the year of publication,
   - then add the pages on which the story or text was found:

Jain, Sunita. "Fly the Friendly Skies." *Short Stories Universal.* **Ed. R.M. Nischik. Stuttgart: Reclam, 1993. 106–111.**

• State what kind of book it is (novel, drama, science fiction, detective story, etc).	Classification
• State what it is about (short information in no more than two sentences).	Topic
• Give an outline of what happens in the book showing the development of the main conflict, its solution and its impact on the character(s).	Synopsis of the content
• Quote one passage that you find most typical of the book's tone and/or message, most interesting, most amusing/horrifying, etc. • View the book from a wider context, discuss the problem and relate it to a specific readership.	Message and problem
• Explain why you like or do not like it, what it does (not) deal with, why you would recommend or not recommend it, etc.	Personal evaluation

(This is only a very brief review. Usually it is more elaborate.)

Example

Book report on *What kind of love?*

Sheila Cole. *What kind of love? Diary of a Pregnant Teenager.* New York: Avon, 1995.	Bibliographical data
This book, a diary, deals with a pregnant teenager's dilemma. Right at the beginning we find the following entry: "What am I going to do? I can't be pregnant. I'm only fifteen."	Classification Topic
In a flash, Valerie's world comes tumbling down. Talented, pretty and popular, she was enjoying life and planning her future. She and Peter, the love of her life, were sharing their dreams. Now she and Peter share a problem. But it turns out to be Val's problem. Peter says he loves her, but has to finish school, go to college, get on with his life. Valerie wishes she could get on with her life and her music career. But she lives each day with the reality Peter wants to forget—and it is she who must make the impossible choices … when love has no answer.	Synopsis of the content
The diary treats a problem quite a few people are confronted with nowadays. It shows, by the example of Valerie and Peter, how teenagers' lives may change overnight and how difficult it is to find solutions.	Message
I like this diary because it is easy to identify with the two characters. Their problems are presented quite realistically, so the book might make young readers aware of the emotional and social conflicts the two have to go through. I think many people should read it—not only young ones.	Personal evaluation

! If you are to present the book report in front of your class, you can make it really impressive with some presentation expertise (→ presentation). It will be a good service for your audience to provide them a hand-out with

a) the bibliographical data; information on the author; topic; short outline (keywords only) of the content and characters,

b) the vocabulary you use from the book that may be new to your classmates.

Hand out the copies and explain the information and vocabulary on it before your report. Only be careful that this doesn't take too long and do not use too many new words.

Essay writing (free or text interpretation)

There are two types of **essays**. The writing process, whether you write a **free essay**, i.e. you are only given a topic to write on, or related to a text (**literary interpretation**) consists of four phases:
1. gathering ideas
2. planning the text
3. writing the text
4. revising and checking it.

What to do

Free essay writing

- Collect ideas and note them down using keywords or short sentences.
- Put your ideas in a logical order (e.g. chronological, order of importance, etc) and plan your paragraphs. Use a topic outline, a ➔ mind map or a ➔ note making chart.
- Start with an introduction to the topic (e.g. by giving a definition or example of the subject), write your text along the lines of your plan and do not forget the conclusion.
- Read the whole text again and check if you have concentrated on the topic and have included all the important ideas. Improve or correct your text if necessary with additional remarks and check your language with a dictionary.

Example

Topic: **Leisure**

Gathering ideas and ordering ideas in a mind map

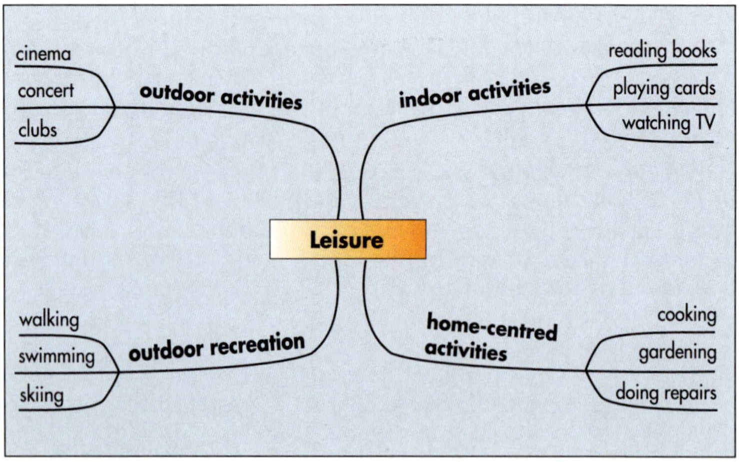

Writing the text

This is only a very short example of how your text could be constructed using the ideas above. To give your essay more substance you should describe some of the activities mentioned in more detail. Here we indicate the passages with [...].

Leisure

It is rather interesting to see how people spend their free time.

Most people spend a great deal of their leisure time at home [as has recently been found out by a survey of ...]. They read books, play cards or watch TV. But they are also regular cinema and concert goers. [xx per cent of the participants said that ...].

A lot of young people belong to clubs [such as ... where they ...] and some to study circles, too. Sports and outdoor recreation are equally popular: walking, swimming and skiing as well as home-centred activities such as gardening, cooking or doing repairs *[better than enumerating is giving examples]*.

There are lots of different and interesting ways of spending your free time. It depends on individual preferences and temperaments if people do more outdoor or indoor activities and sometimes it simply depends on the weather.

Writing a text-related essay (e.g. literary interpretation)

What to do

- Read the text at least twice:
  1. Get the general idea by → skimming,
  2. get the most important details by → scanning and mark them.
- Give your text an **introduction**. There you should refer to the **title** and the **author** of the story. Then add concise information about its topic (abstract meaning of the story) in not more than two sentences **(= short information)**.
- The second step is to write a short → **plot summary** by referring to the **"w"-questions** (who-where-when-what-why). Use the **present simple tense**.
- Write an interpretation, combining facts, analysis and transfer.
- Refer to the text and cite substantial passages to support your arguments.
- Finish your essay with an ending, e.g. with a conclusion, personal statement, outlook on the future and/or a challenging question after your conclusion.

1. Introduction
2. Plot summary
3. Interpretation
4. Ending

! Interpreting a text means to detect the meaning that can be read between the lines. Often the authors use stylistic means (→ Language kit) like metaphors, special sentence structures, etc. You should pay special attention to these. To what effect are they used? Do not forget to write in a logical order and to connect your ideas. You should check what you have written and ask yourself if someone could understand it who has no idea of the text you have interpreted.

Internet research

The **world wide web**, **www**, or the **Internet** is the latest in modern information and communication technology. It can be compared to a worldwide universal, interactive multi-media "dictionary", notice board or chat room. It offers users worldwide, twenty-four-hour a day access to the information centres of universities, libraries, government and private institutions, press organizations and all kinds of periodicals but also to information made available by firms and private persons wishing to share their ideas and views with every-one interested in them. You can get information by directly accessing homepages or by using search engines.
A **search engine** filters through the material in the net looking for the word(s) you have entered. There are several helpful search engines such as *AltaVista*, the *WebCrawler*, etc. The most convenient and efficient ones are *Yahoo!* and *Google*. *Google* is presented below.

What to do

Minding the "netiquette"

- Whenever you download information or texts, graphics, etc from Internet sites you should be fair to those who have had the work of creating them.
- Do not simply copy and take the service for granted. It is a matter of honour to document from where you got your material or ideas. As it is the rule with quotations from books, always state the URL (*uniform resource locator)* address you went to.
- By the way—cheating is out, your teacher probably knows all the addresses where you can get ready-made homework etc. Be careful, there is a lot of "trash" online.

Using homepages

Addresses (URLs) for finding information on Shakespeare and his time:

- www.Shakespeare-online.com
- www.stratford-upon-avon.co.uk
- http://daphne.palomar.edu/Shakespeare
- www.shakespeare.com
- www.luminarium.org/renlit/eliza.htm
- www.verona-world.de

Newspaper addresses, e.g. for the topic *Britain and Europe*:

• www.mirror.co.uk	Daily Mirror
• www.thetimes.co.uk	The Times
• www.independent.co.uk	The Independent
• www.guardian.co.uk	The Guardian

Using a search engine

- Access the Internet.
- Enter http://www.google.com on your starting page.
- You are at the "entrance" of the search engine:

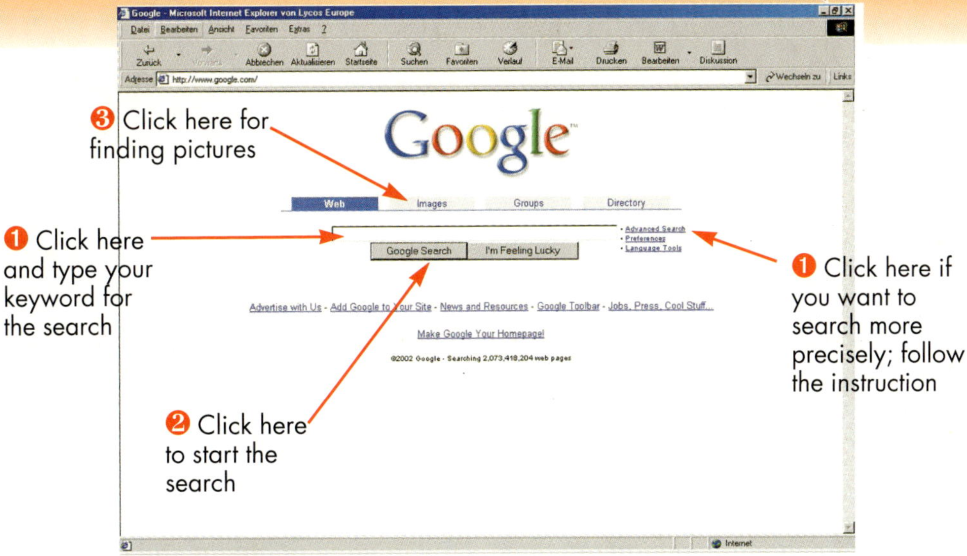

Search results for "Elizabethan England"

Examples

Beginning of a list of about 61,700 results:

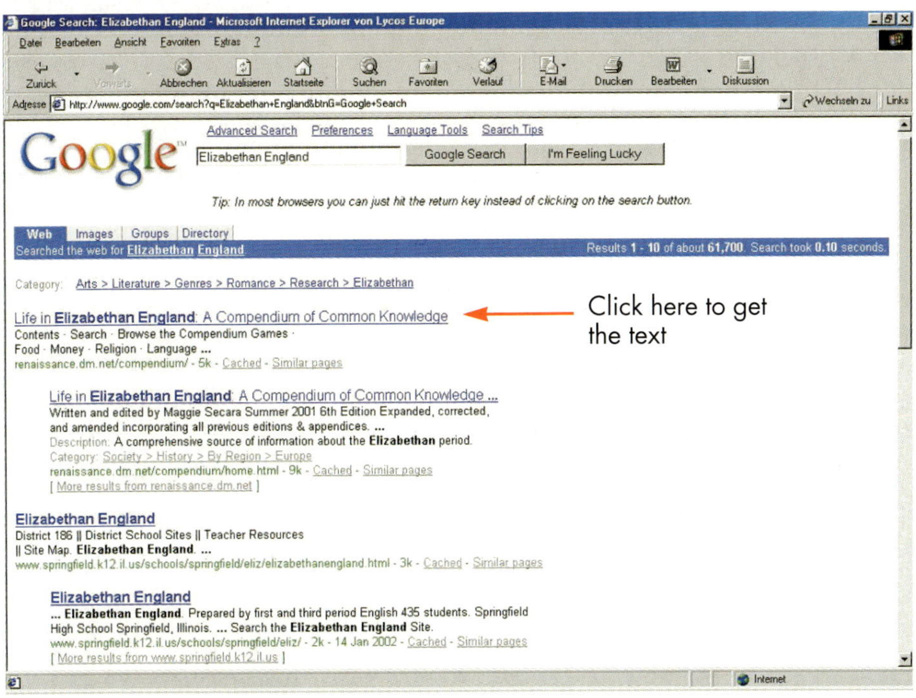

→ Skim the texts and save them in a folder on your computer for closer reading. You should do that offline.

Film analysis

Films consist of many scenes or sequences. Speaking in the director's language the film is a row of **shots**. Film shots give the action from the particular position of the camera or the distance between the camera and the objects being filmed.

What to do

1. When you watch a film scene concentrate on the
   - types of shots,
   - the field size of the shots,
   - the camera movements

   and their function (e.g. drawing the viewer into the action; pointing out important details; creating suspense, etc).
2. Keep the following questions in mind:
   - When do the types of shots change and to what effect?
   - What other effects does the director use in order to create: horror/harmony/atmosphere/ good or bad feelings?

   Therefore pay attention to special effects:
   - the light,
   - the use of space,
   - the props (*Requisiten*),
   - sounds,
   - speed of cuts.
3. How is the story you might have read transformed in the film? Are there any: flashbacks/flashforwards/crosscuts/ freeze frames/slow motions? What is their function or effect?
4. Compare the film with the story in the book.

A long shot gives e.g. a complete view of a setting.

A medium shot zooms closer in on the actors.

A close-up draws the attention to the face, e.g. to show emotions.

An extreme-close up is used to focus on the most important object in the scene.

Camera movements

static shot: camera does not move

to pan left/right (*horizontal schwenken*) to tilt up/down (*vertikal schwenken*)

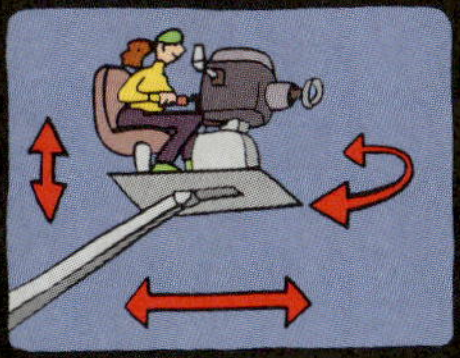

crane shot (*Kranfahrt*): camera moves flexibly in all directions on a crane

to zoom in on/out of sth (e.g. a face)

tracking shot (*Kamerafahrt*): camera is on a vehicle moving on the ground

Camera positions

E.g. a point-of-view shot is seen through a character's eyes. Other examples are:

establishing shot: shows location (long shot/pan) at the start of a scene

overhead shot: bird's eye view

over-the-shoulder shot

reverse-angle shot: from the opposite side, usually shows a dialogue partner

Camera angles

high-angle shot; bird's eye view (from above)

eyelevel shot

low-angle shot; worm's eye view (from below)

Interview

An **interview** is usually a dialogue between a person who asks precise questions and someone who answers. A carefully prepared interview as you may find it on TV or the radio introduces famous persons to the audience and makes them familiar with their private life, their thoughts and dreams, etc. It can also be a form of getting information on special subjects by experts or people who have experienced a special event in life. A modern form of an interview is the **talkshow** on television.

What to do

Interviewing a person:

- Before you interview a person, you should have a preparatory talk with him or her about your intention, the topic you are going to talk about, the place, and how long you are going to talk.
- The first question should be an open invitation to the one being interviewed to talk freely about the subject under discussion. You ask the next question after the person has stopped talking.
- You need a carefully prepared questionnaire. But you should not be fixed on the order of your questions. A good interviewer reacts immediately to the speaker and deals with the questions rather flexibly.
- Your way of questioning is essential for the results. Ask precisely and do not confuse the speaker with too many questions at one time.
- Keep to the time limit. The last question should either be a brief summary of what has been said or a future outlook.

What you need

1. Recording the interview could be helpful. So check if a tape recorder is available and make sure that it works.
2. Work out a **questionnaire** and mind the following types of questions:
   - Polite imperative sentences motivate the speaker to start talking and to carry on for a certain period of time. ("Please, tell us about your time at the genetic engineering laboratory in Toronto!")
   - Yes/No-questions can be useful to check if you got the information right, but they do not really have substance.
   - Rhetorical questions are questions which already carry the answer in themselves. They can be used to clarify or emphasize information. ("So you do not have any bad recollections of your schooldays?")
   - Questions regarding the matter itself (*Sachfragen*) ask for clear answers. ("How many grandchildren have you got?")
   - Questions demanding further information after a piece of information has been given *(Informationsfragen)* want a precise answer. ("Why did you quit the basketball team?")

Making a presentation

After working on a task for example after reading a novel, completing a team activity or doing Internet research, you may be expected to present your results. The **presentation** is a combination of speaking to an audience, showing them your skills and maintaining their interest. Therefore it demands a good command of the language, graphic and/or computer skills and a special self-awareness regarding your behaviour in front of and towards a group of people.

Preparing the presentation

The best weapon against nervousness when speaking in front of a group is being well prepared. Here are some tips:

- You should write down notes for your speech, including keywords only. Cards are helpful. Write only a few terms on one card, so that you can easily read from it without losing your place.
- In order to speak correctly, you should have a general idea of what you are going to say so you can check your grammar, vocabulary and pronunciation with a dictionary beforehand.
- Practise your presentation in front of a friend, your family or use a mirror.
- If your presentation has a time-limit, record your text and time it. That also helps to check your pronunciation and fluency.
- For more help on preparing: → Comment and speech, p. 292.
- Think about material you could use to make your presentation interesting and informative for your listeners. Sometimes a picture says more than a thousand words, so illustrate what you say by using pictures, diagrams, transparencies, maps, drawings, etc.
- If you need an overhead projector, a flip chart, a tape recorder, etc, make sure that all the equipment you need is in the room of your presentation and check if and how they work. Practise using them beforehand.

The presentation

- For the spoken part and how to organize and "pep up" your speech: → Comment and speech, p. 292.
- At the beginning you should tell the audience what you are going to talk about. Give them a short preview of what they are going to hear.
- Provide an attractive handout with an outline of the structure of your presentation, some of the important information, and new vocabulary.
- Tell the audience whether they can interrupt you with questions or if you want them to wait until later.
- If you use new words or difficult ones, do as the teacher does: write them on the board and explain them.
- When you are speaking make sure that everyone can hear you clearly. Do not hurry through your concept, take your time and breath.
- You should not walk around without purpose, but stand still and straight so your listeners can concentrate on what you are saying.

What to do

Overhead projector (for transparencies)

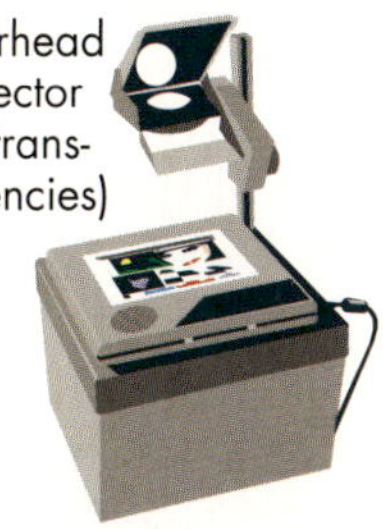

A flip chart can help to take notes during the presentation or serve as a blackboard if there is none in the room (e.g. computer lab).

A multimedia presentation

A **computer presentation** can be a very impressive way of showing one's results to a group. You can use e.g. the programmes Mediator and PowerPoint, which does not take a lot of expertise. You can learn it very quickly. You can create a kind of slide-show (*Diashow*) of pictures and texts.

What to do

Titel durch Klicken hinzufügen

• Titel durch Klicken hinzufügen

Auto-layout transparency (PP 1)

Titel durch Klicken hinzufügen

• Titel durch Klicken hinzufügen

PP 1 with a background picture

Preparing a multimedia presentation

- Prepare texts and pictures with your text programme, scan or download material from the Internet.
- Start the programme, e.g. PowerPoint.
- Choose the second transparency from the auto-layout.
- Fill in your title (PP1) and a text or insert a picture (via copy and paste clipboard function). You can work here as in your text programme.
- Create another transparency (*Bearbeiten—neue Folie*), choose an auto-layout.
- You can also add a special background to your transparencies (z.B. *Format—Entwurfsvorlage übernehmen*).
- Start the presentation (*Bildschirmpräsentation oder unten links kleinen Schalter, mit Maus wird Beschriftung sichtbar*).
- You can learn more tricks by simply clicking through the programme.
- Run your presentation either with a beamer or by printing your texts as transparencies and put them on the overhead projector.

Example

Students read Alan Paton's novel *Cry the Beloved Country*. They made a PP-Presentation to show some of their reading logs and creative work at a special parents' evening and at the "day of the open door" for newcomers and their family at their school:

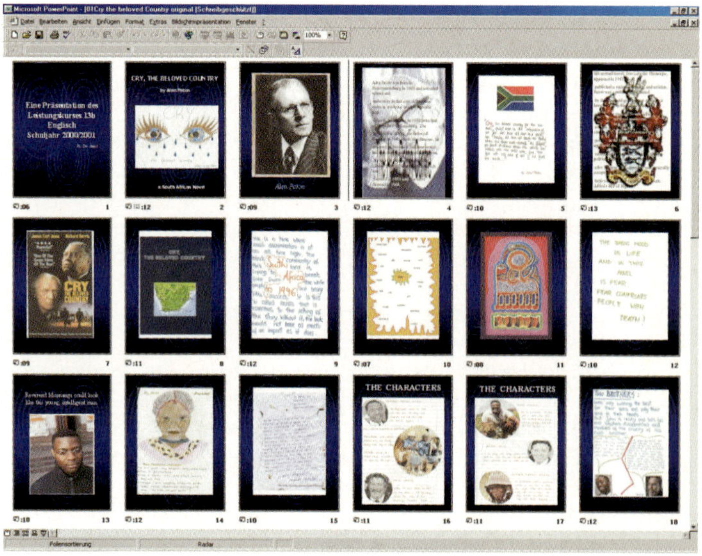

Evaluating a presentation

A **presentation** provides information and results. The best presentations are not only sources of clear and precise information. They can also be very impressive when they are well-organized, interesting and entertaining. An evaluation sheet helps to give feedback to those who were presenting. It also is a check-list for oneself to do it the same way or even better.

What to do

You can use the form below. Copy it and answer the questions after the presentation.

Evaluation sheet – Presentation skills

1. Do you feel sufficiently informed on the subject that was presented by your fellow students?

yes ——— **no**

Why / Why not?

____

____

2. Could you recognize a clear structure in the presentation?

yes ——— **no**

Why / Why not?

____

____

3. Did the speaker show clearly when he/she was moving to a new point, e.g. by means of pauses, summarizing sentences or signposting?

yes ——— **no**

4. Did the language used make it difficult for you to follow the presentation?

yes ——— **no**

For instance ...

____

____

5. What do you think of the visual aids (blackboard, handouts, OH-projector, computer) used?

appropriate ——— **confusing**

Why / Why not?

____

____

6. What about the speed in which he/she spoke?

too fast ——— **too slow**

7. Did the speaker speak clearly enough?

yes ——— **no**

For instance ...

____

____

8. What do you think of the manner in which the speaker spoke?

very natural ——— **as if only reading a printed text**

9. How would you judge the body language of the speaker?

convincing ——— **artificial**

10. General comment on the presentation (use back of the page):

Portfolio

A **portfolio** is a folder with the results of "free-ranging" work such as creative writing, drawings, pictures, poems, elaborate homework etc that have been assembled over a considerable period of time or within a larger project. When applying for a job the portfolio can be a great advantage, if not obligatory in future. The **European Language Portfolio (EPS)**, for example, is an initiative by the European Parliament. Students collect the best products of their school career in a folder. They also evaluate their own performance regularly in the EPS part called foreign language passport.
For more information go to www.learn-line.de/angebote/portfolio/index.html.

European Language Portfolio

Sprachen, die ich in der Schule gelernt habe (Art des Unterrichts: z.B. Fremdsprachenunterricht, Muttersprachlicher Unterricht, Arbeitsgemeinschaften)	**Languages I have learnt at school** (Type of lessons: e.g. modern language instruction, classes in the native language, study groups)	**Langues apprises à l'école** (Type d'enseignement suivi: p. ex. cours de langue étrangère, cours de langue maternelle, groupe de travail/club de langue)

Sprache Language *Langue*	**Art des Unterrichts** Type of lessons *Type d'enseignement*	**JgSt. von – bis** Year (from – to) *Classes ou années de – à*	**durchschn. Anzahl der Wochenstd.** Average number of hours per week *Horaires hebdomadaires (en moyenne)*

Sprachen, die ich außerhalb der Schule gelernt habe (Art des Spracherwerbs: z.B. Fremdsprachenunterricht, Volkshochschule, Telekolleg, Computerkurs, Ferienkurs)	**Languages I have learnt outside school** (Type of language acquisition: e.g. language classes, evening classes, television/correspondence course, computer course, holiday course)	**Langues apprises à l'exterieur de l'école** (Type d'apprentissage: p. ex. cours de langue étrangère, université populaire, téléenseignement, cours sur ordinateur, cours de vacances)
Sprache Language *Langue*	**Art des Spracherwerbs** Type of language acquisition *Type d'apprentissage*	**im Alter von – bis** Age (from – to) *à l'âge de – à*
Auslandsaufenthalte (Art des Auslandaufenthaltes: z.B. Betriebspraktikum, Schüleraustausch, Wohnortwechsel)	**Stays abroad** (Type of stay abroad: e.g. work experience, exchange programme, moving house)	**Séjours à l'étranger** (Type de séjour; p. ex. stage en entreprise, échange scolaire, changement de domicile)
Land Country *Pays*	**Art des Auslandsaufenthaltes** Type of stay abroad *Type de séjour*	**im Alter von – bis** Age (from – to) *à l'âge de – à*

The Council of Europe's European Language Portfolio documents the skills necessary to communicate in a multilingual Europe in such a way that they are readily accepted and understood in different countries. The Portfolio contains three parts:

- The **Language Passport** indicates the level of proficiency reached in all the languages spoken by the holder of the Passport. Language knowledge and skills are differentiated in line with the Council of Europe's competence levels for the teaching and learning of foreign languages. Furthermore, the Language Passport contains information regarding, for example, certificates and diplomas which have been awarded, type and length of language learning, stays abroad in areas where the target language is spoken and projects concerning intercultural and cross-border learning.
  The Language Passport can inform interested parties what the learner can do in different languages and can be used for example when applying for a job, starting a new job, changing schools or educational institutions, taking further education courses.
- The **Language Learning Biography** documents the holder's personal language and intercultural personal language and intercultural learning history and progress and supports self-assessment. It encourages dialogue with teachers and helps young people to organize and take responsibility for their own language learning. At the end of each educational level the data from the Language Learning Biography is summarized and recorded in the Language Passport.
- The **Dossier** contains a listed collection of all types of personal work which the holder of the Portfolio considers to be especially successful. Any kind of work can be brought together in the Dossier—examples of written work in the languages contained in the Language Learning Biography, recordings of oral communication, special productions on audio or video cassette, diskette or CD-ROM. The Dossier has a double function—on the one hand it helps to make the learner conscious of learning progress, on the other hand it can be used to document skills, for example when applying for a job.

Examples from a Dossier

1

2

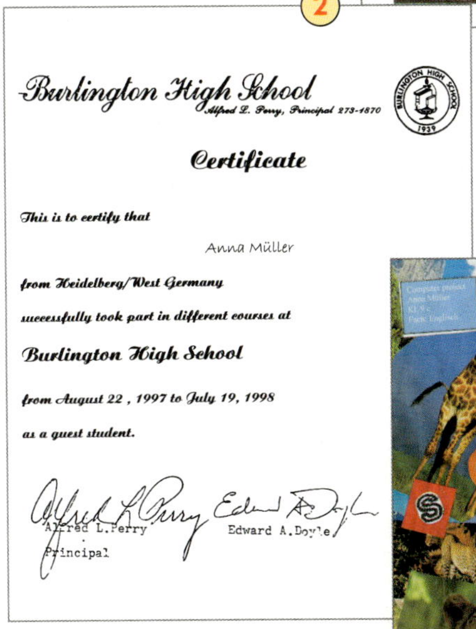
Burlington High School
Alfred L. Perry, Principal 273-4870
Certificate
This is to certify that
Anna Müller
from Heidelberg/West Germany
successfully took part in different courses at
Burlington High School
from August 22, 1997 to July 19, 1998
as a guest student.
Alfred L.Perry
Principal
Edward A.Doyle

3

1. A Willy Russell lecture attended in London
2. A certificate about a school-term spent in the USA
3. A piece of creative work from a lesson at school

Group activities

Working in teams

Rules for our team

1. Don't interrupt while one of the team is speaking.
2. Don't make fun of your partner's English (respect!).
3. Everybody should be involved.
4. No German! ("English-Guard")
5. Keep to the time limit. ("Time-Guard")
6. The teacher sets the time limit and supervises without pressure.

A list on the classroom wall helps everyone observe the rules.

To get the most out of working in small teams you should organize your tasks and think of special functions for each member. Here are some points you should take into consideration when planning your work:

- Who is doing what? Do you all have fair shares of work?
- One of you should be in charge of the "discipline": he or she reminds you to only speak English, to mind the time set by your teacher for fulfilling the task and your own schedules.
- You should set a time limit for yourselves for working on your individual tasks. Such a schedule helps avoid stress when you come close to the time limit.
- Write your "plan of action" and your tasks on a big piece of poster board. Fix it to the wall. Tick off (√) or cross out what has been done.
- One or two of you should be in charge of getting the material you need in time (poster board, text-markers, etc).
- You can appoint one of your team to present your work ("presenter").

Hot seat

Sit in a semi-circle. One of you is put on a chair in front of the class. He or she has slipped into the role of a character in a story. You are asking really pointed questions. The hot seating can be prepared in groups beforehand. One group can help the person to be seated in the middle to think about what kind of questions may come. The others collect questions from the text and beyond. They want to give the one on the seat a challenging time.

Fish bowl

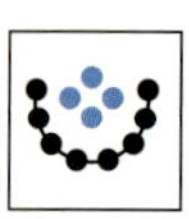

Sit in a semi-circle. Three to five of you sit in the middle and talk about your tasks. There should be one chair left free. Here students from the circle can join the talk spontaneously, add information, comment on what they have heard. After this, they should leave the middle again. After the chosen period of time, first the "fish" are asked how they felt being in the bowl. The observers give a short statement on what they have heard, if they agree or if anything is missing.

Double circle

(*Kugellager*) Divide into two groups. One group sits inside the circle, the other group outside. The teacher tells you when to begin speaking to the partner sitting opposite you and when to stop. When you get the signal to stop, move on to the next partner and begin anew.

Discussion

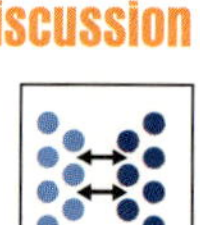

For a discussion you have to mind some rules: One of you is the "moderator." He or she starts the discussion, but does not engage himself or herself in the exchange of opinions.

- The moderator has the function of watching the speakers and reminding them to keep to the time limit.

- The moderator will interrupt when a speaker digresses into mere "babbling" or gets too emotional and perhaps offensive towards other speakers.
- It is the moderator's task to call the speakers one after the other according to the order in which they raised their hands.
- The moderator is in charge of orderly and polite communication. He or she has to take care that all speakers get a fair share of the time.
- The speakers have to listen to the moderator and his or her orders.
- The speakers have their speeches prepared and are aware of keeping to the topic and the time limit.
- The speakers behave in a fair way towards each other. They do not interrupt each other or get loud and offensive.
- The moderator will give a summary of the discussion at the end of the session without criticizing or taking sides with one group. He or she can close the discussion with a look to the future or a motivation, e.g. a challenging question to show that further discussion would be necessary.

Debating

A debate is not a discussion. The place of debates is in politics, e.g. in the House of Commons or the Bundestag. There the speakers argue in favour of or against a motion (*Antrag*).
The speakers should have prepared their speeches (→ Comment and speech). You can start with a "fun debate" e.g. on: "The only good dog is a hot dog." Divide into two groups of supporters and opponents. You either want to convince the opposition of the need to abolish dogs as pets (e.g. because they are dangerous sometimes, bark a lot, etc) or you want to show that you believe in the good of a dog (e.g. as a protector, a friend and helper for blind, disabled or elderly people, etc).

The procedure of a debate:

- You need a chairperson and one or two helpers to conduct the debate and keep order and time.
- Some of the class are the judges, who later decide on who has been most convincing and "won" the debate. They will hand in ballots (*geheime Wahlzettel*) to the Chair after the debate.
- Then take your turns. Present your arguments in 5 to 8 minutes alternately in the order: 1st proposition – 1st opposition – 2nd proposition – 2nd opposition. The timekeeper knocks after the first minute of your speech and then after 7 minutes, a double knock means that you have to stop. While speaking, stand up. The speakers may be interrupted by the listeners, who can throw in "On a point of information ...". You can accept or decline the question. The answer should not be longer than 15 seconds.
- The timekeeper signals the end of the debate. The judges then get a few minutes to discuss their opinions. They can change their minds and vote differently from their ballot. One of them announces the verdict to the Chair and whether it was agreed unanimously (*einstimmig*) or by majority.
  For more information see www.schoolsdebate.com.

Language kit

Terms for text analysis

act: the major unit in the action of a full-length play. Acts in a play are comparable to chapters in a book.

acting time: the time the action of a narrative lasts

action: action in fictional texts is everything that happens in a story, drama, etc. It may be **external**, when the writer describes what the characters do and/or say, or it may be **internal**, when the writer shows the thoughts and feelings of the characters.

anaphora: the repetition of a word or phrase at the beginning of successive clauses

antihero: the main character in a story or play, but one who does not have the qualities typically expected, e.g. courage and strength

antithesis: the presentation of a contrasting idea or argument

alliteration: the repetition of an initial sound in a sequence of words, e.g. **w**ild **w**ater **w**aves **w**ere **w**hirling ...

allusion: a reference to a well-known work of literature, a famous person, or a historical event, which the reader is supposed to know

assonance: the use of the same vowel sound with different consonants or the same consonant with different vowels in successive words or stressed syllables, as in a line of verse; e.g. *time* and *light* or *mystery* and *mastery*

atmosphere: the feeling or mood created by the author through the description of events, setting, situation, etc

blank verse: unrhymed poetry written with an alternating pattern of stressed and unstressed syllables. The rhythm created by this pattern resembles the natural rhythm of spoken English.

catastrophe: the unfortunate or disastrous ending of a story

character: a person who takes part in the action of a fictional text—flat character: a character in a literary work who does not develop in the course of the action; round character: complex individual who may change

characterization: the author may present his characters in two ways:
- directly by describing them, or
- indirectly through their actions, thoughts or feelings and words

climax/crisis: the moment at which the action comes to its point of greatest intensity, the moment that determines whether the situation will improve or grow worse (→ turning-point). Crisis refers to the highest point of reader interest.

comedy: a type of play which deals with a light or serious topic in an amusing way, always with a happy ending

comic relief: a humorous scene, incident, or speech in the course of a serious literary work that relieves the tension momentarily

conflict: the struggle between opposing forces, which is the basis of the plot of a story or play. External conflict occurs between two characters, or between a character and society. Internal conflict occurs when a character struggles within himself or herself in order to make a decision.

content: the kind of information a text contains

couplet: two lines of verse of equal length one after the other: rhyming couplets (➔ rhyme); heroic couplet (➔ sonnet)

dénouement: the last part, esp. of a book, play, etc, in which everything is settled or made clear

dialect: the form of a language used in a part of a country or by a class of people with grammar, words and pronunciation that may be different from other forms of the same language. Accents are national, local or individual ways of pronouncing words.

dialogue: a conversation between two or more characters

drama: ➔ play

dystopia: opposite of ➔ utopia

ellipsis: the omission of essential grammatical elements (e.g. So early come?)

exaggeration: an extreme overstatement

exposition: the first part in a story or play, that provides background information and introduces the story's setting, its conflict and often its main character or characters

eye rhyme: ➔ rhyme

falling action: the part of a story or play following the climax/crisis and leading to the dénouement or catastrophe

fiction: a piece of writing that comes from a writer's imagination. Fiction is not factual but may be sometimes based on facts, real experiences or people the writer has known.

figurative language: language that conveys meaning beyond the literal meaning of the words. Writers often use figurative language to create effects, to emphasize ideas and to call upon emotions (➔ simile, metaphor, or personification).

free verse: poetry without regular patterns of rhyme or metre. It often sounds like everyday language when it is read aloud.

function of a text: intention of a text; possible functions are to amuse, to criticize, to inform, to persuade, etc

genre: the term used to specify the distinct types or categories into which literary works are grouped. The four main literary genres are fiction, poetry, drama and non-fiction.

humour: in literature: an amusing description, an exaggeration, or a sarcastic remark

image: a picture in words. Images (➔ symbol, simile, and metaphor) are examples of figurative language. The words that are used mean more than their usual definition in a dictionary.

interpolated story: a story within a story which frames it (➔ short story)

introduction: the beginning of a text (➔ exposition)

irony: the contrast between what is said and what is really meant

metaphor: an implicit comparison between two things or ideas, not introduced by "as" or "like" (e.g. the river of life)

metre: the regular pattern of stressed and unstressed syllables in a line of poetry, e.g.

iambic metre [aɪ'æmbɪk]: short (unstressed) syllable followed by a long (stressed) one (stress like *tawúm*: avóid)

trochaic metre: long (stressed) syllable followed by a short (unstressed) one (stress like *wúmta*: lóvely)

mood: the feeling that the writer tries to evoke in a work of literature, such as excitement, anger, sadness, happiness, pity, etc

motive: a character's reason for action

narrative: any writing that tells a story

narrator: a fictitious person who tells the story

non-fiction: prose writing about real people, places, things and ideas

onomatopoeia [ˌɒnəˌmætəˈpiːə]: a combination of sounds in a word that resembles or suggests what the word refers to, e.g. hiss, cuckoo, thud

parallelism: a parallel construction of sentences like: He came. He saw. He conquered.

personification: type of figurative language in which human qualities are attributed to an object, animal or idea

play: a piece of literature that is written to be presented on a stage. In a drama or play actors and actresses play the roles of the characters, telling the story through their words and actions. Like fiction, a play contains character(s), setting, plot and theme. A full-length play is divided into acts and scenes.

poetry: special type of literature in which words are chosen and arranged in single lines to create a certain effect. Poems often reflect the speaker's experiences or like fiction, they can also tell stories.

point of view: the perspective from which a story is presented. The story can be told by a first-person or by a third-person narrator. The narrator can be a character or be outside the story.

props (properties): objects and things on a stage like chairs, tables, etc needed for the setting of a scene or as decoration (➔ stage directions)

protagonist: the main character in a fictional text

pun: the humorous use of a word that has two meanings, or of different words that sound the same; a play on words

register: level of language, e.g. standard, informal, colloquial English

rhyme: the repetition of sounds at the end of two or more lines or in the middle of a poem's lines (internal rhyme):
- **full rhyme**: show – blow
- **eye rhyme**: dies – stories (only the spelling suggests a rhyming pattern)

rhyme scheme: the pattern created by rhymes

rhyming couplets:

recall	(a)	sky	(a)
all	(a)	show	(b)
night	(b)	blow	(b)
light	(b)		

alternate rhyme:		**embracing rhyme:**	
crow	(a)	tree	(a)
me	(b)	another	(b)
snow	(a)	brother	(b)
tree	(b)	me	(a)

rhythm: the regular or irregular stress pattern in a line of a poem (➔ metre)

rising action: the part of a play or story following the exposition and leading to the climax

satire [ˈsætaɪə⁽ʳ⁾]: a piece of writing, a play, a film, etc that uses the art or practice of mocking people, institutions, etc and making them appear ridiculous in order to show how foolish, wicked or incompetent they are

scene: part of an act in a play

setting: the place where and time at which the action takes place and the social background of the characters

short play: a (one-act) play concentrating on a single dramatic situation, one place, a short time-span, a small cast of characters and one main conflict. Normally a short play is not divided into smaller parts like a full-length play.

short story: a work of fiction which usually deals with one or two major characters and one major conflict. The elements of a short story are character, plot, setting and theme. It gives a snap-shot of life and often uses figurative language and techniques like flashbacks or interpolated stories.

simile: a comparison between different things or ideas indicated by "like" or "as", e.g.: Her lips are as red as roses.

slang: very informal, often vulgar but lively level of speech outside the standard version of a language

soliloquy: (an act of) speaking one's thoughts aloud, esp. in a play when a character does this without another character being present on stage

sonnet: a poem with 14 verses, each of ten syllables and a fixed pattern of → rhyme. The two last rhyming lines of a Shakespearian sonnet are called a "heroic couplet."

stage directions: notes in a play telling the actors how to speak and act. They also say what the characters and the stage should look like (→ props) and where and when the action takes place.

stanza: a group of lines that form a unit in a poem; verse

stereotype: a fixed idea, image, etc that many people have of a particular type of person or thing, but which is often not true in reality; a special kind of prejudice

style: the special, often personal and individual way in which a writer expresses ideas, often in close connection with the type of text he/she has chosen

suspense: growing feeling of excitement that makes a reader curious about the outcome of a story

symbol: an object, a character or an event that stands for an abstract idea or suggests something greater than itself, e.g. the cross as the symbol of Christianity

tension: the feeling caused by the conflict of opposing forces in a text

text form: the classification of a text according to the form in which it is presented, e.g. as a poem, a short story, a play, a report, etc

text type: the classification of the text according to the writer's intentions. There are five different models of text types: description (presenting the characteristics of living things, objects or processes), narration (presenting actions or events in a logical temporal order), exposition (explaining relatively complex matter in an objective and precise way), argumentation (dealing with problems and expressing reasons for a particular opinion), instruction (telling sb what to do).

theme: the main generalized idea the writer wants to present. As the theme is usually not stated directly, the reader has to figure it out. One way of discovering the theme of a story is to consider what happens to the main character(s) and what it all means to him/her/them.

topic sentence: the sentence that expresses the main idea of the paragraph in which it occurs

turning point: the point at which the action takes a different, often unexpected direction

utopia: a fictional narration about an imaginary place or state of things in which everything is perfect; [from Greek *ou-*: no, later as well from *eu*: good and *topos*: place]. The name for that kind of literature is taken from Sir Thomas More's satirical novel *Utopia*. Utopias are the classical form of science fiction. Later on in the tradition, designs of negative mostly totalitarian future states have been created like George Orwell's *1984* or Aldous Huxley's *Brave New World*. They are anti-utopias or so-called dystopias.

Vocabulary for text analysis and text production

The following words and phrases will help you to talk about texts, to interpret short stories, plays and poems, to analyse texts and to do written tasks.

Fictional texts: short story, play, poem

theme

The	story play poem	deals with …

The theme of the	story play poem	is …

action and plot

The setting of the	story play	is …

The action of the	story play	is set in …

The action takes place in …

The events of the story happen …

The main elements of the plot are …

The	stages phases	of the action are …

The	turning point climax	is reached when …

The action reaches its climax when …

The story has a	surprise tragic happy	ending.

atmosphere

The atmosphere of the	play story	is … because …

The | setting / description of … | creates a/an … atmosphere

calm	*(ruhig)*	aggressive	*(aggressiv)*
carefree	*(sorgenfrei)*	cold	*(kalt)*
peaceful	*(friedlich)*	dark	*(dunkel)*
safe	*(sicher)*	gloomy	*(schwermütig)*
serene	*(heiter)*	tense	*(gespannt)*
		threatening	*(drohend)*
		sad	*(traurig)*

The | author / narrator | describes the | characteristic features / activities / outward appearance | of …

characterization

The following characteristics are typical | aspects / features | of …

The main character's behaviour is | polite. / …

character: trait (positive/negative)

positive		**negative**	
balanced	*(ausgeglichen)*	aggressive	*(aggressiv)*
calm	*(ruhig)*	brutal	*(brutal)*
courageous	*(mutig)*	cruel	*(grausam)*
friendly	*(freundlich)*	desperate	*(verzweifelt)*
good-natured	*(gutmütig)*	impatient	*(ungeduldig)*
moderate	*(gemäßigt)*	impolite	*(unhöflich)*
modest	*(bescheiden)*	impulsive	*(impulsiv)*
patient	*(geduldig)*	intemperate	*(unbeherrscht)*
polite	*(höflich)*	intolerant	*(intolerant)*
reasonable	*(vernünftig)*	irritable	*(reizbar)*
self-controlled	*(beherrscht)*	obstinate	*(eigensinnig)*
self-assured	*(selbstbewusst)*	ruthless	*(rücksichtslos)*
sensible	*(vernünftig)*	self-centred	*(ichbezogen)*
sensitive	*(empfindsam)*	stubborn	*(halsstarrig)*
tolerant	*(tolerant)*		

feeling

to be |

concerned	*(besorgt)*	excited	*(aufgeregt)*
confident	*(zuversichtlich)*	fearful	*(furchtsam)*
content	*(zufrieden)*	frightened	*(erschrocken)*
hopeful	*(hoffnungsvoll)*	nervous	*(nervös)*
optimistic	*(optimistisch)*	pessimistic	*(pessimistisch)*
pleased	*(erfreut)*	upset	*(aufgeregt)*
satisfied	*(zufrieden)*	sad	*(traurig)*
worried	*(beunruhigt)*	shocked	*(schockiert)*
bothered	*(verärgert)*		

Stylistic features and rhetorical devices

choice of words

The text is full of	abstract unusual colourful	words/expressions.

The author uses	images. poetic expressions.

The	figurative metaphorical	language creates an atmosphere of …

The word … is	effective to the point vague	because …

tone

The tone of the passage is	aggressive. alarming. colloquial. humorous. ironical. light. neutral. playful. serious. …

imagination

The author seems to have a	powerful vivid	imagination

when he says …

The author	employs uses	vivid images in order to …

simile/comparison

A (e.g. he) is like B (e.g. his father).

This simile is	drawn taken	from the world of …

The simile indicates that …

metaphor

The author uses	metaphors metaphorical language	in order to …

The metaphor … conveys the meaning of …

symbol

A	symbolizes is a symbol of	B.

repetition

The writer uses repetition to drive his message home.

The repetition of the word … emphasizes the fact that …

The author is repetitive when he says …

This text contains	unnecessary monotonous	repetitions.

flashback

The author	employs uses	flashbacks in order to …

This flashback helps the reader to understand that …

The character's past is	evoked recalled	in a series of flashbacks.

Non-fictional texts

topic

The	topic main idea	of the text is …

The	text deals with is about	…

The	main general …	idea expressed in the text is …

structure

The text	is can be	divided into … parts.

The text	consists of has	… paragraphs.

The	paragraph passage	can be subdivided into … parts.

The main	parts elements	of the text are …

The …	paragraph contains the	introduction. central problem. conclusion/solution.

A possible heading for this	section paragraph	is …

author and text: the content of the text	The author	deals with discusses	…		
	The author gives an exact	analysis description	of …		
the author's intention	The author wants to	show convince	the reader that …		
the author's opinion	The author gives his	personal opinion idea	on the	problem question	of …
	The author	thinks believes	that …		
	The author's	opinion	is based on …		
argumentation	The author	uses	the following argument(s):		
	The author	rejects	the following argument(s):		
	The author	comes to draws	the conclusion that …		

Acknowledgements

Illustrations

p. 9/10, 172/173 top, 306, 307: Reinhild Kassing/Verlagsarchiv Schöningh; p. 10: John Tenniel; p. 12/13: David Crystal, The Cambridge Encyclopedia of the English Language, Cambridge, Cambridge University Press, 1995, p. 107; p. 17, 200 bottom, 226 bottom left, 231, 236, 252: Archiv für Kunst und Geschichte, Berlin; p. 20: © mediacolor's/Füger; p. 21, 22, 23, 209, 210, 254 (4 illustrations), 264 bottom, 265, 266 (3 photos), 267, 268: CINETEXT Bildarchiv, Frankfurt; p. 24 left: Alan Paton: Cry, the Beloved Country, London, Penguin 1999, www.penguinreaders.com; p. 25 bottom: Ministry of External Affairs, Government of India; p. 27: copyright © Dimension N; p. 29: Christina Waltz/Verlagsarchiv Schöningh; p. 34: National Thai Studies Centre/The Australian National University; p. 40 top left: taken from www.rugby7.com/7Commonwealth.asp; p. 40 bottom: taken from Newsweek, December 20, 1999, p. 89; p. 40/41, 59: Ullstein Bilderdienst, Berlin; p. 41 top right: taken from The Daily Telegraph, June 11, 2001; p. 42: Fotograf: Klaus Ludes, www.classical-reggae-interviews.org; p. 43: Packaging Design © 2001 Cinema Club, London; p. 45, 54, 55 top, 75 bottom, 93, 123 bottom, 195: © dpa-Fotoreport; p. 47 top: Paul's Pub & Cybercafé, Republica Dominicana; p. 47 bottom: © Anna Weise; p. 51, 98, 115, 121 top, 122 top, 122 center: © dpa-Bildarchiv; p. 55 bottom: Copyright Brigitte Gastel Lloyd; p. 56: BCM "Conservative" London; p. 58: New York World, repr. Literary Digest 17 (Nov. 26, 1898); p. 60: Royal Engineers; p. 66: © mediacolor's/Gisela Damm; p. 69 top: Lutz Braun/Bildarchiv Preußischer Kulturbesitz; p. 69 bottom, 143 bottom: © dpa-Sportreport; p. 70: © Reinhard-Tierfoto; p. 71 bottom: Matthew Kneale: English Passengers. London, Penguin 2001; p. 72: taken from: The Koori Mail, February 8, 1995; p. 76: Guardian Unlimited © Guardian Newspapers Limited 2001; p. 77: Dennis Connolly, Bulletin, June 3, 1920. Courtesy: Australian Consolidated Press; p. 79 top: Lou Beach/Time; p. 80: Benoit Decout – REA; p. 82: © European Communities, 1995–2001; p. 84, 86: taken from Jonathan Lynn, Anthony Jay: The Complete Yes Prime Minister. London, BBC Books, 1989; p. 87: © 2001 Steven Breen - Asbury Park Press; p. 88: Peter Preston: 51st State. London, Penguin, 1999. Cover photographs: Big Ben, London © Telegraph Colour Library; US flag © Walter Rawlings/Robert Harding Picture Library; p. 91 top, 121 bottom: Keystone; p. 91 bottom (4 illustrations): © European Communities, 1995–2003; p. 95: Evening Standard, June 8, 2000, p. 4; p. 96: © 1999 Gurmit Flora; p. 101: from Sue Townsend: The Queen and I, London, Reed Consumer Books, 1993, p. 11, drawing by Martin Honeysett; p. 103: taken from The Sun, January 29, 1954, drawing by Emile Mercier; p. 104: Ian Jones – St. James Palace – PA; p. 106 top left: Drawing by James Montgomery Flagg; p. 106 top: Dieter Klaas, Gerd Köhncke/Verlagsarchiv Schöningh; p. 106 bottom: © mediacolor's/Reto Socorro; p. 107 left: © DC Comics; p. 107 right: Corbis/BZ-Grafik; p. 107 bottom: Michael Marks – Camera 5; p. 114 top: Culver Pictures; p. 114 bottom: Grison-Pasquier/Rapho/Agentur Focus; p. 118, 200 top: Bildarchiv Preußischer Kulturbesitz, Berlin; p. 120 top: New York Historical Society, New York; p. 120 bottom: Yale University Art Gallery, New Haven, Conn.; p. 121 center: © AP Photo; p. 122 bottom, 123 top: Barry Fitzgerald, USIA; p. 125: Umschlag: Arthur Miller: Death of a Salesman, Klettbuch 3-12-577630-9, Ernst Klett Verlag GmbH, Stuttgart 1988; p. 127: Library of Congress USZ62-43605; p. 131: © VG Bild-Kunst, Bonn 2002; p. 132: © 2001 Creators Syndicate, Inc.; p. 135: Thomas Höpker; p. 136: HEMO/mediacolor's; p. 139: Eric Swanson; p. 142 (8 illustrations): General Mills; p. 143 top, 150: Illustration: KAL;

p. 144: Photograph by Mathew Black; p. 146: Illustration by Cathie Bleck; p. 147: © mediacolor's/BU; p. 153: Charles Moore – Black Star; p. 159: Walter Hanel/CCC; p. 161 top: Greg Lovett – Palm Beach Post; p. 161 center and bottom: Lannis Waters – Palm Beach Post; p. 166 left: Fred Slavin/Index/KEY; p. 166 right: Alex Fuchs/AP/KEY; p. 172/173 bottom: Cathy © Cathy Guisewite. Reprinted with permission of UNIVERSAL PRESS SYNDICATE. All rights reserved; p. 175 top left: Karl Brack/Verlagsarchiv Schöningh; p. 175 top right: Getty Images/David Harry Sterwart; p. 175 center right: © Anthony/Guderjahn; p. 175 bottom, 226 bottom right, 227 center (2 illustrations), 272: Verlagsarchiv Schöningh; p. 176: dpa; p. 179: Getty Images/Bruce Ayres; p. 183: Lauren Uram, Artwork for Time; p. 184: entnommen aus: Carsten Feeser: Erfinde mit Erfindern, Düsseldorf, Hoch Verlag, 1973; p. 185: taken from: English Journal, Vol. 90, November 2000, p. 80; p. 186: © 1999 Electronic Arts; p. 187: Siemens AG; p. 188: David Goldin; p. 192: Baloo, in: Wall Street Journal Europe, 1.3.01; p. 193: K.H. Wagner, P. Dieckow/Verlagsarchiv Schöningh; p. 194: Gerhard Mester/CCC; p. 196 top left: Adrian Arbib – Corbis; p. 196 top right: Mark Edwards – Still Pictures; p. 196 center left: Dan Borris – Corbis Outline; p. 196 center: taken from: Time, February 1, 1999, front cover; p. 196 center right: Timothy Reagan; p. 196 bottom left: Jeff Mitchell – Reuters; p. 196 bottom right: Thomas Haley – SIPA; p. 197 left: Claus Meyer – Black Star; p. 197 center left: David Frazier – Photo Researchers; p. 197 center right: Hank Morgan – Science Source-Photo Researchers; p. 197 right: Index Stock; p. 201 top: © Succession Picasso/VG Bild-Kunst, Bonn 2002; p. 201 bottom left: Frankfurt, Städelsches Kunstinstitut; p. 201 bottom right: John Michell, London; p. 202, 226 top: inaki/Christoph Knecht; p. 205: Martin Brockhoff; p. 206: Getty Images/Brian Stablyk; p. 207: Dr. Karola Aust/Verlagsarchiv Schöningh; p. 211: Günter Schlottmann/Verlagsarchiv Schöningh; p. 213: Getty Images/V.C.L.; p. 215: CDC; p. 217: Illustration by Peter Schrank, © The Independent, 22.5.1995; p. 219: Foto: Gisèle Freund; p. 220: Virginia Woolf: A Room of One's Own, London, Grafton Books 1989; p. 222 top, 224 left, 225: Folger Shakespeare Library; p. 222 bottom, 223 top: Shakespeare Birthplace Trust, Stratford-upon-Avon; p. 223 bottom: Royal Shakespeare Theatre Collection, Stratford-upon-Avon; p. 224 right: Corpus Christi College, Cambridge, UK/Bridgeman Art Library; p. 227 bottom (facsimile): Public Record Office, London; p. 228: British Travel Association; p. 229 top: taken from Punch, May 2, 1984; p. 229 bottom: Louisa Hare; p. 232: GP/mediacolor's; p. 233: Anthony – Weißer; p. 234: Dr. Eberhard Schallhorn/Verlagsarchiv Schöningh; p. 235: Photographs of the 1955 Stratford-upon-Avon production, Macbeth by Angus McBean, in the Harvard Theatre Collection, Harvard University, Cambridge, Mass.; p. 238, 264 top: J. Freeman; p. 239: taken from Ulric Molitor, "De Lamiis et phitonicis mulieribus" (1489); p. 240, 243, 250: Theatergruppe des Melanchthon-Gymnasiums, Bretten, Foto: Dr. Eberhard Schallhorn; p. 244: The Shakespeare Centre Library, Stratford-upon-Avon; p. 247 (4 photos), 248: Columbia Pictures & Castle Rock Entertainment; p. 251: Roman Beniaminson/Bildarchiv PreußischerKulturbesitz; p. 255: King Lear (1984), directed by Michael Elliott; p. 258: Graham Arnold; p. 260: Kaveh Golestan; p. 261: C. Walter Hodges, 1965; p. 262 top: Badisches Staatstheater Karlsruhe; p. 262 bottom, 263: Badisches Staatstheater Karlsruhe, Foto: Jochen Klenk; p. 269: taken from: Humphrey Carpenter: Shakespaere Without the Boring Bits. London: Penguin 1994. Illustrations: The Big i, 1994; p. 270 (2 illustrations), 271 (2 illustrations): taken from Anna Claybourne and Rebecca Treays: The World of Shakespeare, Usborne Publishing, 1996, p. 16; p. 273: Veronika Wypior/ Verlagsarchiv Schöningh; p. 274: Illustration: Oxford University Press 1977

Texts

p. 10: Lewis Carroll: "Jabberwocky" from *Alice's Adventures in the Wonderland / Through the Looking Glass*, Harmondsworth, Puffin, 1983, p. 202; **p. 11:** Lewis Carroll: "Der Zipferlake" from *Alice hinter den Spiegeln* by Lewis Caroll, translated by Christian Enzensberger, Frankfurt am Main, Insel, 1992; **p. 14:** David Crystal: "Why Do People Everywhere Learn English?" from *The Cambridge Encyclopedia of The English Language*, Cambridge, Cambridge University Press, 1997, p. 106; **p. 16:** Anonymous: "Let's Do The Tongue Twist" from a letter published in *Sunday Times*, January 3, 1965; **p. 17:** Robert Mc Crum, William Cran, Robert MacNeil: "The Spread of RP" from *The Story of English* by Robert McCrum, William Cran, and Robert MacNeil, London, Faber and Faber, 1986, pp. 26–28; **p. 20:** Alan Paton: "Growing Apart" from *Cry, The Beloved Country* by Alan Paton, London, Penguin, 1987, pp. 32–36; **p. 25:** Nissim Ezekiel: "All Men Are Brothers, No?" from *The Patriot by Nissim Ezekiel, in: The Arnold Anthology of Post-Colonial Literatures in English*, ed. by John Thieme, London, Arnold, 1996, pp. 710f.; **p. 27:** Benjamin Zephaniah: "Dis Poetry" from *Penguin Book of Poetry: From Britain and Ireland Since 1945*, ed. by Simon Armitage, Viking Press, 1998; **p. 47:** Zadie Smith: "The Burning of Books" from *White Teeth* by Zadie Smith, London, Penguin, 2001, pp. 230–234; **p. 55:** Margaret Atwood: "Rule Britannia" from *Cat's Eye* by Margaret Atwood, New York, Doubleday, 1988; **p. 59:** George Orwell: "A Hanging" from *The Collected Essays, Journalism and Letters of George Orwell*, Volume 1, London, Penguin, 1968, pp. 66–71; **p. 70:** Hyllus Maris: "Spiritual Song of the Aborigine" from *Inside Black Australia*, ed. by Kevin Gilbert, Ringwood, Penguin Books Australia Ltd., 1988, p. 60; **p. 71:** Matthew Kneale: "Sunday Services" from *English Passengers* by Matthew Kneale, London, Penguin, 2001, pp. 249–250; **p. 72:** "A Letter from England" from *The Koori Mail*, No. 94, February 8, 1995; **p. 84:** Jonathan Lynn and Anthony Jay: "Food is a Weapon" from *The Complete Yes Prime Minister*, London, BBC Books, 1989, pp. 30–33; **p. 88:** Peter Preston: "51st State" from *51st State* by Peter Preston, London, Penguin, 1999, pp. 58–60; **p. 100:** Sue Townsend: "Mrs Windsor" from *The Queen and I* by Sue Townsend, London, Mandarin Paperbacks/Reed Consumer Books, 1993, pp. 15–17; **p. 108:** "Everything is Different in America", first edition; **p. 112:** J. Hector St. John de Crèvecœur: "What is an American?" from *Letters from an American Farmer* by J. Hector St. John de Crèvecœur, Philadelphia, Matthew Carey, 1793, pp. 46–47; **p. 114:** "The Contrapuntal Civilization" from *The Contrapuntal Civilization. Essays Toward a New Understanding of the American Experience*, ed. by Michael Kammen, New York, Crowell, 1971; **p. 120:** "Dreams in a Land of Opportunity", first edition; **p. 127:** Langston Hughes: "Let America Be America Again" from *The collected Poems of Langston Hughes*, New York, Alfred A. Knopf, Inc. Copyright 1994 the Estate of Langston Hughes. Used with permission; **p. 132:** Daphne Spain: "How Healthy is Immigration?" from *Electronic Journals of the U.S. Information Agency*, Vol. 4, No. 2, 2000; **p. 135:** Sunita Jain: "Fly the Friendly Skies" from *Eunuch of Time and Other Stories* by Sunita Jain, New Delhi, Vikas, 1982, pp. 16–20, © 1982 Sunita Jain; **p. 153:** Martin Luther King Jr.: "Letter From a Birmingham Jail" from *A Documentary History of the United States*, ed. by Richard D. Heffner, New York, Mentor, 51991, pp. 333–341, © Estate of Dr. Martin Luther King Jr., Atlanta; **p. 156:** Rudolph Kizerman: "Martians" from *Stand up in the World* by Rudolph Kizerman, London, Blackbird Books, 1969; **p. 160:** "Voices on Votes", first edition; **p. 161:** "Suggestions for Improving the Electoral System", first edition; **p. 163:** "The Case of the Oklahoma City Bombing", first edition; **p. 176:** Douglas Coupland: "A Day in the Life of danielu@microsoft.com" from *Microserfs* by Douglas Coupland, New, York, Flamingo, 1995, pp. 1–4; **p. 181:** "Life Before the Computer" from http://dapatchy.com/chuckles/computer.html; **p. 186:** Lillian E. Carlton: "TV or Not TV—A Modern Soliloquy" from *The Saturday Evening Post*, 1971; **p. 196:** "Fighting for the Environment—Actions From all Over the World", first edition; **p. 199:** "Another Day in Paradise" Words and Music by Phil Collins © 1989, Philip Collins Ltd / Hit & Run Music (Publishing) Ltd, London WC2H 0QY; **p. 202:** John Berger: "An Old Woman with a Pram" from

Photocopies by John Berger, London, Bloomsbury, 1996, pp. 31–33; **p. 205:** Aaron Medres: "I'm Still a Man" from *Dear World* by Aaron Medres, © SOON Educational Publications, June 1999; **p. 207:** Simon Trump: "A Single Mum Struggles to Keep her Family out of the Underclass" from *www.clarionnews.com/sinmumstrugt.html*, ClarionNews in Association with EthnikNet; **p. 209:** Anne Fine: "Madame Doubtfire" from *Madame Doubtfire* by Anne Fine, Harmondsworth, London, Puffin, 1987, pp. 17–26; **p. 211:** Nick Hornby: "About a Boy" from *About a Boy* by Nick Hornby, London, Penguin, 2000, pp. 44–48; **p. 215:** Caryl Churchill: "Top Girls" from *Top Girls* by Caryl Churchill, London, Methuen, 1991, pp. 57–60; **p. 218:** Virginia Woolf: "Shakespeare's Sister" from *A Room of One's Own* by Virginia Woolf, London, Grafton Books, 1989, pp. 45–47; **p. 224:** "An Investigation", first edition; **p. 265:** Marc Norman, Tom Stoppard: "Shakespeare in Love" from *Shakespeare in Love* by Marc Norman and Tom Stoppard, ed. by B. Puschmann-Nalenz, Stuttgart, Reclam, 2000, pp. 38–42; **p. 266:** Arthur Laurents, Leonard Bernstein, Stephen Sondheim: "West Side Story—The Musical" from *Westside Story. A Musical* by Arthur Laurents, Leonard Bernstein, Stephen Sondheim, based on a conception of Jerome Robbins, London, Heinemann, 1972; **p. 269:** Humphrey Carpenter: "Macbeth—Told by Macbeth" from *Shakespeare Without the Boring Bits* by Humphrey Carpenter, London, Penguin, 1994; **p. 278:** "Corporal Punishment in British Schools", © Verlag Ferdinand Schöningh 2001; **p. 282:** Toni Morrison: "Song of Solomon" from *Song of Solomon* by Toni Morrison, New York, Random House, 1977; **p. 292:** George Orwell: "Serious Sport is War Minus the Shooting" from *Shooting an Elephant and Other Essays* by George Orwell, Harcourt Trade Publishers, 1950